The Angel of Elhamburgh

of

Aki

Translation: Adair Trask † Lettering: Tania Biswas
++

ERUHANBURUGU NO TENSHI © 2013 by AKI. All rights reserved. First published in Japan in 2013 by SHODENSHA PUBLISHING CO., LTD., Tokyo. English translation rights in USA, Canada, and UK arranged with SHODENSHA PUBLISHING CO., LTD. through Tuttle-Mori Agency, Inc., Tokyo.

Translation © 2015 by Hachette Book Group, Inc.

Yen Press
Hachette Book Group
1290 Avenue of the Americas
New York, NY 10104

www.HachetteBookGroup.com • www.YenPress.com

Yen Press is an imprint of Hachette Book Group, Inc. The Yen Press name and logo are trademarks of Hachette Book Group, Inc.

The publisher is not responsible for websites (or their content) that are not owned by the publisher.

First Yen Press Edition: March 2015

ISBN: 978-0-316-34046-5

10 9 8 7 6 5 4 3 2 1

BUG

Printed in the United States of America

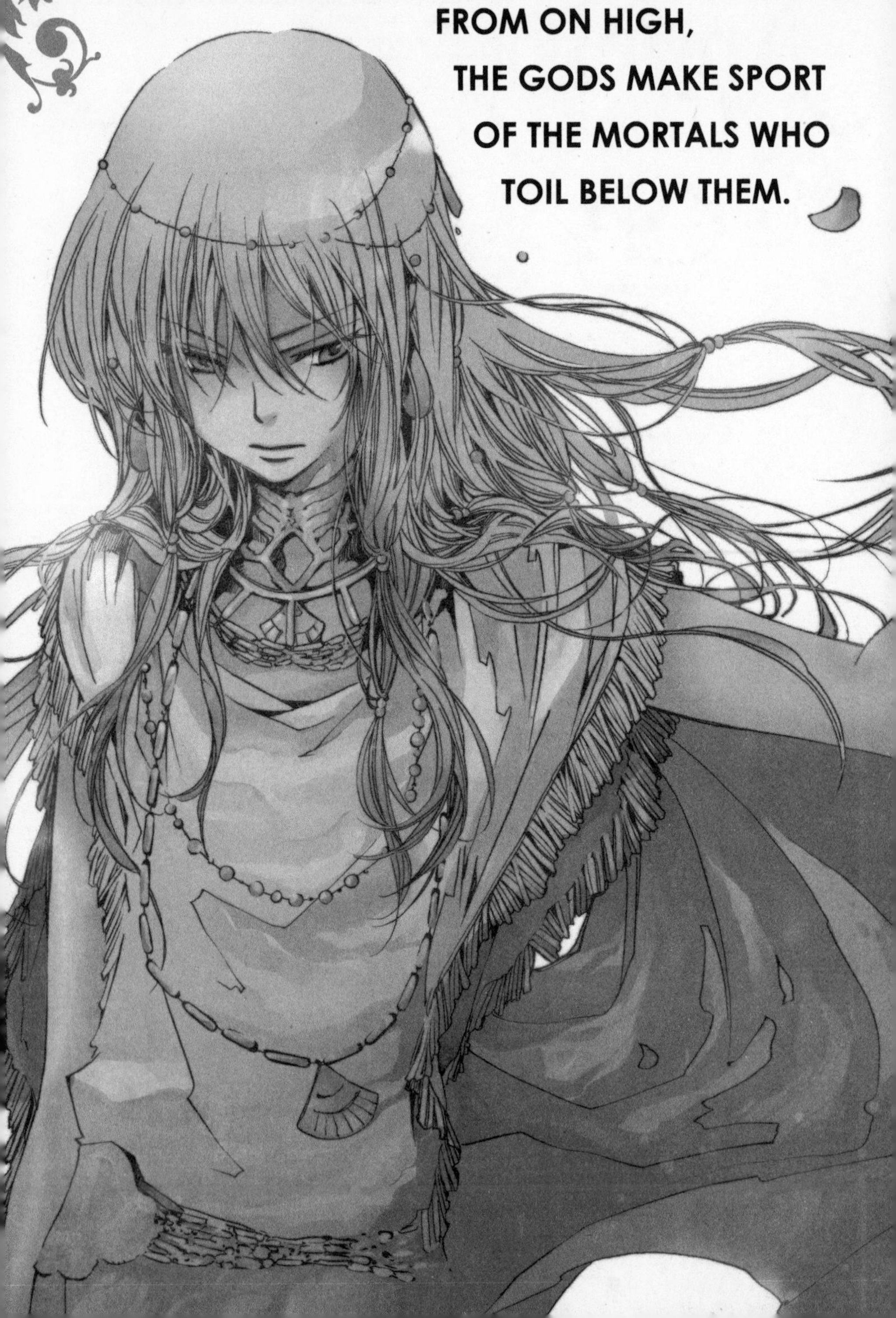
FROM ON HIGH,
THE GODS MAKE SPORT
OF THE MORTALS WHO
TOIL BELOW THEM.

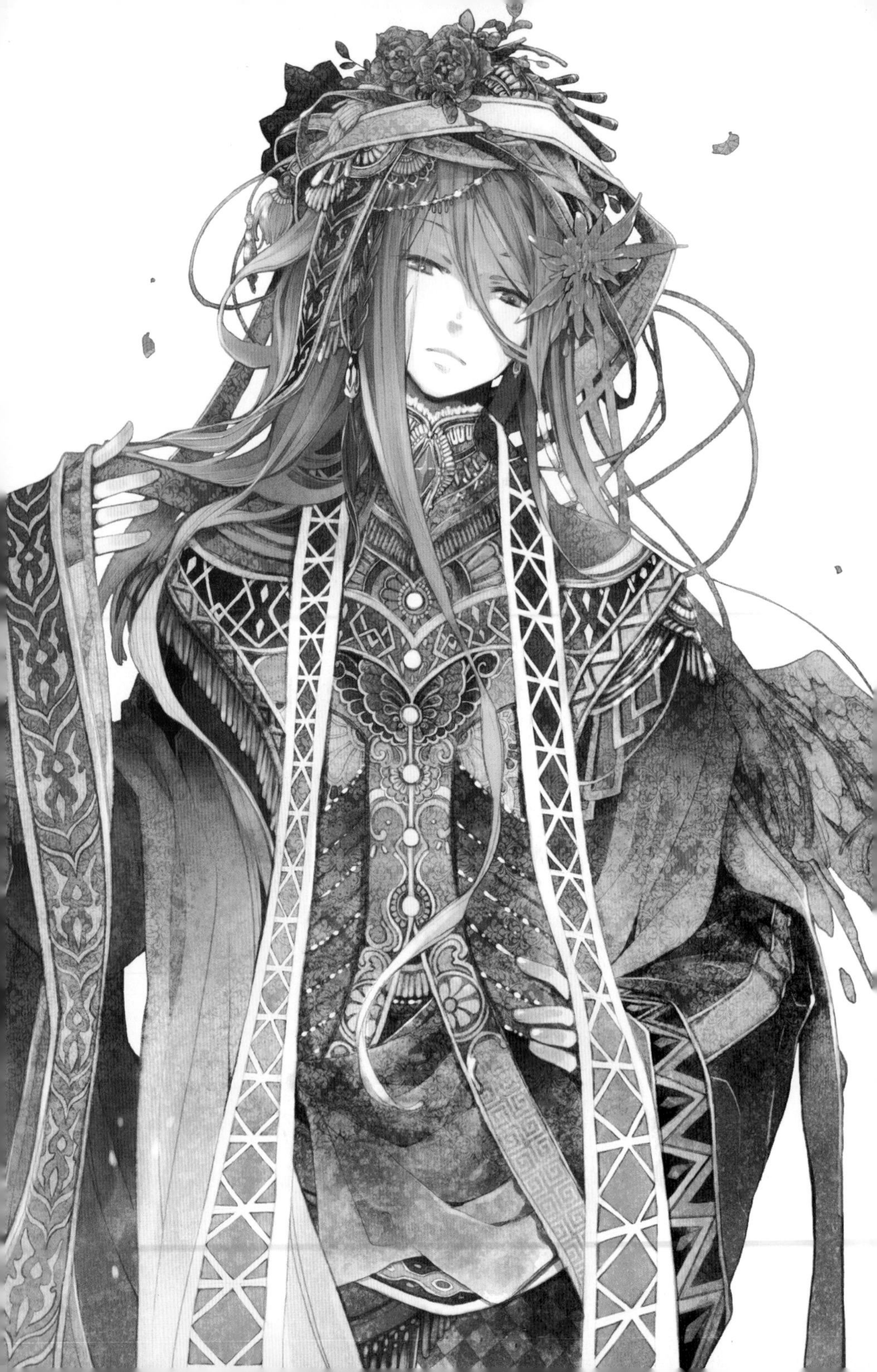

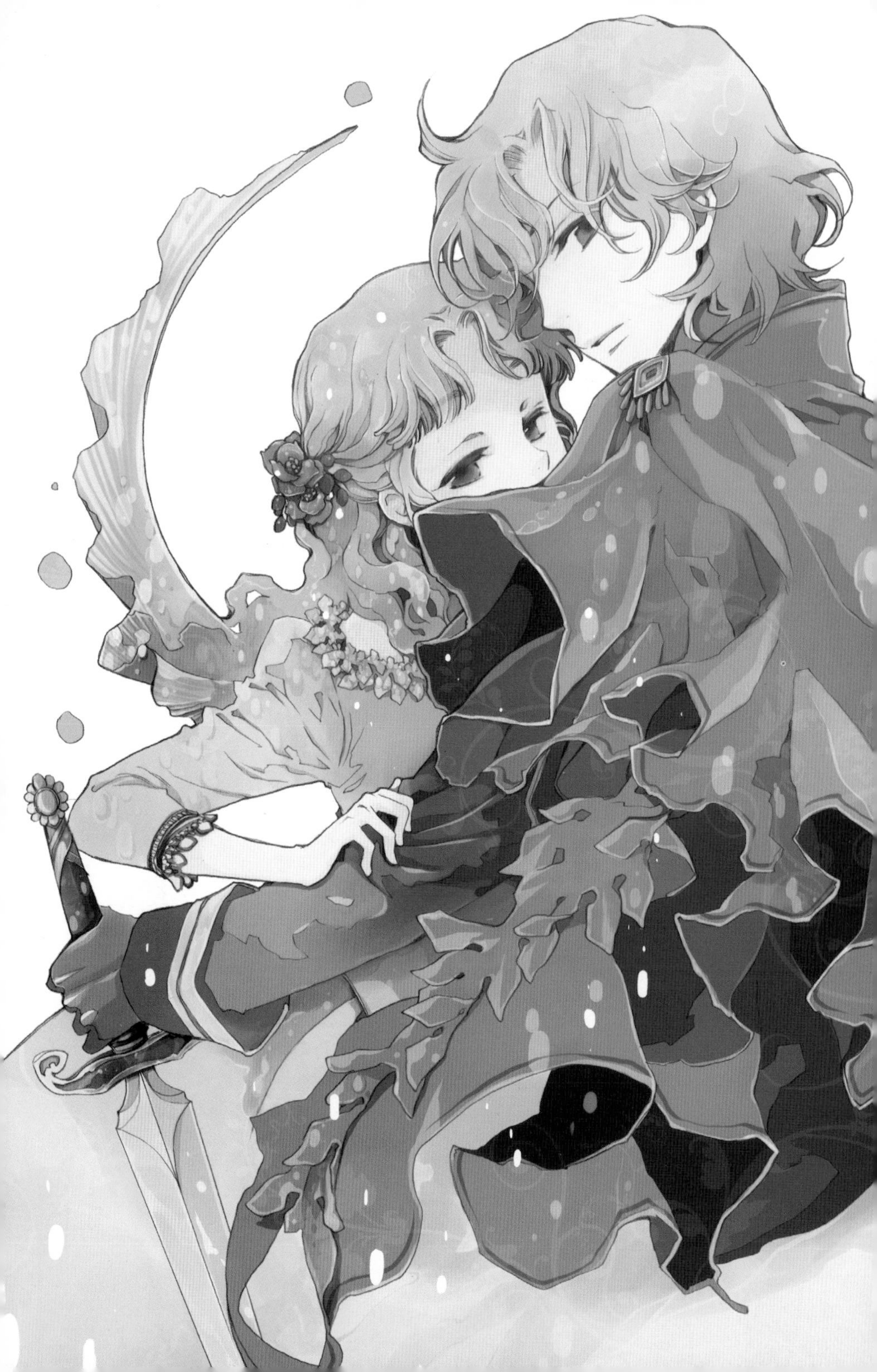

The Angel of Elhamburg

Aki

scene.1   005

scene.2   033

scene.3   061

scene.4   089

scene.5   121

AFTERWORD   158

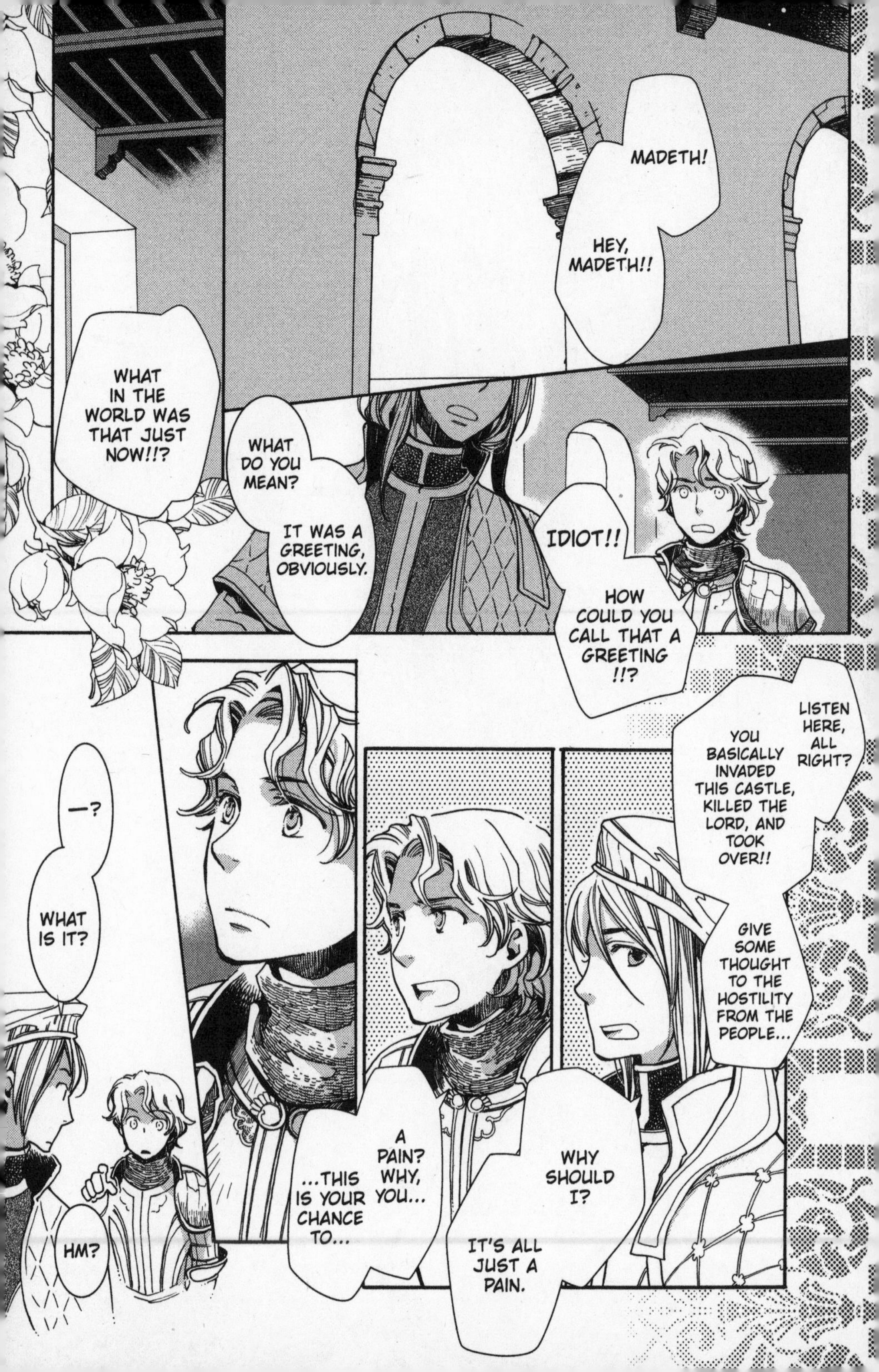
MADETH!
HEY, MADETH!!
WHAT IN THE WORLD WAS THAT JUST NOW!!?
WHAT DO YOU MEAN?
IT WAS A GREETING, OBVIOUSLY.
IDIOT!!
HOW COULD YOU CALL THAT A GREETING!!?
LISTEN HERE, ALL RIGHT?
YOU BASICALLY INVADED THIS CASTLE, KILLED THE LORD, AND TOOK OVER!!
GIVE SOME THOUGHT TO THE HOSTILITY FROM THE PEOPLE...
WHY SHOULD I?
IT'S ALL JUST A PAIN.
A PAIN? WHY, YOU...
...THIS IS YOUR CHANCE TO...
—?
WHAT IS IT?
HM?

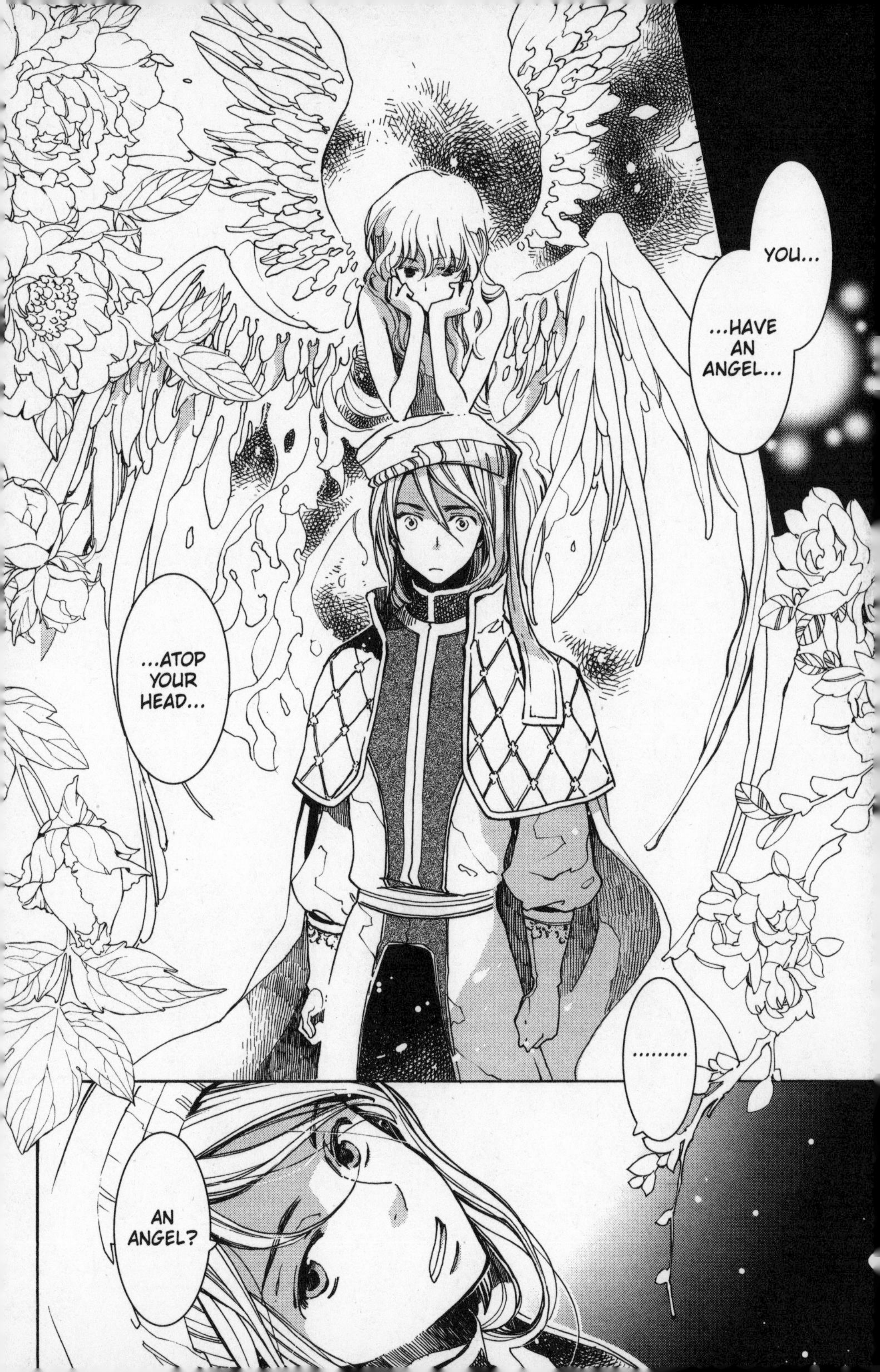
YOU...
...HAVE AN ANGEL...
...ATOP YOUR HEAD...
....
AN ANGEL?

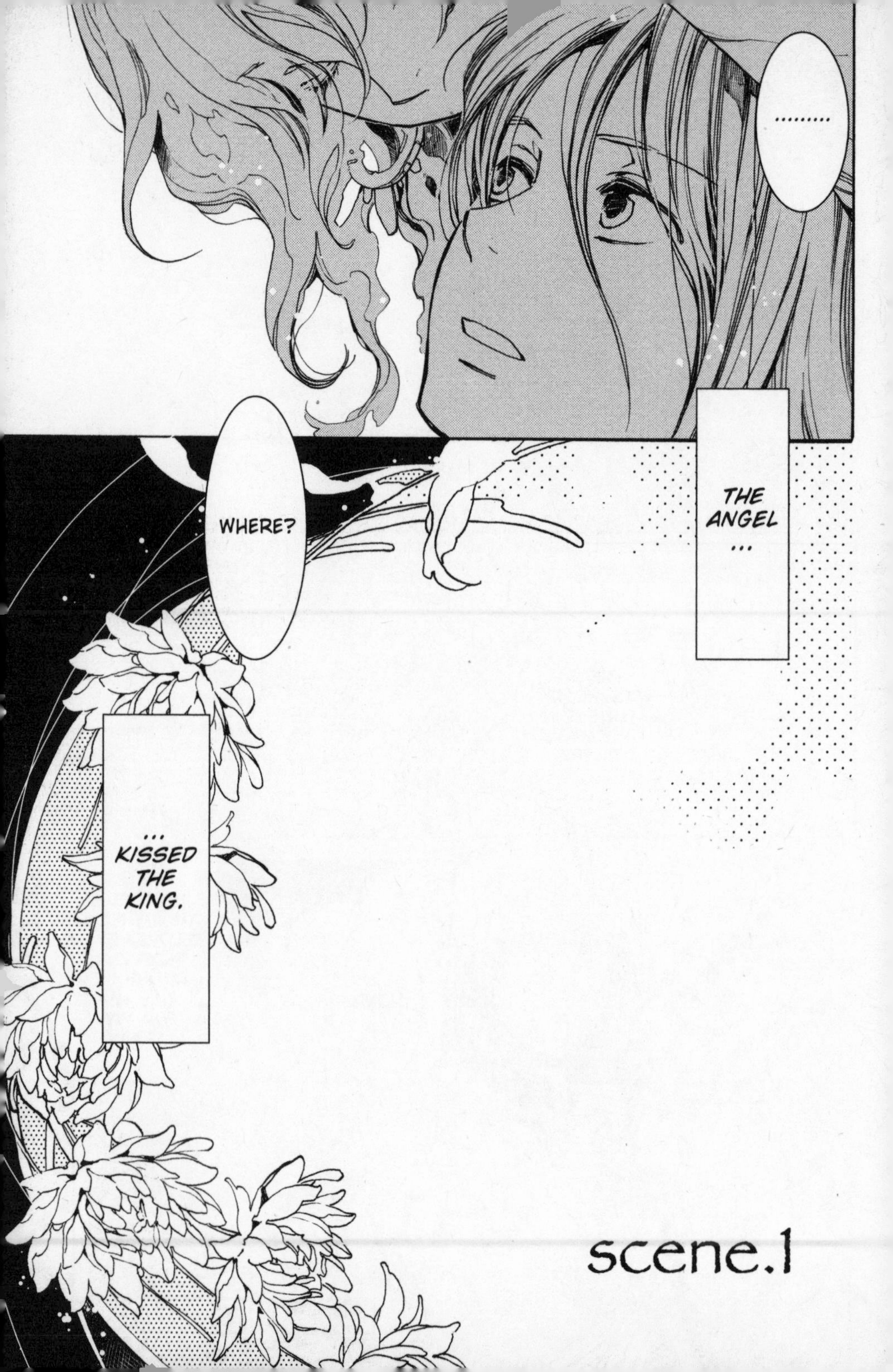
....
THE ANGEL ...
WHERE?
... KISSED THE KING.

scene.1

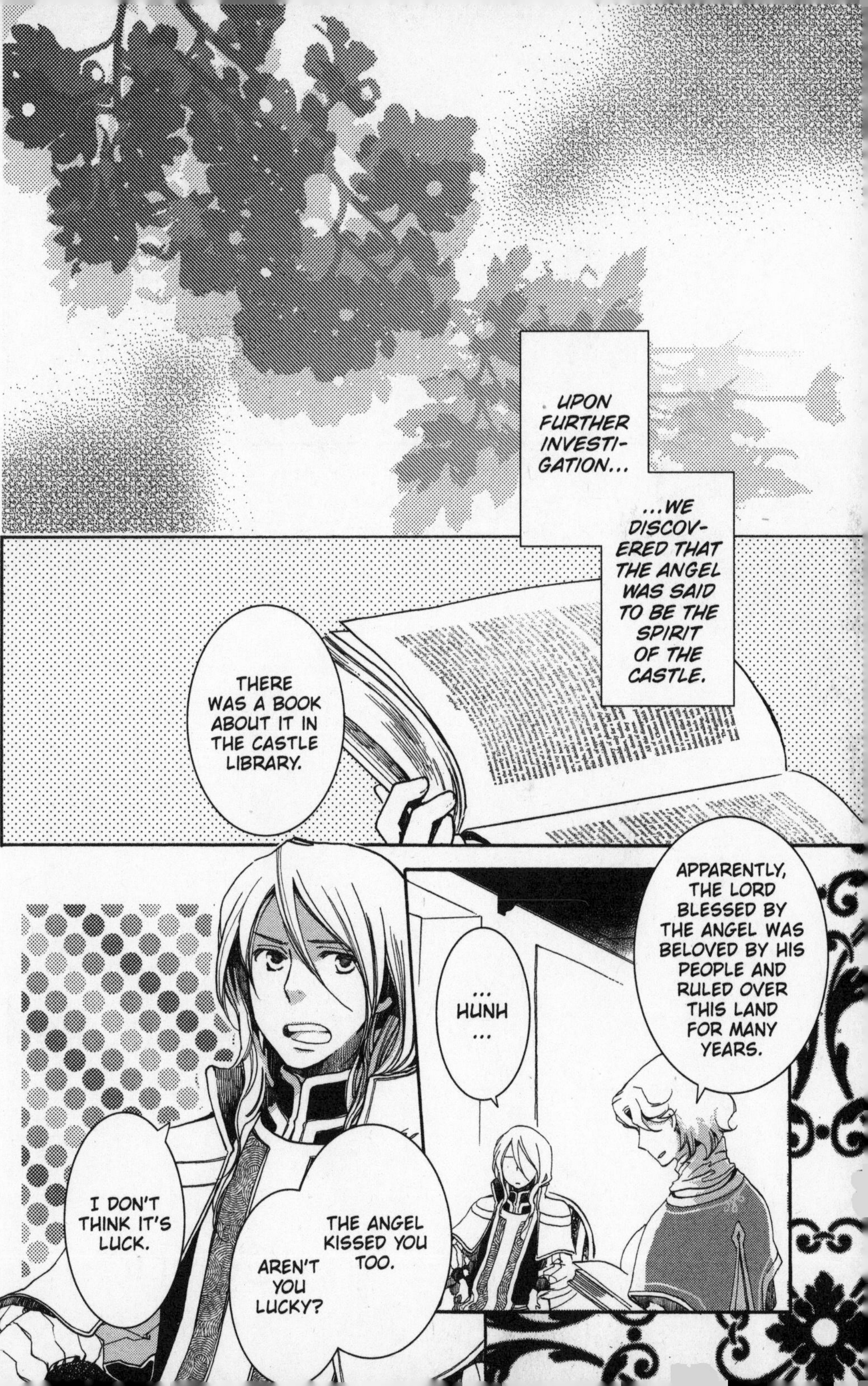
UPON FURTHER INVESTIGATION...
...WE DISCOVERED THAT THE ANGEL WAS SAID TO BE THE SPIRIT OF THE CASTLE.
THERE WAS A BOOK ABOUT IT IN THE CASTLE LIBRARY.
APPARENTLY, THE LORD BLESSED BY THE ANGEL WAS BELOVED BY HIS PEOPLE AND RULED OVER THIS LAND FOR MANY YEARS.
...HUNH...
THE ANGEL KISSED YOU TOO.
AREN'T YOU LUCKY?
I DON'T THINK IT'S LUCK.

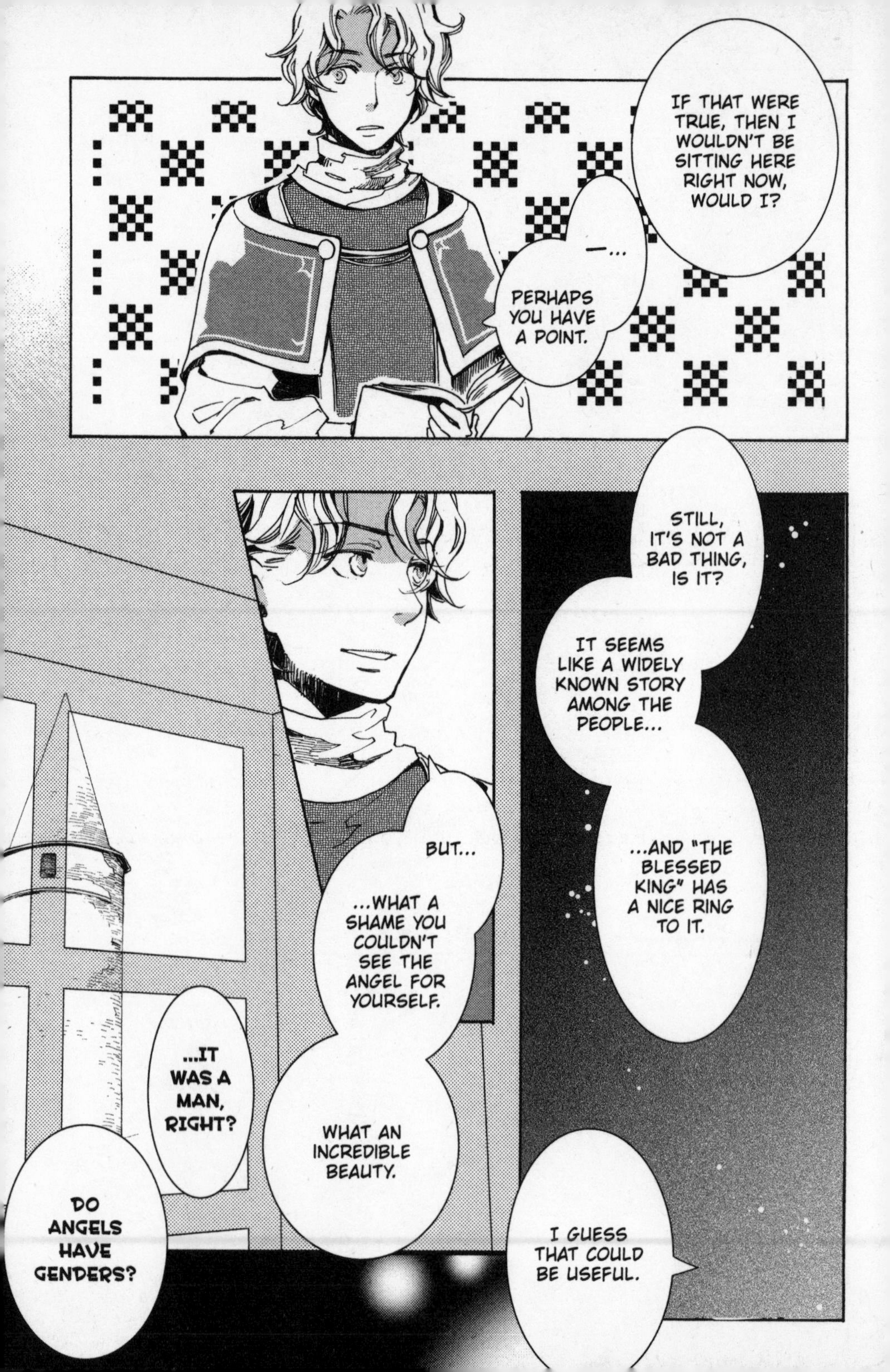
IF THAT WERE TRUE, THEN I WOULDN'T BE SITTING HERE RIGHT NOW, WOULD I?
—...
PERHAPS YOU HAVE A POINT.
STILL, IT'S NOT A BAD THING, IS IT?
IT SEEMS LIKE A WIDELY KNOWN STORY AMONG THE PEOPLE...
...AND "THE BLESSED KING" HAS A NICE RING TO IT.
I GUESS THAT COULD BE USEFUL.
BUT...
...WHAT A SHAME YOU COULDN'T SEE THE ANGEL FOR YOURSELF.
WHAT AN INCREDIBLE BEAUTY.
...IT WAS A MAN, RIGHT?
DO ANGELS HAVE GENDERS?

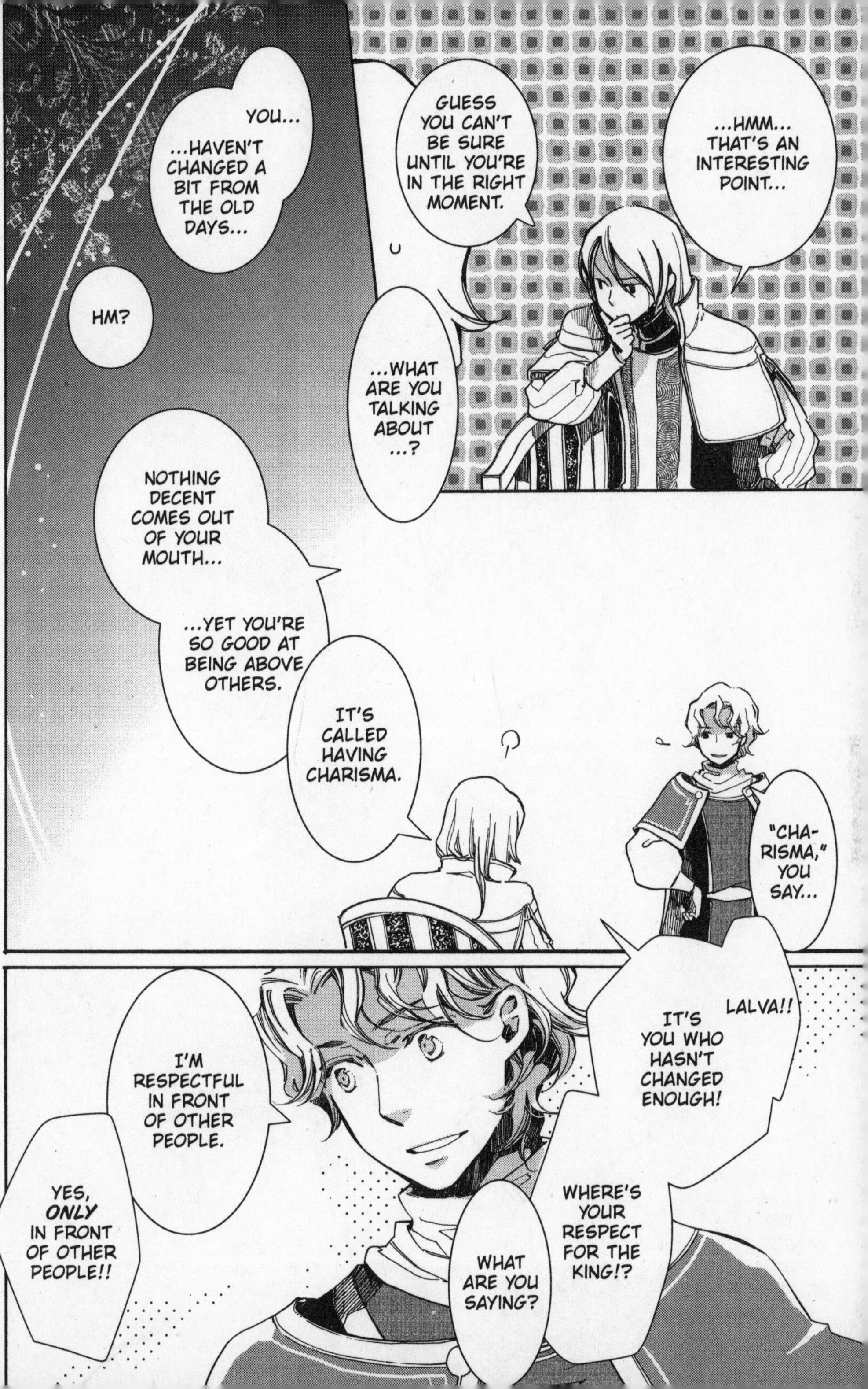
...HMM... THAT'S AN INTERESTING POINT...
GUESS YOU CAN'T BE SURE UNTIL YOU'RE IN THE RIGHT MOMENT.
...WHAT ARE YOU TALKING ABOUT ...?
YOU...
...HAVEN'T CHANGED A BIT FROM THE OLD DAYS...
HM?
NOTHING DECENT COMES OUT OF YOUR MOUTH...
...YET YOU'RE SO GOOD AT BEING ABOVE OTHERS.
IT'S CALLED HAVING CHARISMA.
"CHA-RISMA," YOU SAY...
LALVA!!
IT'S YOU WHO HASN'T CHANGED ENOUGH!
I'M RESPECTFUL IN FRONT OF OTHER PEOPLE.
WHERE'S YOUR RESPECT FOR THE KING!?
WHAT ARE YOU SAYING?
YES, ***ONLY*** IN FRONT OF OTHER PEOPLE!!

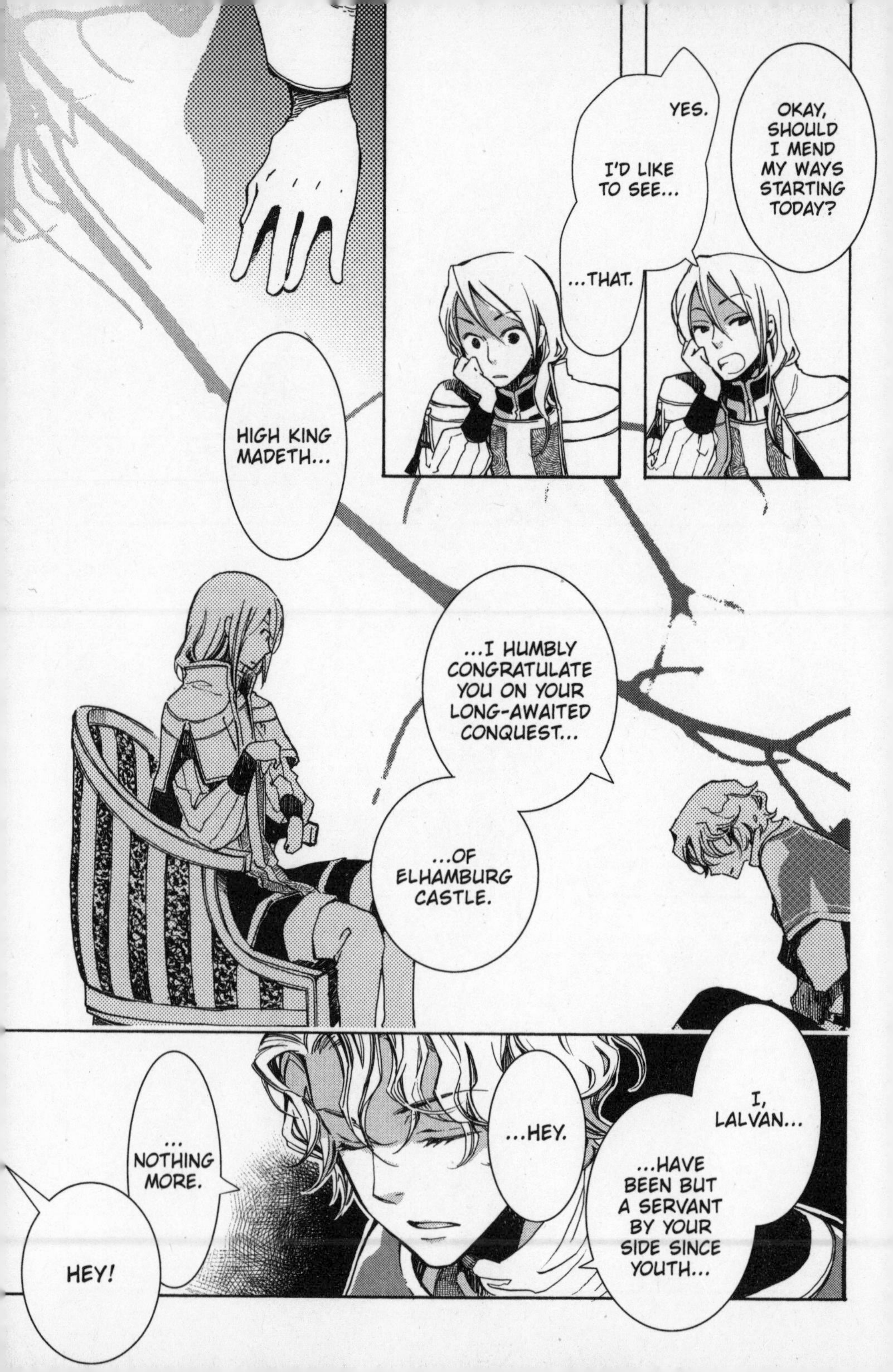
OKAY, SHOULD I MEND MY WAYS STARTING TODAY?
YES.
I'D LIKE TO SEE...
...THAT.
HIGH KING MADETH...
...I HUMBLY CONGRATULATE YOU ON YOUR LONG-AWAITED CONQUEST...
...OF ELHAMBURG CASTLE.
I, LALVAN...
...HAVE BEEN BUT A SERVANT BY YOUR SIDE SINCE YOUTH...
...HEY.
... NOTHING MORE.
HEY!

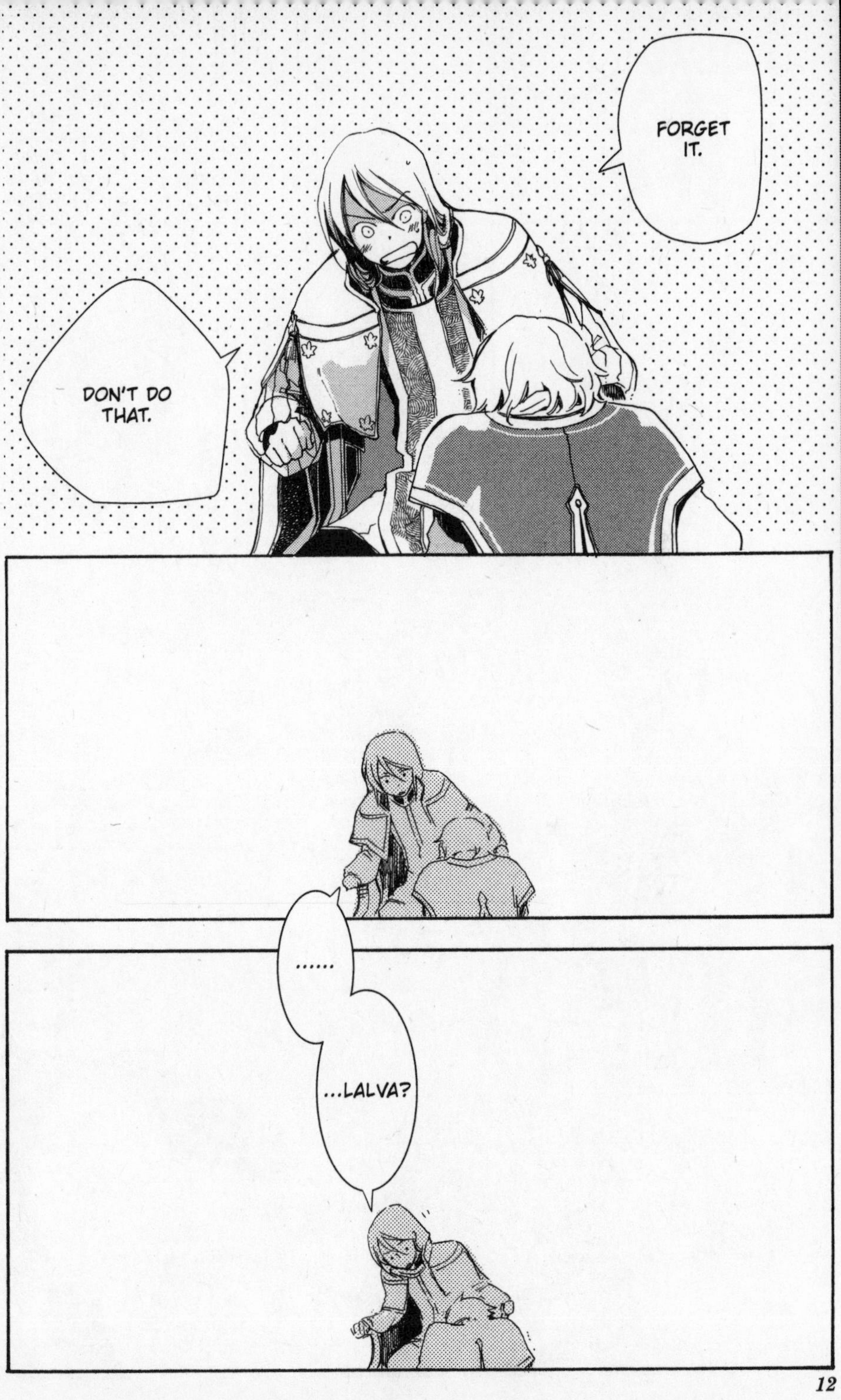
FORGET IT.
DON'T DO THAT.
......
...LALVA?

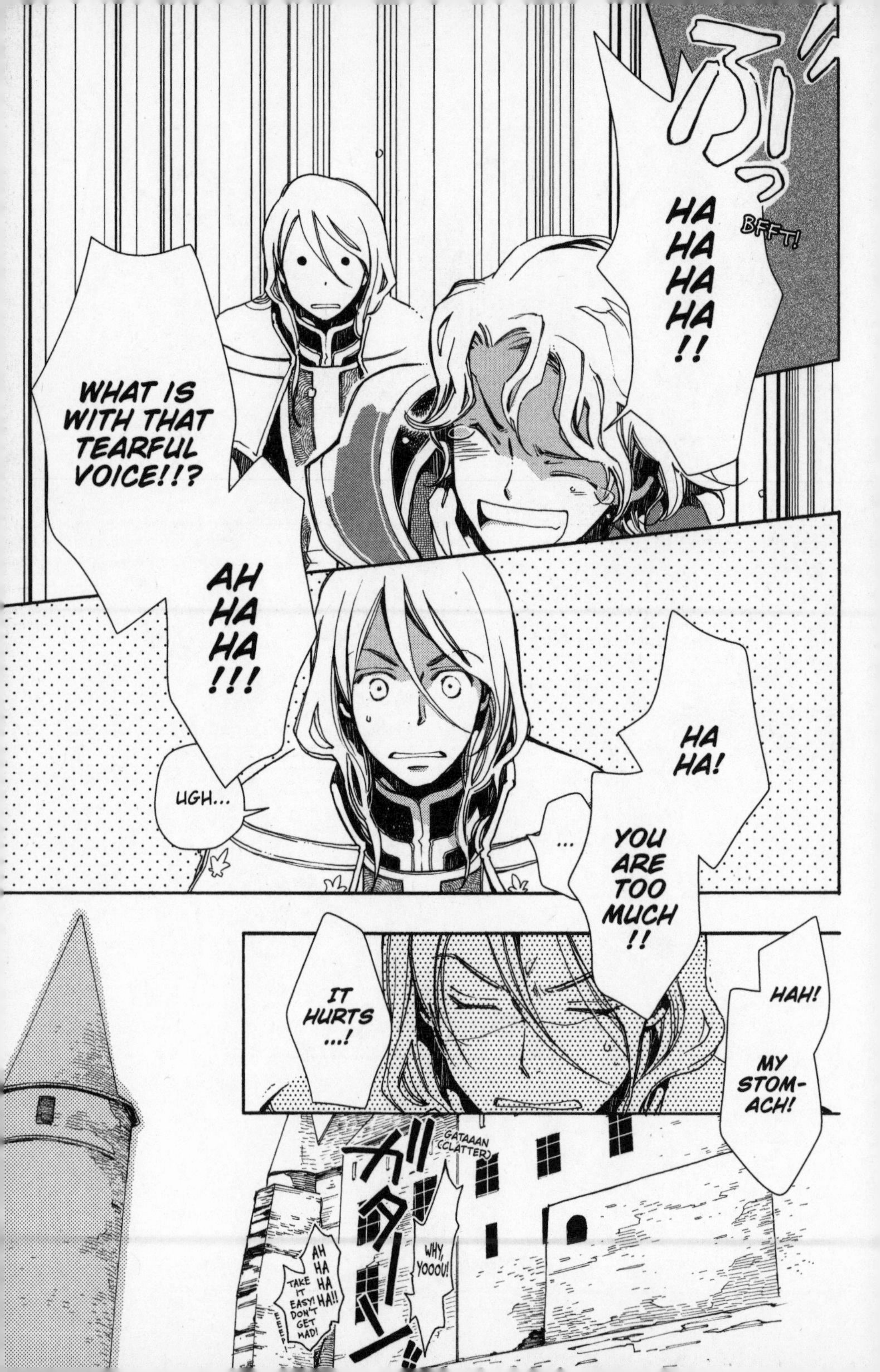
ふっ
BFFT!
HA HA HA HA!!
WHAT IS WITH THAT TEARFUL VOICE!!?
AH HA HA!!!
HA HA!
UGH...
...
YOU ARE TOO MUCH!!
HAH! MY STOMACH!
IT HURTS...!
GATAAAN (CLATTER)
ガターン
WHY, YOOOU!
AH HA HA HA!!
TAKE IT EASY! DON'T GET MAD!
EEEEP!

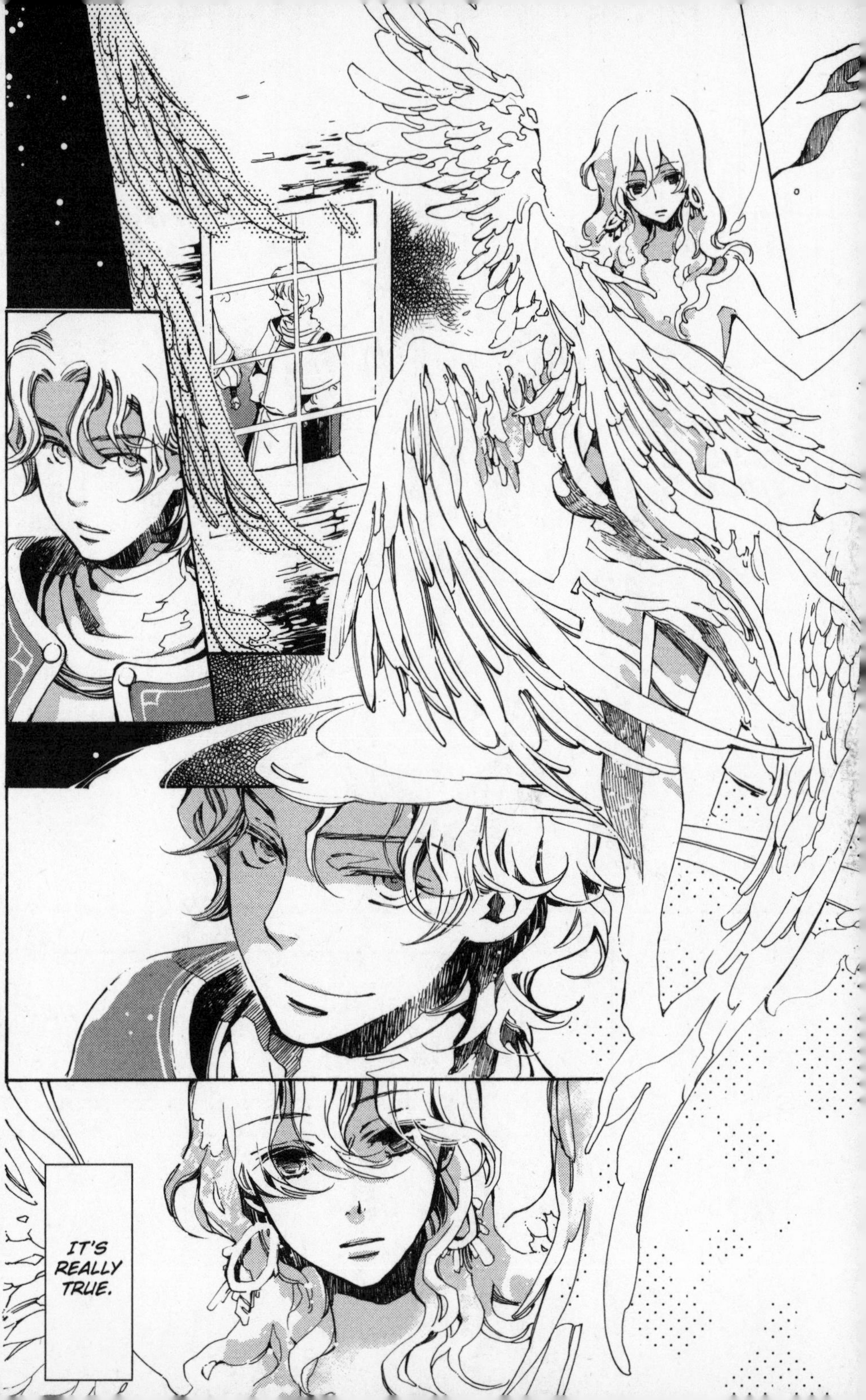
IT'S REALLY TRUE.

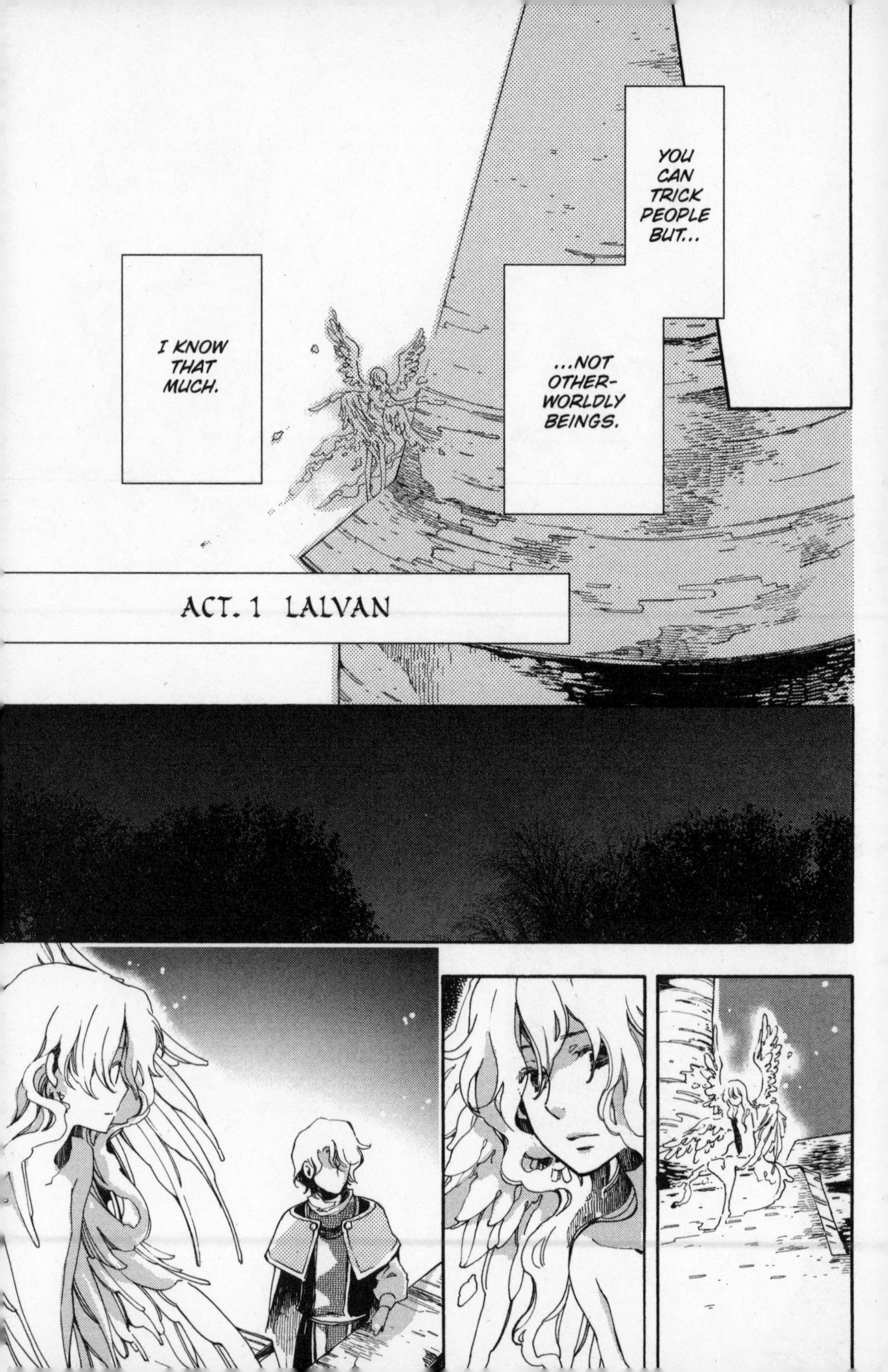
YOU CAN TRICK PEOPLE BUT...
...NOT OTHER-WORLDLY BEINGS.
I KNOW THAT MUCH.
ACT. 1 LALVAN

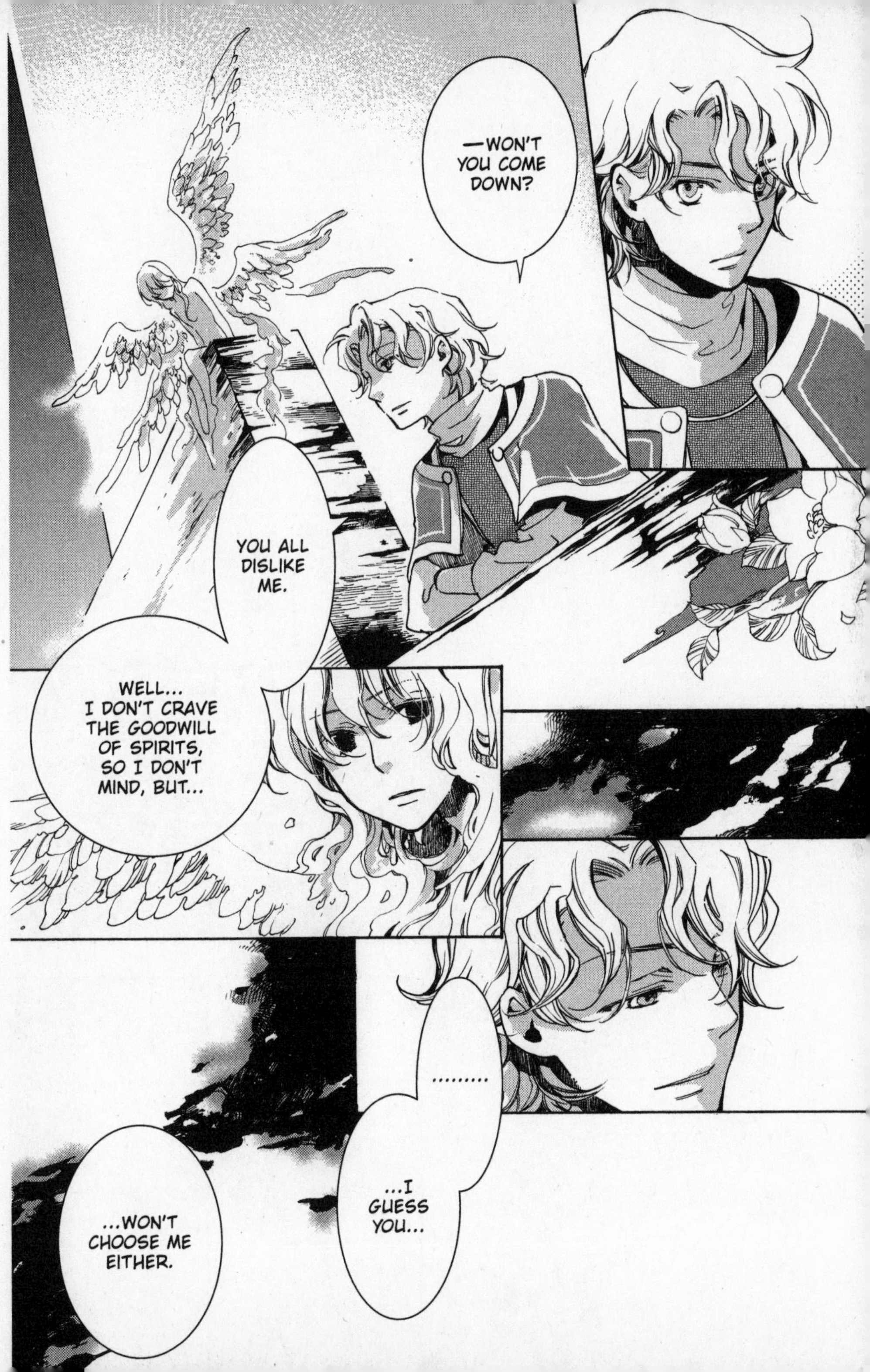
—WON'T YOU COME DOWN?
YOU ALL DISLIKE ME.
WELL... I DON'T CRAVE THE GOODWILL OF SPIRITS, SO I DON'T MIND, BUT...
....
...I GUESS YOU...
...WON'T CHOOSE ME EITHER.

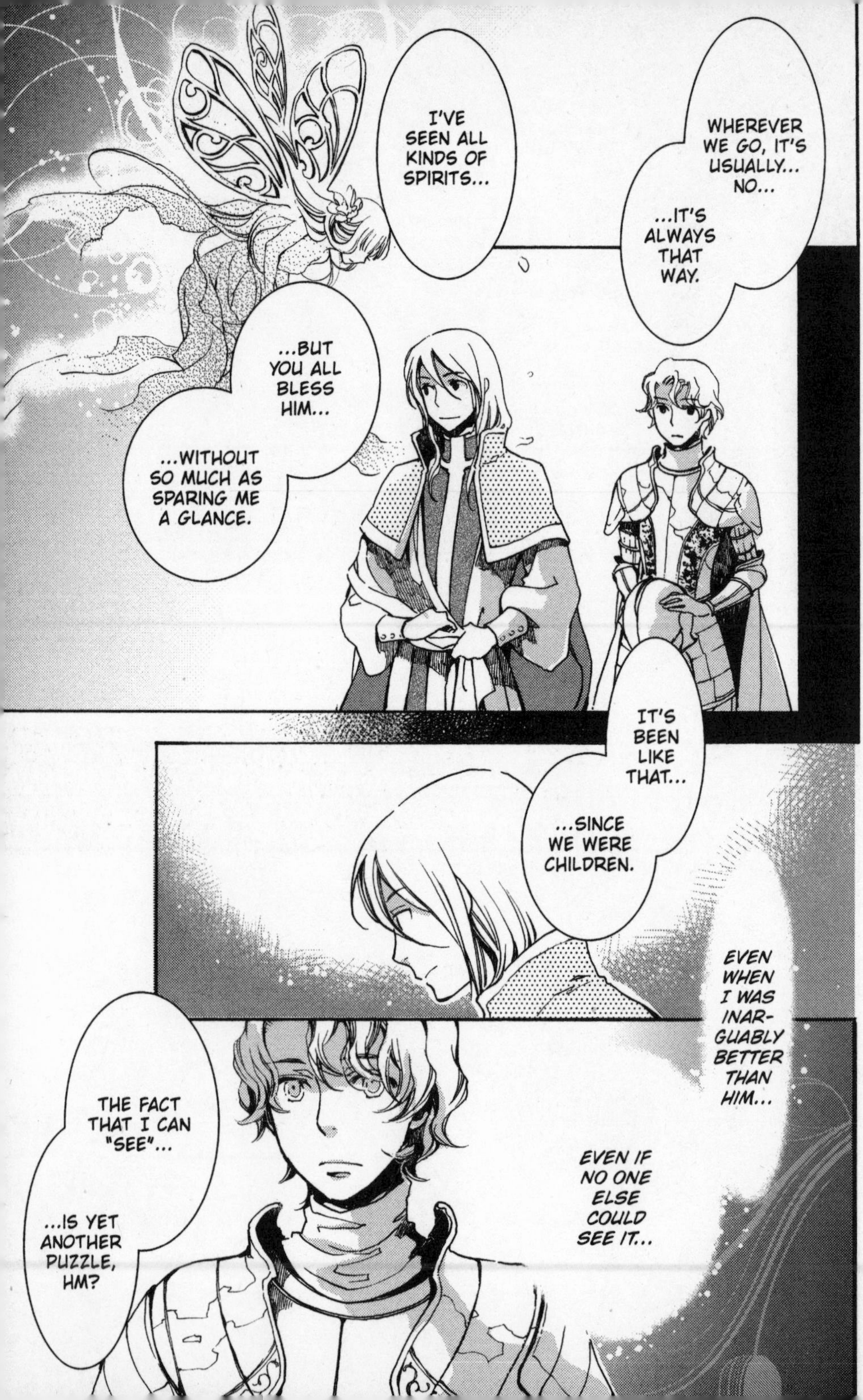
WHEREVER WE GO, IT'S USUALLY... NO...
...IT'S ALWAYS THAT WAY.
I'VE SEEN ALL KINDS OF SPIRITS...
...BUT YOU ALL BLESS HIM...
...WITHOUT SO MUCH AS SPARING ME A GLANCE.
IT'S BEEN LIKE THAT...
...SINCE WE WERE CHILDREN.
EVEN WHEN I WAS INARGUABLY BETTER THAN HIM...
EVEN IF NO ONE ELSE COULD SEE IT...
THE FACT THAT I CAN "SEE"...
...IS YET ANOTHER PUZZLE, HM?

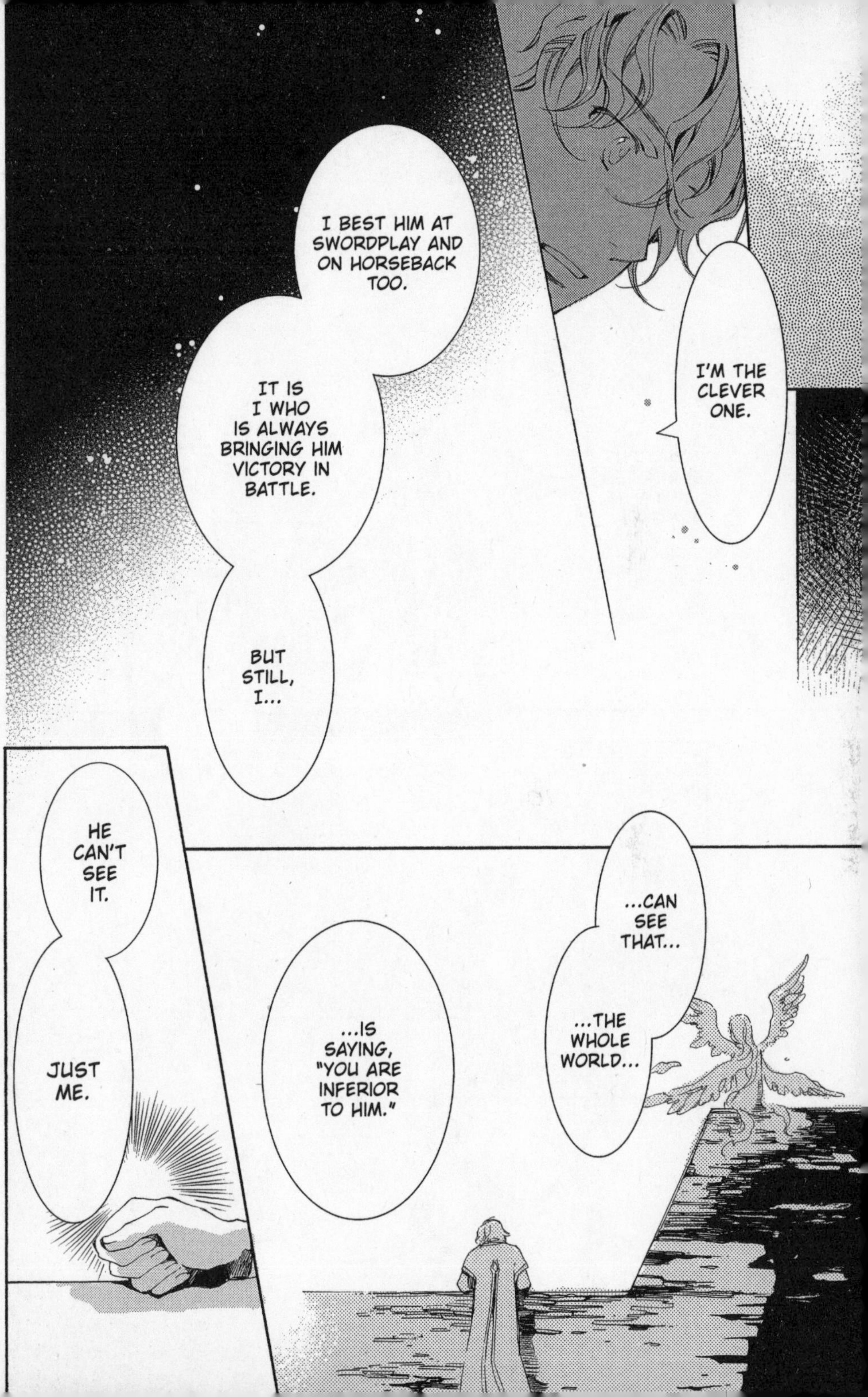
I'M THE CLEVER ONE.
I BEST HIM AT SWORDPLAY AND ON HORSEBACK TOO.
IT IS I WHO IS ALWAYS BRINGING HIM VICTORY IN BATTLE.
BUT STILL, I...
...CAN SEE THAT...
...THE WHOLE WORLD...
...IS SAYING, "YOU ARE INFERIOR TO HIM."
HE CAN'T SEE IT.
JUST ME.

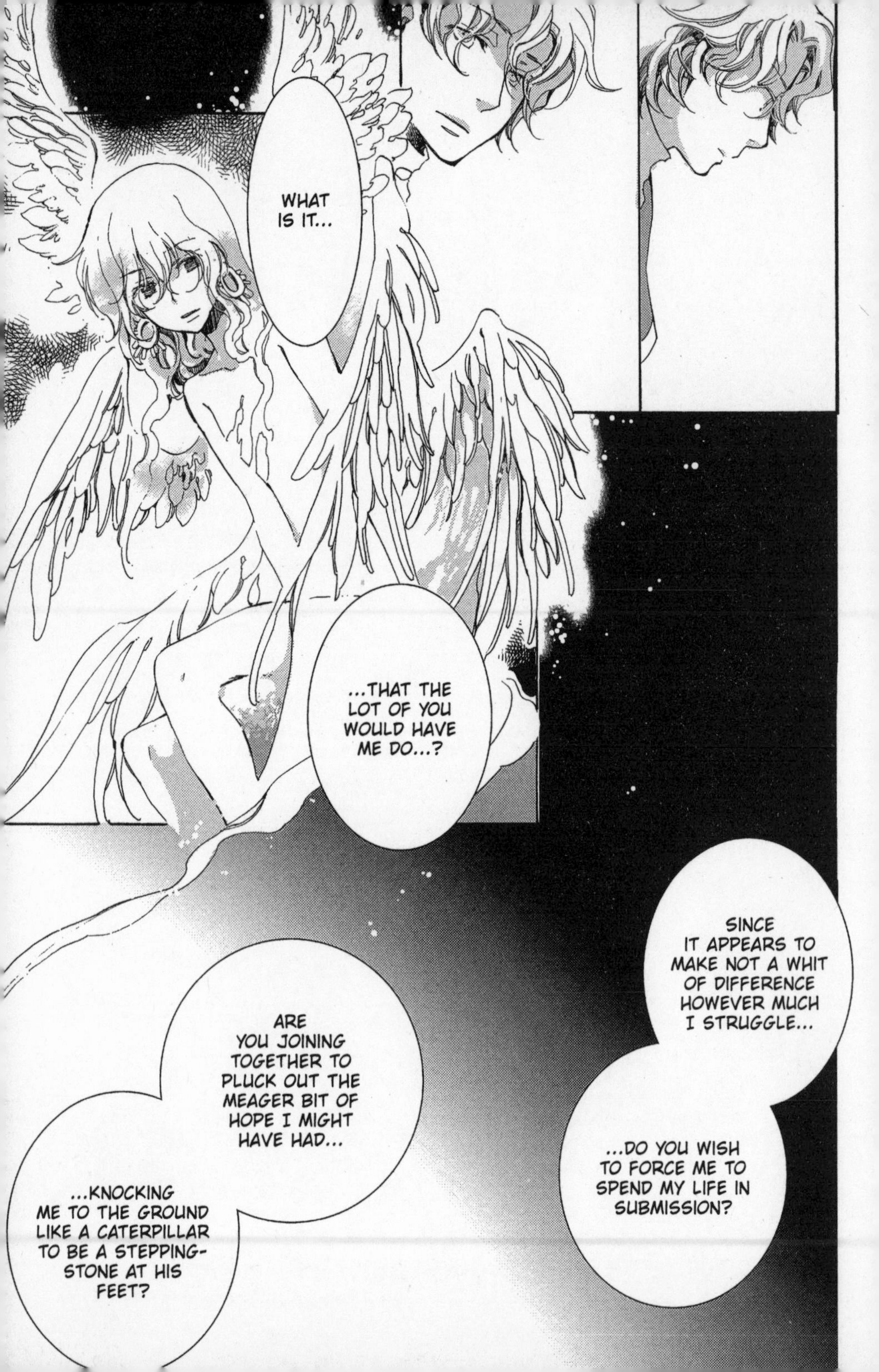
WHAT IS IT...
...THAT THE LOT OF YOU WOULD HAVE ME DO...?
SINCE IT APPEARS TO MAKE NOT A WHIT OF DIFFERENCE HOWEVER MUCH I STRUGGLE...
...DO YOU WISH TO FORCE ME TO SPEND MY LIFE IN SUBMISSION?
ARE YOU JOINING TOGETHER TO PLUCK OUT THE MEAGER BIT OF HOPE I MIGHT HAVE HAD...
...KNOCKING ME TO THE GROUND LIKE A CATERPILLAR TO BE A STEPPING-STONE AT HIS FEET?

DO YOU THINK I...

...WOULD SIMPLY ACQUIESCE TO SUCH A THING?

ACT. 2 HIGH KING MADETH

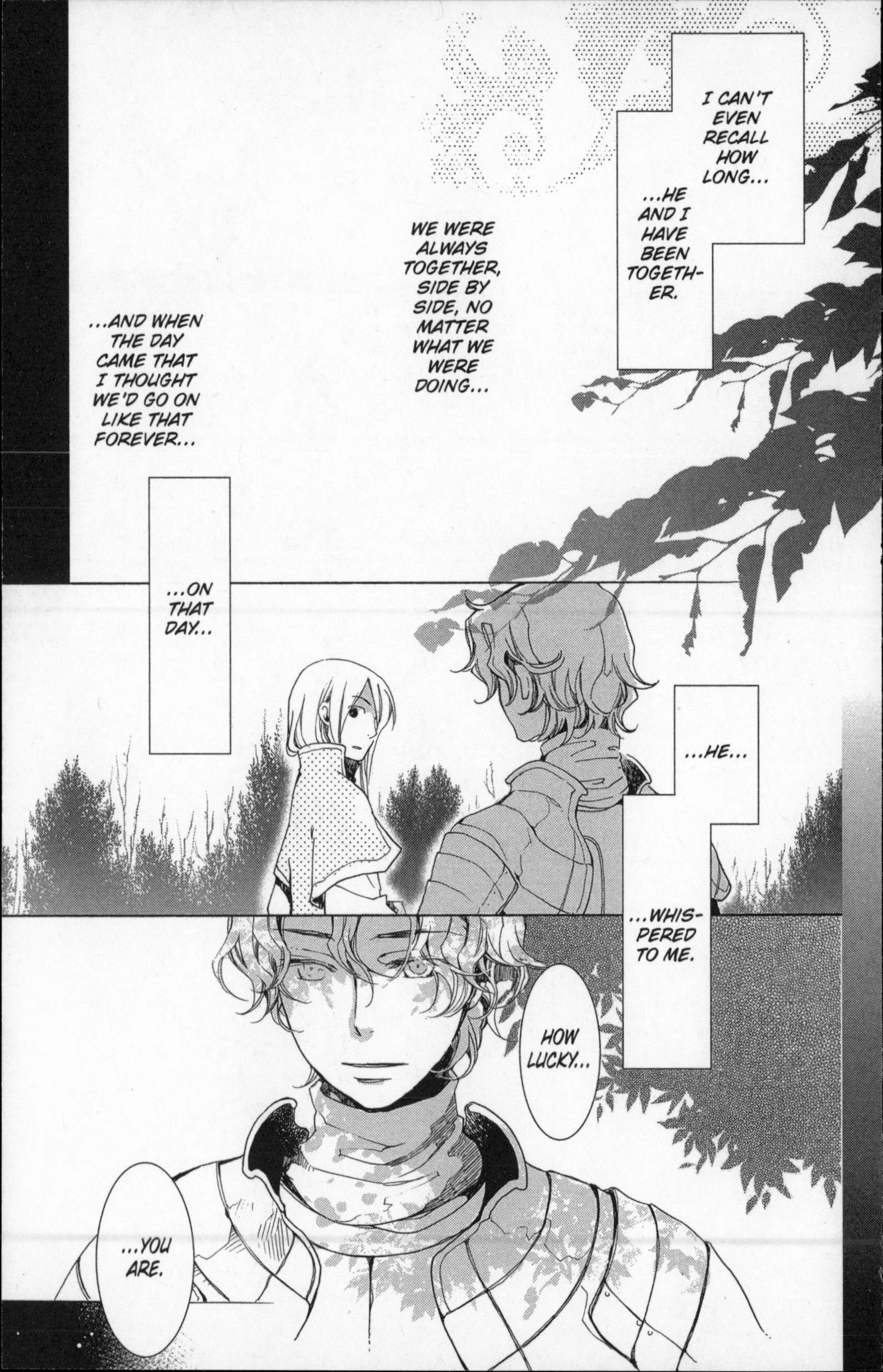

I CAN'T EVEN RECALL HOW LONG...
...HE AND I HAVE BEEN TOGETH-ER.
WE WERE ALWAYS TOGETHER, SIDE BY SIDE, NO MATTER WHAT WE WERE DOING...
...AND WHEN THE DAY CAME THAT I THOUGHT WE'D GO ON LIKE THAT FOREVER...
...ON THAT DAY...
...HE...
...WHIS-PERED TO ME.
HOW LUCKY...
...YOU ARE.

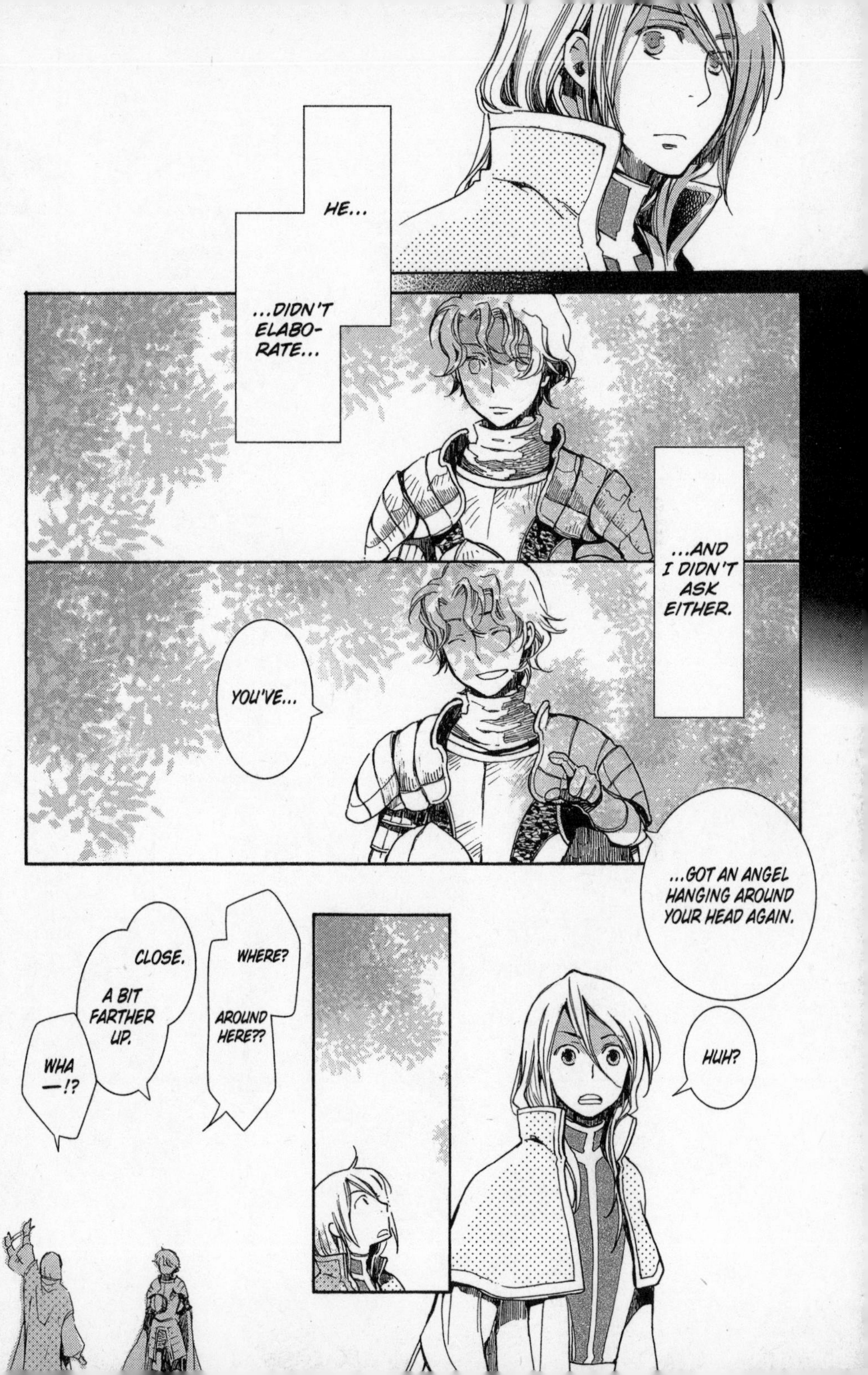
HE...
...DIDN'T ELABORATE...
...AND I DIDN'T ASK EITHER.
YOU'VE...
...GOT AN ANGEL HANGING AROUND YOUR HEAD AGAIN.
HUH?
WHERE? AROUND HERE??
CLOSE. A BIT FARTHER UP.
WHA—!?

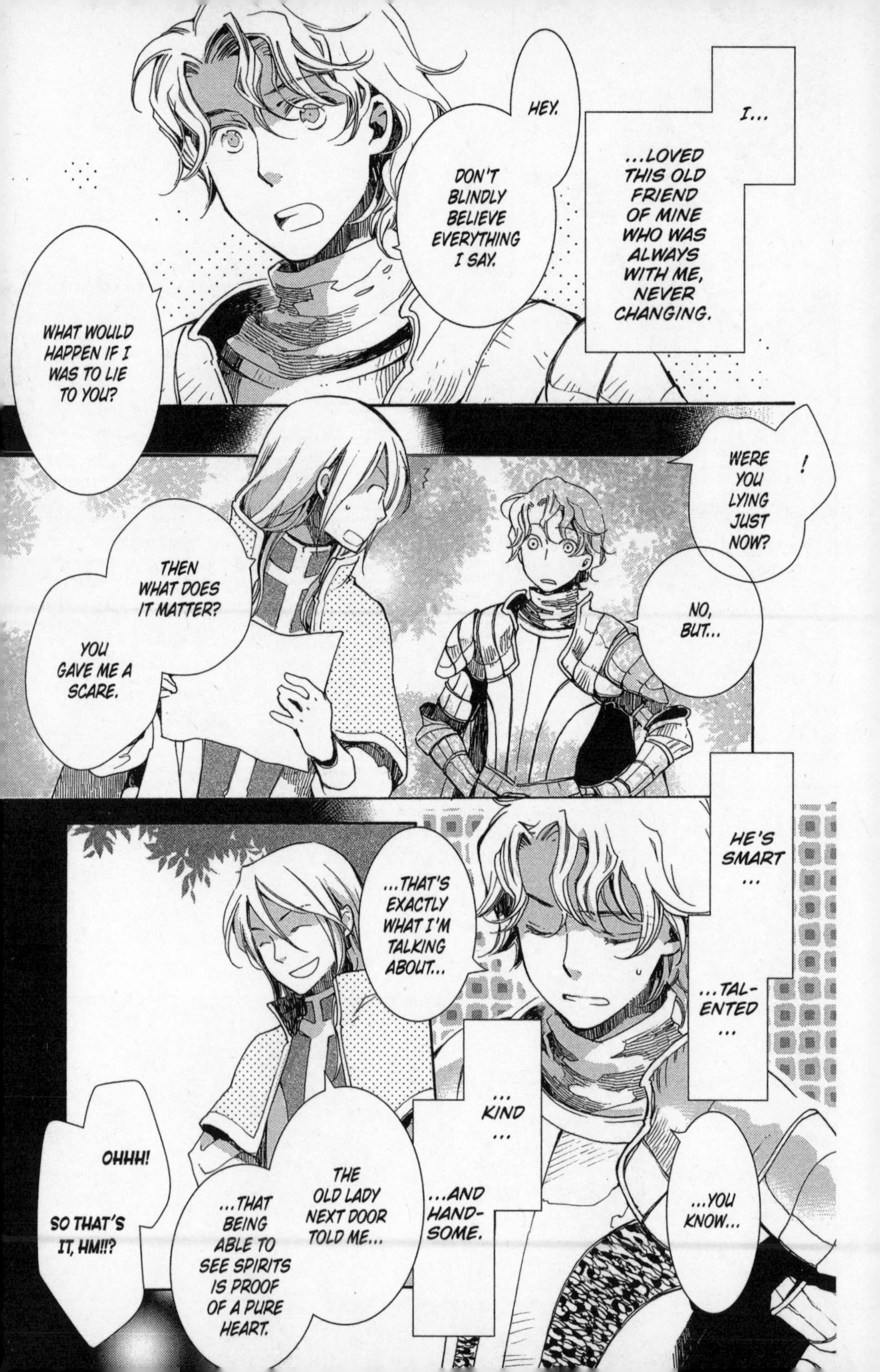
I...
...LOVED THIS OLD FRIEND OF MINE WHO WAS ALWAYS WITH ME, NEVER CHANGING.
HEY.
DON'T BLINDLY BELIEVE EVERYTHING I SAY.
WHAT WOULD HAPPEN IF I WAS TO LIE TO YOU?
!
WERE YOU LYING JUST NOW?
NO, BUT...
THEN WHAT DOES IT MATTER?
YOU GAVE ME A SCARE.
HE'S SMART...
...TALENTED...
...THAT'S EXACTLY WHAT I'M TALKING ABOUT...
...KIND...
...YOU KNOW...
...AND HANDSOME.
THE OLD LADY NEXT DOOR TOLD ME...
...THAT BEING ABLE TO SEE SPIRITS IS PROOF OF A PURE HEART.
OHHH!
SO THAT'S IT, HM!!?

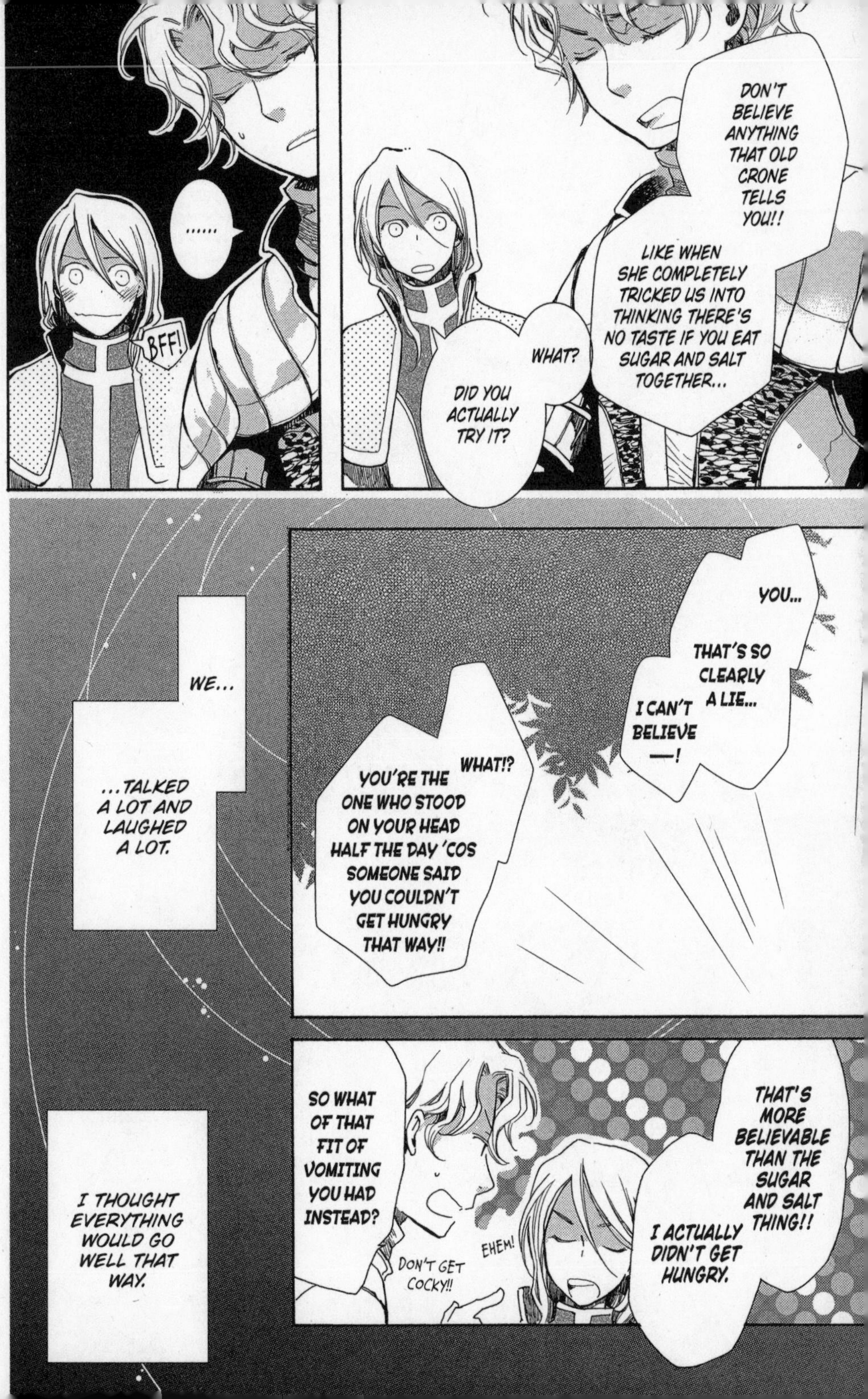
DON'T BELIEVE ANYTHING THAT OLD CRONE TELLS YOU!!
LIKE WHEN SHE COMPLETELY TRICKED US INTO THINKING THERE'S NO TASTE IF YOU EAT SUGAR AND SALT TOGETHER...
WHAT?
DID YOU ACTUALLY TRY IT?
......
BFF!
YOU...
THAT'S SO CLEARLY A LIE...
I CAN'T BELIEVE —!
WHAT!?
YOU'RE THE ONE WHO STOOD ON YOUR HEAD HALF THE DAY 'COS SOMEONE SAID YOU COULDN'T GET HUNGRY THAT WAY!!
THAT'S MORE BELIEVABLE THAN THE SUGAR AND SALT THING!!
I ACTUALLY DIDN'T GET HUNGRY.
EHEM!
SO WHAT OF THAT FIT OF VOMITING YOU HAD INSTEAD?
DON'T GET COCKY!!
WE...
...TALKED A LOT AND LAUGHED A LOT.
I THOUGHT EVERYTHING WOULD GO WELL THAT WAY.

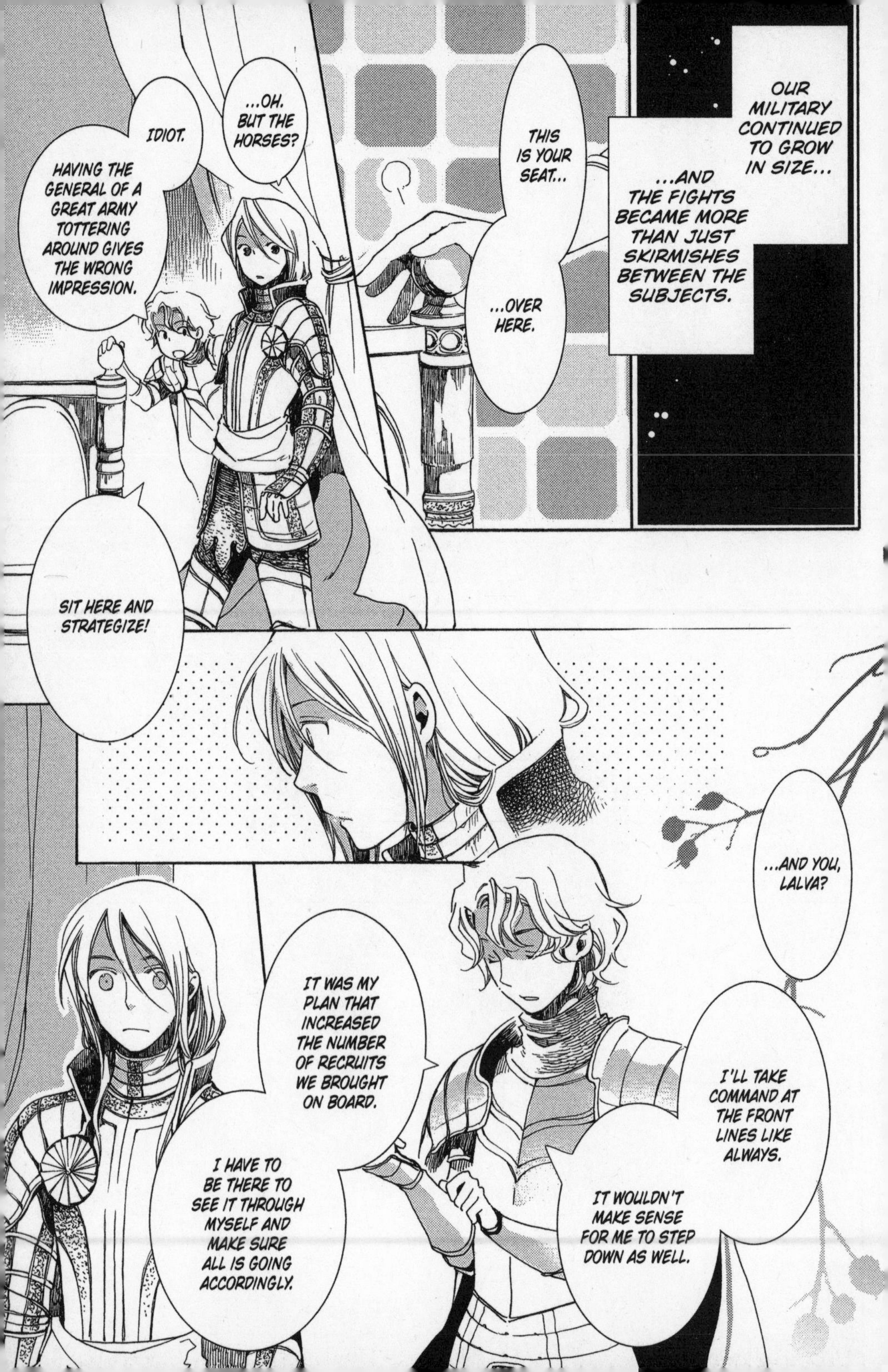
OUR MILITARY CONTINUED TO GROW IN SIZE...
...AND THE FIGHTS BECAME MORE THAN JUST SKIRMISHES BETWEEN THE SUBJECTS.
THIS IS YOUR SEAT...
...OVER HERE.
...OH. BUT THE HORSES?
IDIOT.
HAVING THE GENERAL OF A GREAT ARMY TOTTERING AROUND GIVES THE WRONG IMPRESSION.
SIT HERE AND STRATEGIZE!
...AND YOU, LALVA?
IT WAS MY PLAN THAT INCREASED THE NUMBER OF RECRUITS WE BROUGHT ON BOARD.
I HAVE TO BE THERE TO SEE IT THROUGH MYSELF AND MAKE SURE ALL IS GOING ACCORDINGLY.
I'LL TAKE COMMAND AT THE FRONT LINES LIKE ALWAYS.
IT WOULDN'T MAKE SENSE FOR ME TO STEP DOWN AS WELL.

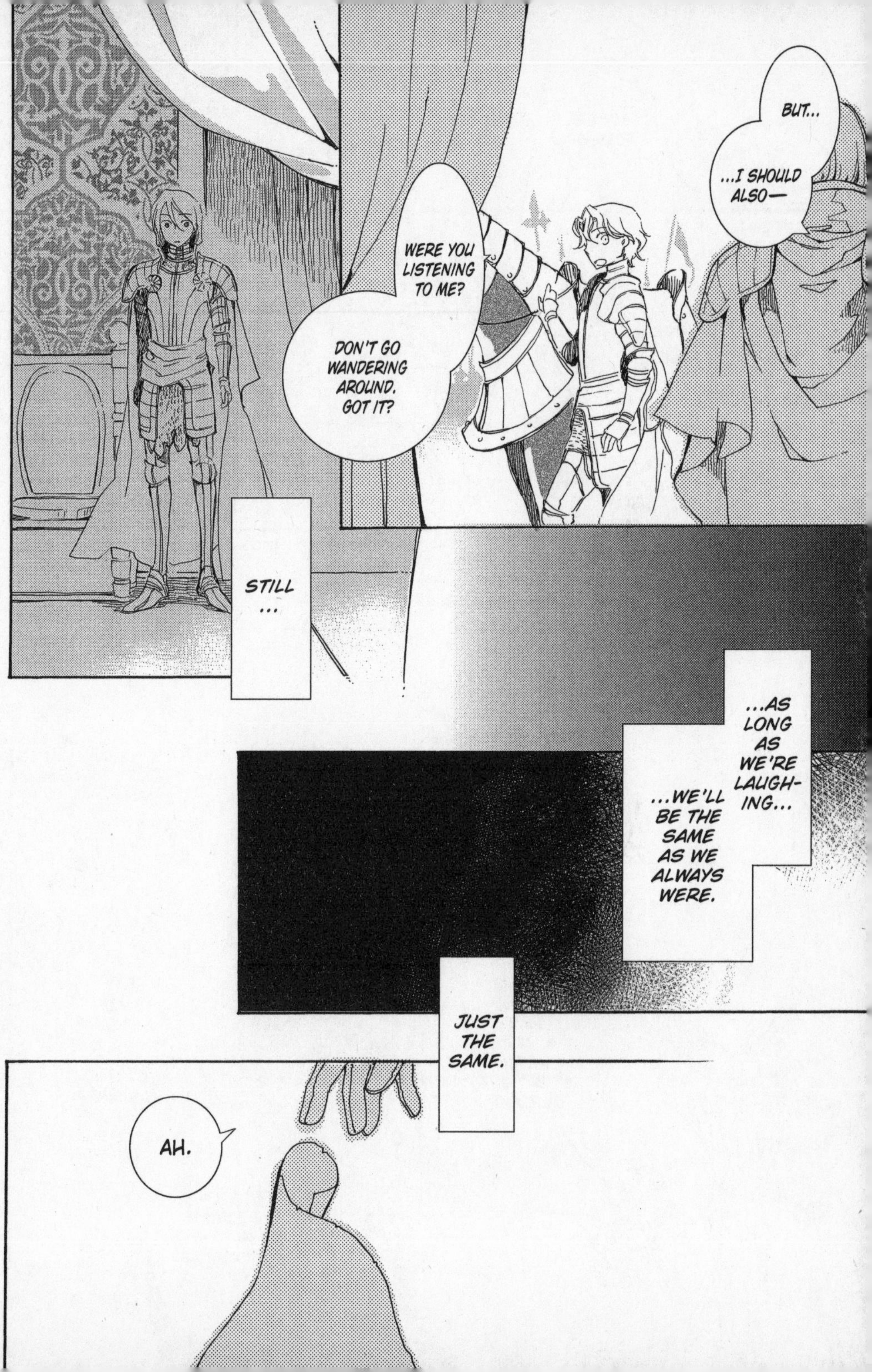
BUT...
...I SHOULD ALSO—
WERE YOU LISTENING TO ME?
DON'T GO WANDERING AROUND. GOT IT?
STILL...
...AS LONG AS WE'RE LAUGH-ING...
...WE'LL BE THE SAME AS WE ALWAYS WERE.
JUST THE SAME.
AH.

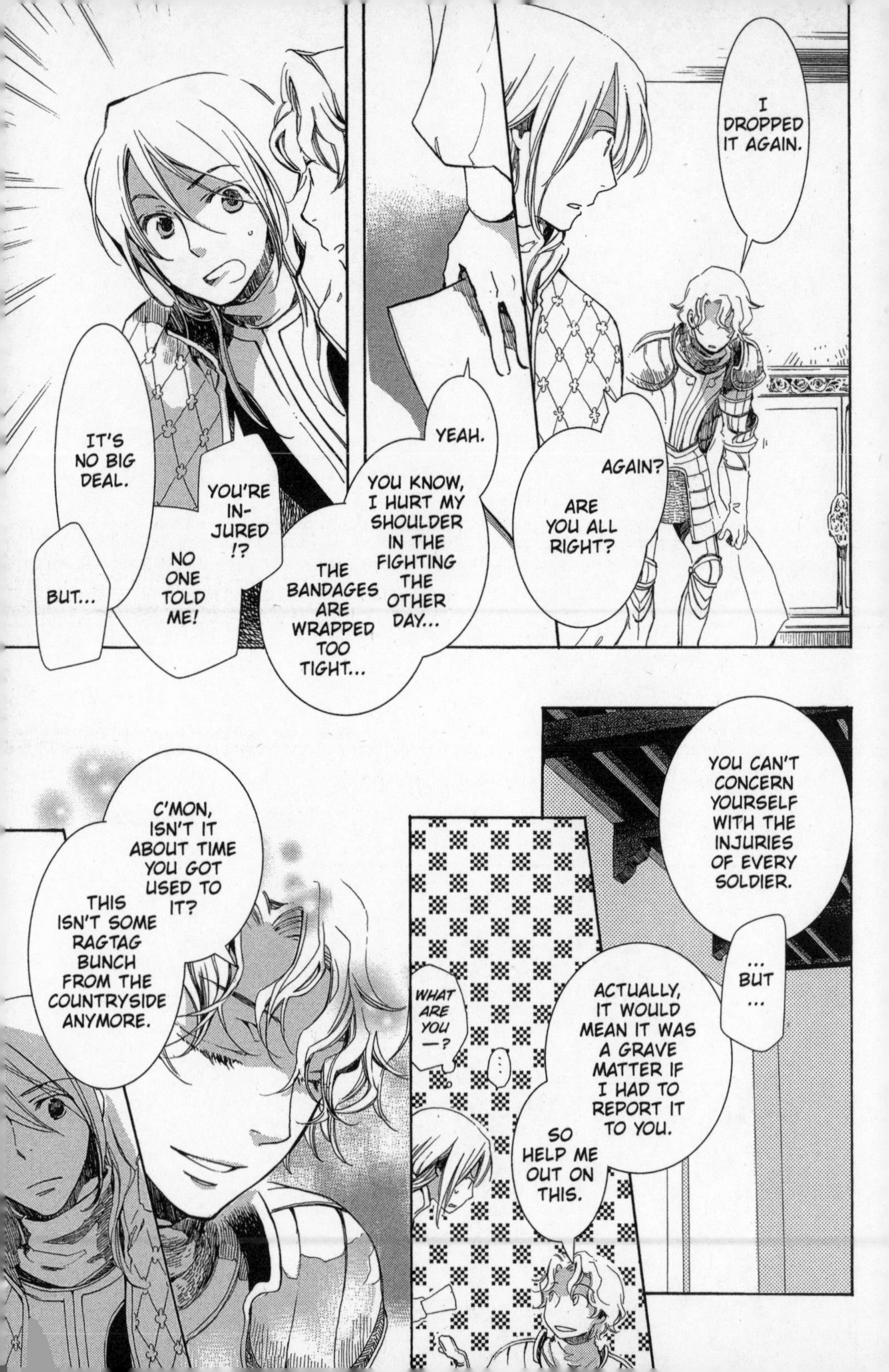
I DROPPED IT AGAIN.
AGAIN?
ARE YOU ALL RIGHT?
YEAH.
YOU KNOW, I HURT MY SHOULDER IN THE FIGHTING THE OTHER DAY...
THE BANDAGES ARE WRAPPED TOO TIGHT...
YOU'RE IN-JURED!?
NO ONE TOLD ME!
IT'S NO BIG DEAL.
BUT...
YOU CAN'T CONCERN YOURSELF WITH THE INJURIES OF EVERY SOLDIER.
...BUT...
ACTUALLY, IT WOULD MEAN IT WAS A GRAVE MATTER IF I HAD TO REPORT IT TO YOU.
SO HELP ME OUT ON THIS.
WHAT ARE YOU—?
...
C'MON, ISN'T IT ABOUT TIME YOU GOT USED TO IT?
THIS ISN'T SOME RAGTAG BUNCH FROM THE COUNTRYSIDE ANYMORE.

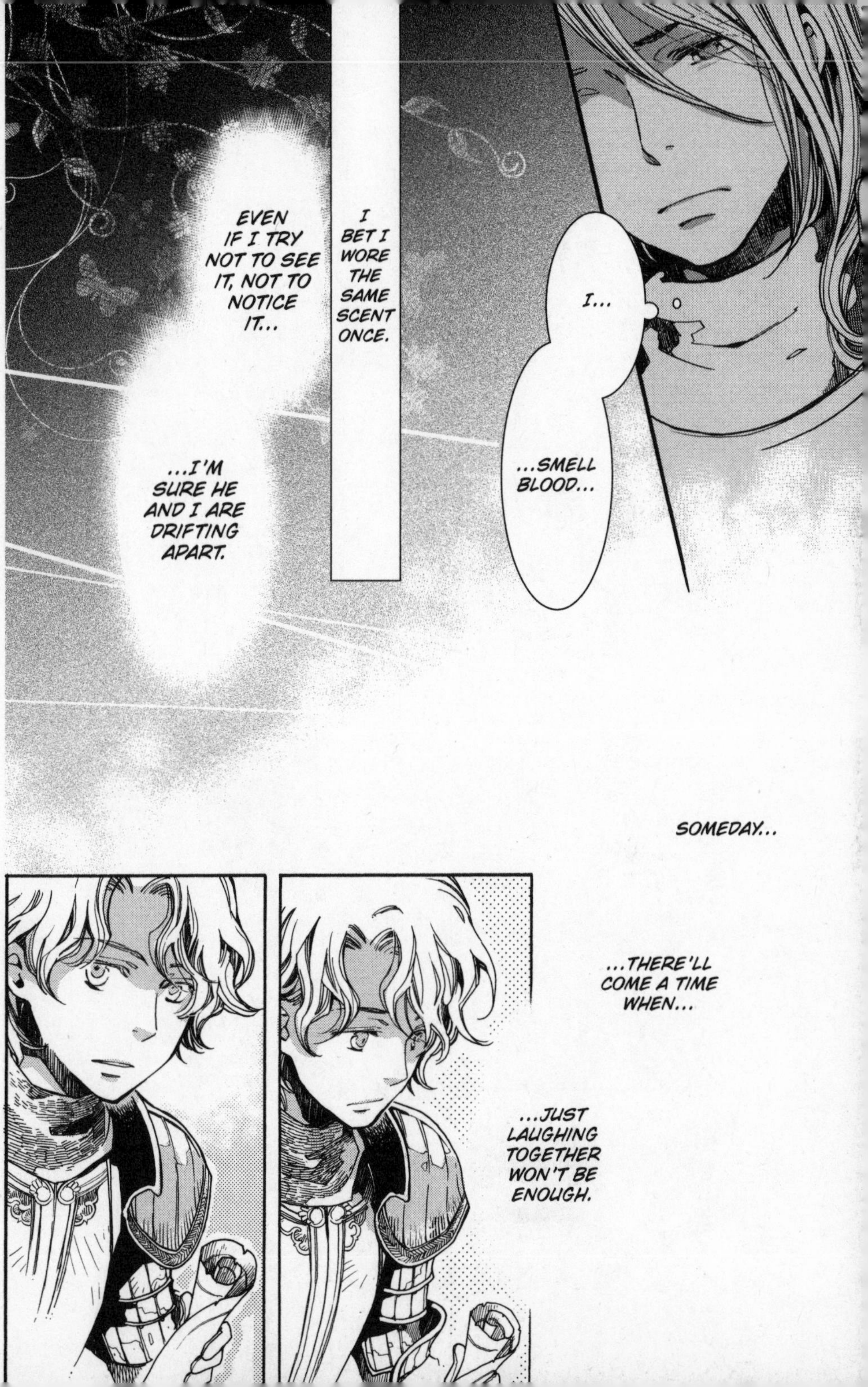
I... ...SMELL BLOOD...
I BET I WORE THE SAME SCENT ONCE.
EVEN IF I TRY NOT TO SEE IT, NOT TO NOTICE IT...
...I'M SURE HE AND I ARE DRIFTING APART.
SOMEDAY...
...THERE'LL COME A TIME WHEN...
...JUST LAUGHING TOGETHER WON'T BE ENOUGH.

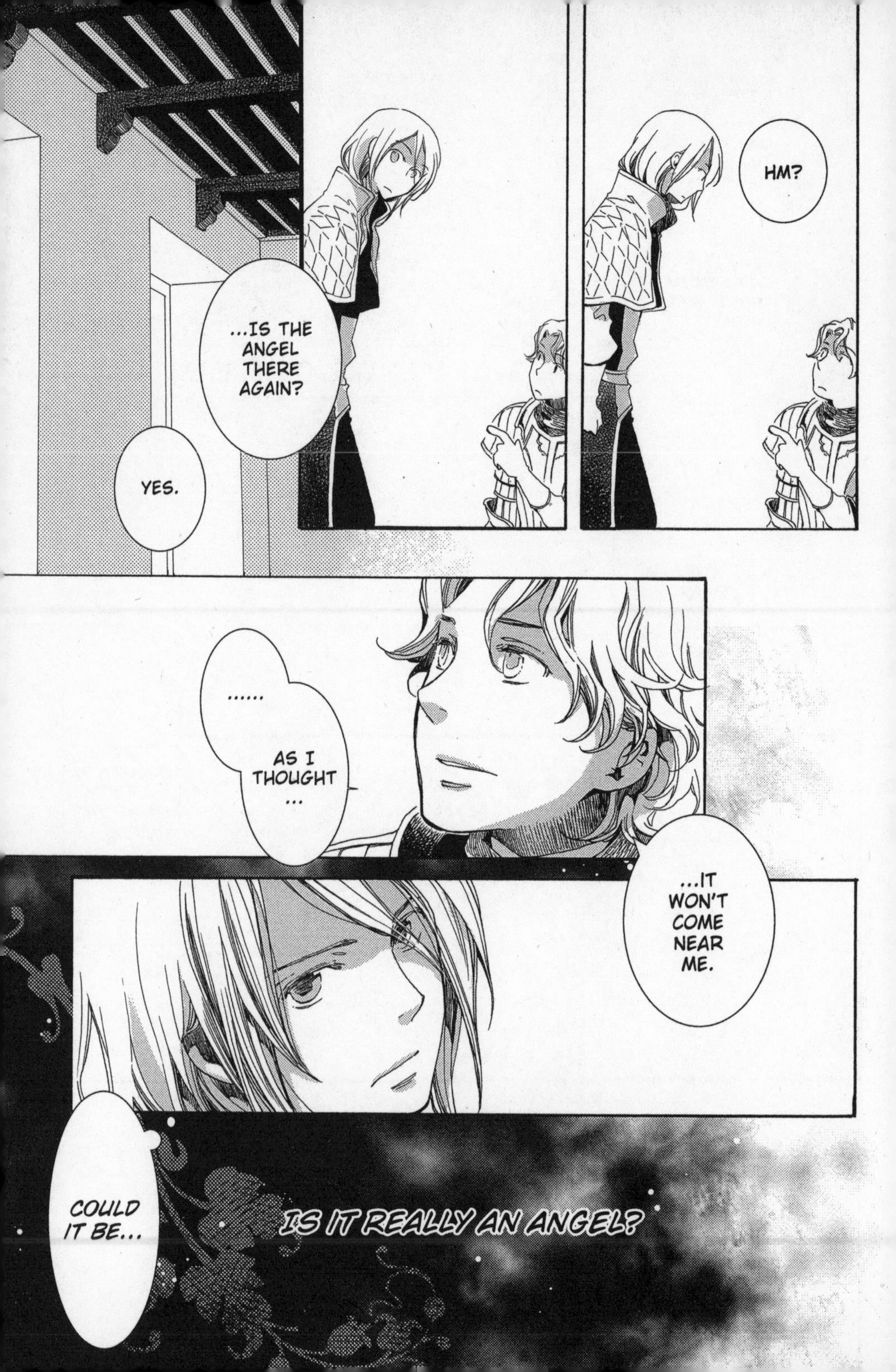
HM?
...IS THE ANGEL THERE AGAIN?
YES.
......
AS I THOUGHT ...
...IT WON'T COME NEAR ME.
IS IT REALLY AN ANGEL?
COULD IT BE...

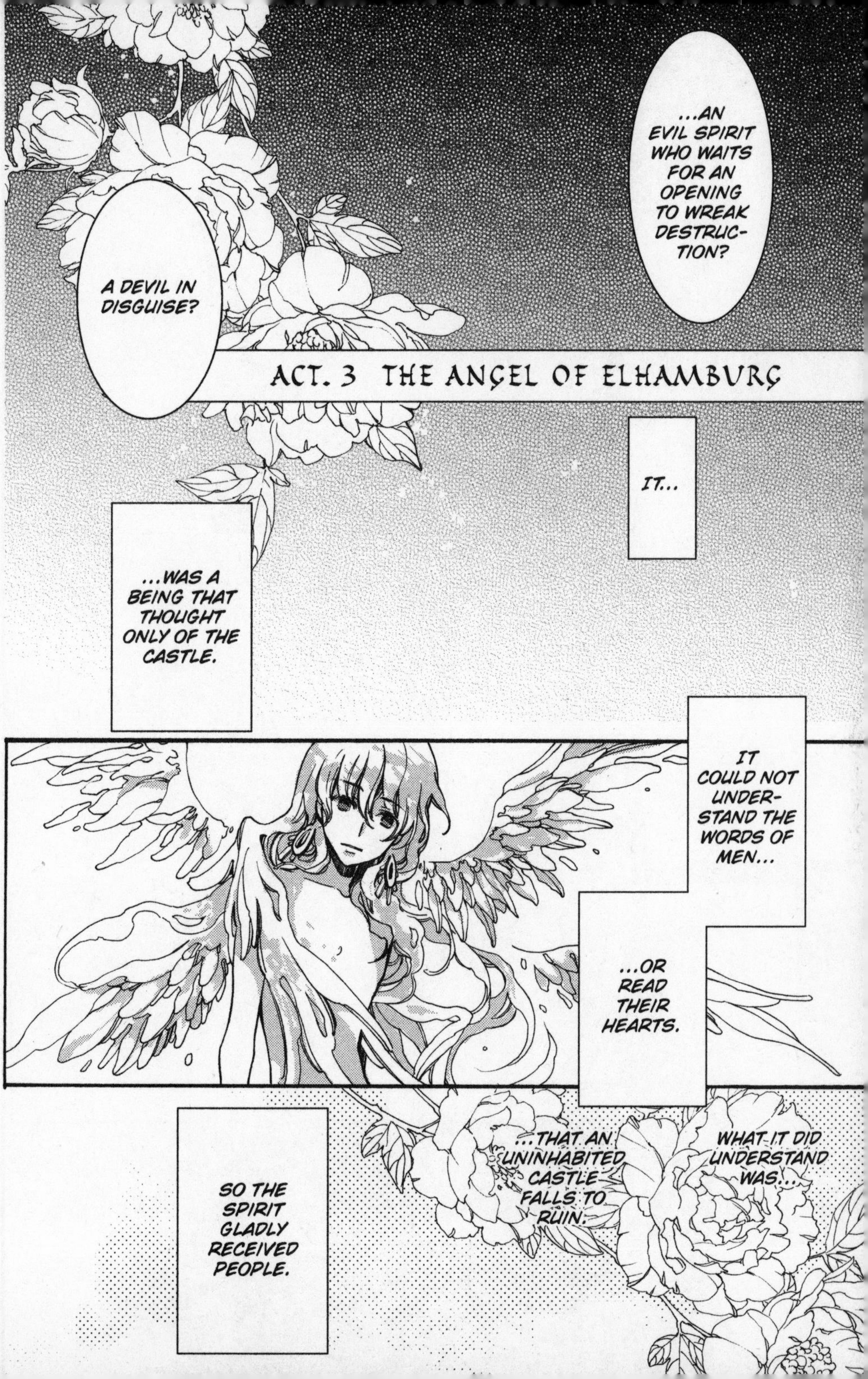
...AN EVIL SPIRIT WHO WAITS FOR AN OPENING TO WREAK DESTRUC-TION?
A DEVIL IN DISGUISE?
ACT. 3 THE ANGEL OF ELHAMBURG
IT...
...WAS A BEING THAT THOUGHT ONLY OF THE CASTLE.
IT COULD NOT UNDER-STAND THE WORDS OF MEN...
...OR READ THEIR HEARTS.
WHAT IT DID UNDERSTAND WAS...
...THAT AN UNINHABITED CASTLE FALLS TO RUIN.
SO THE SPIRIT GLADLY RECEIVED PEOPLE.

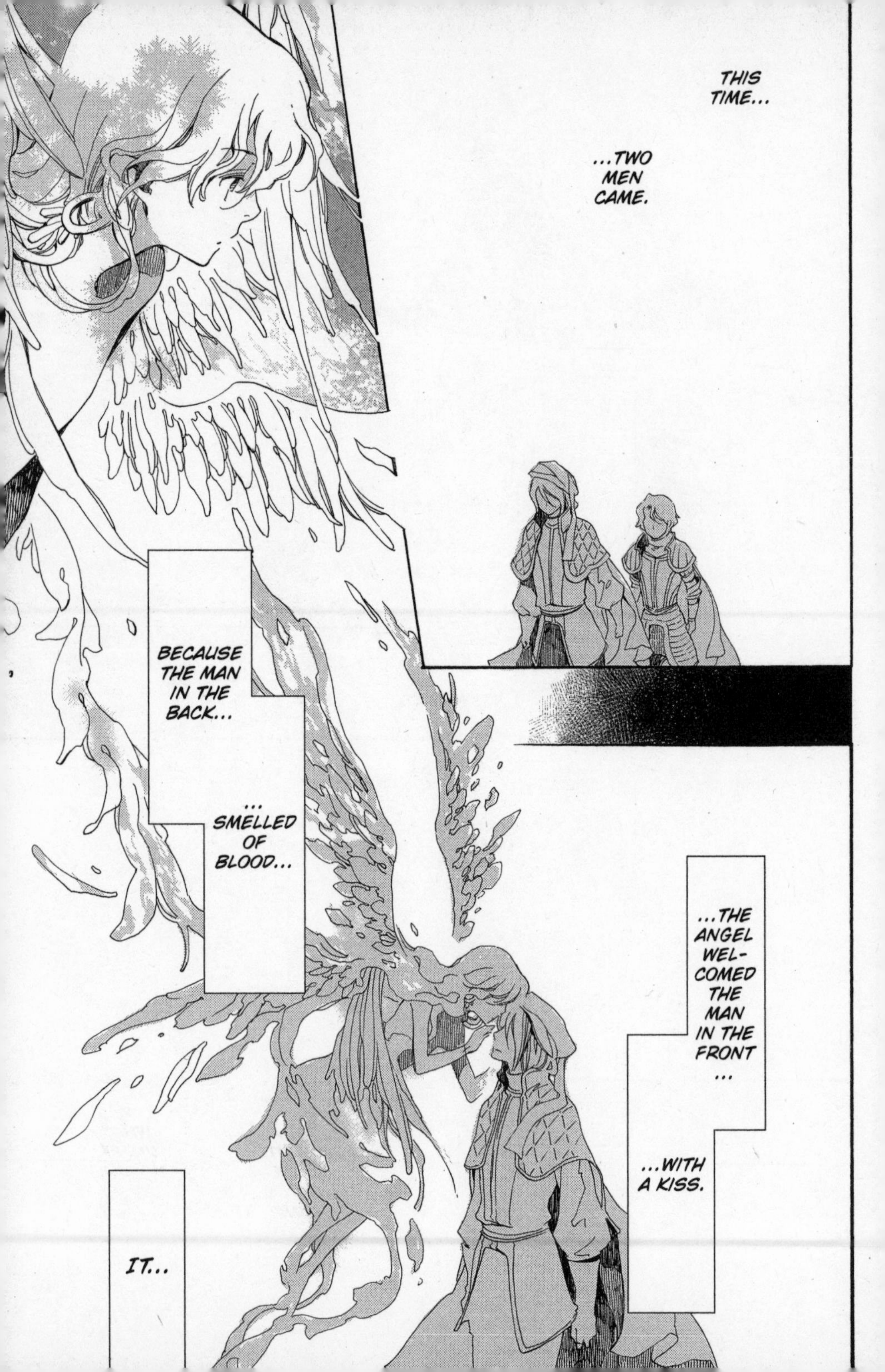
THIS TIME...
...TWO MEN CAME.
...THE ANGEL WEL-COMED THE MAN IN THE FRONT ...
...WITH A KISS.
BECAUSE THE MAN IN THE BACK...
...SMELLED OF BLOOD...
IT...

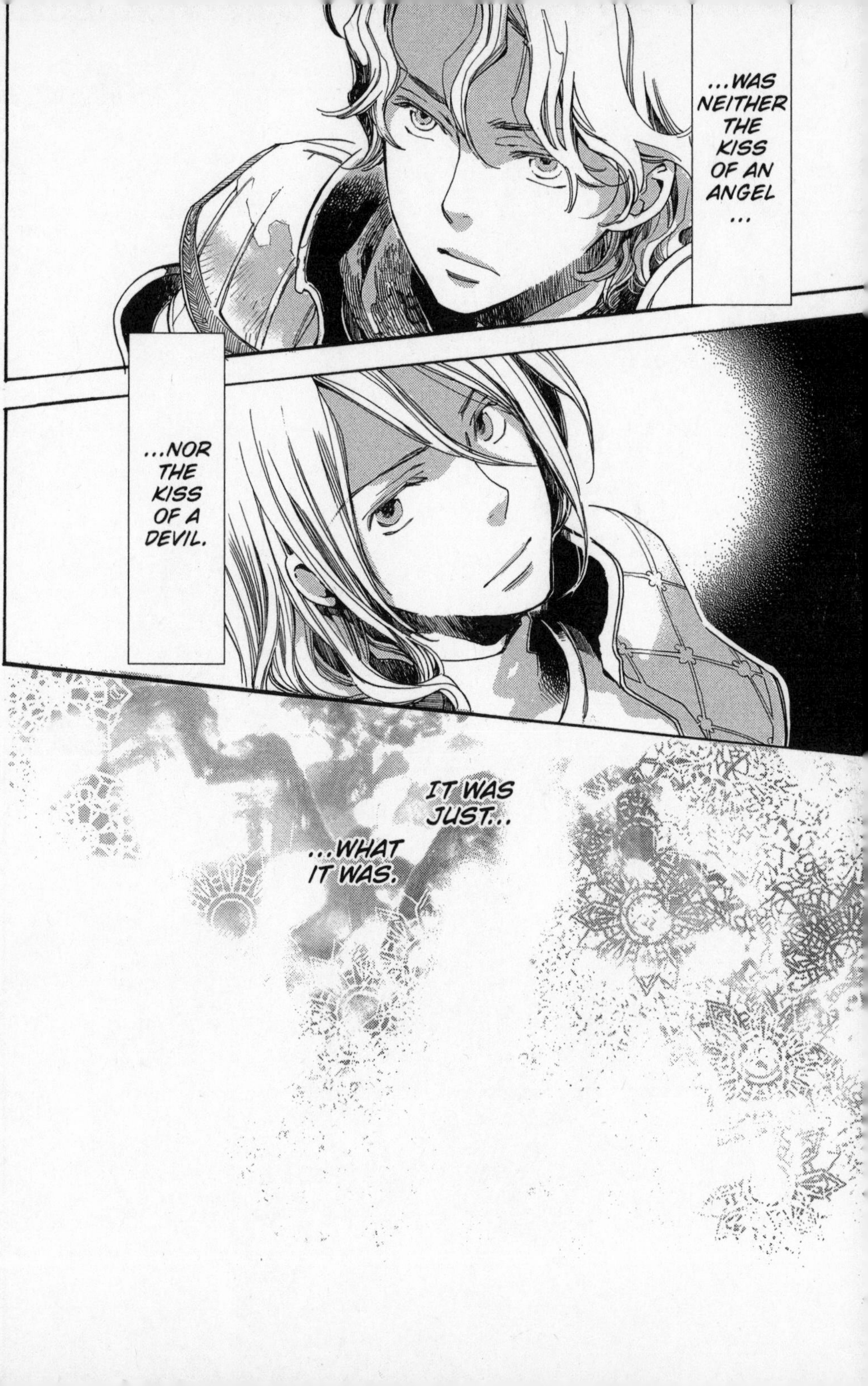
...WAS NEITHER THE KISS OF AN ANGEL ...
...NOR THE KISS OF A DEVIL.
IT WAS JUST...
...WHAT IT WAS.

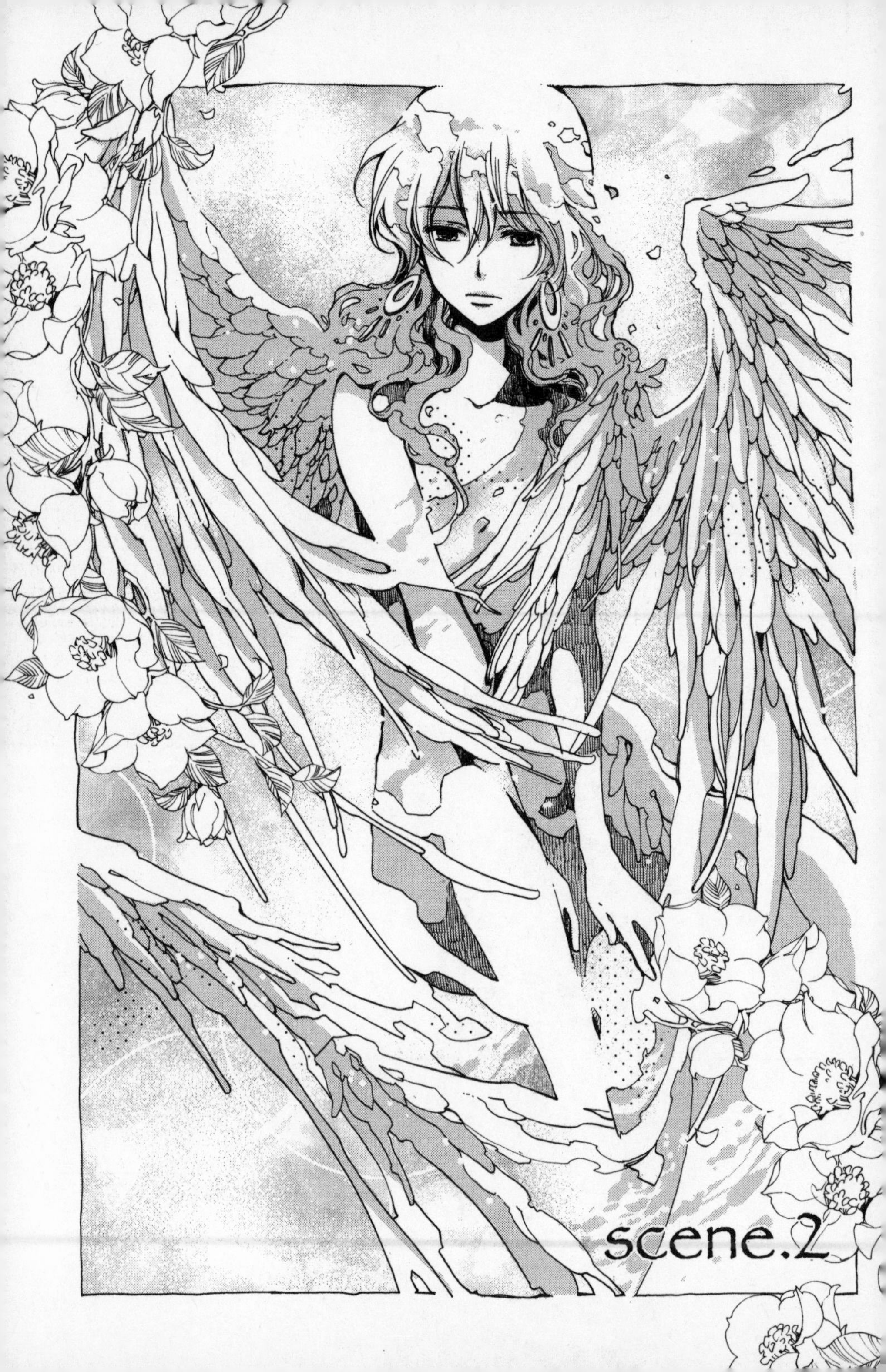
scene.2

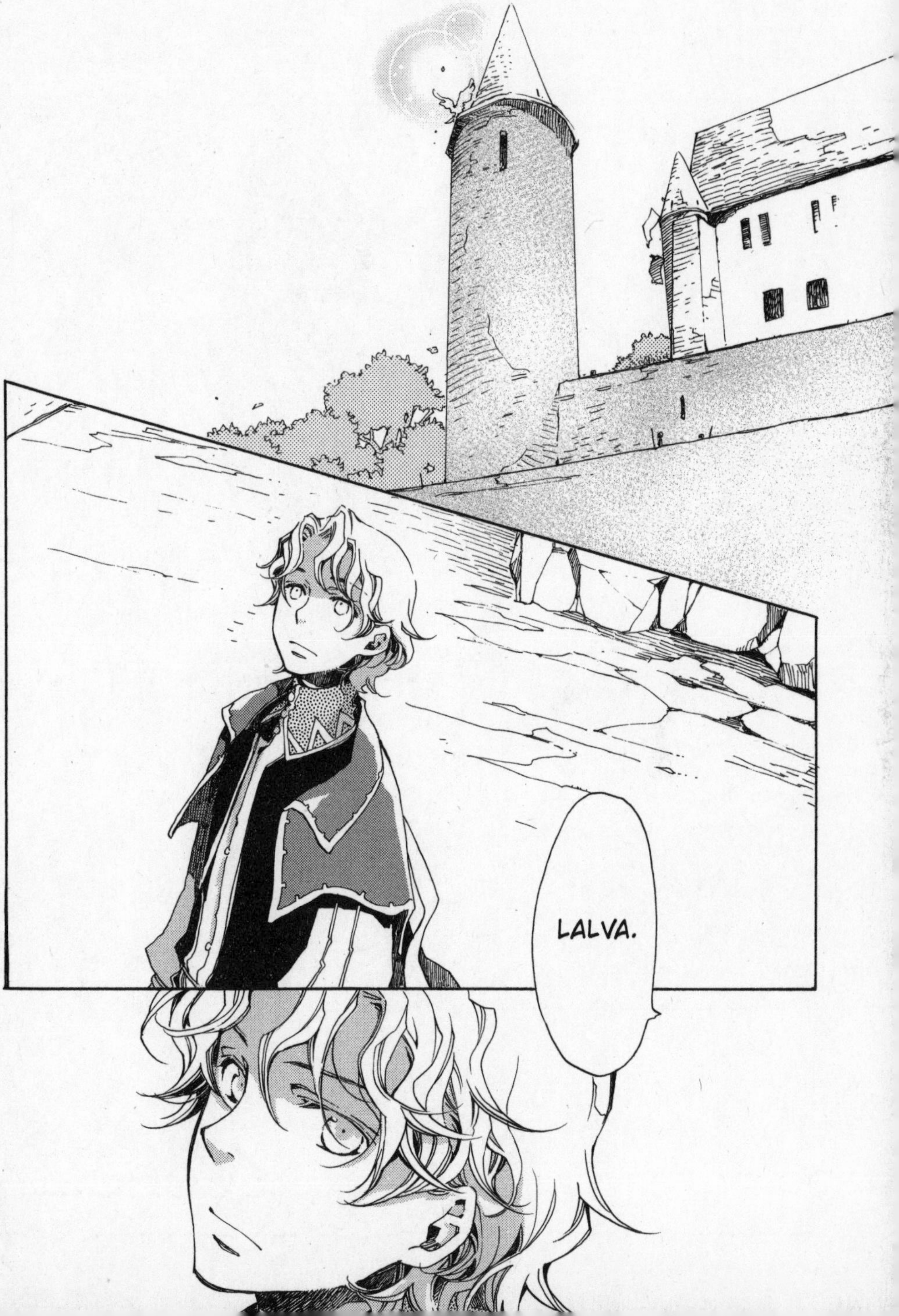
LALVA.

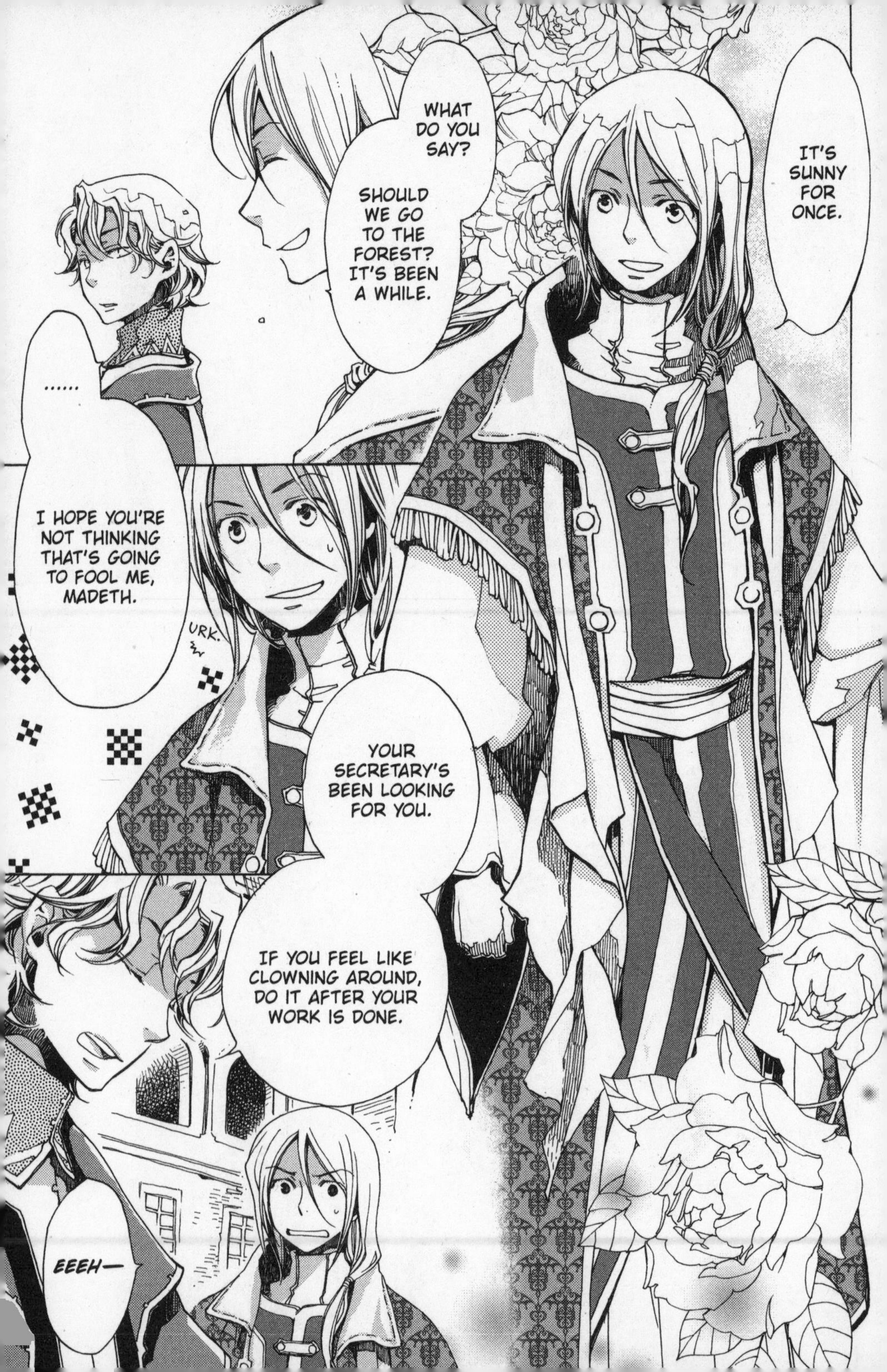
IT'S SUNNY FOR ONCE.
WHAT DO YOU SAY?
SHOULD WE GO TO THE FOREST? IT'S BEEN A WHILE.
......
I HOPE YOU'RE NOT THINKING THAT'S GOING TO FOOL ME, MADETH.
URK.
YOUR SECRETARY'S BEEN LOOKING FOR YOU.
IF YOU FEEL LIKE CLOWNING AROUND, DO IT AFTER YOUR WORK IS DONE.
EEEH—

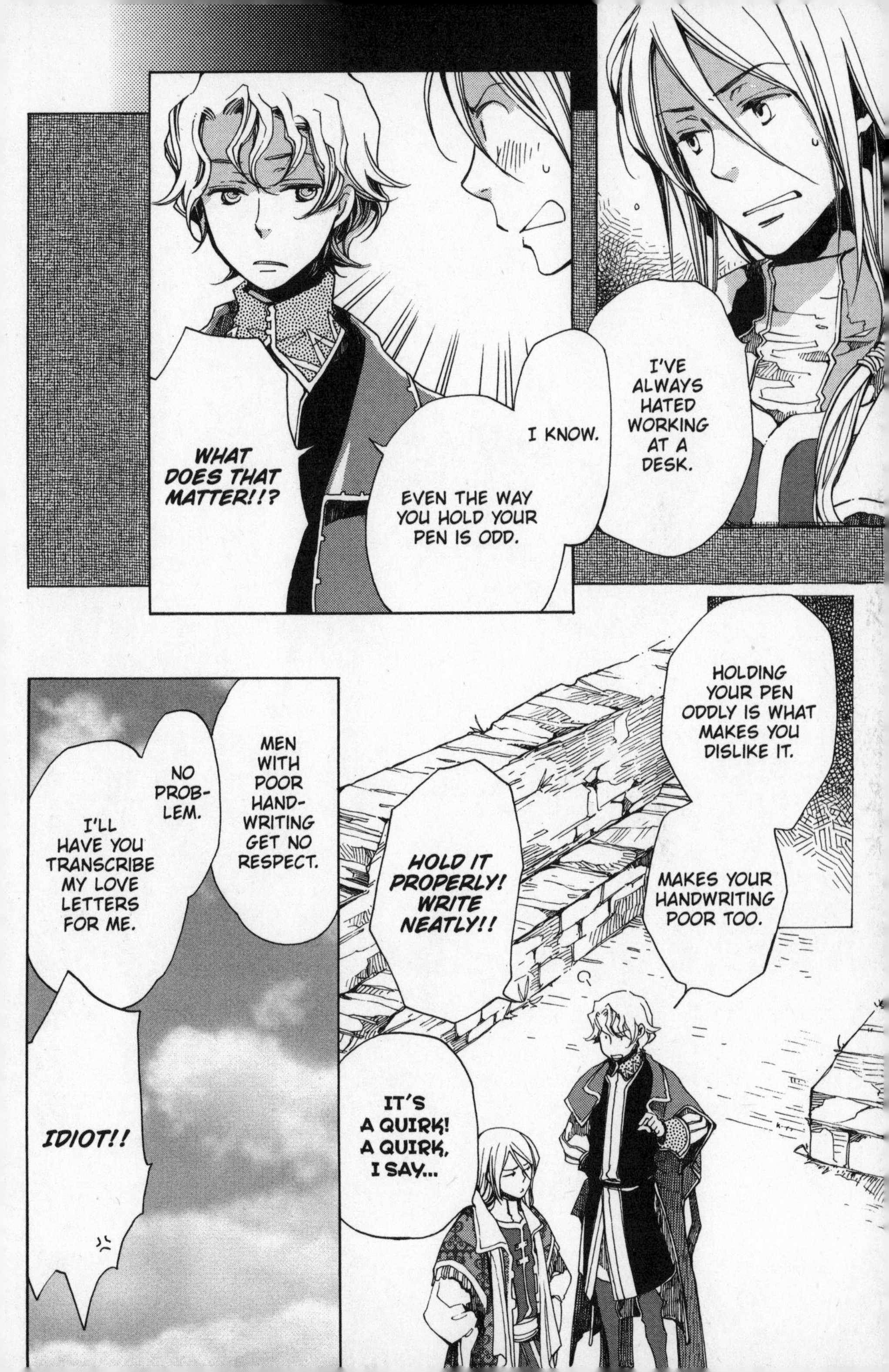

I'VE ALWAYS HATED WORKING AT A DESK.
I KNOW.
EVEN THE WAY YOU HOLD YOUR PEN IS ODD.
WHAT DOES THAT MATTER!!?
HOLDING YOUR PEN ODDLY IS WHAT MAKES YOU DISLIKE IT.
MAKES YOUR HANDWRITING POOR TOO.
HOLD IT PROPERLY! WRITE NEATLY!!
IT'S A QUIRK! A QUIRK, I SAY...
MEN WITH POOR HAND-WRITING GET NO RESPECT.
NO PROB-LEM.
I'LL HAVE YOU TRANSCRIBE MY LOVE LETTERS FOR ME.
IDIOT!!

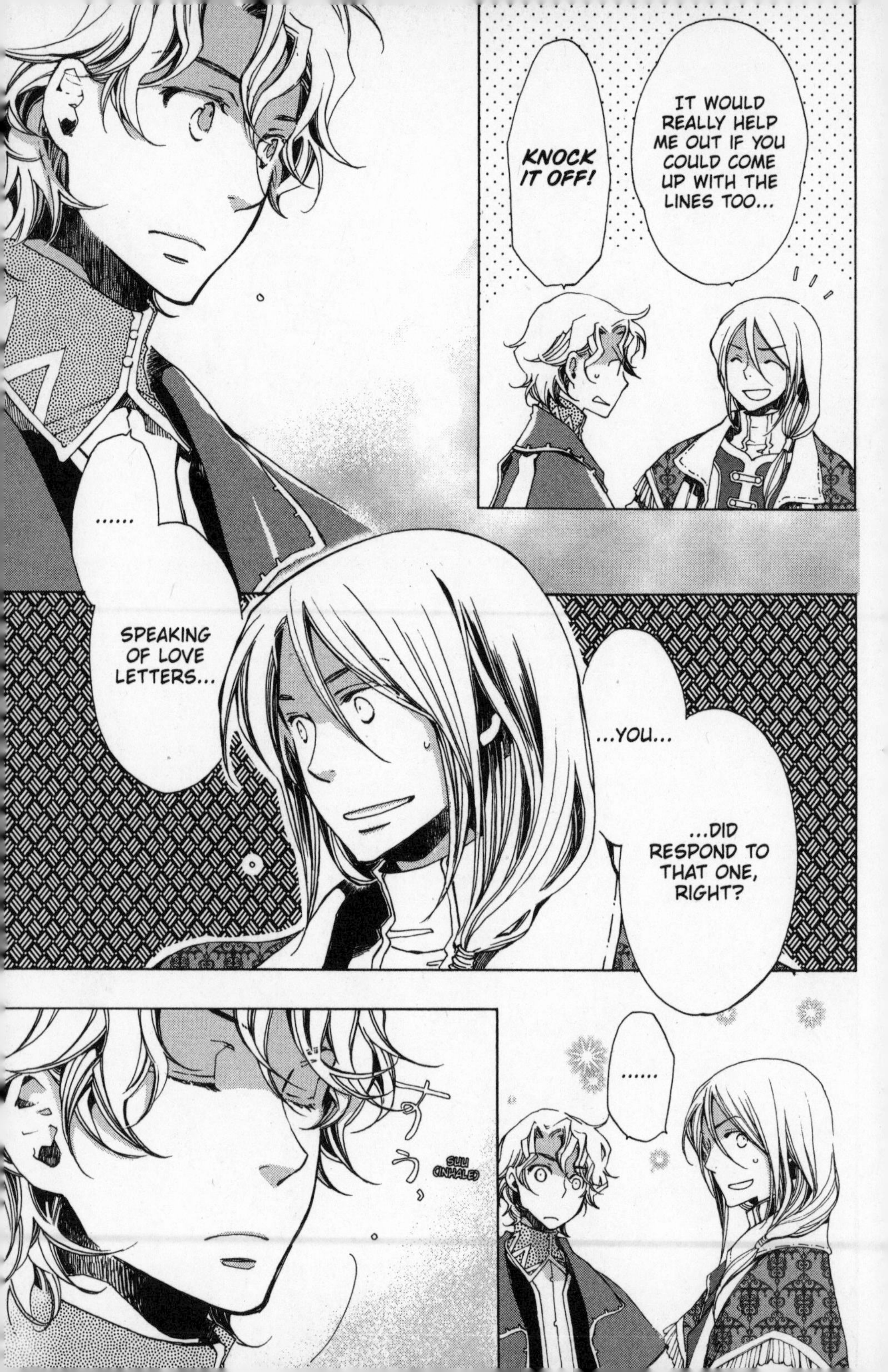
IT WOULD REALLY HELP ME OUT IF YOU COULD COME UP WITH THE LINES TOO...
KNOCK IT OFF!
......
SPEAKING OF LOVE LETTERS...
...YOU...
...DID RESPOND TO THAT ONE, RIGHT?
......
SUU (INHALED)

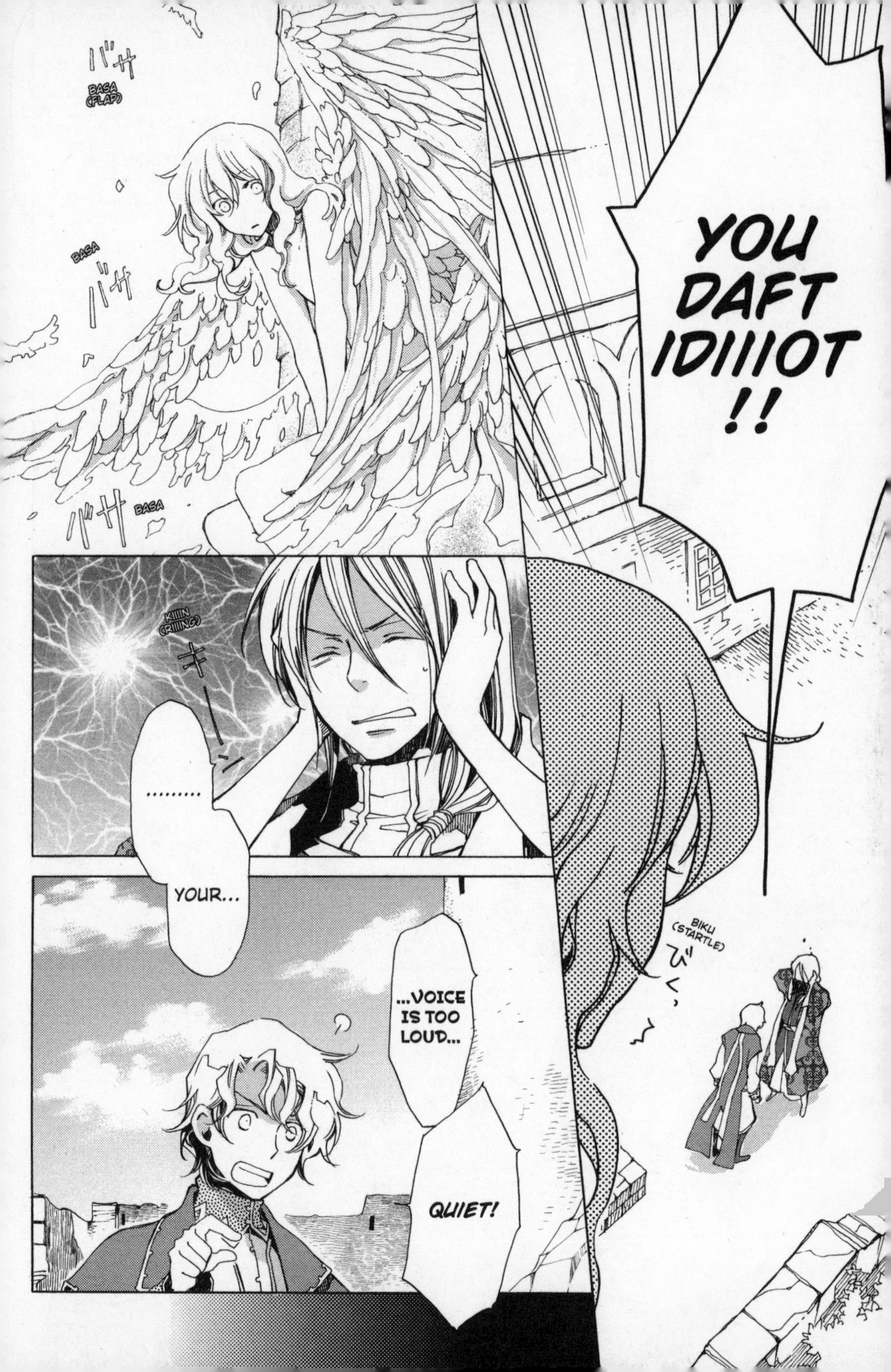
YOU DAFT IDIIIIOT!!
BIKU (STARTLE)
BASA (FLAP)
BASA
BASA
KIIIN (RIIING)
....
YOUR...
...VOICE IS TOO LOUD...
QUIET!

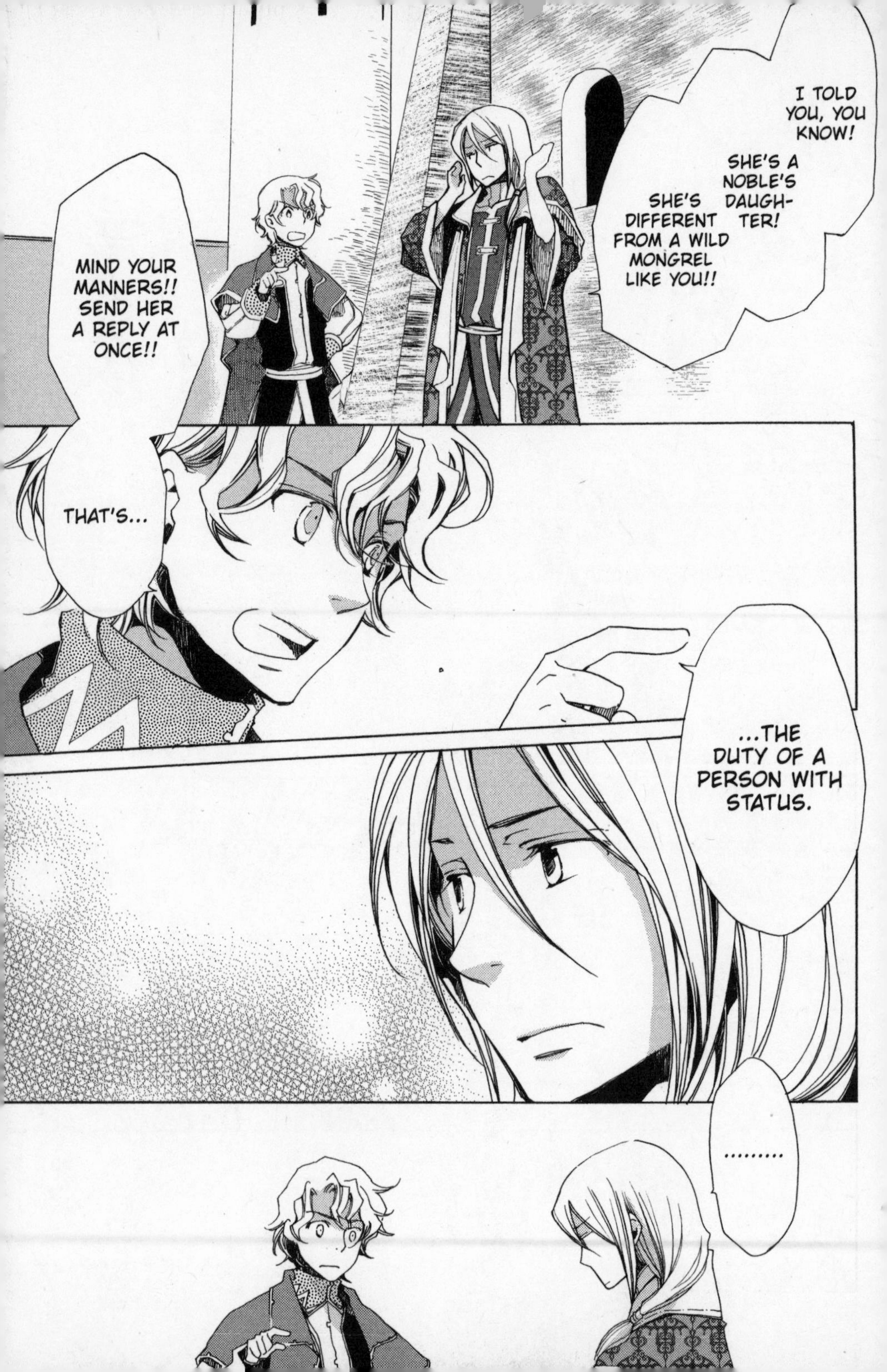
I TOLD YOU, YOU KNOW!
SHE'S A NOBLE'S DAUGHTER!
SHE'S DIFFERENT FROM A WILD MONGREL LIKE YOU!!
MIND YOUR MANNERS!! SEND HER A REPLY AT ONCE!!
THAT'S...
...THE DUTY OF A PERSON WITH STATUS.
....

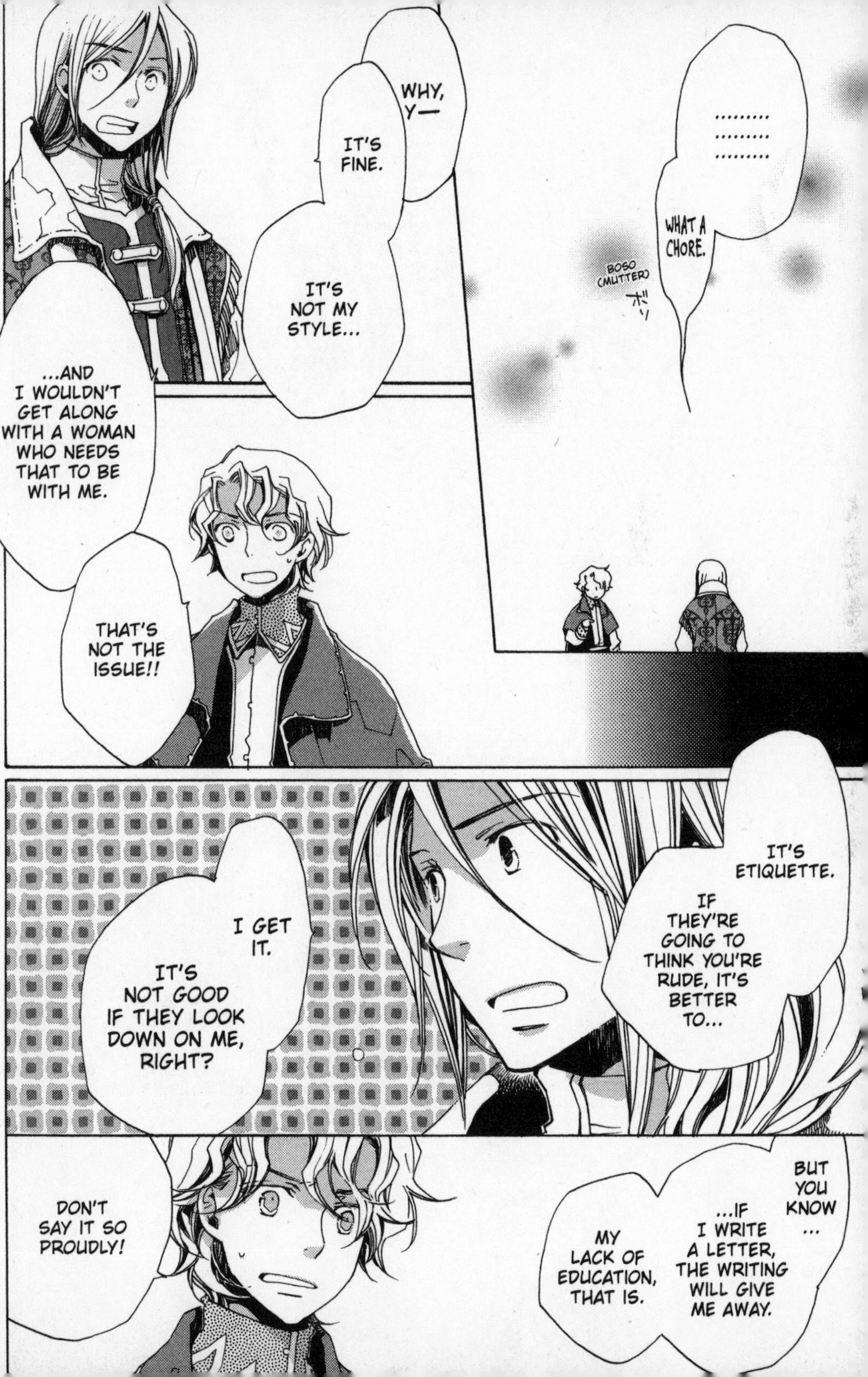
....
....
....
WHAT A CHORE.
BOSO (MUTTER)
WHY, Y—
IT'S FINE.
IT'S NOT MY STYLE...
...AND I WOULDN'T GET ALONG WITH A WOMAN WHO NEEDS THAT TO BE WITH ME.
THAT'S NOT THE ISSUE!!
IT'S ETIQUETTE.
IF THEY'RE GOING TO THINK YOU'RE RUDE, IT'S BETTER TO...
I GET IT.
IT'S NOT GOOD IF THEY LOOK DOWN ON ME, RIGHT?
BUT YOU KNOW...
...IF I WRITE A LETTER, THE WRITING WILL GIVE ME AWAY.
MY LACK OF EDUCATION, THAT IS.
DON'T SAY IT SO PROUDLY!

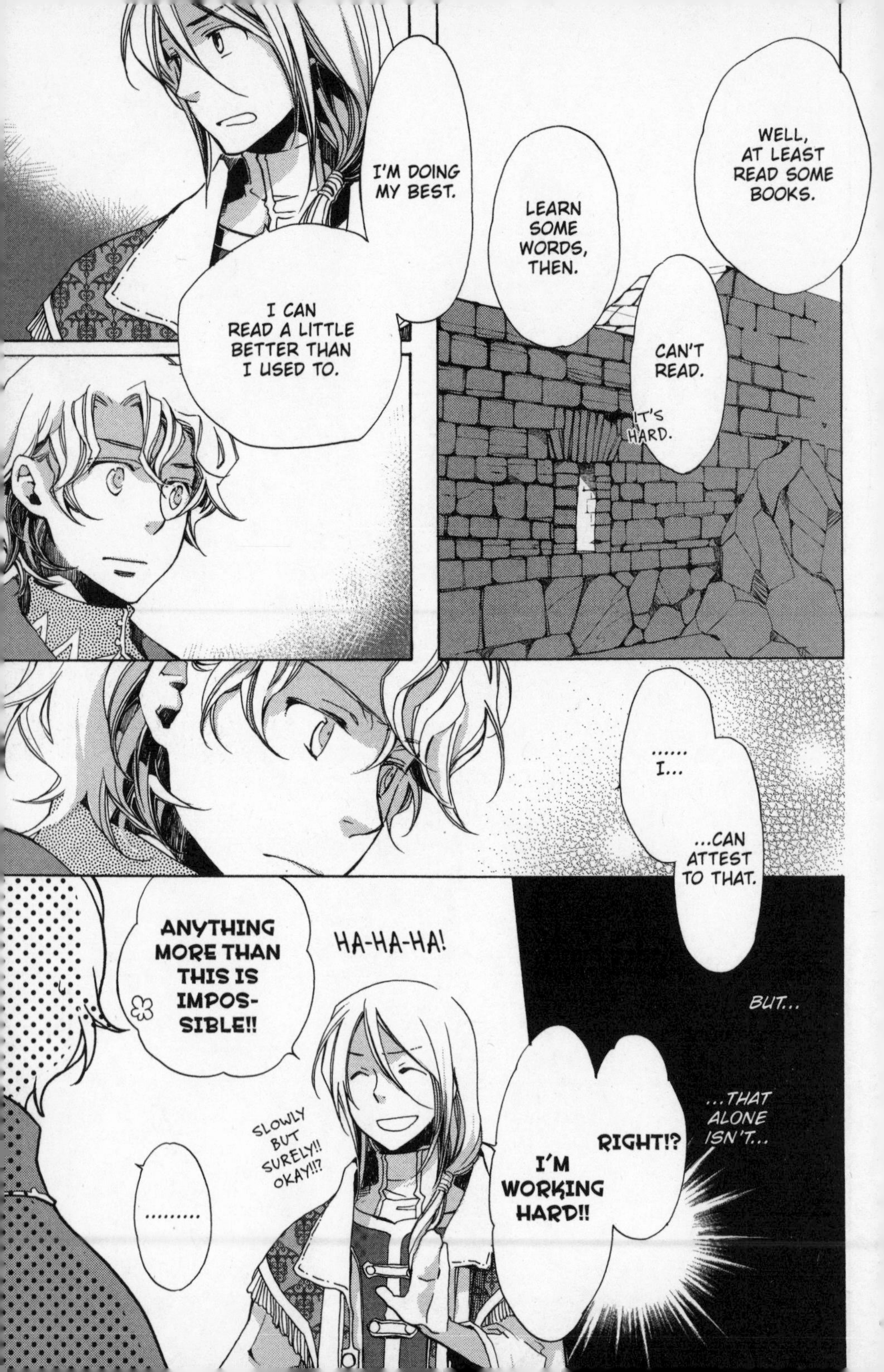
WELL, AT LEAST READ SOME BOOKS.
CAN'T READ.
IT'S HARD.
LEARN SOME WORDS, THEN.
I'M DOING MY BEST.
I CAN READ A LITTLE BETTER THAN I USED TO.
...... I...
...CAN ATTEST TO THAT.
BUT...
...THAT ALONE ISN'T...
I'M WORKING HARD!! RIGHT!?
SLOWLY BUT SURELY!! OKAY!!?
HA-HA-HA!
ANYTHING MORE THAN THIS IS IMPOS-SIBLE!!
....

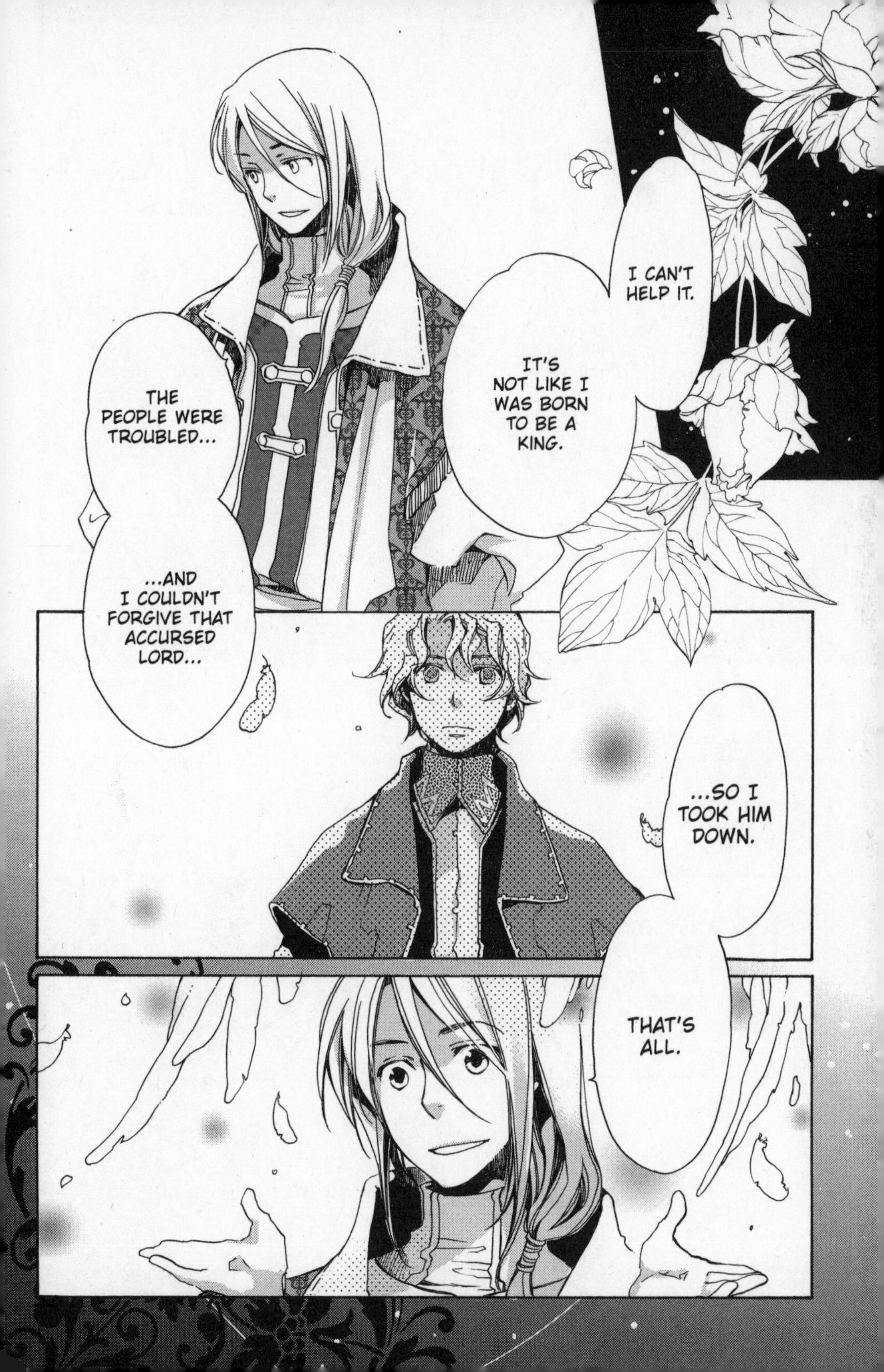
I CAN'T HELP IT.
IT'S NOT LIKE I WAS BORN TO BE A KING.
THE PEOPLE WERE TROUBLED...
...AND I COULDN'T FORGIVE THAT ACCURSED LORD...
...SO I TOOK HIM DOWN.
THAT'S ALL.

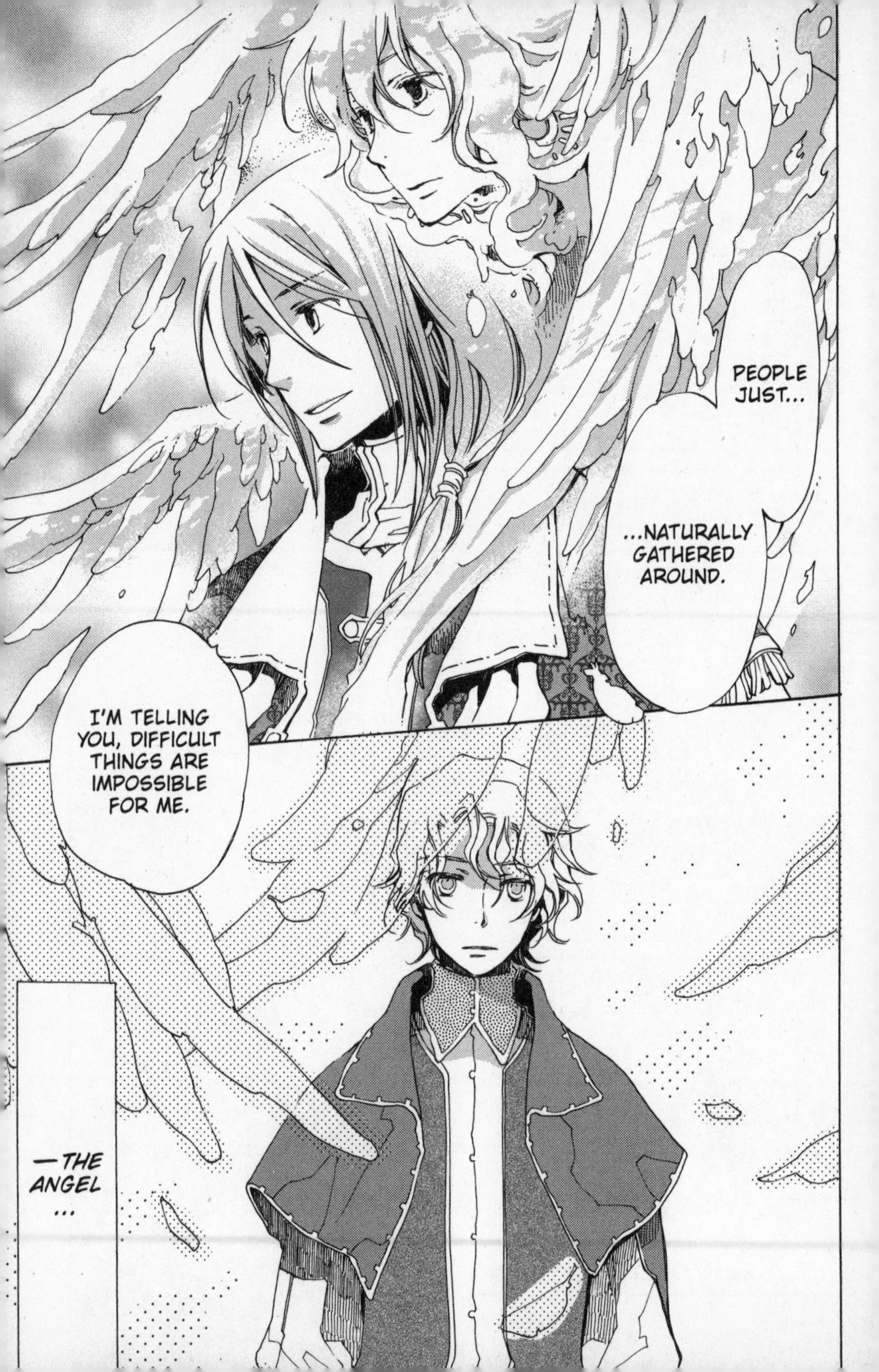
PEOPLE JUST...
...NATURALLY GATHERED AROUND.
I'M TELLING YOU, DIFFICULT THINGS ARE IMPOSSIBLE FOR ME.
—THE ANGEL ...

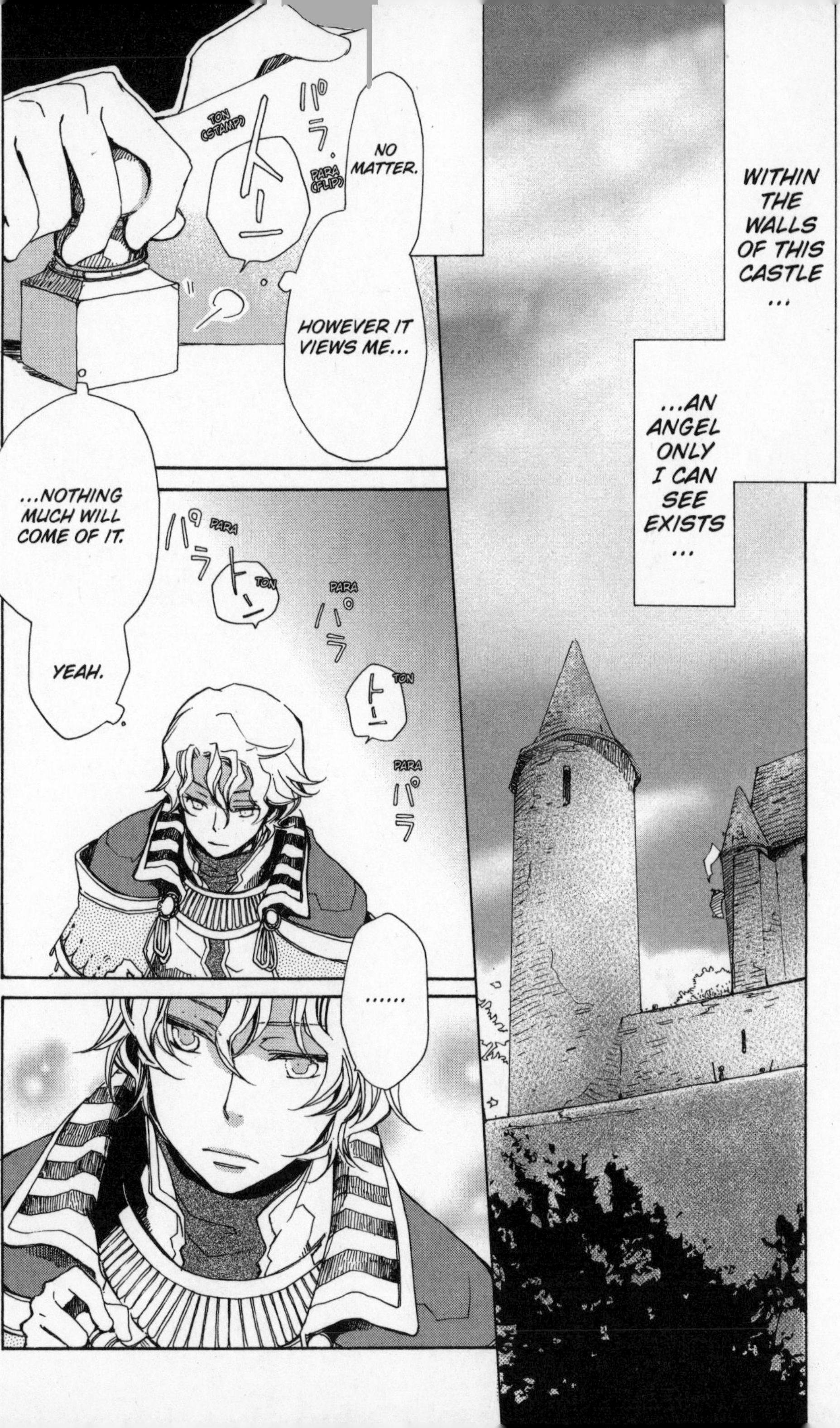
WITHIN THE WALLS OF THIS CASTLE...
...AN ANGEL ONLY I CAN SEE EXISTS...
パラ
PARA (FLIP)
NO MATTER.
トン
TON (STAMP)
HOWEVER IT VIEWS ME...
...NOTHING MUCH WILL COME OF IT.
YEAH.
パラ
PARA
トン
TON
パラ
PARA
トン
TON
パラ
PARA
......

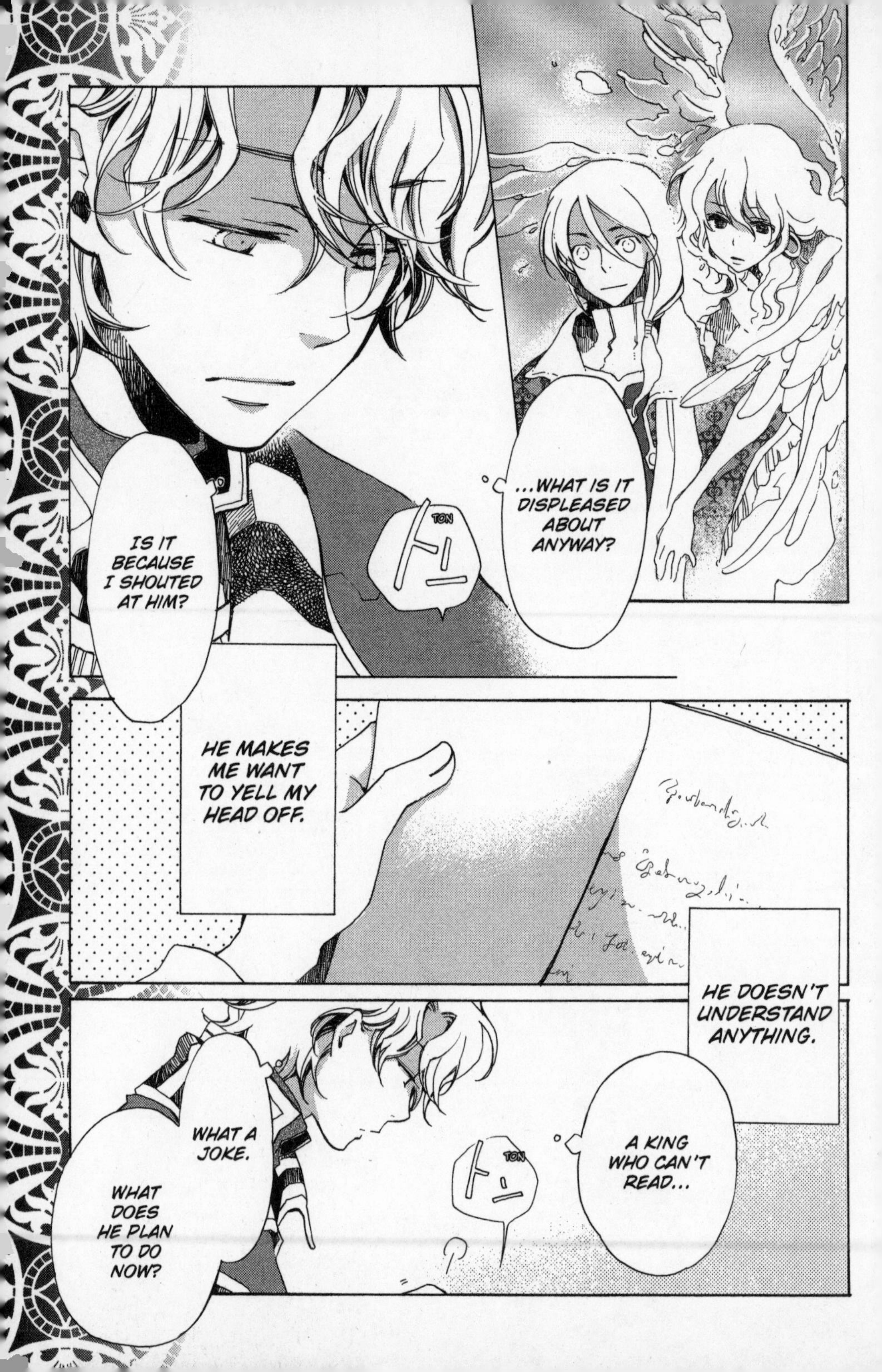
...WHAT IS IT DISPLEASED ABOUT ANYWAY?
TON
IS IT BECAUSE I SHOUTED AT HIM?
HE MAKES ME WANT TO YELL MY HEAD OFF.
HE DOESN'T UNDERSTAND ANYTHING.
A KING WHO CAN'T READ...
TON
WHAT A JOKE.
WHAT DOES HE PLAN TO DO NOW?

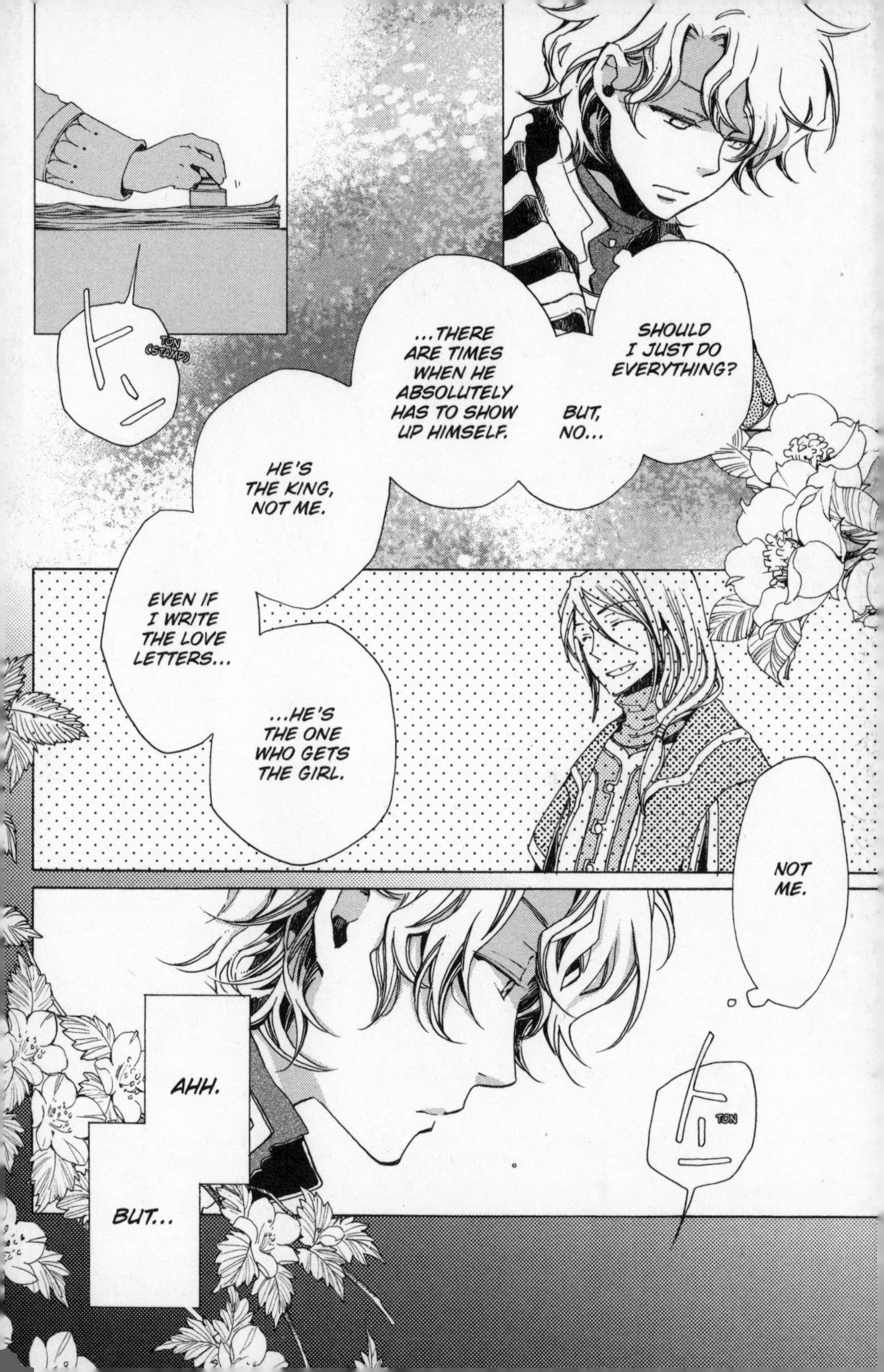
SHOULD I JUST DO EVERYTHING?
BUT, NO...
...THERE ARE TIMES WHEN HE ABSOLUTELY HAS TO SHOW UP HIMSELF.
TON (STAMP)
HE'S THE KING, NOT ME.
EVEN IF I WRITE THE LOVE LETTERS...
...HE'S THE ONE WHO GETS THE GIRL.
NOT ME.
TON
AHH.
BUT...

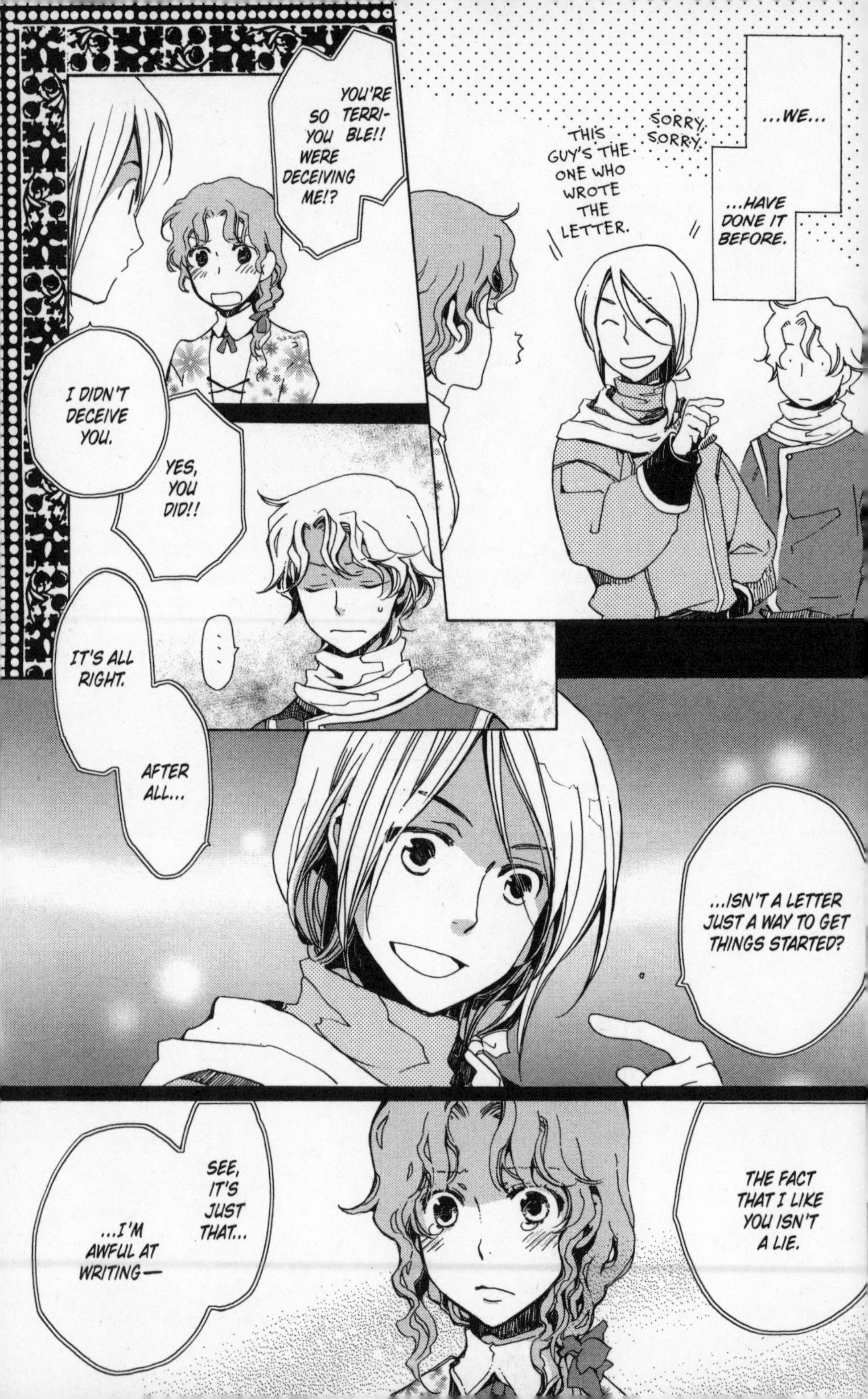
...WE...
...HAVE DONE IT BEFORE.
SORRY, SORRY.
THIS GUY'S THE ONE WHO WROTE THE LETTER.
YOU'RE TERRI-BLE!!
SO YOU WERE DECEIVING ME!?
I DIDN'T DECEIVE YOU.
YES, YOU DID!!
...
IT'S ALL RIGHT.
AFTER ALL...
...ISN'T A LETTER JUST A WAY TO GET THINGS STARTED?
THE FACT THAT I LIKE YOU ISN'T A LIE.
SEE, IT'S JUST THAT...
...I'M AWFUL AT WRITING—

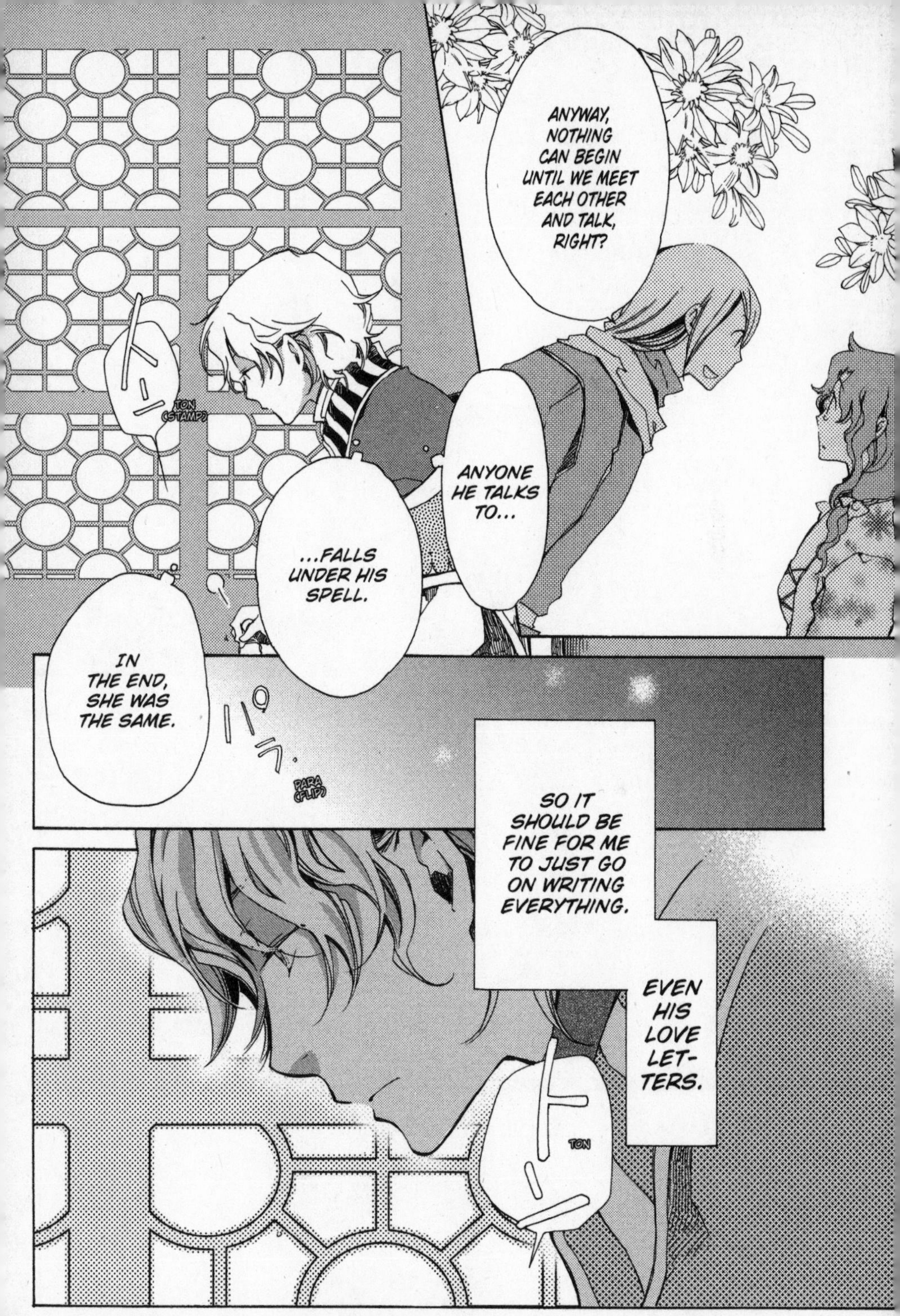
ANYWAY, NOTHING CAN BEGIN UNTIL WE MEET EACH OTHER AND TALK, RIGHT?
ANYONE HE TALKS TO...
...FALLS UNDER HIS SPELL.
TON (STAMP)
IN THE END, SHE WAS THE SAME.
PARA (FLIP)
SO IT SHOULD BE FINE FOR ME TO JUST GO ON WRITING EVERYTHING.
EVEN HIS LOVE LET-TERS.
TON

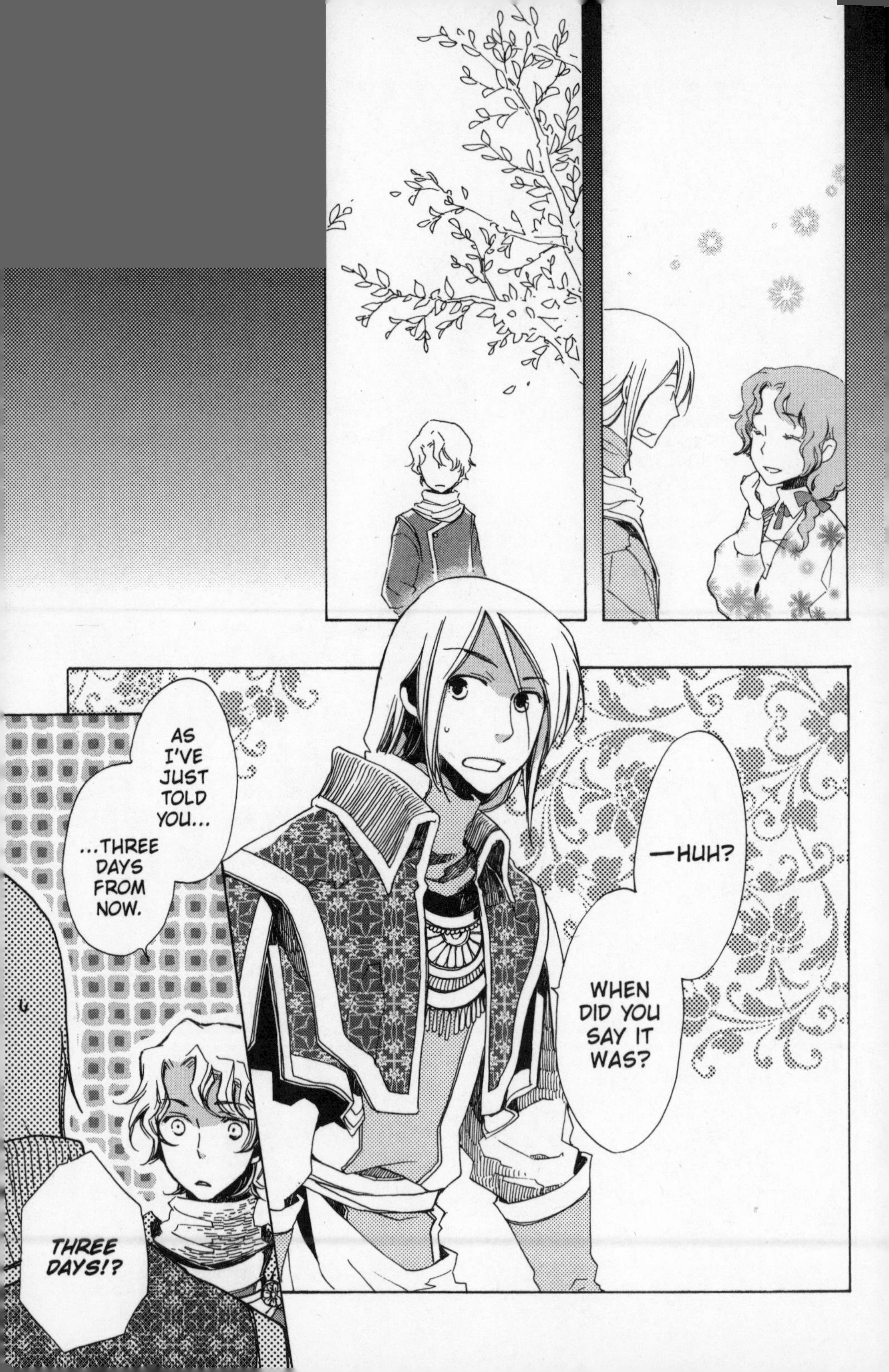
—HUH?
WHEN DID YOU SAY IT WAS?
AS I'VE JUST TOLD YOU...
...THREE DAYS FROM NOW.
THREE DAYS!?

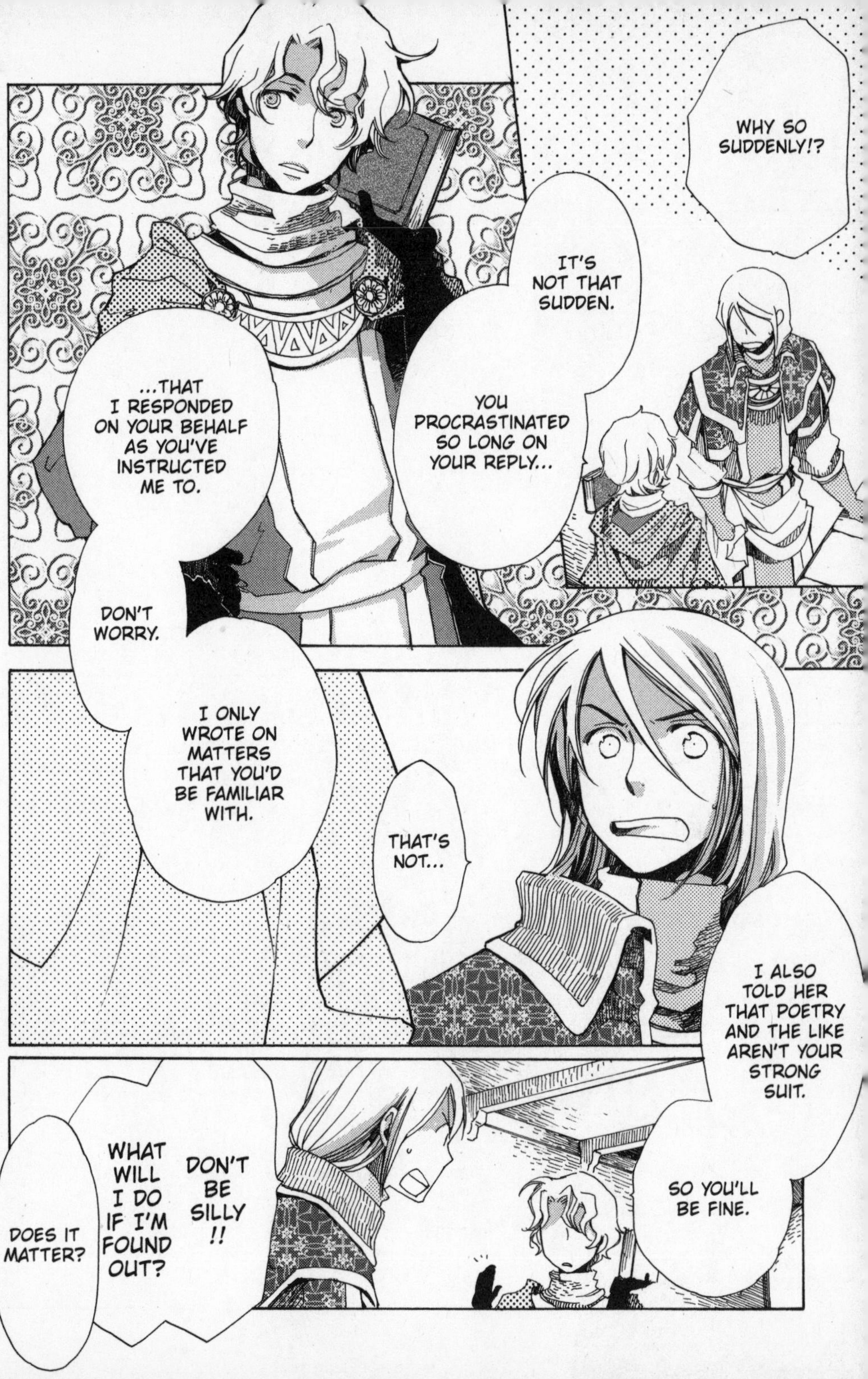
WHY SO SUDDENLY!?
IT'S NOT THAT SUDDEN.
YOU PROCRASTINATED SO LONG ON YOUR REPLY...
...THAT I RESPONDED ON YOUR BEHALF AS YOU'VE INSTRUCTED ME TO.
DON'T WORRY.
I ONLY WROTE ON MATTERS THAT YOU'D BE FAMILIAR WITH.
THAT'S NOT...
I ALSO TOLD HER THAT POETRY AND THE LIKE AREN'T YOUR STRONG SUIT.
SO YOU'LL BE FINE.
DON'T BE SILLY !!
WHAT WILL I DO IF I'M FOUND OUT?
DOES IT MATTER?

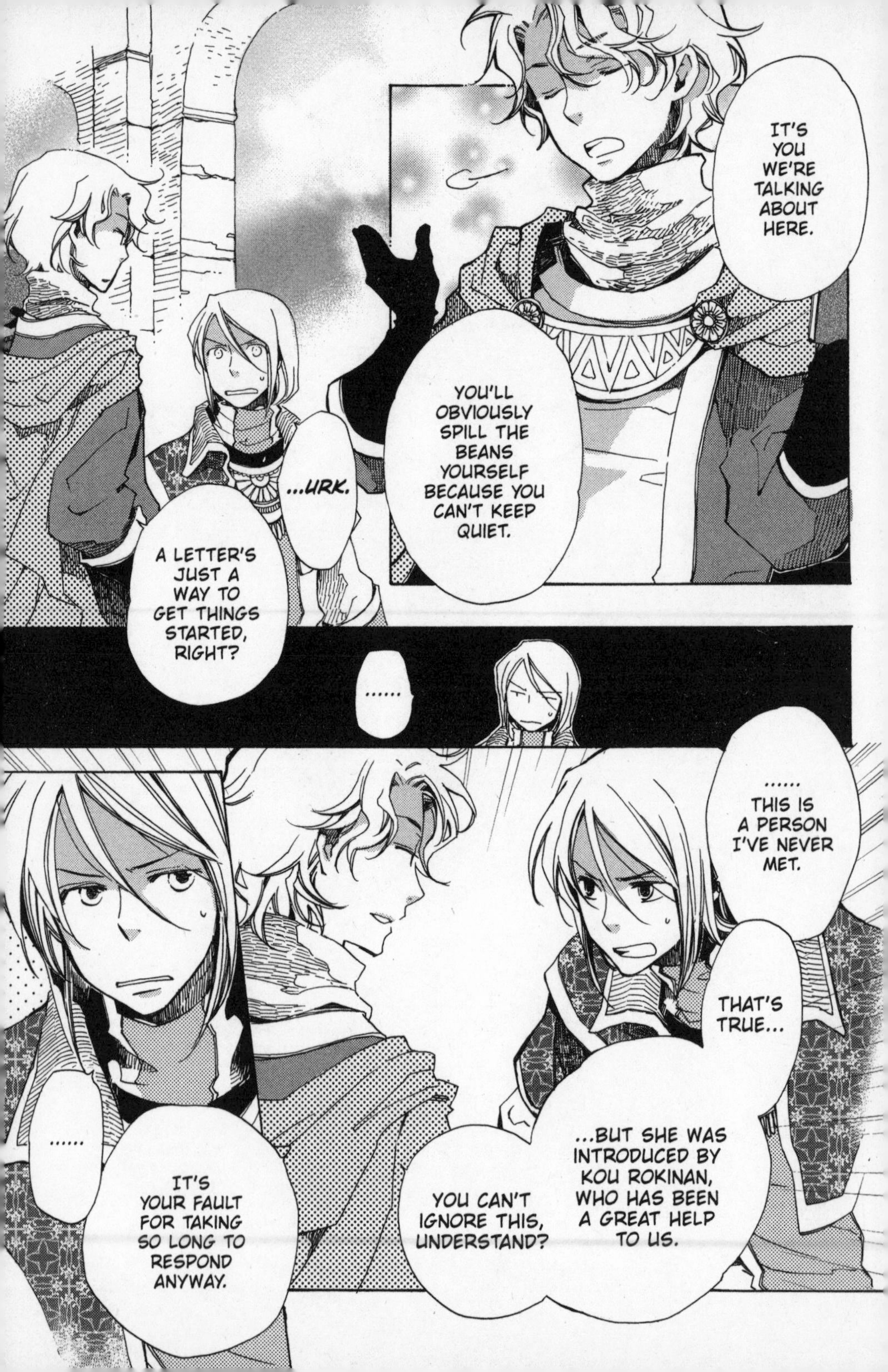
IT'S YOU WE'RE TALKING ABOUT HERE.
YOU'LL OBVIOUSLY SPILL THE BEANS YOURSELF BECAUSE YOU CAN'T KEEP QUIET.
...URK.
A LETTER'S JUST A WAY TO GET THINGS STARTED, RIGHT?
......
...... THIS IS A PERSON I'VE NEVER MET.
THAT'S TRUE...
...BUT SHE WAS INTRODUCED BY KOU ROKINAN, WHO HAS BEEN A GREAT HELP TO US.
YOU CAN'T IGNORE THIS, UNDERSTAND?
......
IT'S YOUR FAULT FOR TAKING SO LONG TO RESPOND ANYWAY.

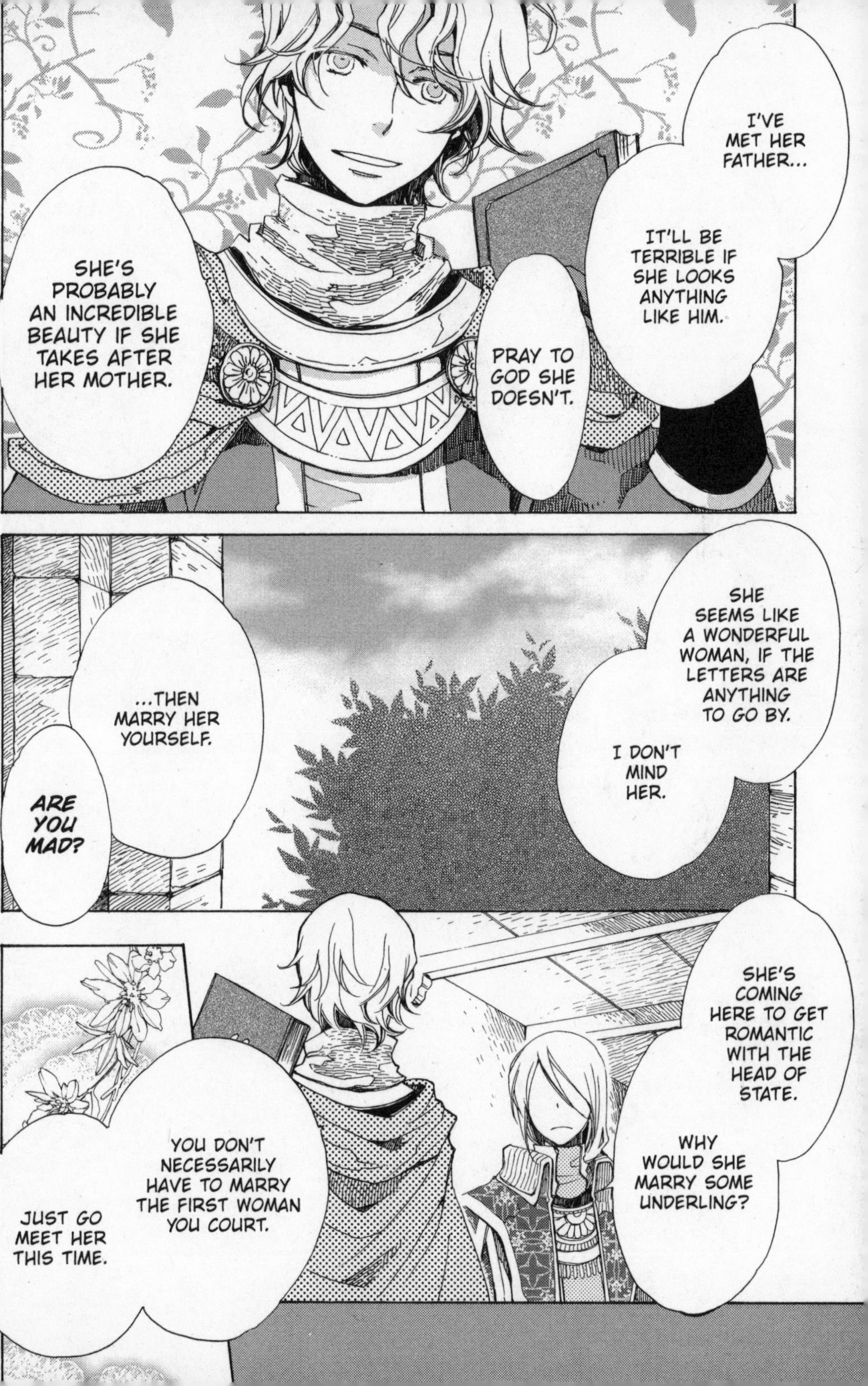
I'VE MET HER FATHER...
IT'LL BE TERRIBLE IF SHE LOOKS ANYTHING LIKE HIM.
PRAY TO GOD SHE DOESN'T.
SHE'S PROBABLY AN INCREDIBLE BEAUTY IF SHE TAKES AFTER HER MOTHER.
SHE SEEMS LIKE A WONDERFUL WOMAN, IF THE LETTERS ARE ANYTHING TO GO BY.
I DON'T MIND HER.
...THEN MARRY HER YOURSELF.
ARE YOU MAD?
SHE'S COMING HERE TO GET ROMANTIC WITH THE HEAD OF STATE.
WHY WOULD SHE MARRY SOME UNDERLING?
YOU DON'T NECESSARILY HAVE TO MARRY THE FIRST WOMAN YOU COURT.
JUST GO MEET HER THIS TIME.

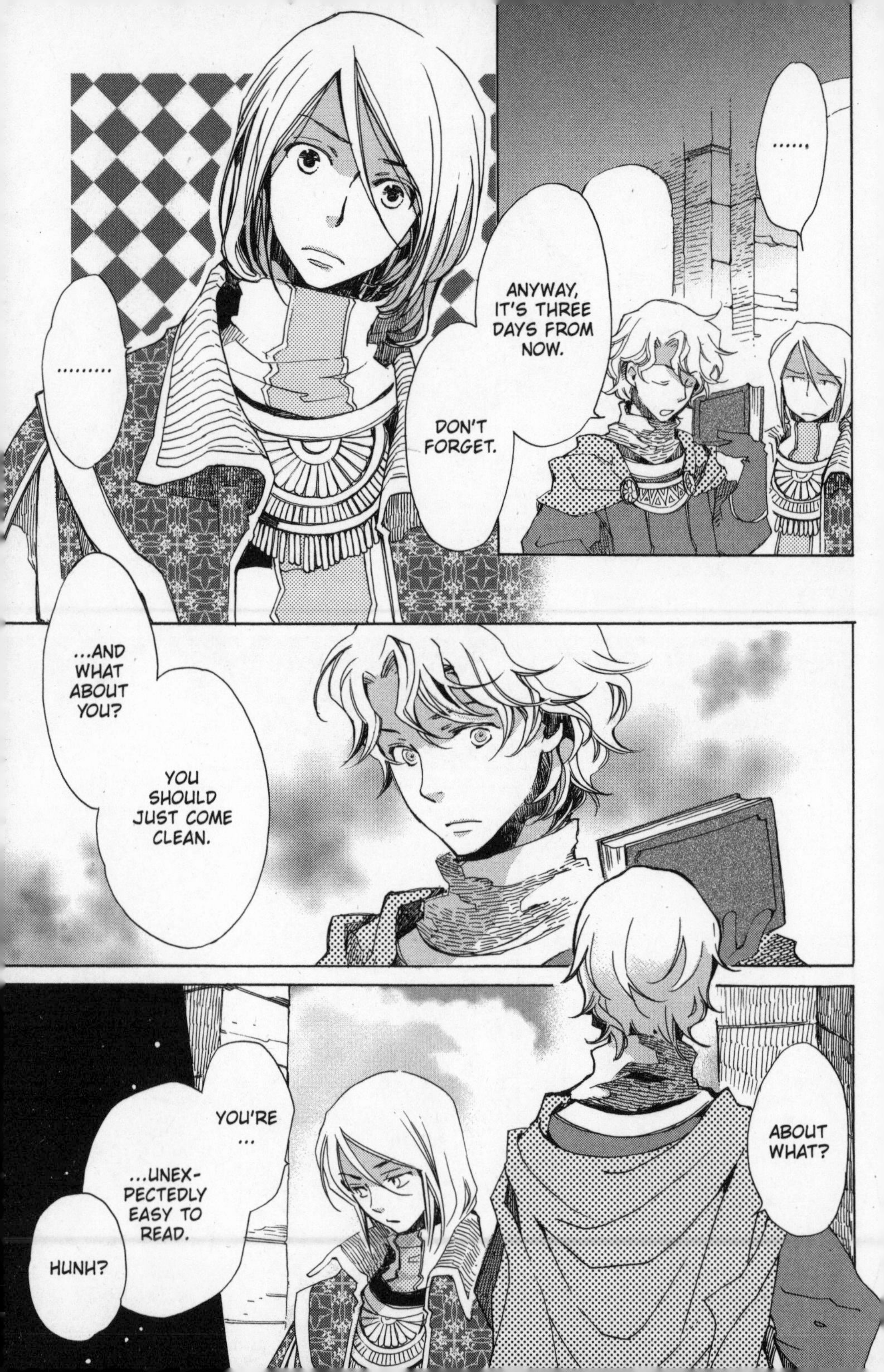
......
ANYWAY, IT'S THREE DAYS FROM NOW.
DON'T FORGET.
....
...AND WHAT ABOUT YOU?
YOU SHOULD JUST COME CLEAN.
ABOUT WHAT?
YOU'RE ...
...UNEX-PECTEDLY EASY TO READ.
HUNH?

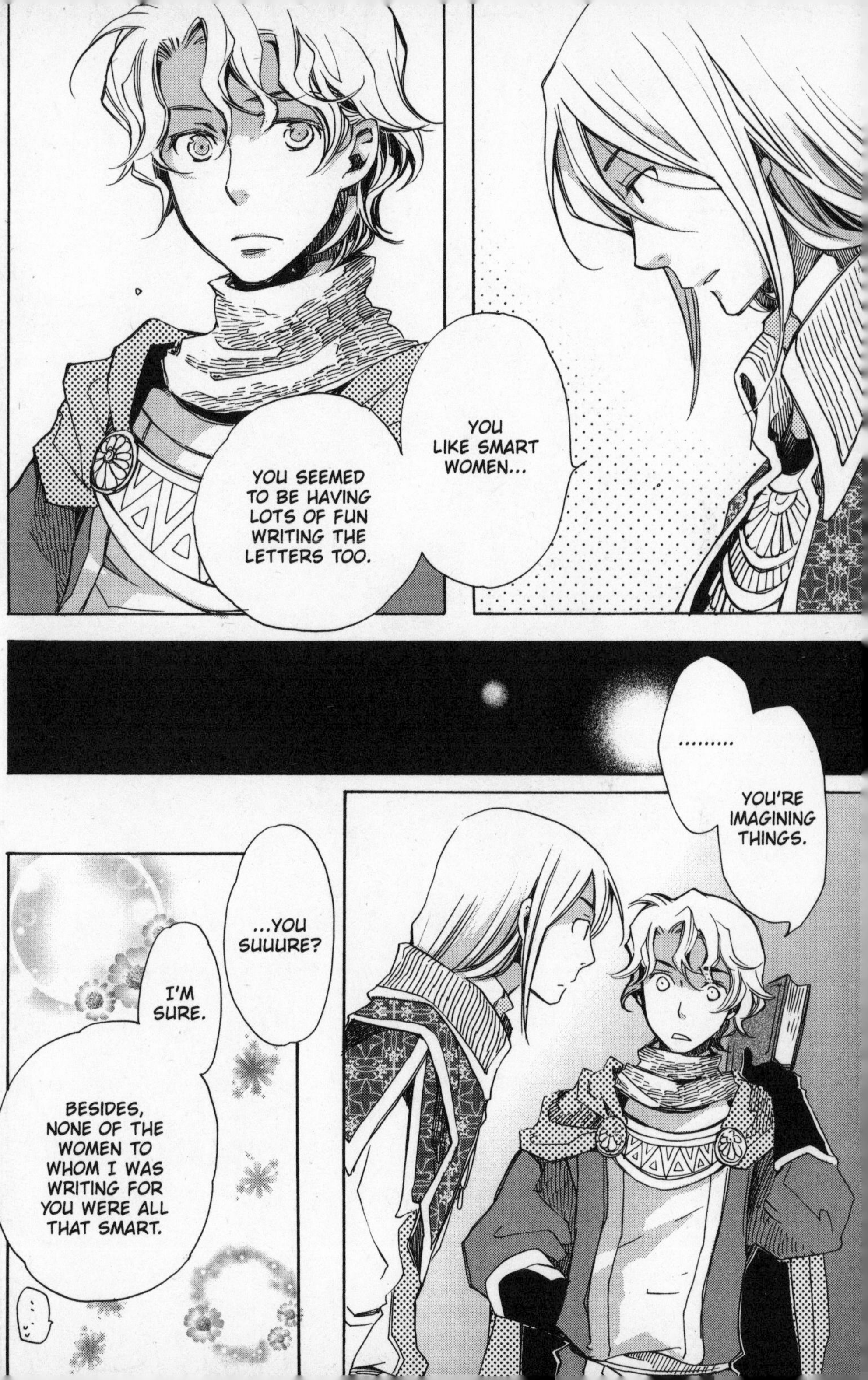
YOU LIKE SMART WOMEN...
YOU SEEMED TO BE HAVING LOTS OF FUN WRITING THE LETTERS TOO.
....
YOU'RE IMAGINING THINGS.
...YOU SUUURE?
I'M SURE.
BESIDES, NONE OF THE WOMEN TO WHOM I WAS WRITING FOR YOU WERE ALL THAT SMART.

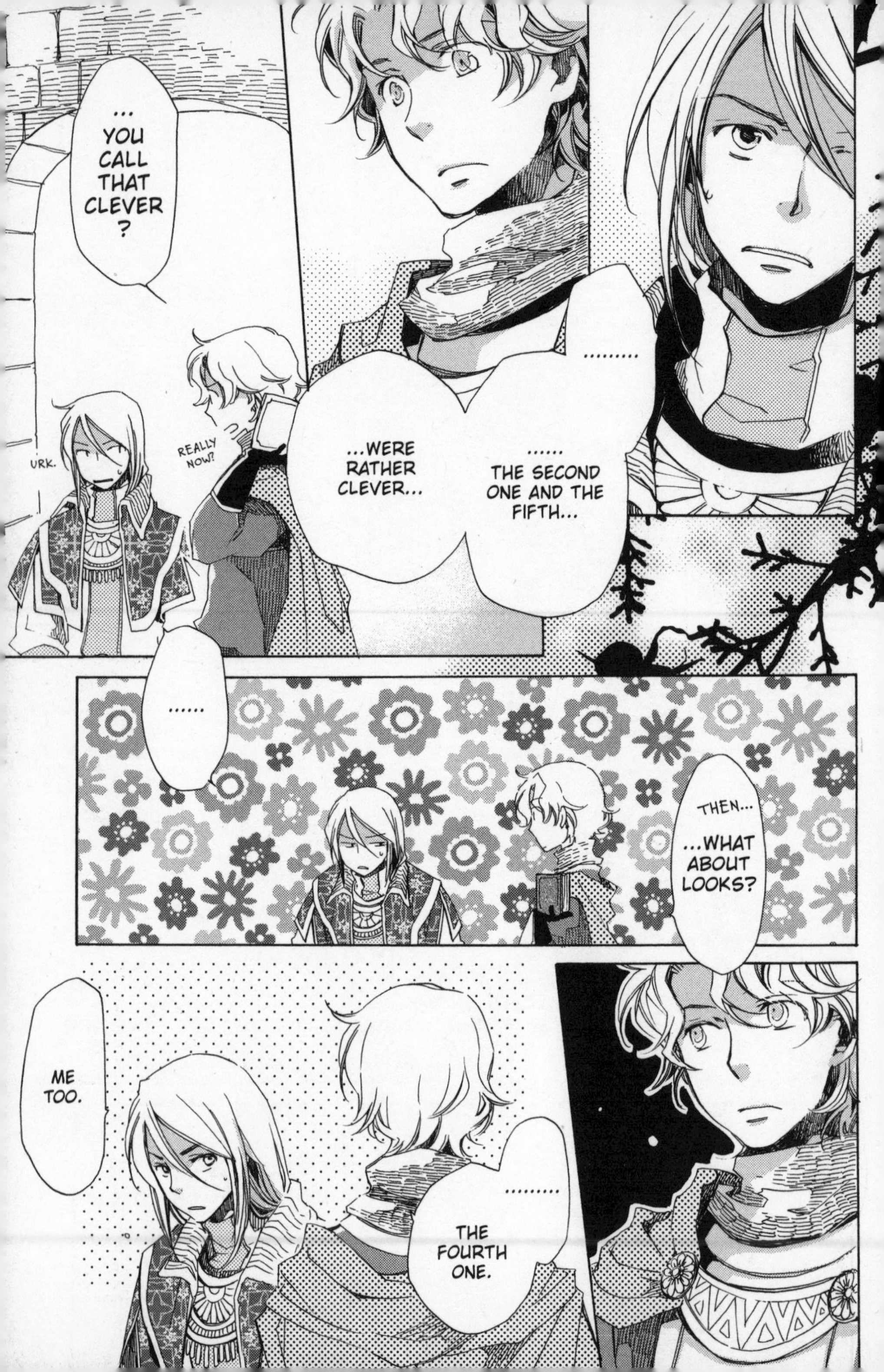
....
......
THE SECOND ONE AND THE FIFTH...
...WERE RATHER CLEVER...
...
YOU CALL THAT CLEVER?
REALLY NOW?
URK.
......
THEN...
...WHAT ABOUT LOOKS?
....
THE FOURTH ONE.
ME TOO.

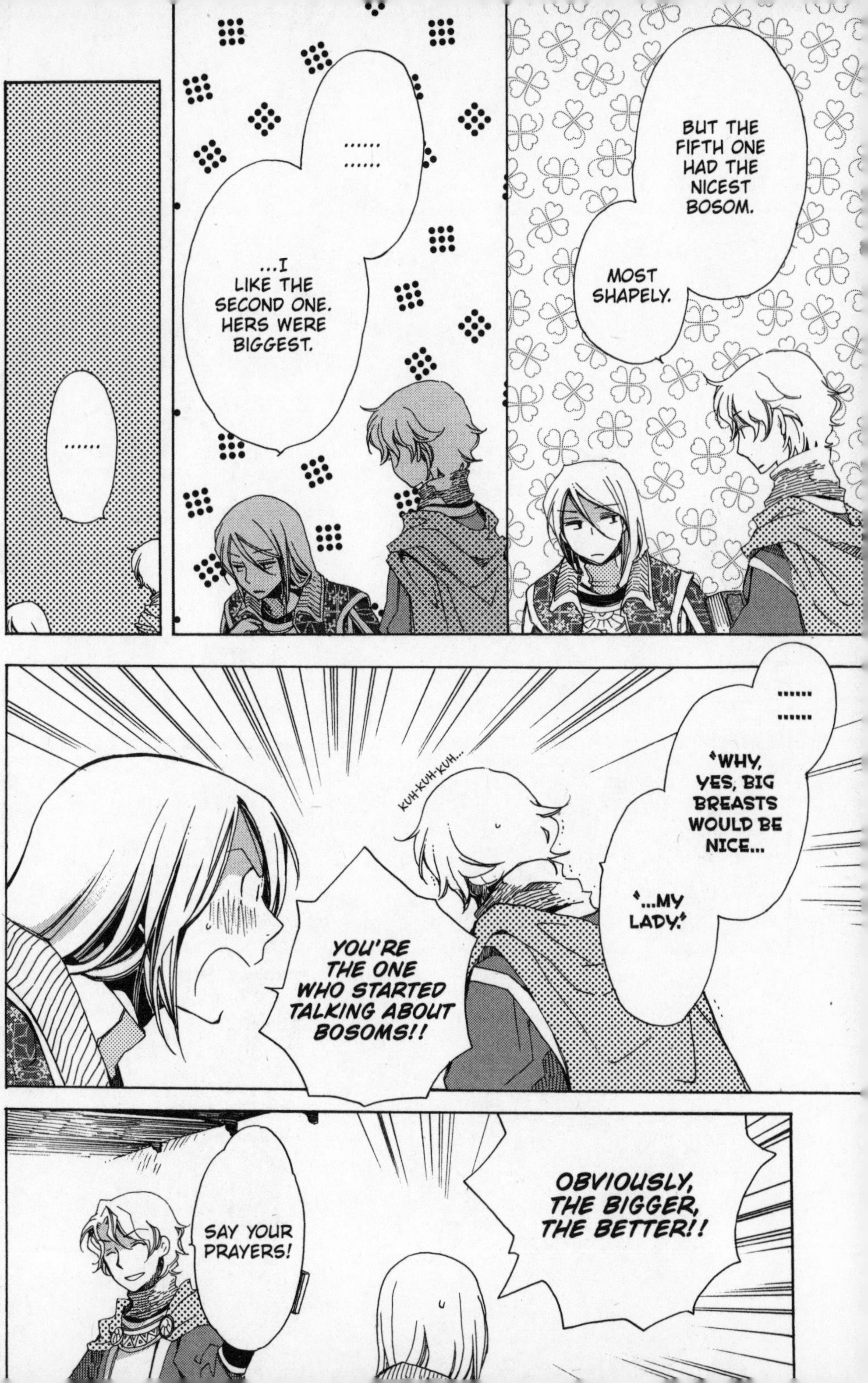
BUT THE FIFTH ONE HAD THE NICEST BOSOM.
MOST SHAPELY.
....
...I LIKE THE SECOND ONE. HERS WERE BIGGEST.
......
....
WHY, YES, BIG BREASTS WOULD BE NICE...
...MY LADY.
KUH-KUH-KUH...
YOU'RE THE ONE WHO STARTED TALKING ABOUT BOSOMS!!
OBVIOUSLY, THE BIGGER, THE BETTER!!
SAY YOUR PRAYERS!

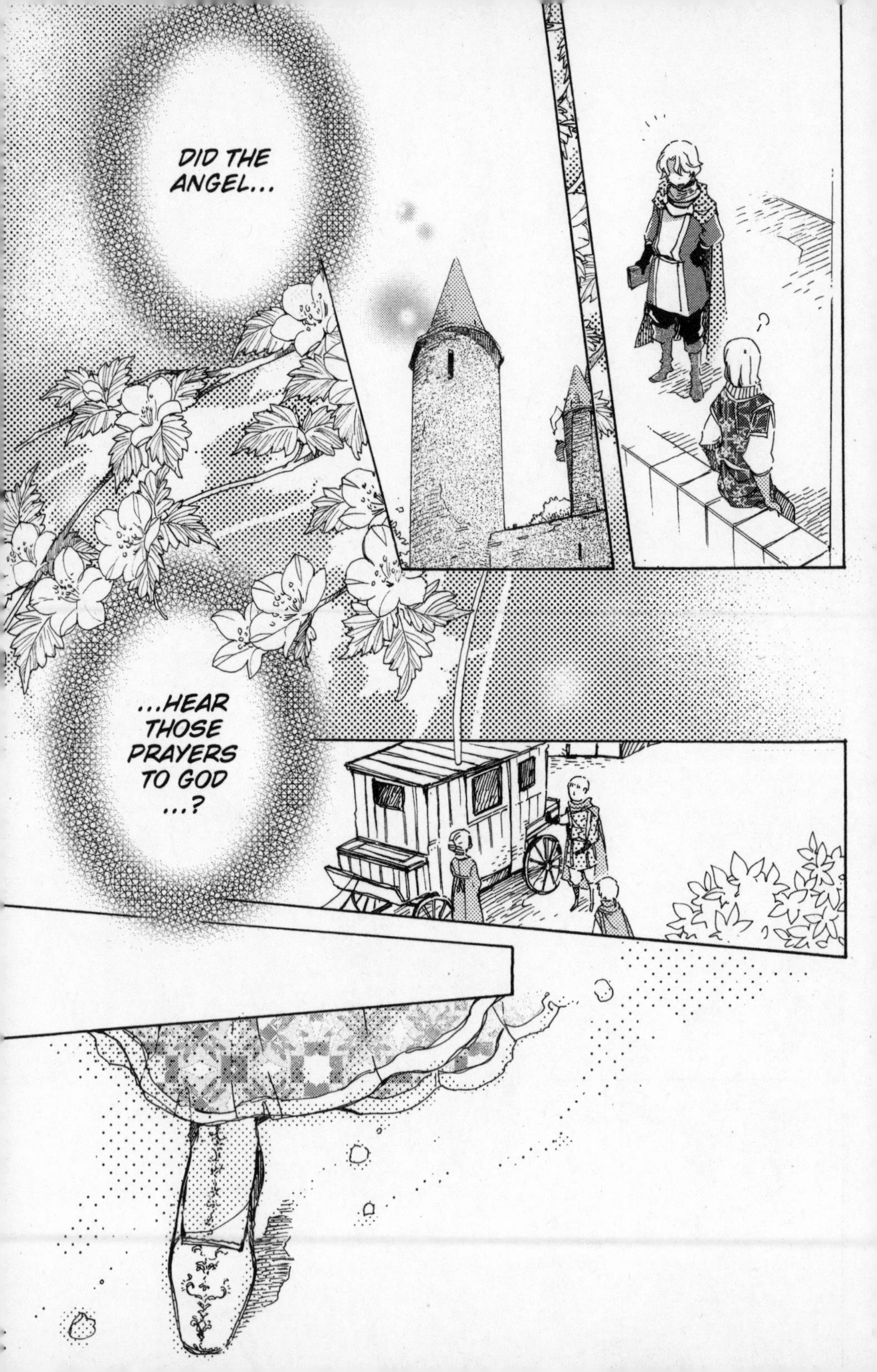
DID THE ANGEL...
...HEAR THOSE PRAYERS TO GOD ...?

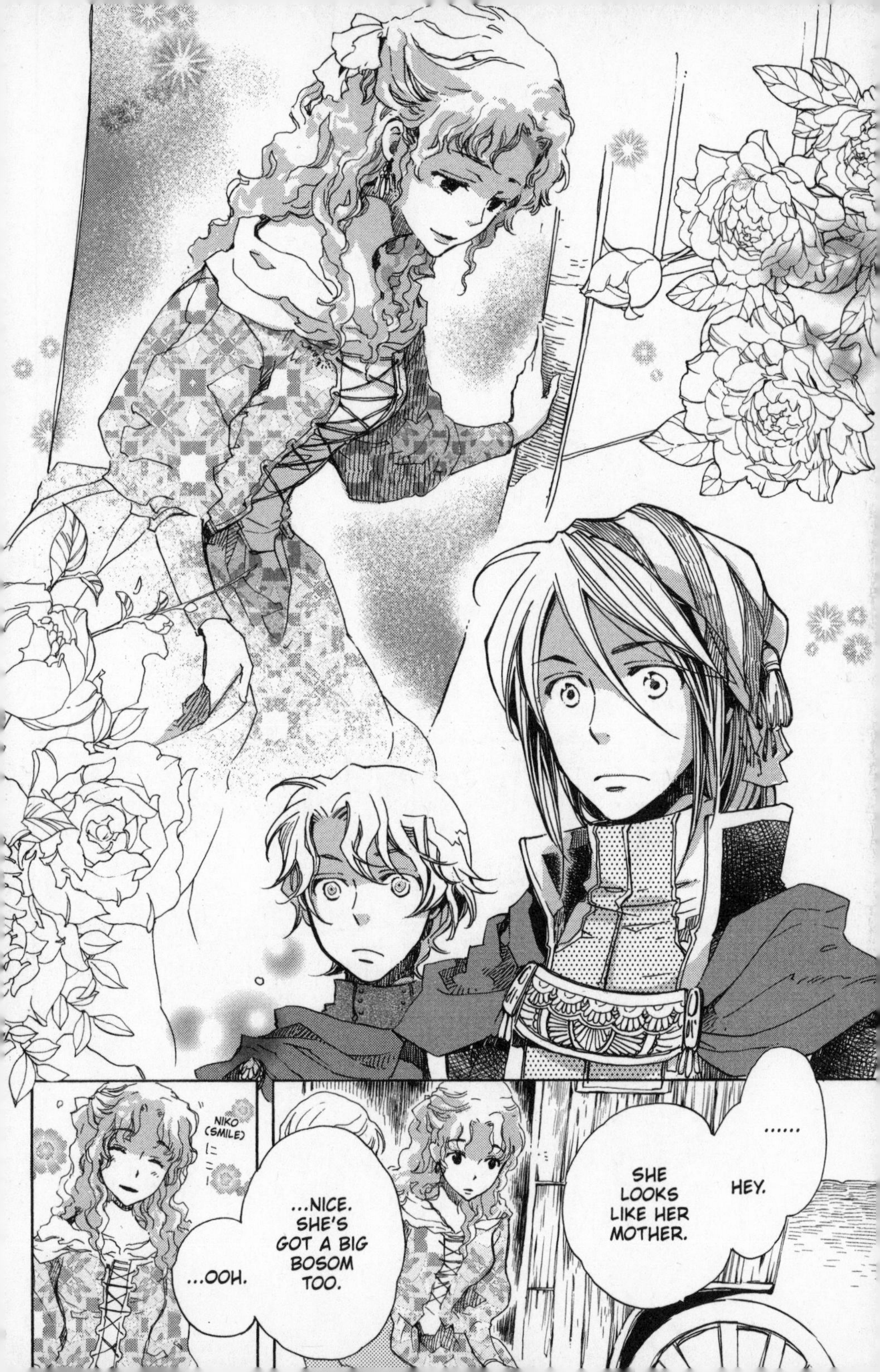
......
HEY.
SHE LOOKS LIKE HER MOTHER.
...NICE. SHE'S GOT A BIG BOSOM TOO.
NIKO (SMILE)
...OOH.

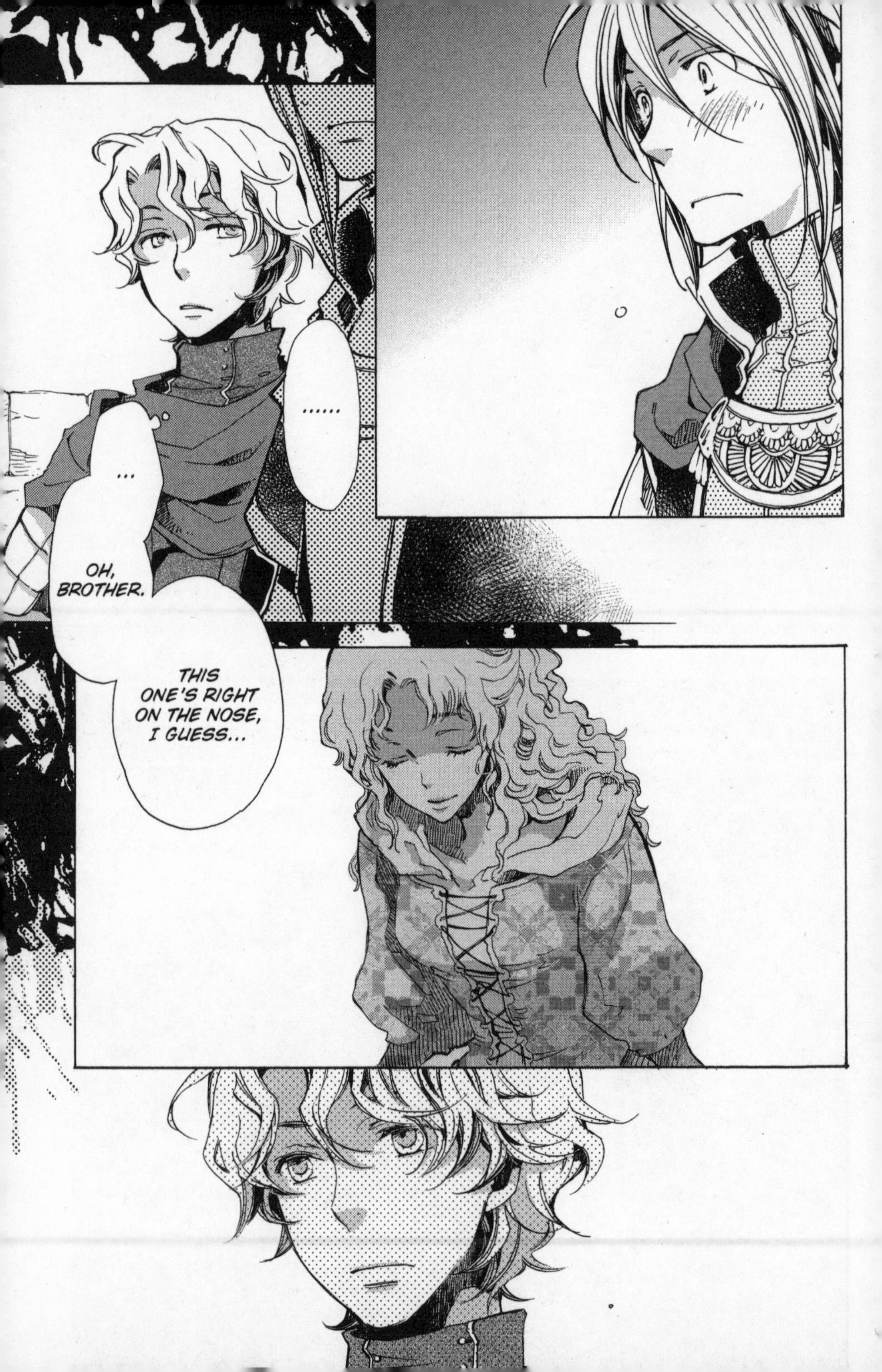
......
...
OH, BROTHER.
THIS ONE'S RIGHT ON THE NOSE, I GUESS...

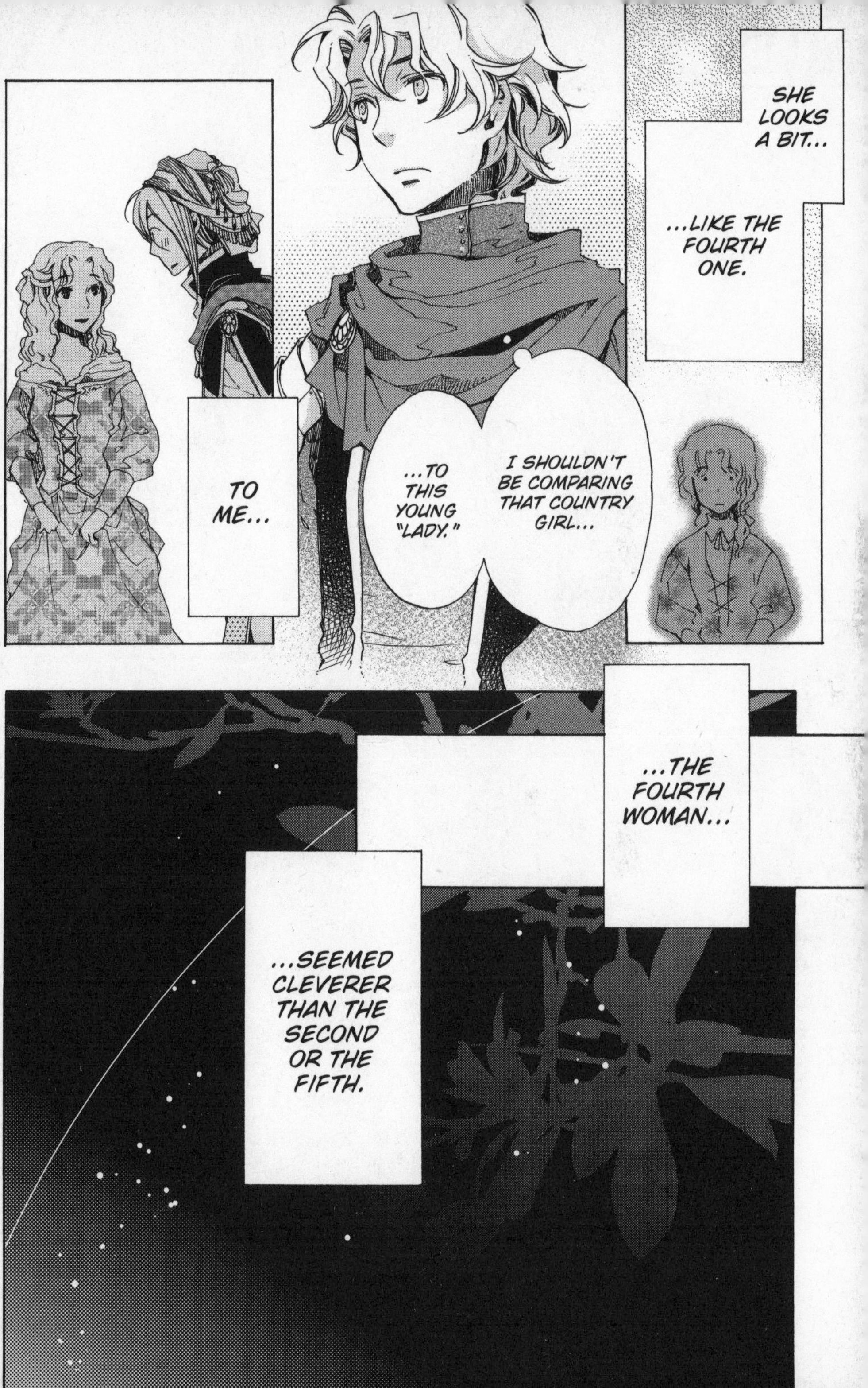
SHE LOOKS A BIT...
...LIKE THE FOURTH ONE.
I SHOULDN'T BE COMPARING THAT COUNTRY GIRL...
...TO THIS YOUNG "LADY."
TO ME...
...THE FOURTH WOMAN...
...SEEMED CLEVERER THAN THE SECOND OR THE FIFTH.

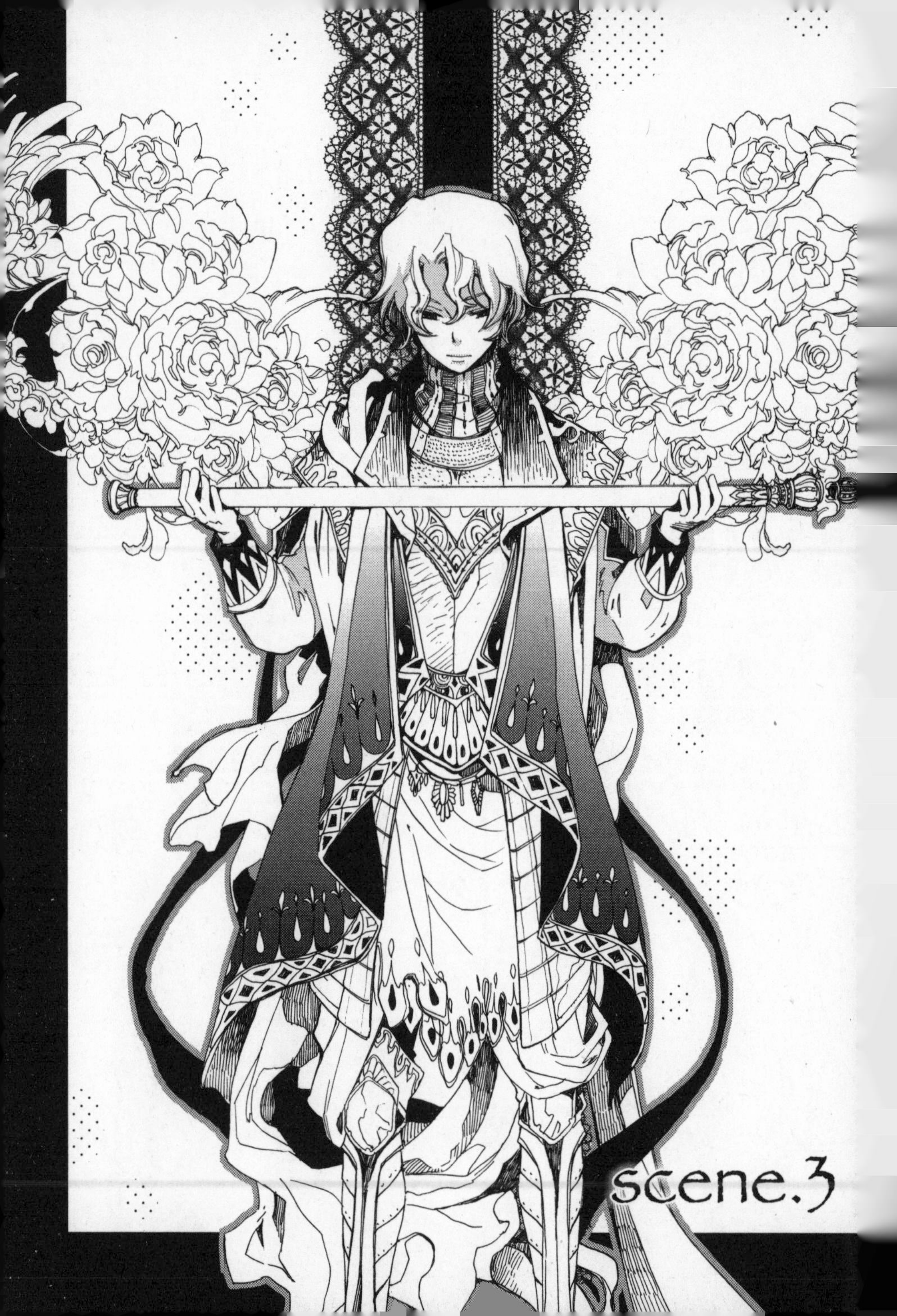
scene.3

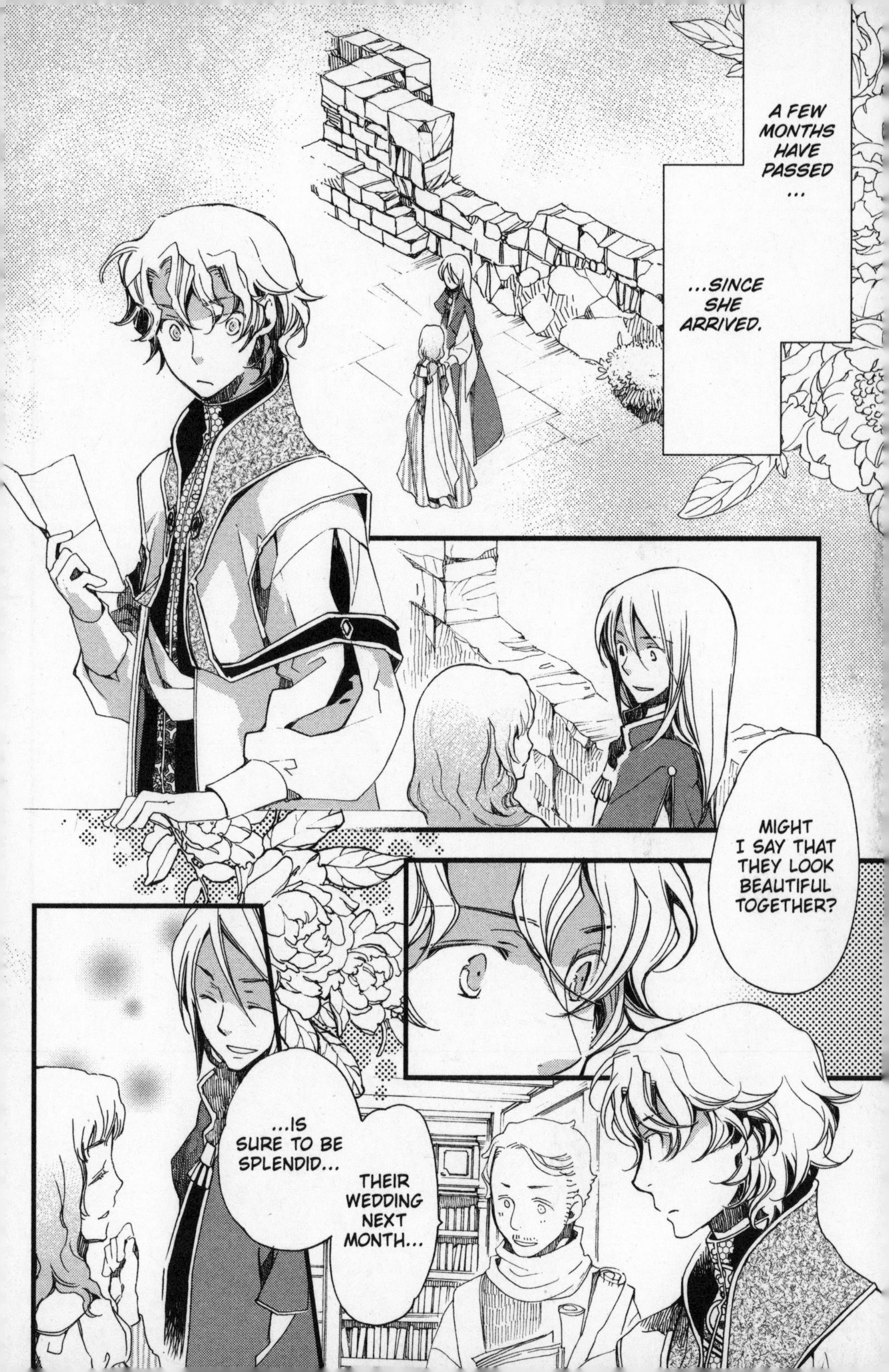
A FEW MONTHS HAVE PASSED ...
...SINCE SHE ARRIVED.
MIGHT I SAY THAT THEY LOOK BEAUTIFUL TOGETHER?
THEIR WEDDING NEXT MONTH...
...IS SURE TO BE SPLENDID...

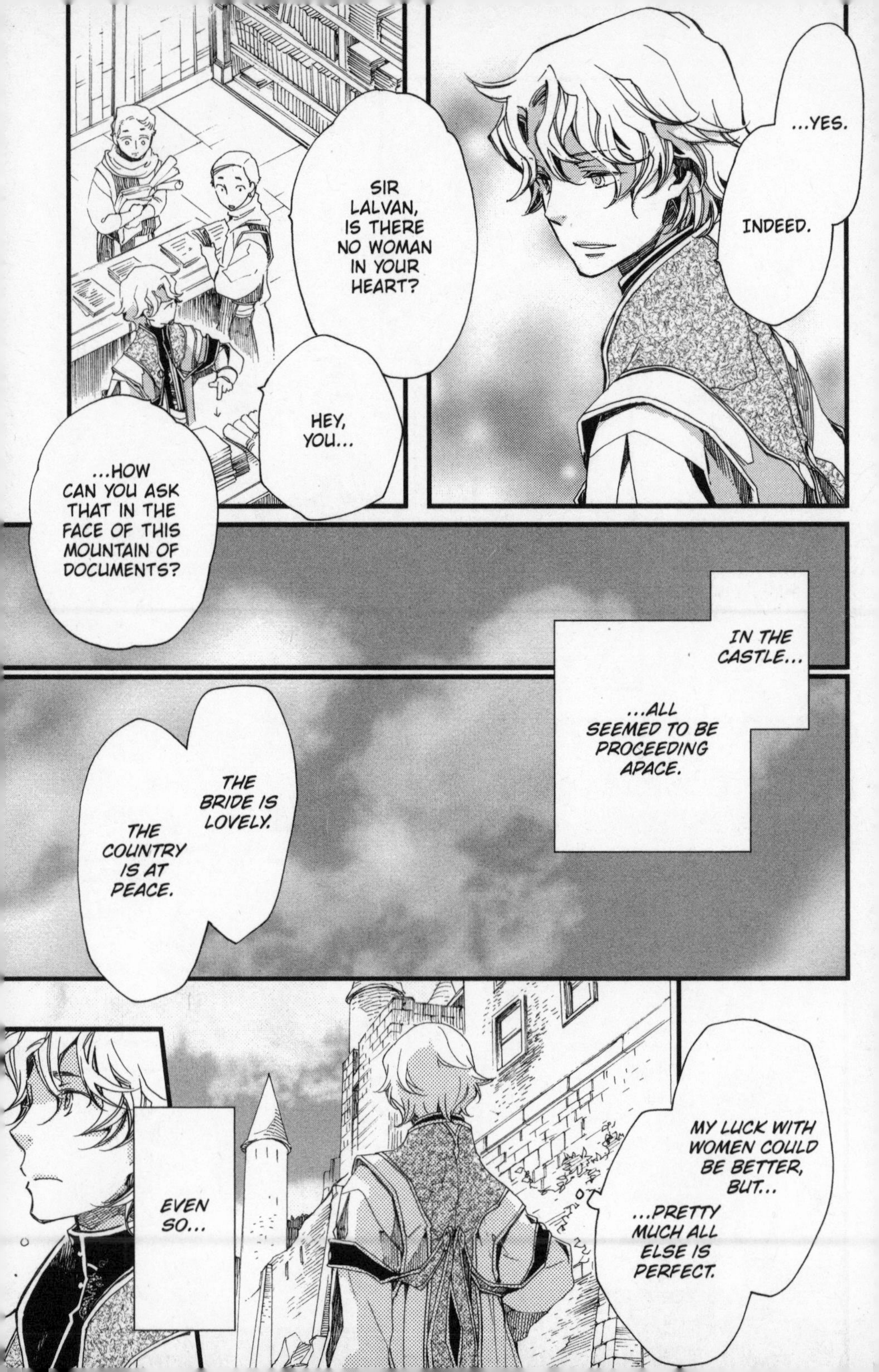
...YES.
INDEED.
SIR LALVAN, IS THERE NO WOMAN IN YOUR HEART?
HEY, YOU...
...HOW CAN YOU ASK THAT IN THE FACE OF THIS MOUNTAIN OF DOCUMENTS?
IN THE CASTLE...
...ALL SEEMED TO BE PROCEEDING APACE.
THE BRIDE IS LOVELY.
THE COUNTRY IS AT PEACE.
MY LUCK WITH WOMEN COULD BE BETTER, BUT...
...PRETTY MUCH ALL ELSE IS PERFECT.
EVEN SO...

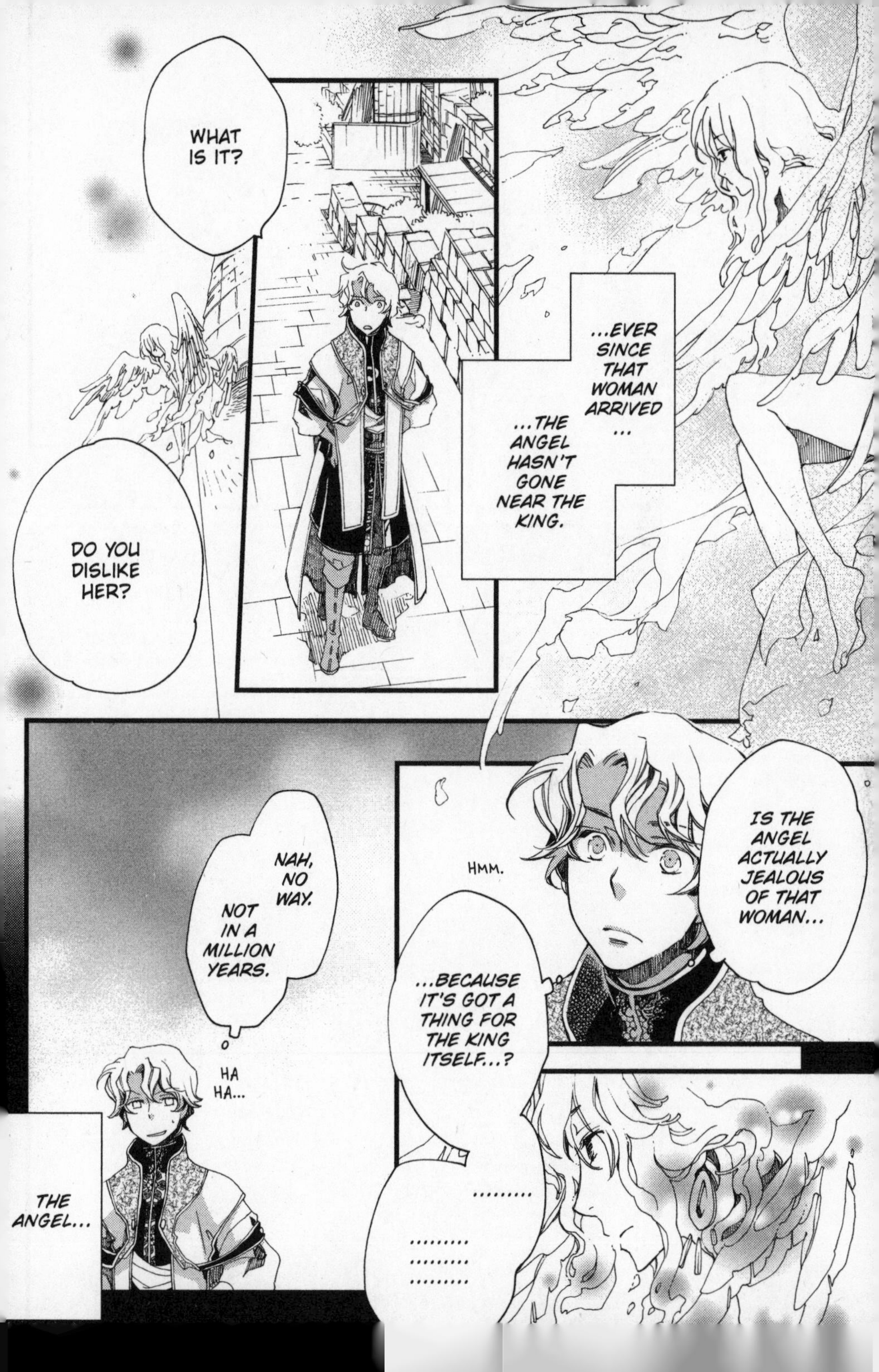
...EVER SINCE THAT WOMAN ARRIVED ...
...THE ANGEL HASN'T GONE NEAR THE KING.
WHAT IS IT?
DO YOU DISLIKE HER?
IS THE ANGEL ACTUALLY JEALOUS OF THAT WOMAN...
HMM.
...BECAUSE IT'S GOT A THING FOR THE KING ITSELF...?
....
....
....
....
NAH, NO WAY.
NOT IN A MILLION YEARS.
HA HA...
THE ANGEL...

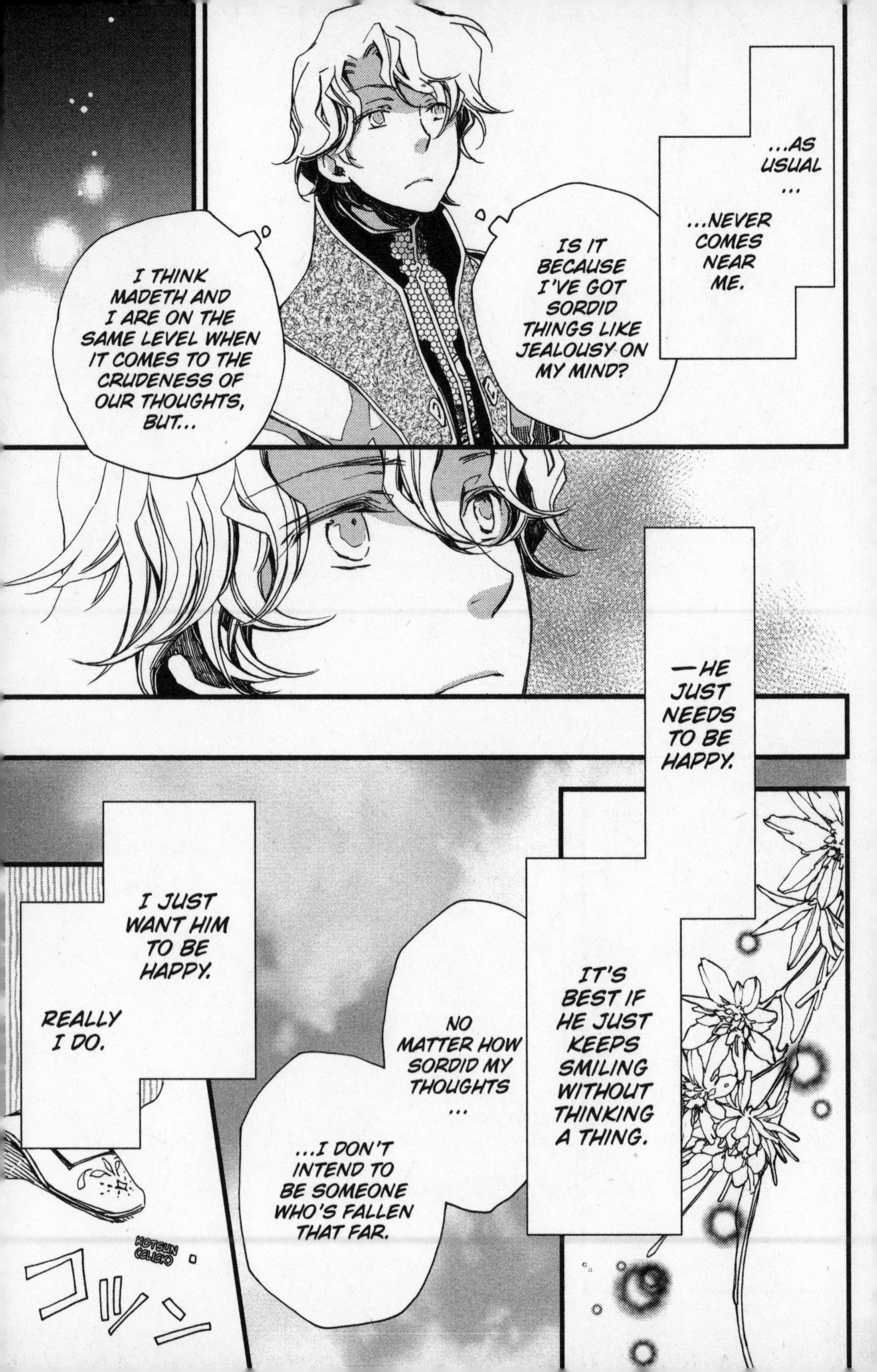
...AS USUAL ... ...NEVER COMES NEAR ME.
IS IT BECAUSE I'VE GOT SORDID THINGS LIKE JEALOUSY ON MY MIND?
I THINK MADETH AND I ARE ON THE SAME LEVEL WHEN IT COMES TO THE CRUDENESS OF OUR THOUGHTS, BUT...
—HE JUST NEEDS TO BE HAPPY.
IT'S BEST IF HE JUST KEEPS SMILING WITHOUT THINKING A THING.
NO MATTER HOW SORDID MY THOUGHTS ...
...I DON'T INTEND TO BE SOMEONE WHO'S FALLEN THAT FAR.
I JUST WANT HIM TO BE HAPPY.
REALLY I DO.
KOTSUN (CLICK)

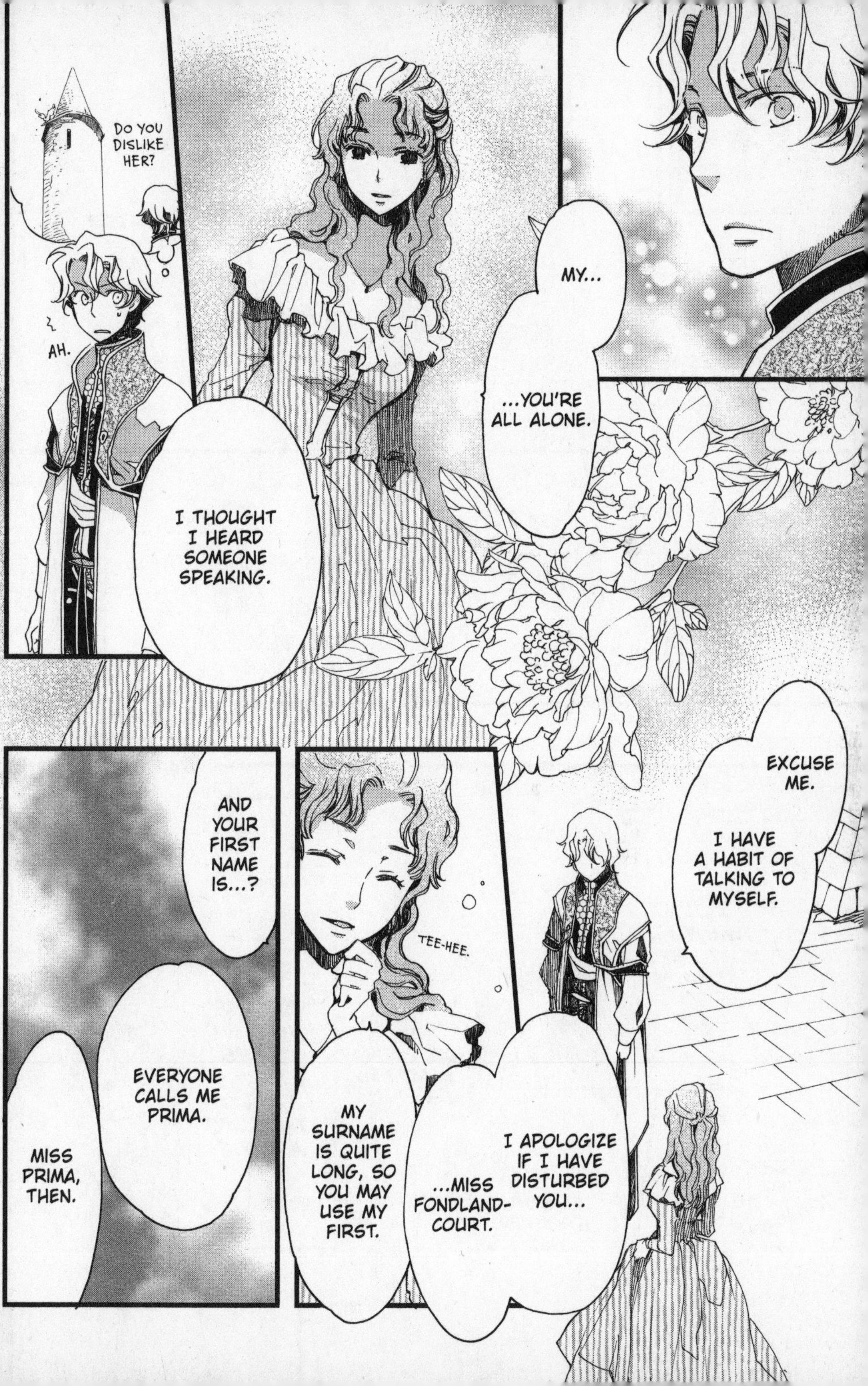
MY...
...YOU'RE ALL ALONE.
I THOUGHT I HEARD SOMEONE SPEAKING.
DO YOU DISLIKE HER?
AH.
EXCUSE ME.
I HAVE A HABIT OF TALKING TO MYSELF.
I APOLOGIZE IF I HAVE DISTURBED YOU...
...MISS FONDLAND-COURT.
MY SURNAME IS QUITE LONG, SO YOU MAY USE MY FIRST.
TEE-HEE.
AND YOUR FIRST NAME IS...?
EVERYONE CALLS ME PRIMA.
MISS PRIMA, THEN.

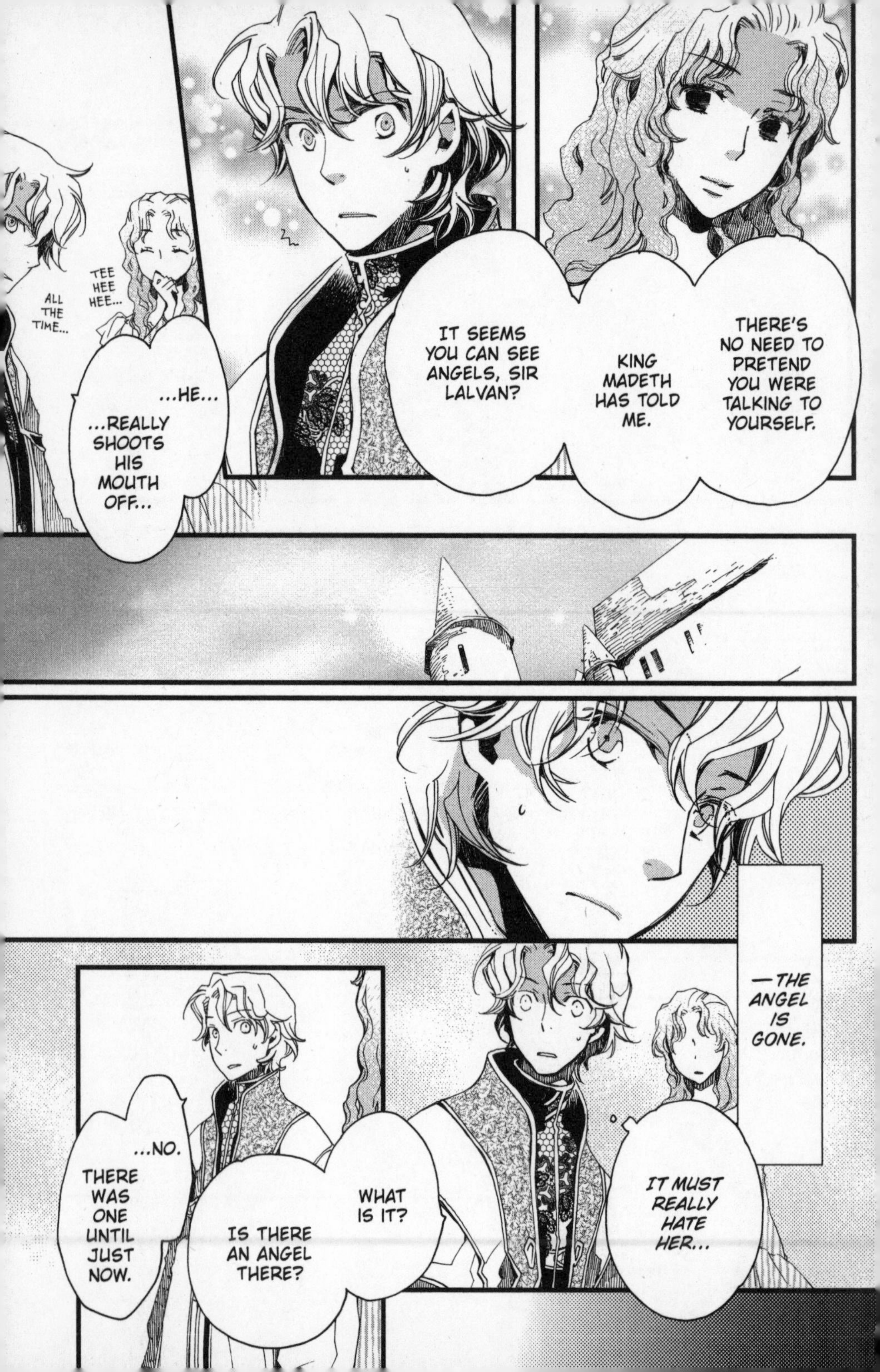
THERE'S NO NEED TO PRETEND YOU WERE TALKING TO YOURSELF.
KING MADETH HAS TOLD ME.
IT SEEMS YOU CAN SEE ANGELS, SIR LALVAN?
TEE HEE HEE...
...HE...
...REALLY SHOOTS HIS MOUTH OFF...
ALL THE TIME...
—THE ANGEL IS GONE.
IT MUST REALLY HATE HER...
WHAT IS IT?
IS THERE AN ANGEL THERE?
...NO.
THERE WAS ONE UNTIL JUST NOW.

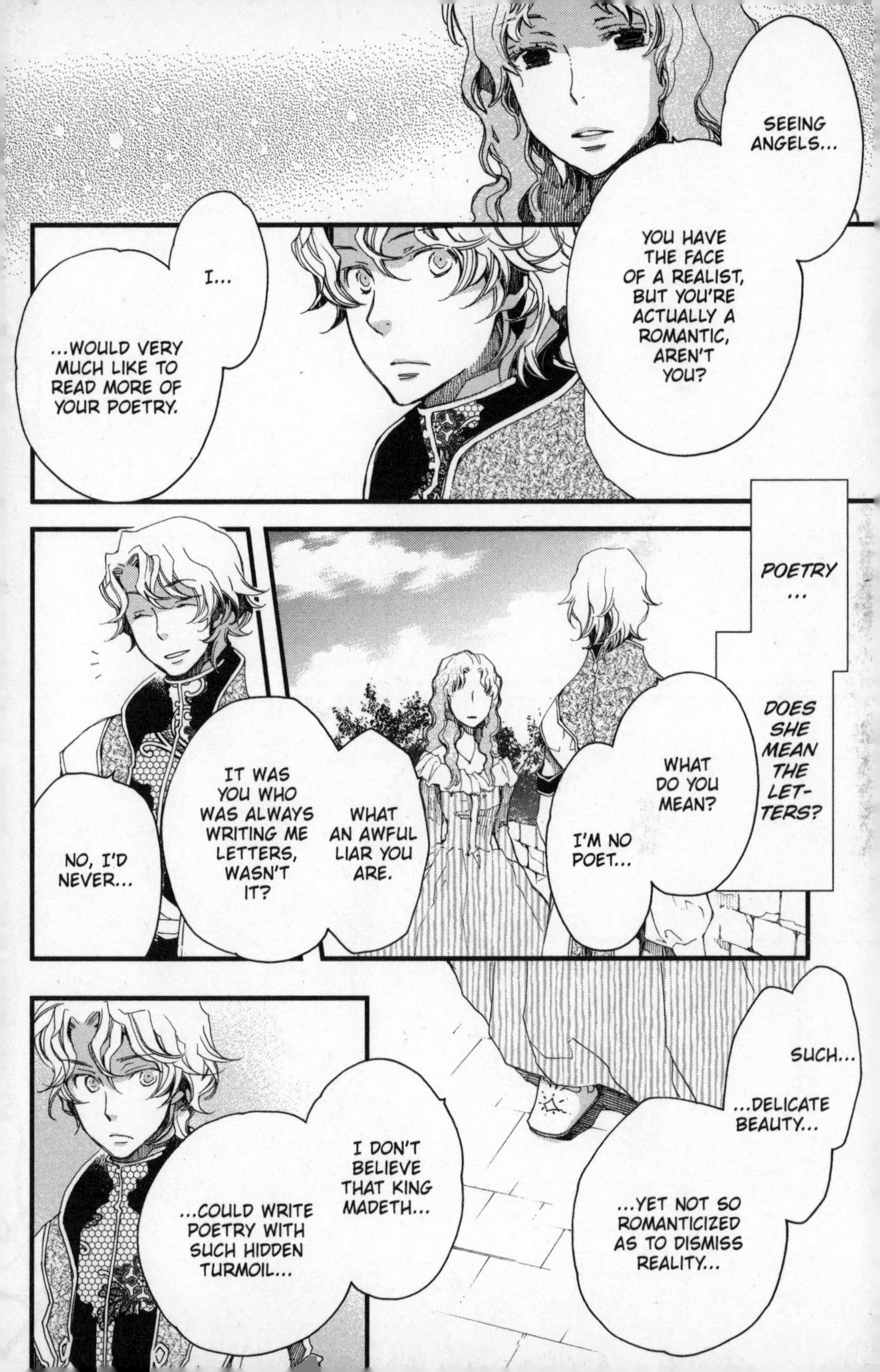
SEEING ANGELS...
YOU HAVE THE FACE OF A REALIST, BUT YOU'RE ACTUALLY A ROMANTIC, AREN'T YOU?
I...
...WOULD VERY MUCH LIKE TO READ MORE OF YOUR POETRY.
POETRY...
DOES SHE MEAN THE LET-TERS?
WHAT DO YOU MEAN?
I'M NO POET...
WHAT AN AWFUL LIAR YOU ARE.
IT WAS YOU WHO WAS ALWAYS WRITING ME LETTERS, WASN'T IT?
NO, I'D NEVER...
SUCH...
...DELICATE BEAUTY...
...YET NOT SO ROMANTICIZED AS TO DISMISS REALITY...
I DON'T BELIEVE THAT KING MADETH...
...COULD WRITE POETRY WITH SUCH HIDDEN TURMOIL...

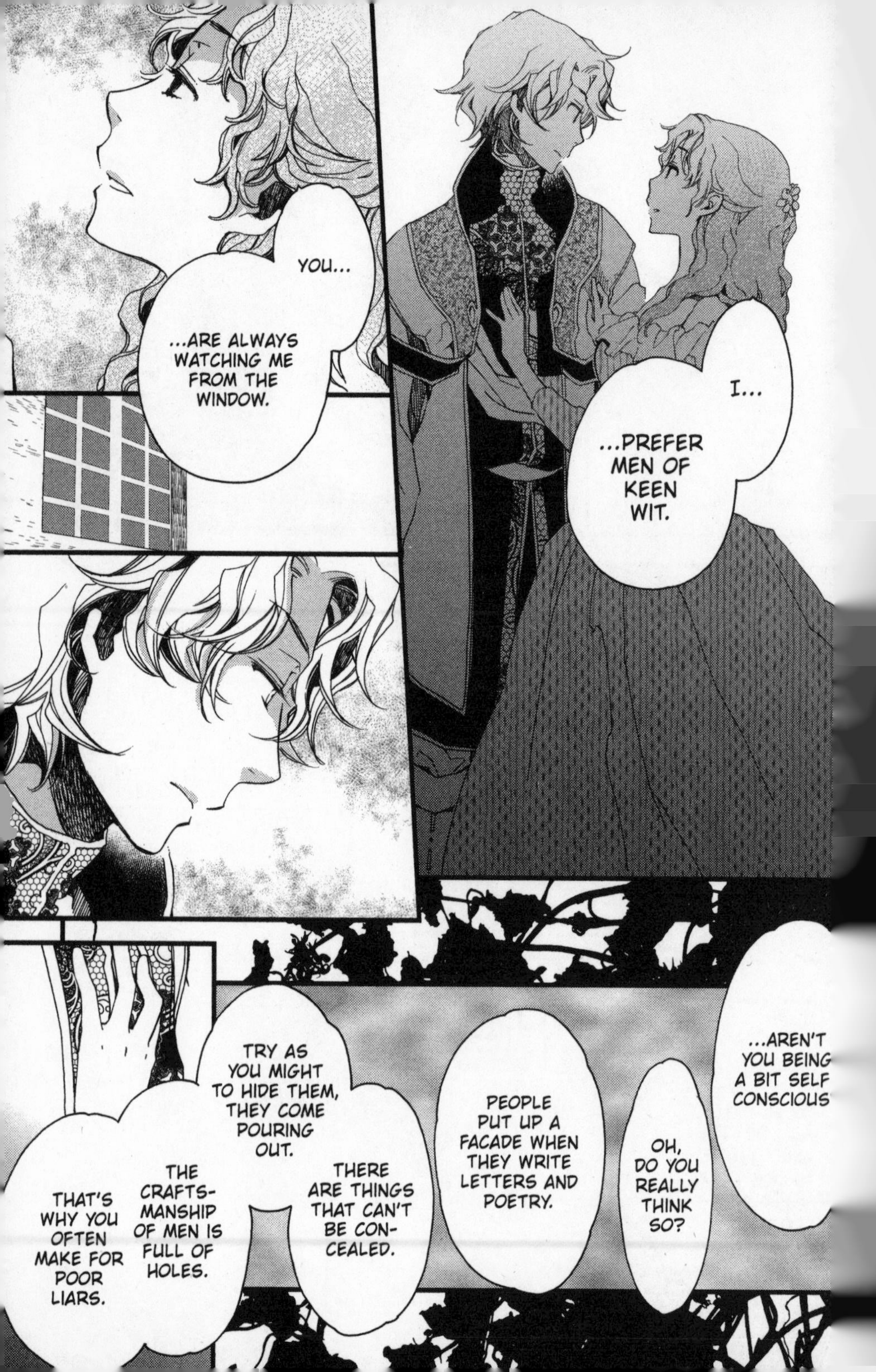
I...
...PREFER MEN OF KEEN WIT.
YOU...
...ARE ALWAYS WATCHING ME FROM THE WINDOW.
...AREN'T YOU BEING A BIT SELF CONSCIOUS
OH, DO YOU REALLY THINK SO?
PEOPLE PUT UP A FACADE WHEN THEY WRITE LETTERS AND POETRY.
THERE ARE THINGS THAT CAN'T BE CON-CEALED.
TRY AS YOU MIGHT TO HIDE THEM, THEY COME POURING OUT.
THE CRAFTS-MANSHIP OF MEN IS FULL OF HOLES.
THAT'S WHY YOU OFTEN MAKE FOR POOR LIARS.

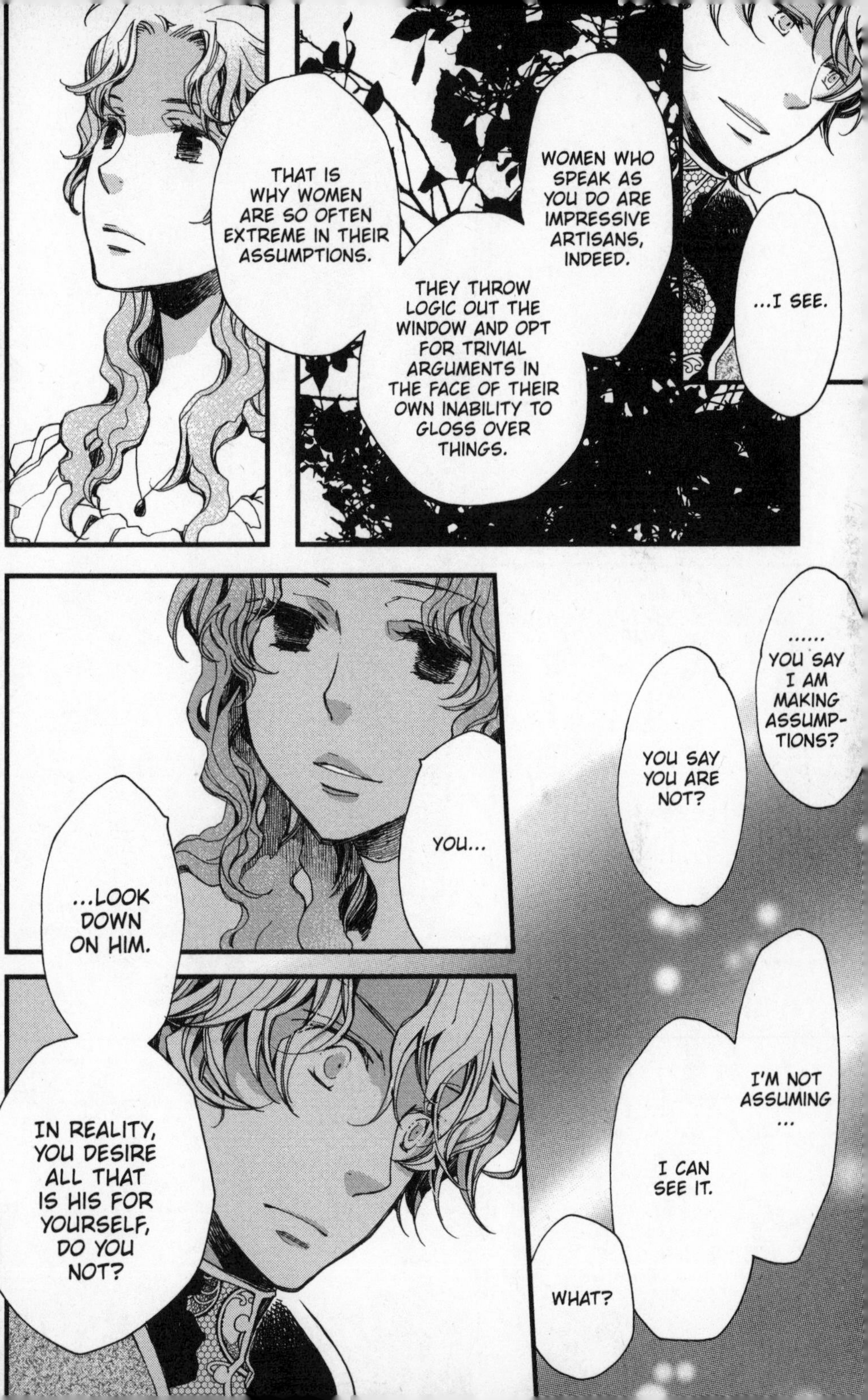
...I SEE.
WOMEN WHO SPEAK AS YOU DO ARE IMPRESSIVE ARTISANS, INDEED.
THAT IS WHY WOMEN ARE SO OFTEN EXTREME IN THEIR ASSUMPTIONS.
THEY THROW LOGIC OUT THE WINDOW AND OPT FOR TRIVIAL ARGUMENTS IN THE FACE OF THEIR OWN INABILITY TO GLOSS OVER THINGS.
...... YOU SAY I AM MAKING ASSUMP-TIONS?
YOU SAY YOU ARE NOT?
YOU...
...LOOK DOWN ON HIM.
I'M NOT ASSUMING ...
I CAN SEE IT.
WHAT?
IN REALITY, YOU DESIRE ALL THAT IS HIS FOR YOURSELF, DO YOU NOT?

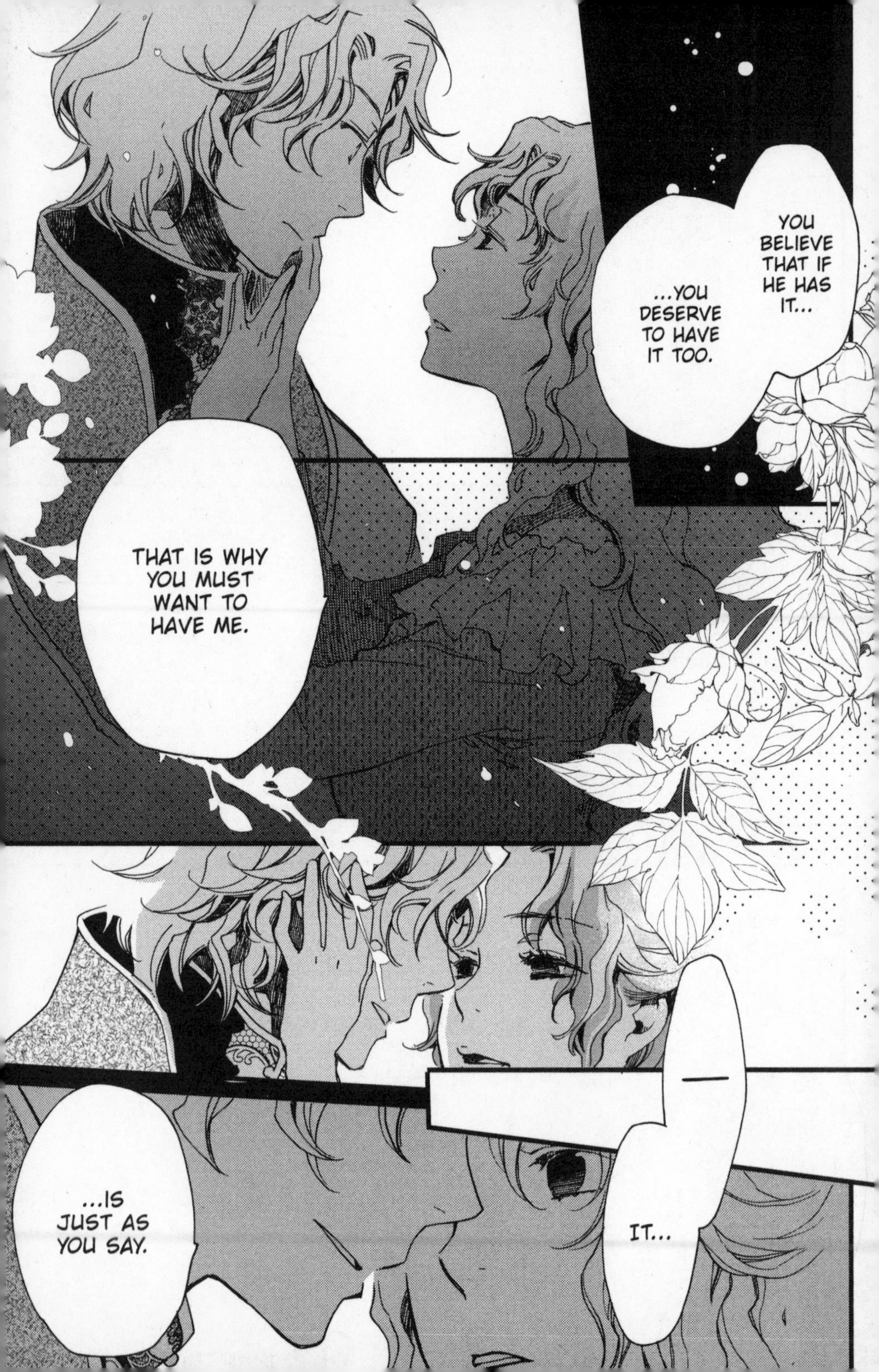
YOU BELIEVE THAT IF HE HAS IT...
...YOU DESERVE TO HAVE IT TOO.
THAT IS WHY YOU MUST WANT TO HAVE ME.
—
IT...
...IS JUST AS YOU SAY.

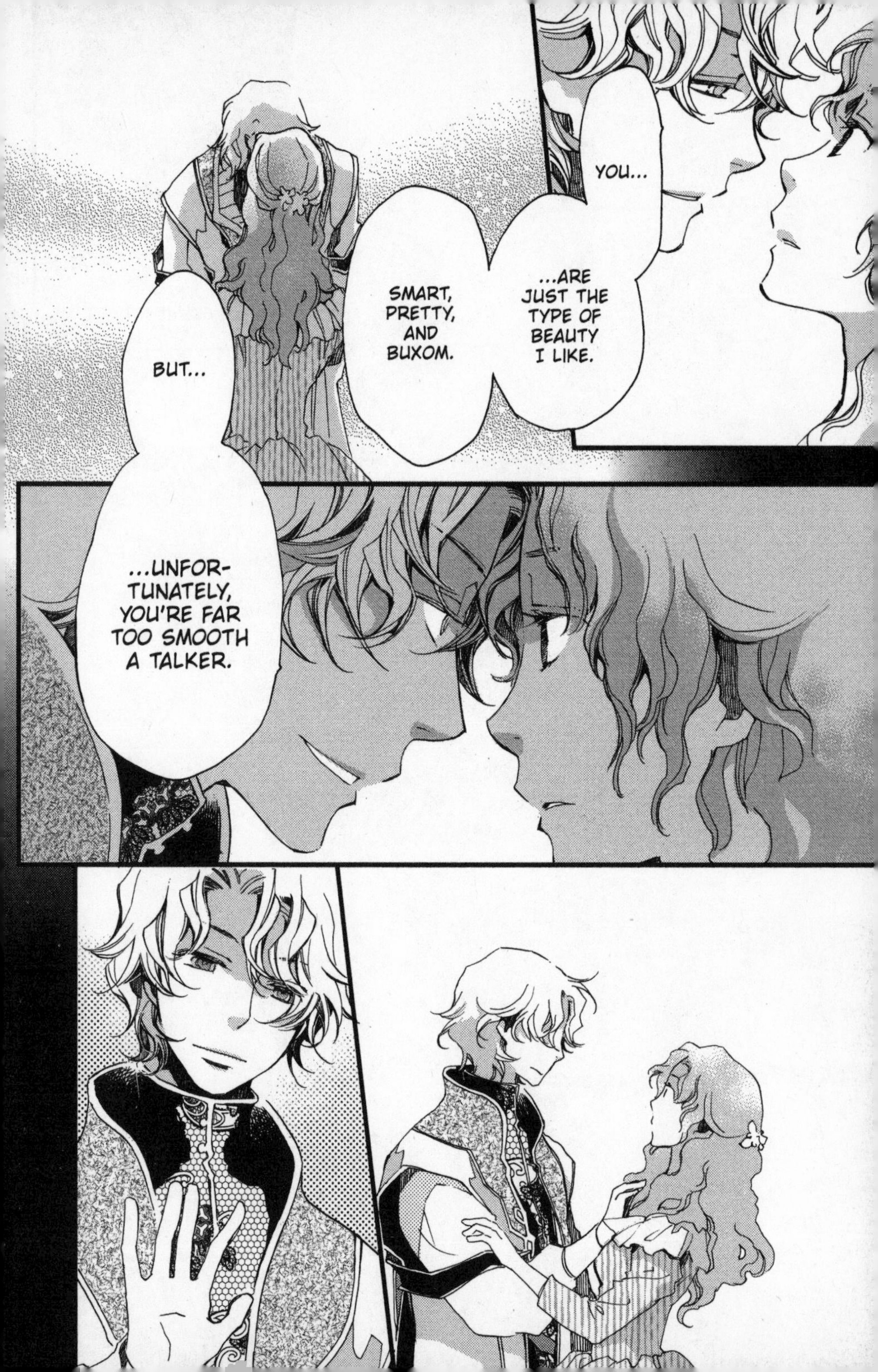
YOU...
...ARE JUST THE TYPE OF BEAUTY I LIKE.
SMART, PRETTY, AND BUXOM.
BUT...
...UNFOR-TUNATELY, YOU'RE FAR TOO SMOOTH A TALKER.

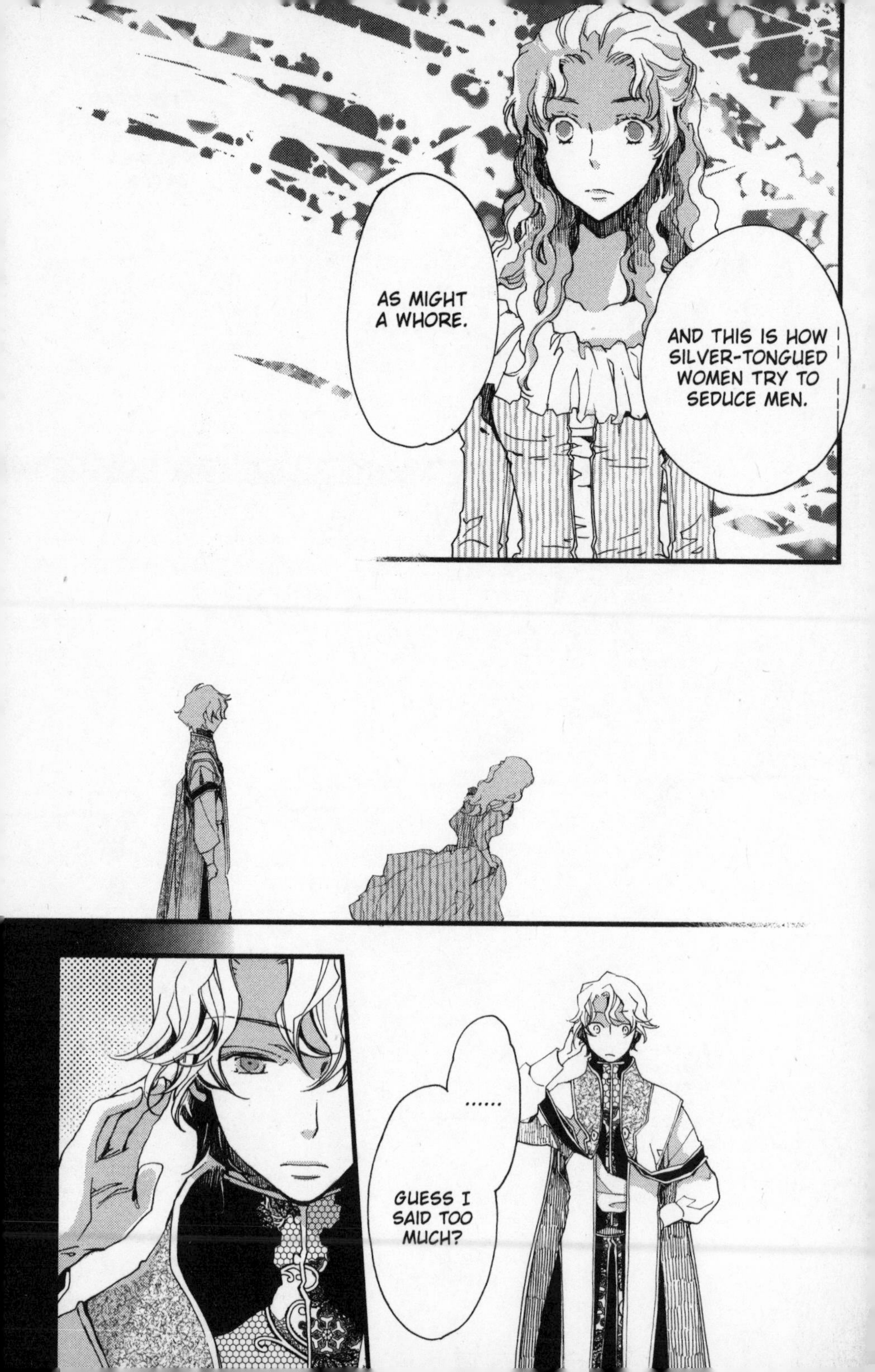
AND THIS IS HOW SILVER-TONGUED WOMEN TRY TO SEDUCE MEN.
AS MIGHT A WHORE.
......
GUESS I SAID TOO MUCH?

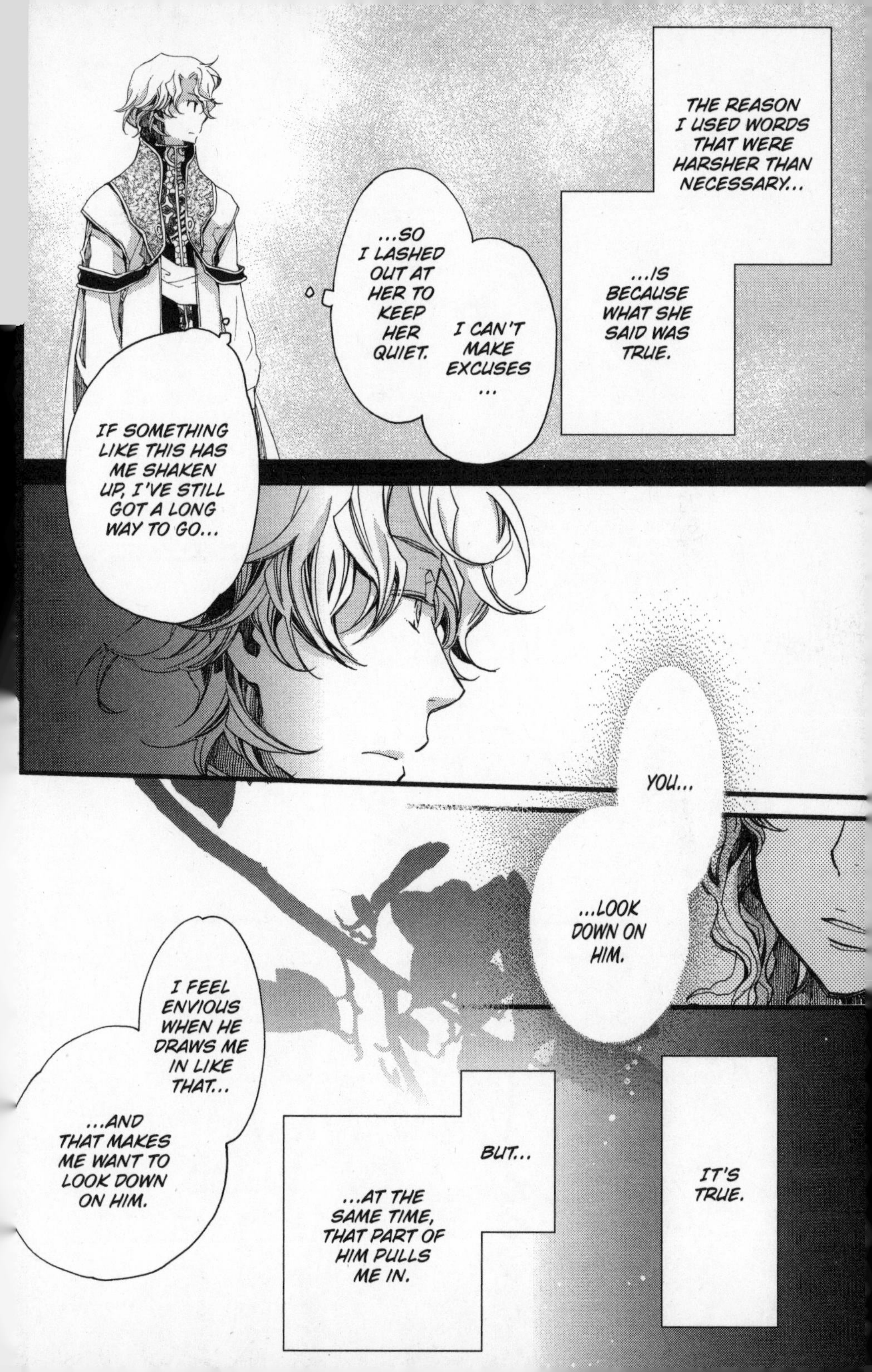
THE REASON I USED WORDS THAT WERE HARSHER THAN NECESSARY...
...IS BECAUSE WHAT SHE SAID WAS TRUE.
I CAN'T MAKE EXCUSES...
...SO I LASHED OUT AT HER TO KEEP HER QUIET.
IF SOMETHING LIKE THIS HAS ME SHAKEN UP, I'VE STILL GOT A LONG WAY TO GO...
YOU...
...LOOK DOWN ON HIM.
IT'S TRUE.
BUT...
...AT THE SAME TIME, THAT PART OF HIM PULLS ME IN.
I FEEL ENVIOUS WHEN HE DRAWS ME IN LIKE THAT...
...AND THAT MAKES ME WANT TO LOOK DOWN ON HIM.

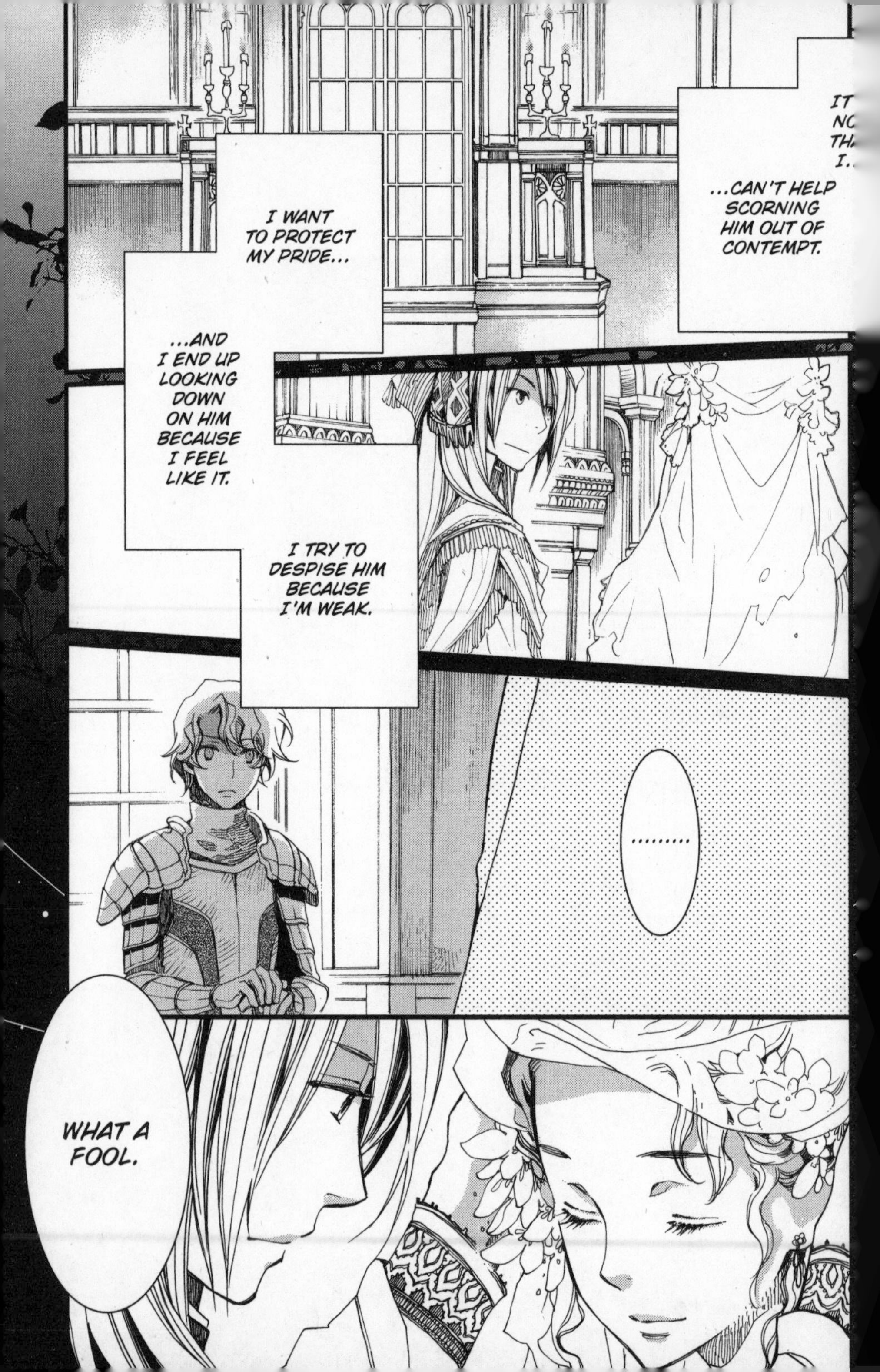
IT NO THA I..
...CAN'T HELP SCORNING HIM OUT OF CONTEMPT.
I WANT TO PROTECT MY PRIDE...
...AND I END UP LOOKING DOWN ON HIM BECAUSE I FEEL LIKE IT.
I TRY TO DESPISE HIM BECAUSE I'M WEAK.
....
WHAT A FOOL.

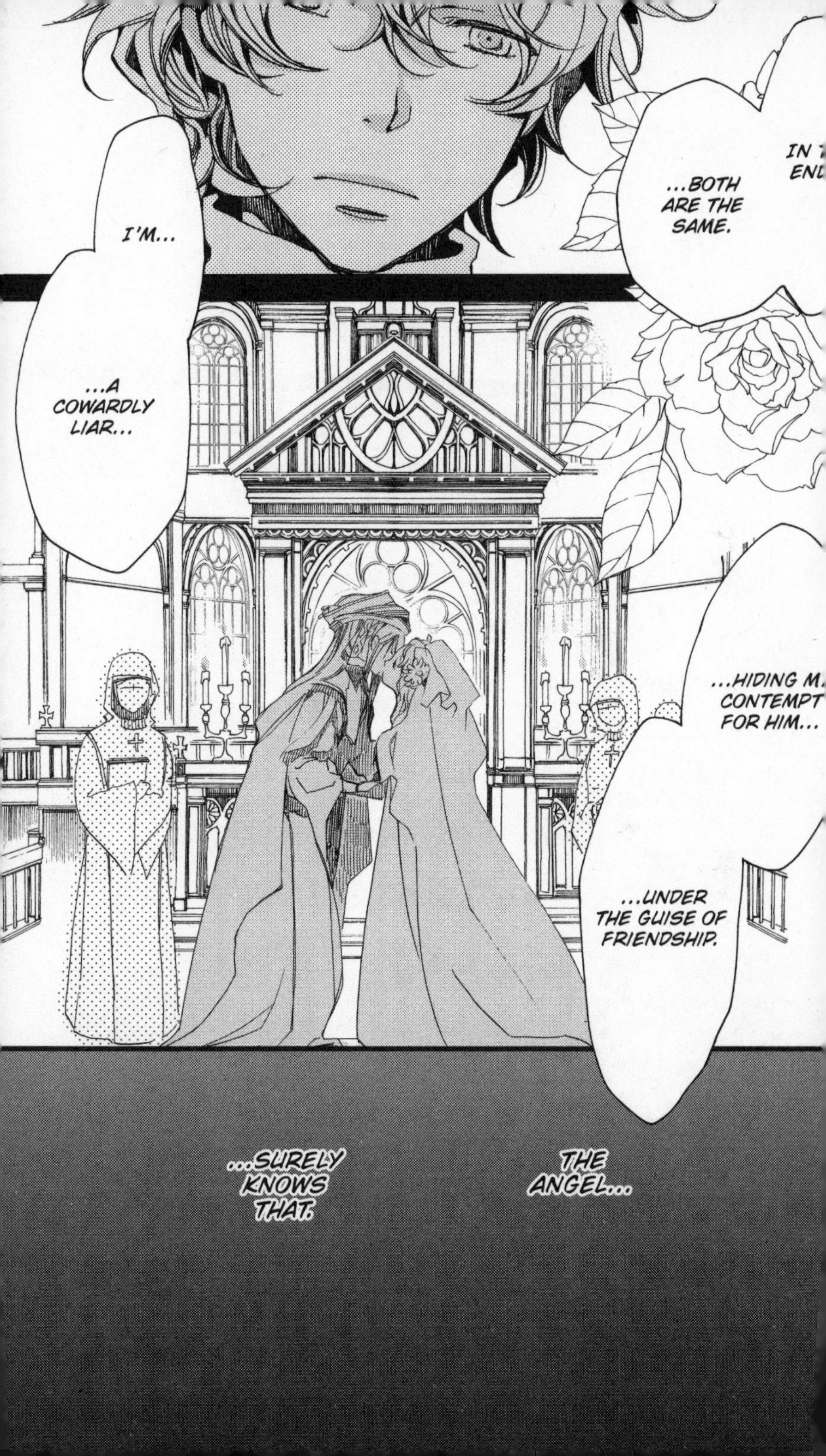
IN T
EN
...BOTH ARE THE SAME.
I'M...
...A COWARDLY LIAR...
...HIDING M
CONTEMPT FOR HIM...
...UNDER THE GUISE OF FRIENDSHIP.
THE ANGEL...
...SURELY KNOWS THAT.

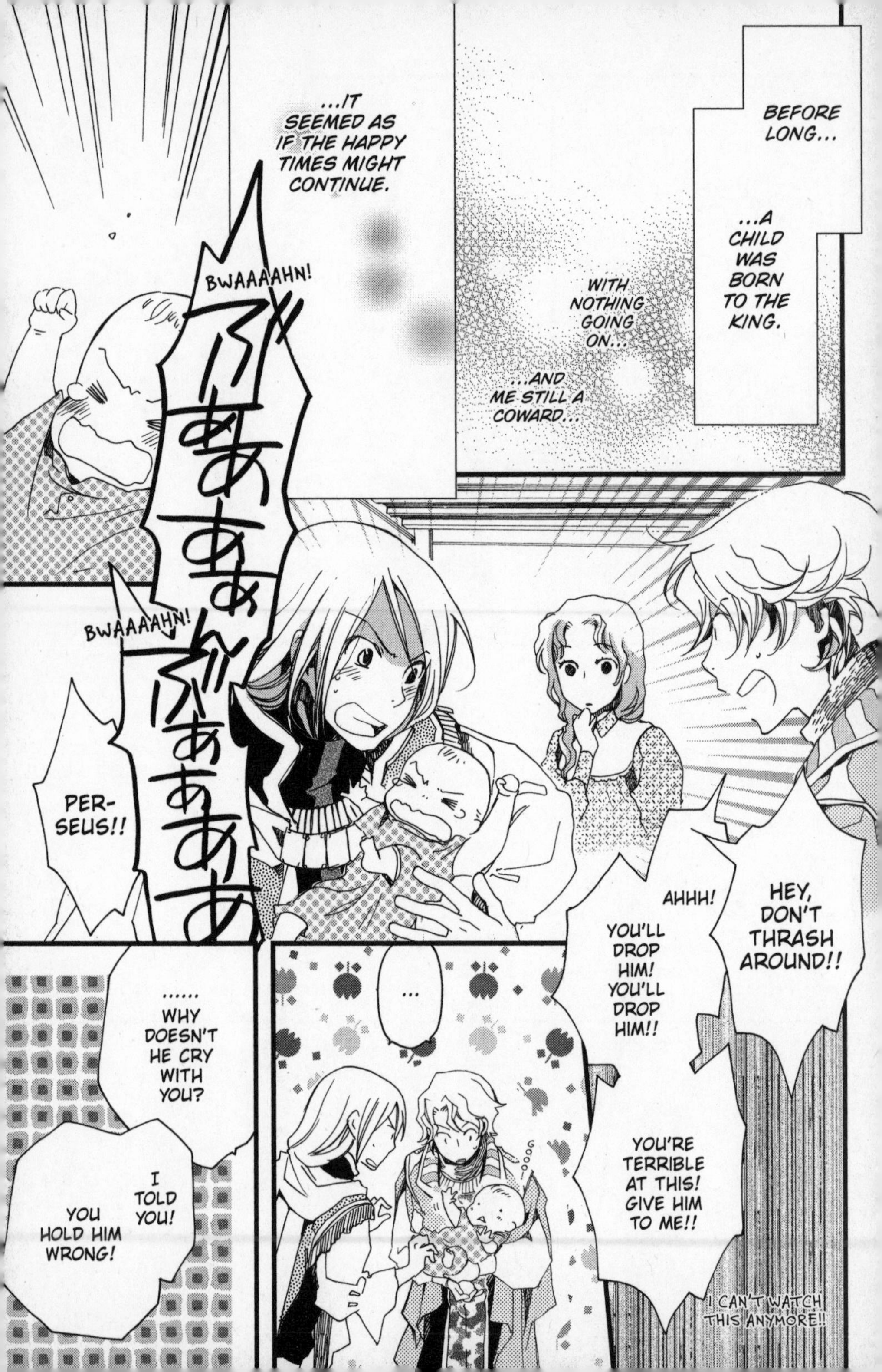
BEFORE LONG...
...A CHILD WAS BORN TO THE KING.
WITH NOTHING GOING ON...
...AND ME STILL A COWARD...
...IT SEEMED AS IF THE HAPPY TIMES MIGHT CONTINUE.
BWAAAAHN!
ぶあああん
BWAAAAHN!
ぶああああ
PER-SEUS!!
HEY, DON'T THRASH AROUND!!
AHHH!
YOU'LL DROP HIM! YOU'LL DROP HIM!!
YOU'RE TERRIBLE AT THIS! GIVE HIM TO ME!!
I CAN'T WATCH THIS ANYMORE!!
GOOO!
...
...... WHY DOESN'T HE CRY WITH YOU?
I TOLD YOU!
YOU HOLD HIM WRONG!

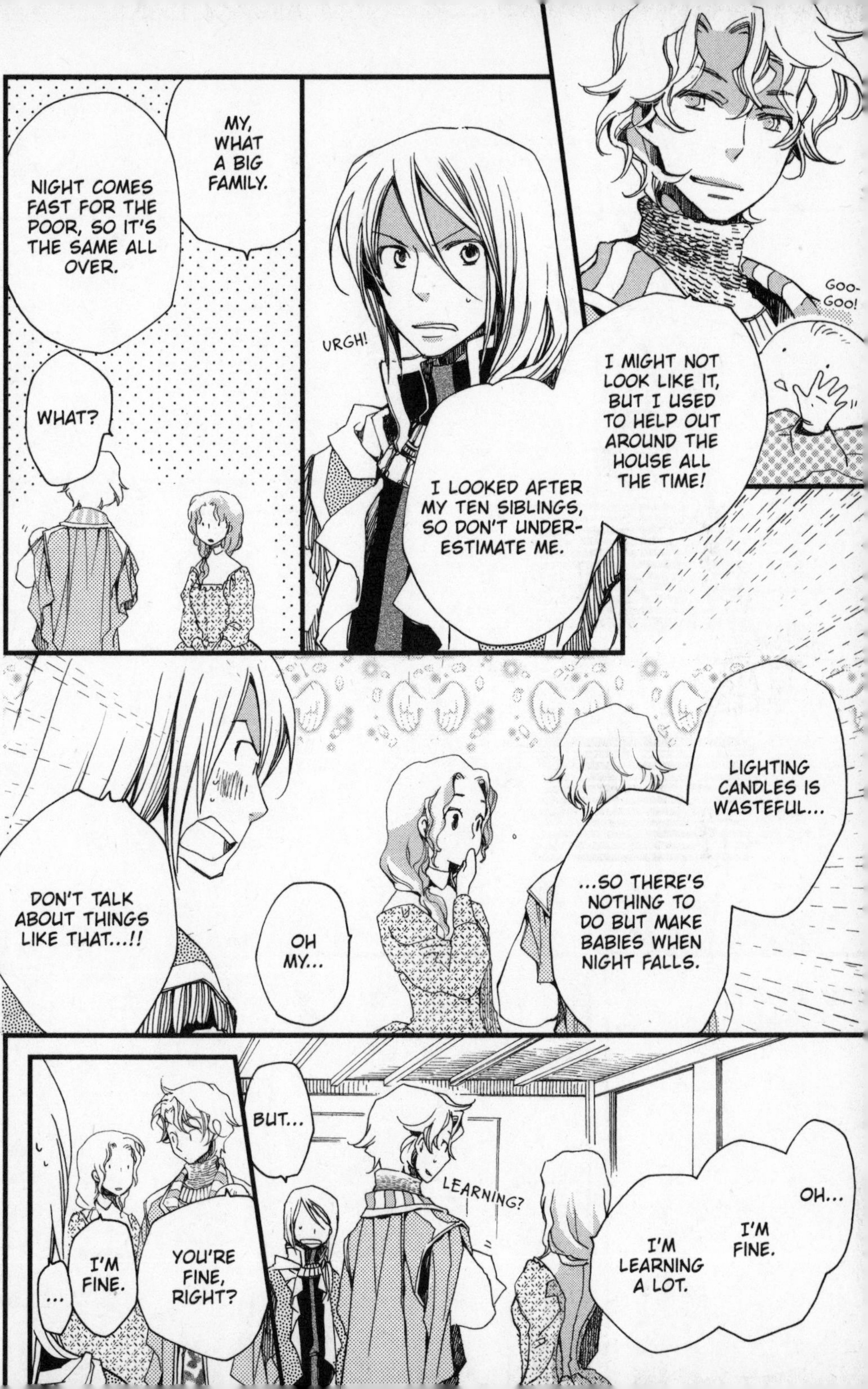
GOO-GOO!
I MIGHT NOT LOOK LIKE IT, BUT I USED TO HELP OUT AROUND THE HOUSE ALL THE TIME!
URGH!
I LOOKED AFTER MY TEN SIBLINGS, SO DON'T UNDER-ESTIMATE ME.
MY, WHAT A BIG FAMILY.
NIGHT COMES FAST FOR THE POOR, SO IT'S THE SAME ALL OVER.
WHAT?
LIGHTING CANDLES IS WASTEFUL...
...SO THERE'S NOTHING TO DO BUT MAKE BABIES WHEN NIGHT FALLS.
OH MY...
DON'T TALK ABOUT THINGS LIKE THAT...!!
OH...
I'M FINE.
I'M LEARNING A LOT.
LEARNING?
BUT...
YOU'RE FINE, RIGHT?
I'M FINE.
...

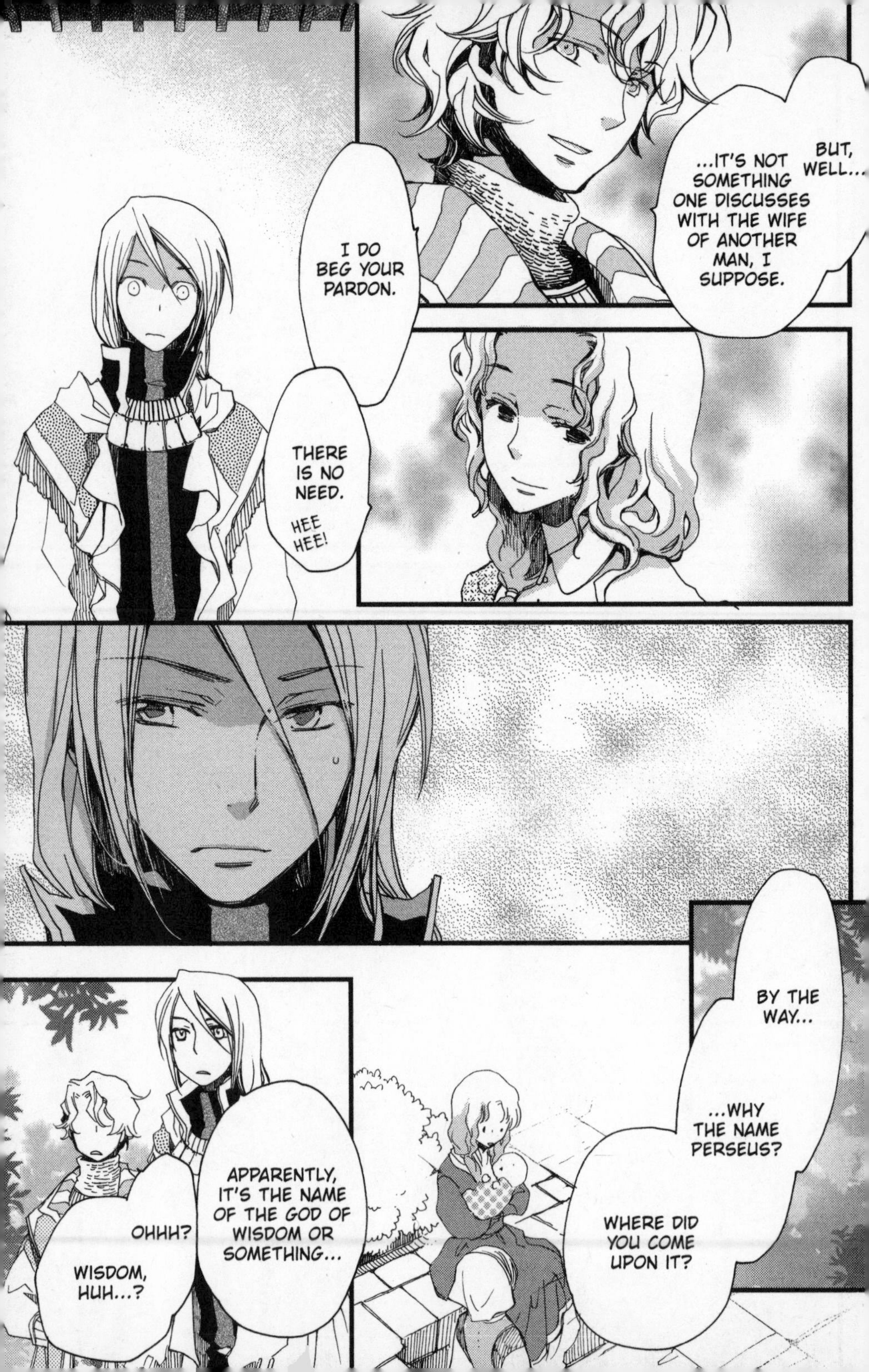
BUT, WELL...
...IT'S NOT SOMETHING ONE DISCUSSES WITH THE WIFE OF ANOTHER MAN, I SUPPOSE.
I DO BEG YOUR PARDON.
THERE IS NO NEED.
HEE HEE!
BY THE WAY...
...WHY THE NAME PERSEUS?
WHERE DID YOU COME UPON IT?
APPARENTLY, IT'S THE NAME OF THE GOD OF WISDOM OR SOMETHING...
OHHH?
WISDOM, HUH...?

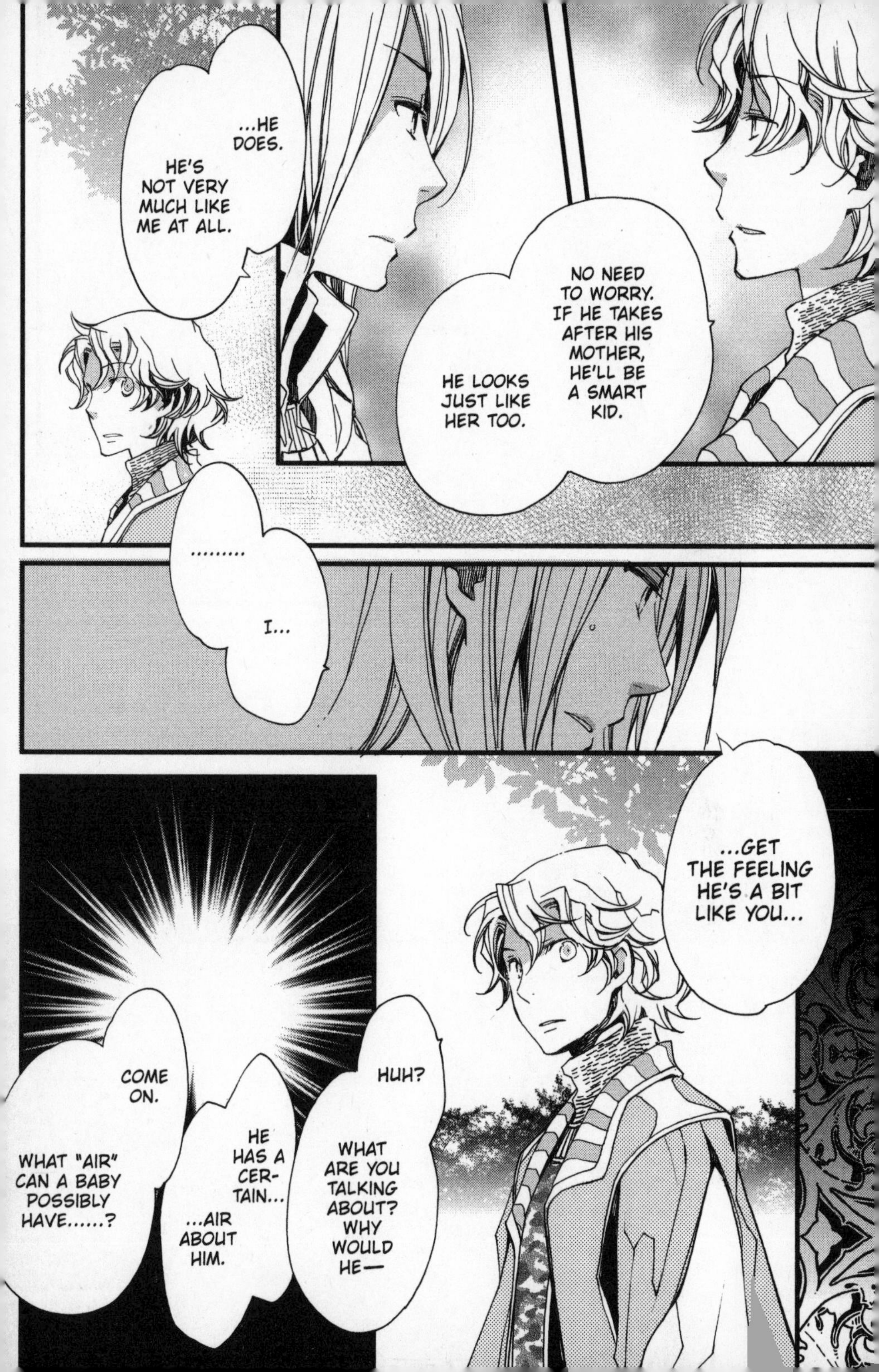
NO NEED TO WORRY. IF HE TAKES AFTER HIS MOTHER, HE'LL BE A SMART KID.
HE LOOKS JUST LIKE HER TOO.
...HE DOES.
HE'S NOT VERY MUCH LIKE ME AT ALL.
....
I...
...GET THE FEELING HE'S A BIT LIKE YOU...
HUH?
WHAT ARE YOU TALKING ABOUT? WHY WOULD HE—
HE HAS A CER-TAIN...
...AIR ABOUT HIM.
COME ON.
WHAT "AIR" CAN A BABY POSSIBLY HAVE......?

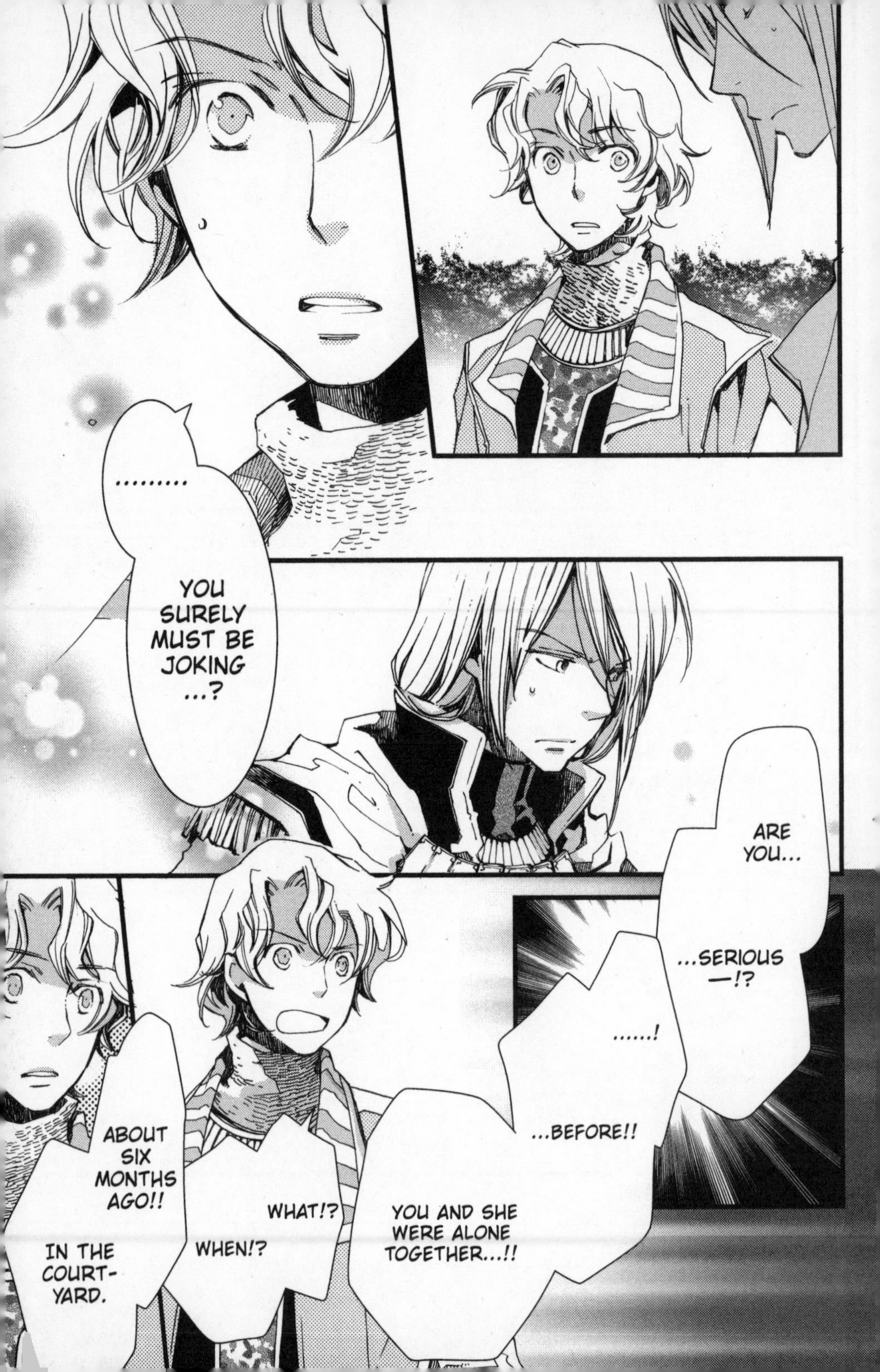
....
YOU SURELY MUST BE JOKING...?
ARE YOU...
...SERIOUS—!?
......!
...BEFORE!!
YOU AND SHE WERE ALONE TOGETHER...!!
WHAT!?
WHEN!?
ABOUT SIX MONTHS AGO!!
IN THE COURTYARD.

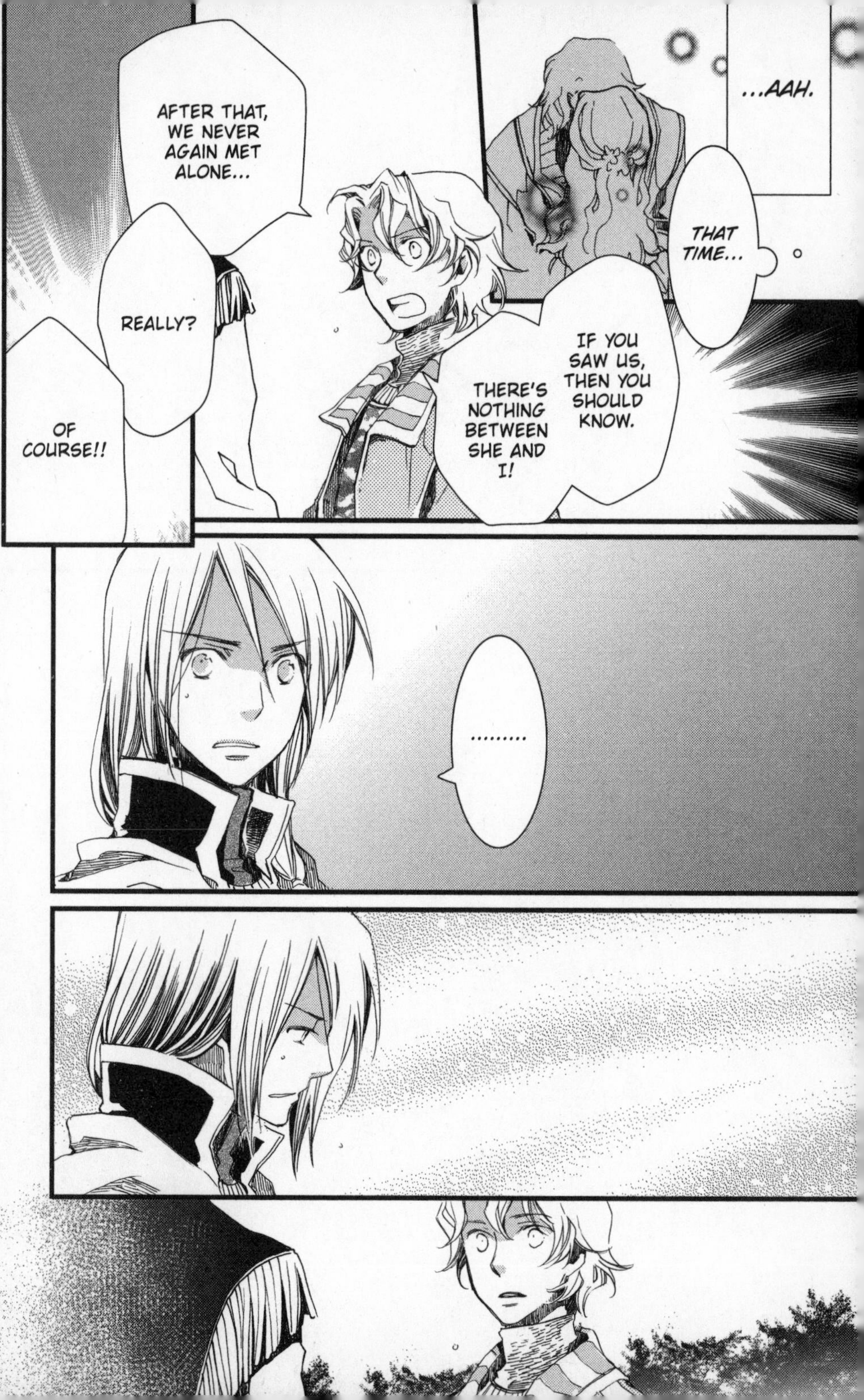
...AAH.
THAT TIME...
IF YOU SAW US, THEN YOU SHOULD KNOW.
THERE'S NOTHING BETWEEN SHE AND I!
AFTER THAT, WE NEVER AGAIN MET ALONE...
REALLY?
OF COURSE!!
....

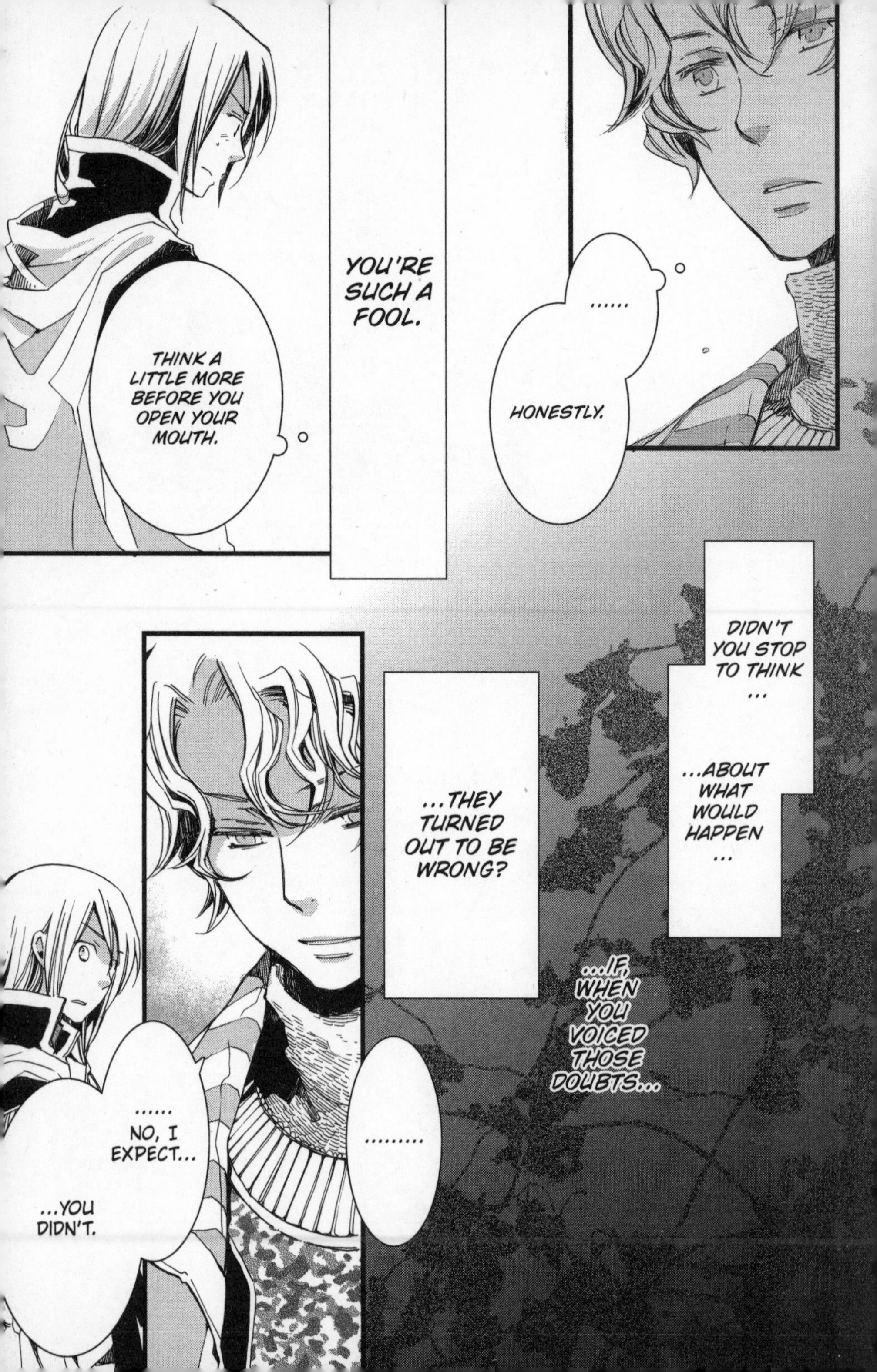
......
HONESTLY.
YOU'RE SUCH A FOOL.
THINK A LITTLE MORE BEFORE YOU OPEN YOUR MOUTH.
DIDN'T YOU STOP TO THINK ...
...ABOUT WHAT WOULD HAPPEN ...
...IF, WHEN YOU VOICED THOSE DOUBTS...
...THEY TURNED OUT TO BE WRONG?
....
...... NO, I EXPECT...
...YOU DIDN'T.

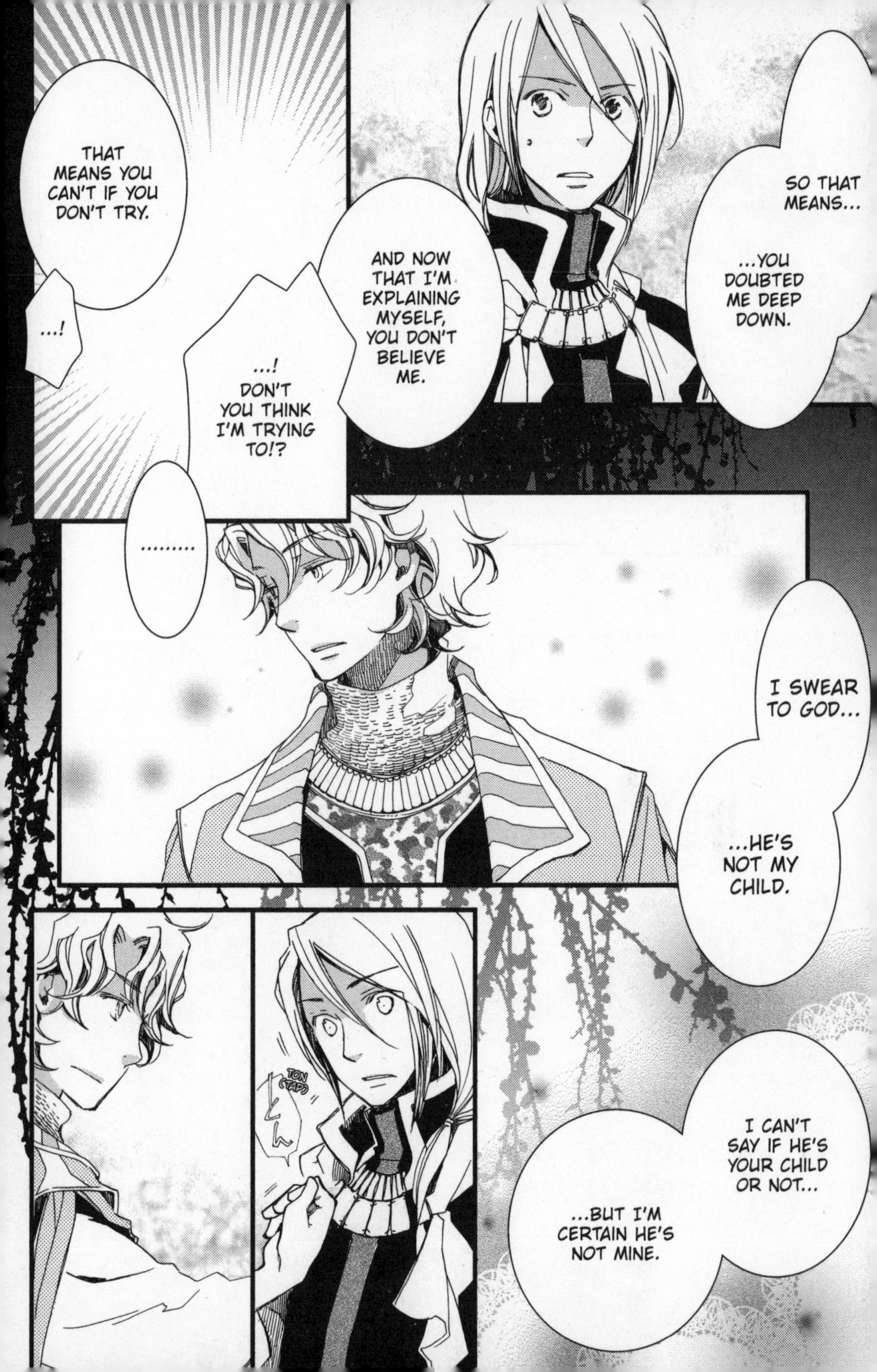
SO THAT MEANS...
...YOU DOUBTED ME DEEP DOWN.
AND NOW THAT I'M EXPLAINING MYSELF, YOU DON'T BELIEVE ME.
THAT MEANS YOU CAN'T IF YOU DON'T TRY.
...!
...! DON'T YOU THINK I'M TRYING TO!?
....
I SWEAR TO GOD...
...HE'S NOT MY CHILD.
I CAN'T SAY IF HE'S YOUR CHILD OR NOT...
...BUT I'M CERTAIN HE'S NOT MINE.
TON (TAP)

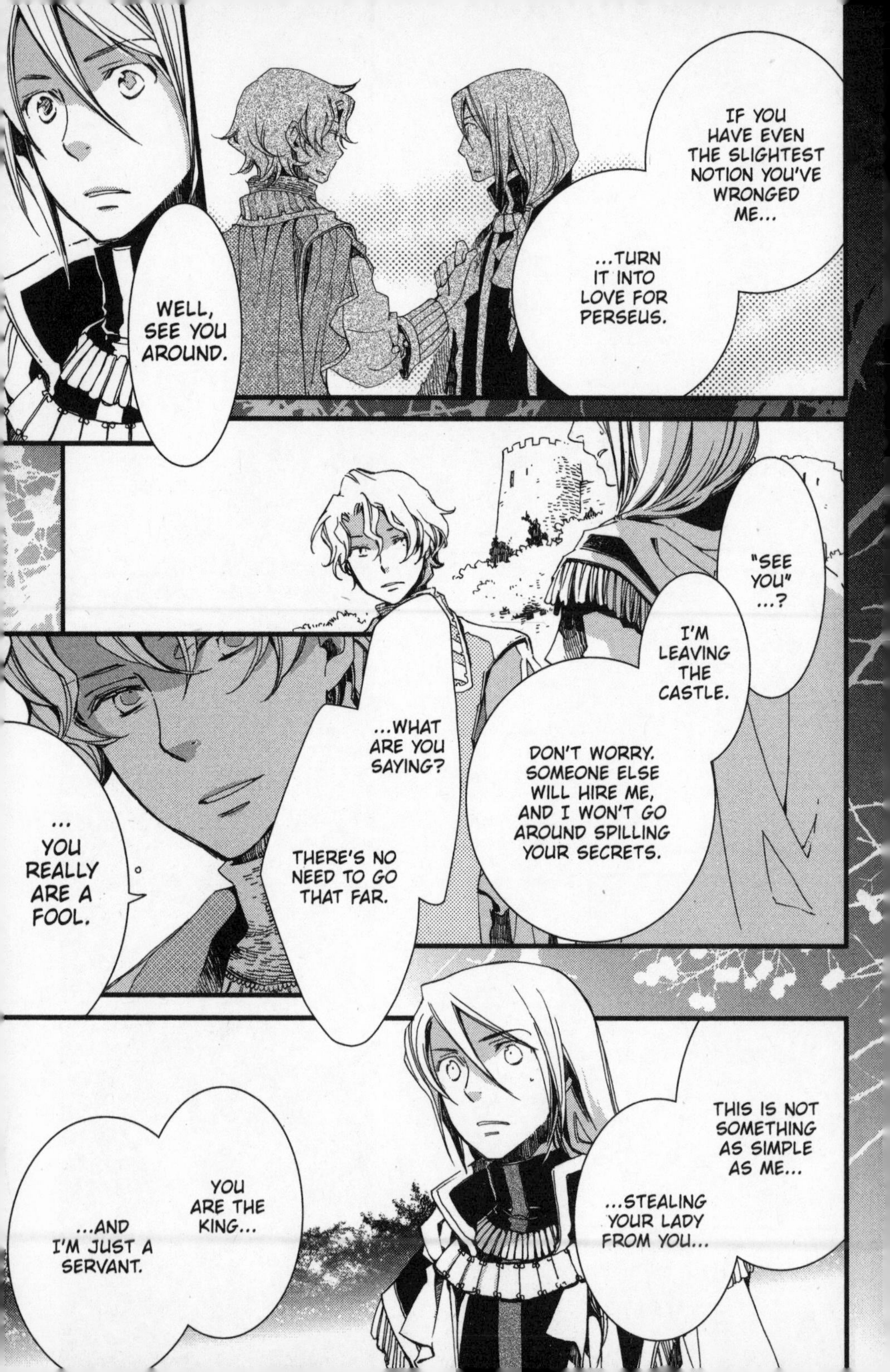
IF YOU HAVE EVEN THE SLIGHTEST NOTION YOU'VE WRONGED ME...
...TURN IT INTO LOVE FOR PERSEUS.
WELL, SEE YOU AROUND.
"SEE YOU" ...?
I'M LEAVING THE CASTLE.
DON'T WORRY. SOMEONE ELSE WILL HIRE ME, AND I WON'T GO AROUND SPILLING YOUR SECRETS.
...WHAT ARE YOU SAYING?
THERE'S NO NEED TO GO THAT FAR.
... YOU REALLY ARE A FOOL.
THIS IS NOT SOMETHING AS SIMPLE AS ME...
...STEALING YOUR LADY FROM YOU...
YOU ARE THE KING...
...AND I'M JUST A SERVANT.

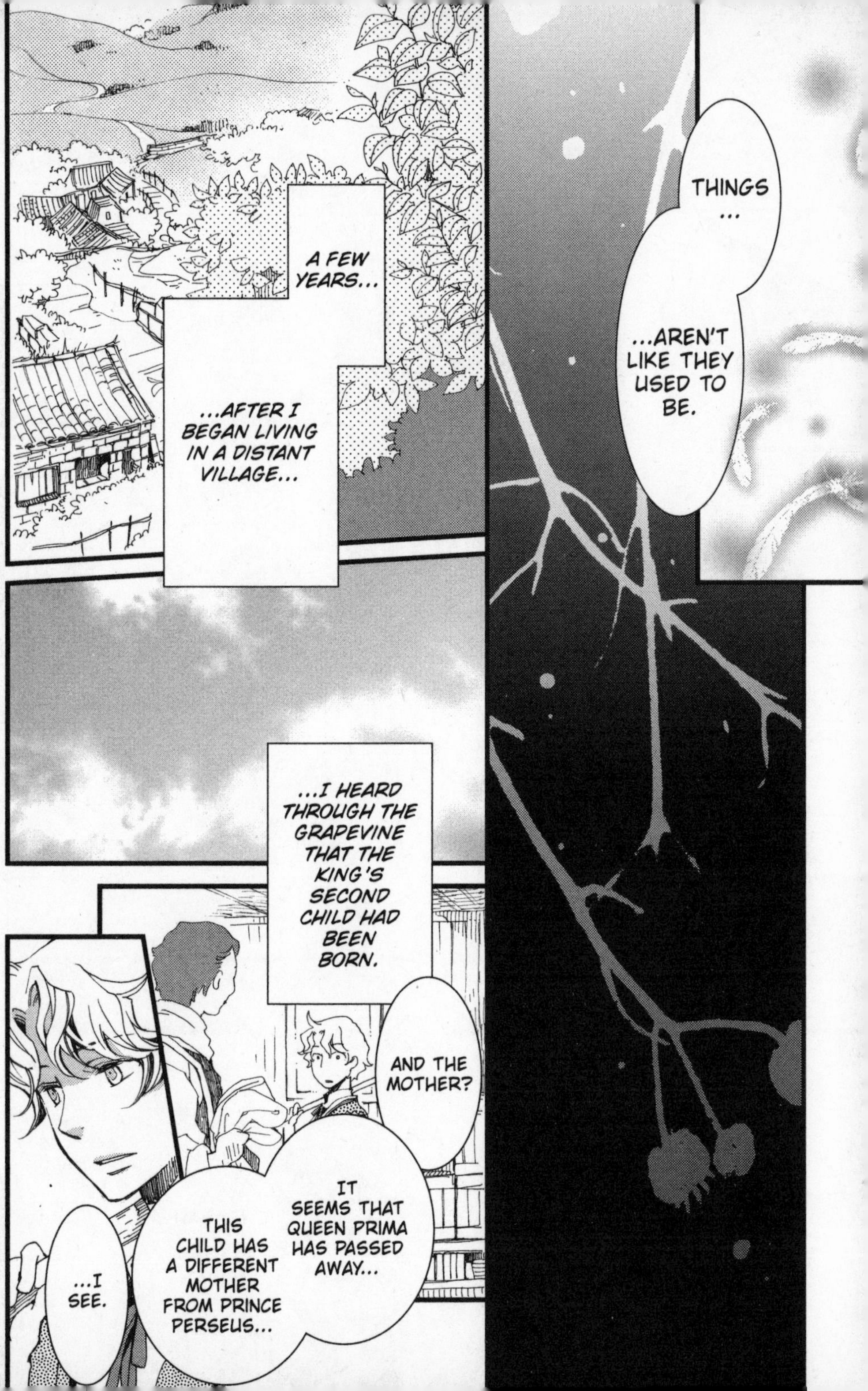
THINGS...
...AREN'T LIKE THEY USED TO BE.
A FEW YEARS...
...AFTER I BEGAN LIVING IN A DISTANT VILLAGE...
...I HEARD THROUGH THE GRAPEVINE THAT THE KING'S SECOND CHILD HAD BEEN BORN.
AND THE MOTHER?
IT SEEMS THAT QUEEN PRIMA HAS PASSED AWAY...
THIS CHILD HAS A DIFFERENT MOTHER FROM PRINCE PERSEUS...
...I SEE.

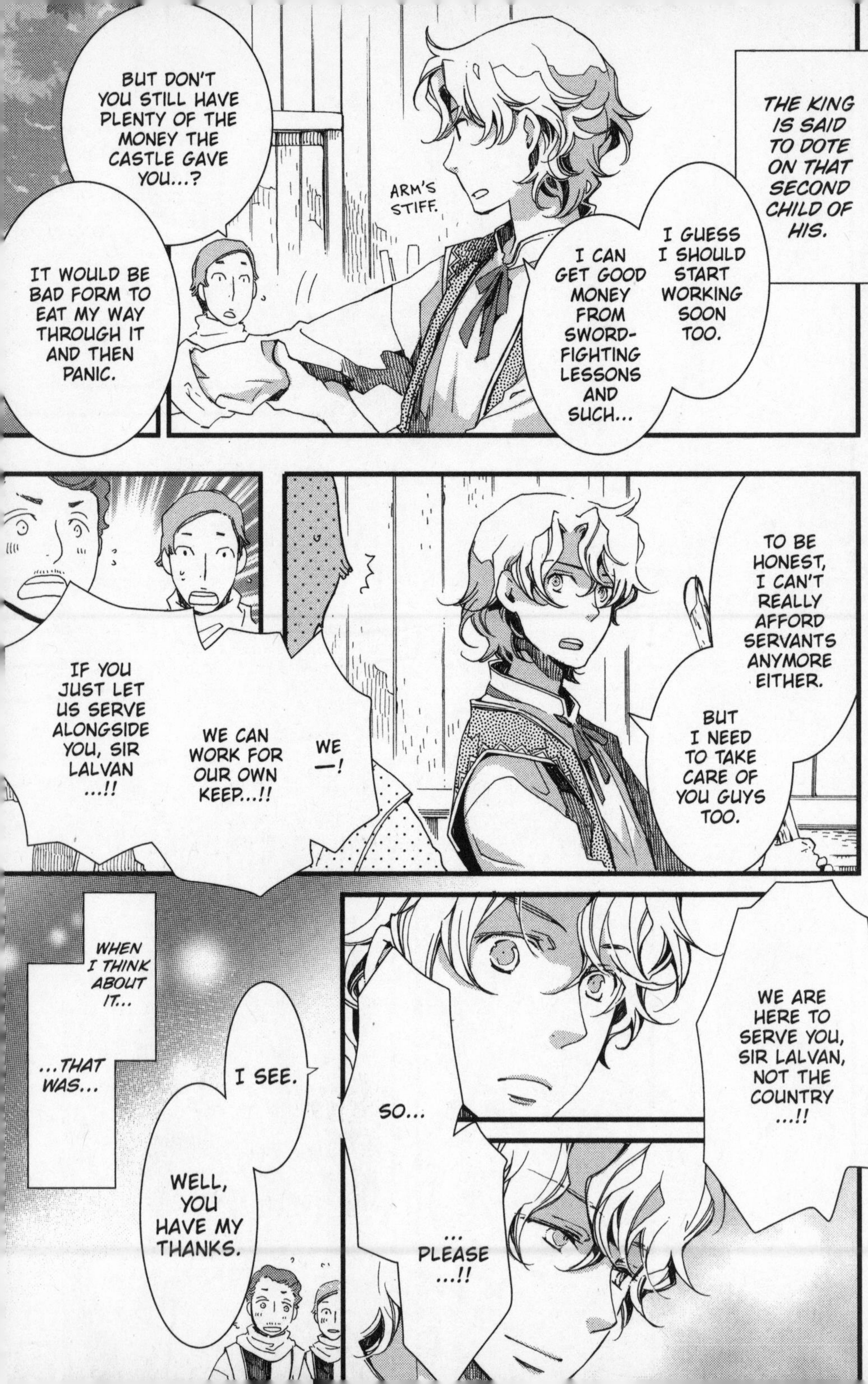
THE KING IS SAID TO DOTE ON THAT SECOND CHILD OF HIS.
I GUESS I SHOULD START WORKING SOON TOO.
I CAN GET GOOD MONEY FROM SWORD-FIGHTING LESSONS AND SUCH...
ARM'S STIFF.
BUT DON'T YOU STILL HAVE PLENTY OF THE MONEY THE CASTLE GAVE YOU...?
IT WOULD BE BAD FORM TO EAT MY WAY THROUGH IT AND THEN PANIC.
TO BE HONEST, I CAN'T REALLY AFFORD SERVANTS ANYMORE EITHER.
BUT I NEED TO TAKE CARE OF YOU GUYS TOO.
WE—!
WE CAN WORK FOR OUR OWN KEEP...!!
IF YOU JUST LET US SERVE ALONGSIDE YOU, SIR LALVAN...!!
WE ARE HERE TO SERVE YOU, SIR LALVAN, NOT THE COUNTRY...!!
SO...
...PLEASE...!!
I SEE.
WELL, YOU HAVE MY THANKS.
WHEN I THINK ABOUT IT...
...THAT WAS...

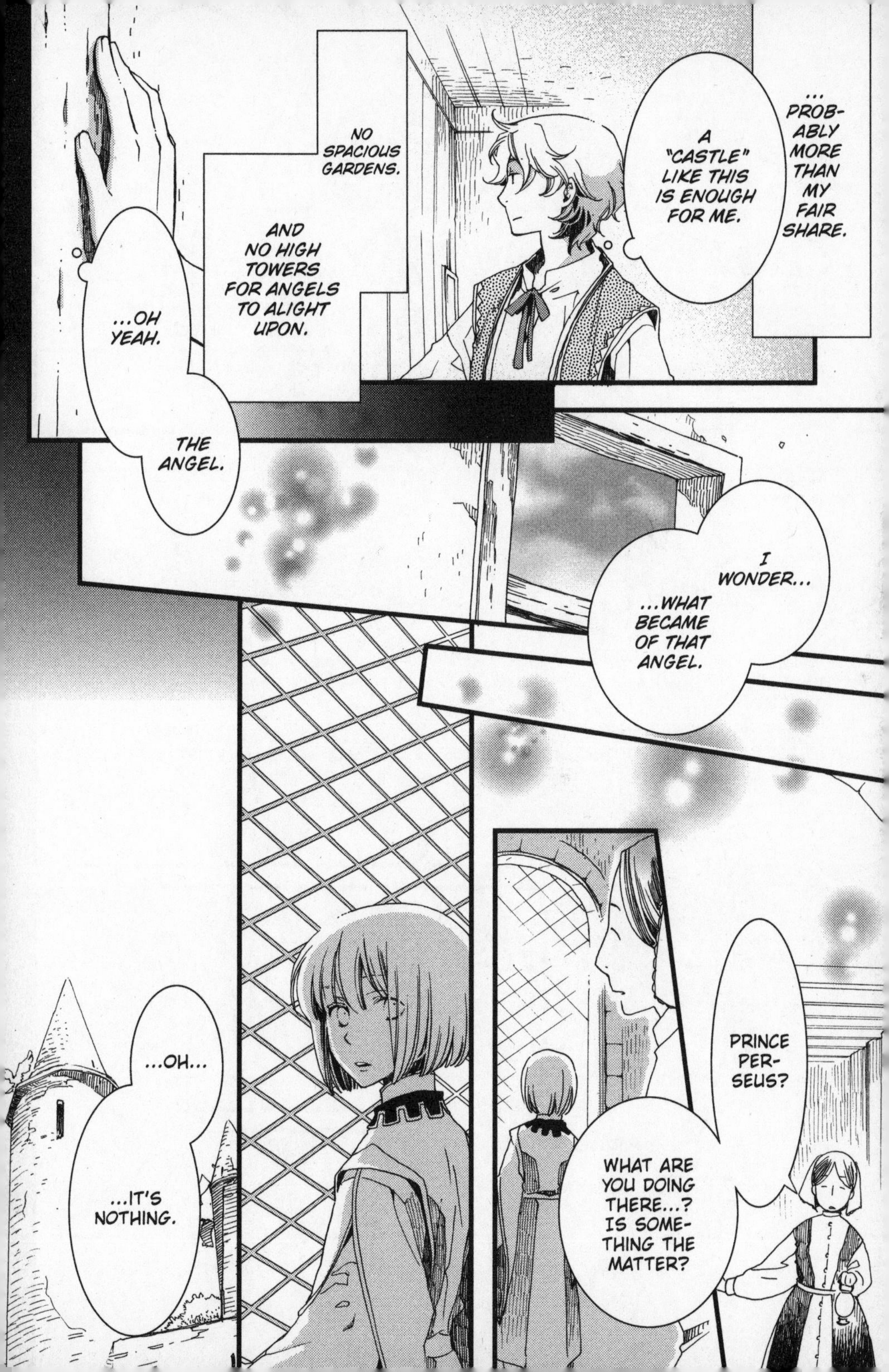
...PROBABLY MORE THAN MY FAIR SHARE.
A "CASTLE" LIKE THIS IS ENOUGH FOR ME.
NO SPACIOUS GARDENS.
AND NO HIGH TOWERS FOR ANGELS TO ALIGHT UPON.
...OH YEAH.
THE ANGEL.
I WONDER...
...WHAT BECAME OF THAT ANGEL.
PRINCE PERSEUS?
WHAT ARE YOU DOING THERE...? IS SOMETHING THE MATTER?
...OH...
...IT'S NOTHING.

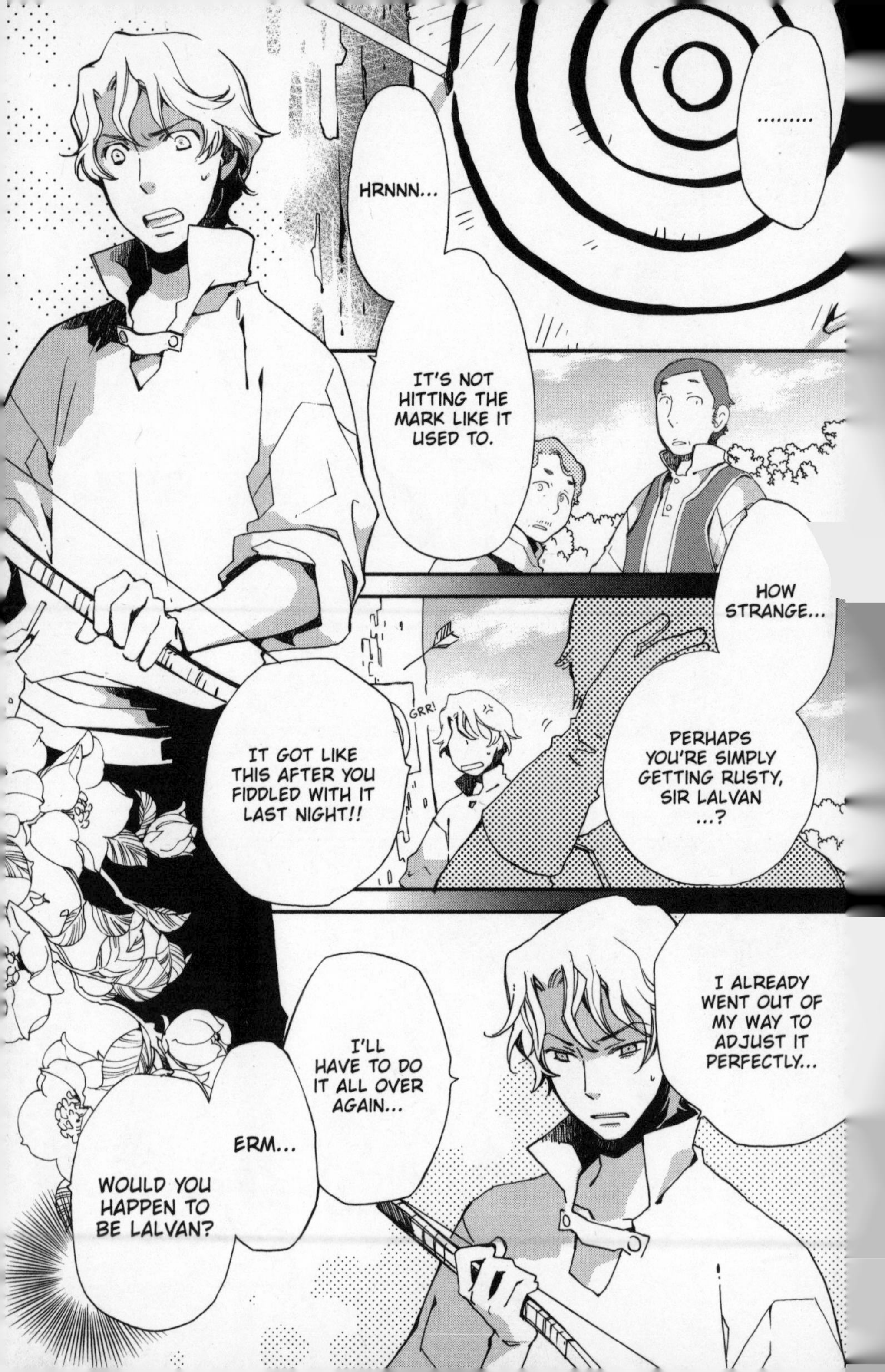
....
HRNNN...
IT'S NOT HITTING THE MARK LIKE IT USED TO.
HOW STRANGE...
PERHAPS YOU'RE SIMPLY GETTING RUSTY, SIR LALVAN ...?
GRR!
IT GOT LIKE THIS AFTER YOU FIDDLED WITH IT LAST NIGHT!!
I ALREADY WENT OUT OF MY WAY TO ADJUST IT PERFECTLY...
I'LL HAVE TO DO IT ALL OVER AGAIN...
ERM...
WOULD YOU HAPPEN TO BE LALVAN?

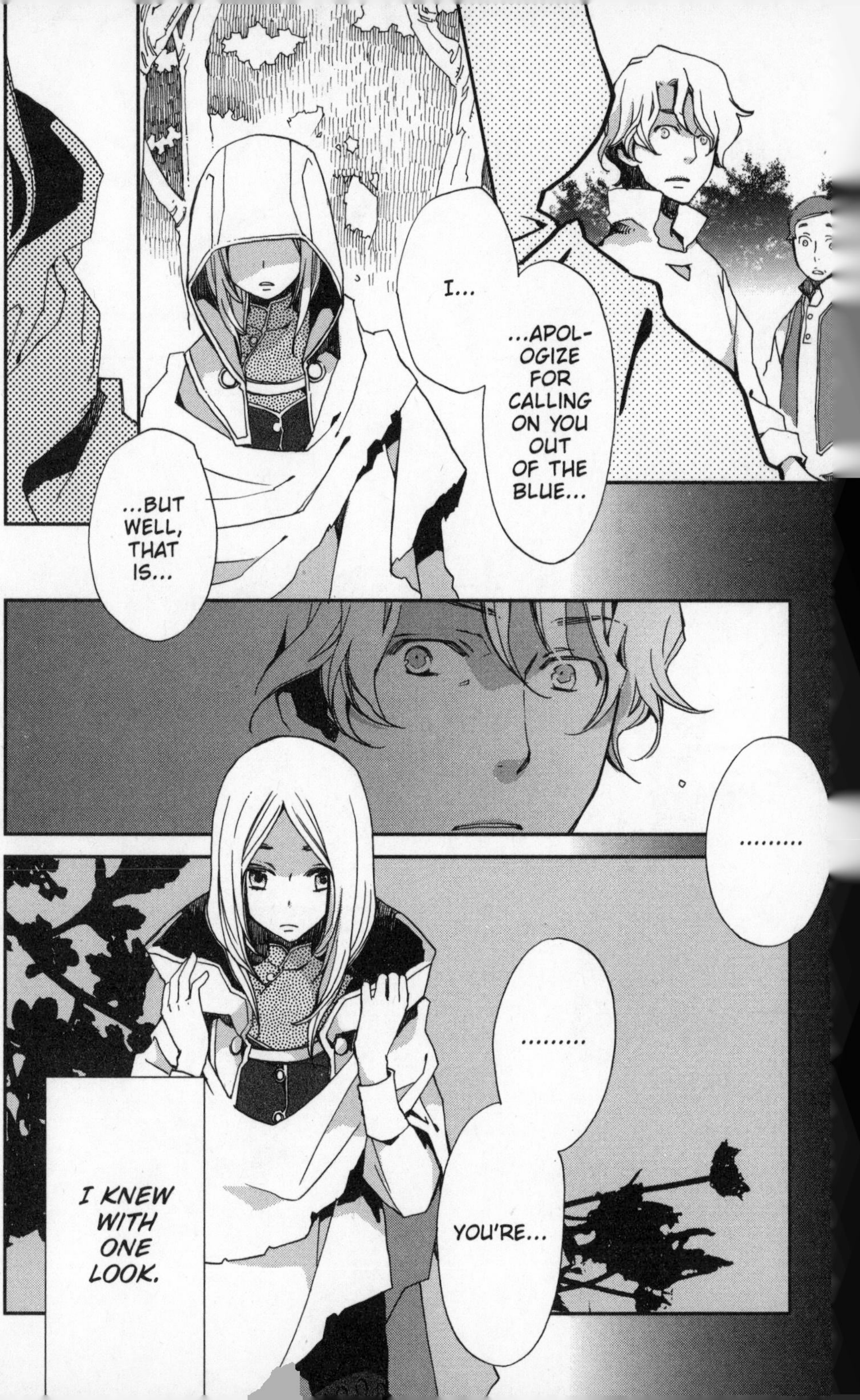
I...
...APOLOGIZE FOR CALLING ON YOU OUT OF THE BLUE...
...BUT WELL, THAT IS...
....
....
YOU'RE...
I KNEW WITH ONE LOOK.

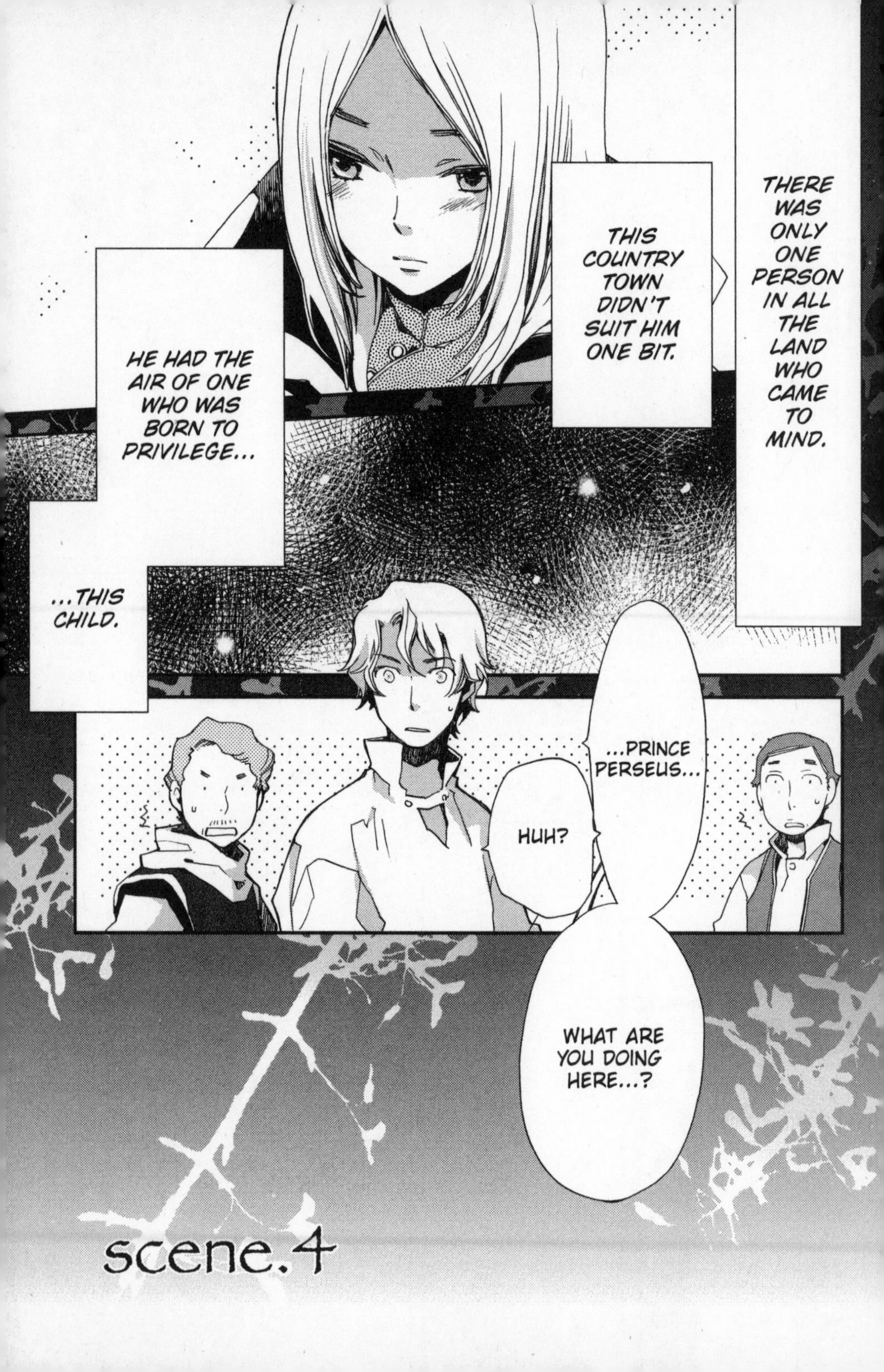
THERE WAS ONLY ONE PERSON IN ALL THE LAND WHO CAME TO MIND.
THIS COUNTRY TOWN DIDN'T SUIT HIM ONE BIT.
HE HAD THE AIR OF ONE WHO WAS BORN TO PRIVILEGE...
...THIS CHILD.
...PRINCE PERSEUS...
HUH?
WHAT ARE YOU DOING HERE...?
scene.4

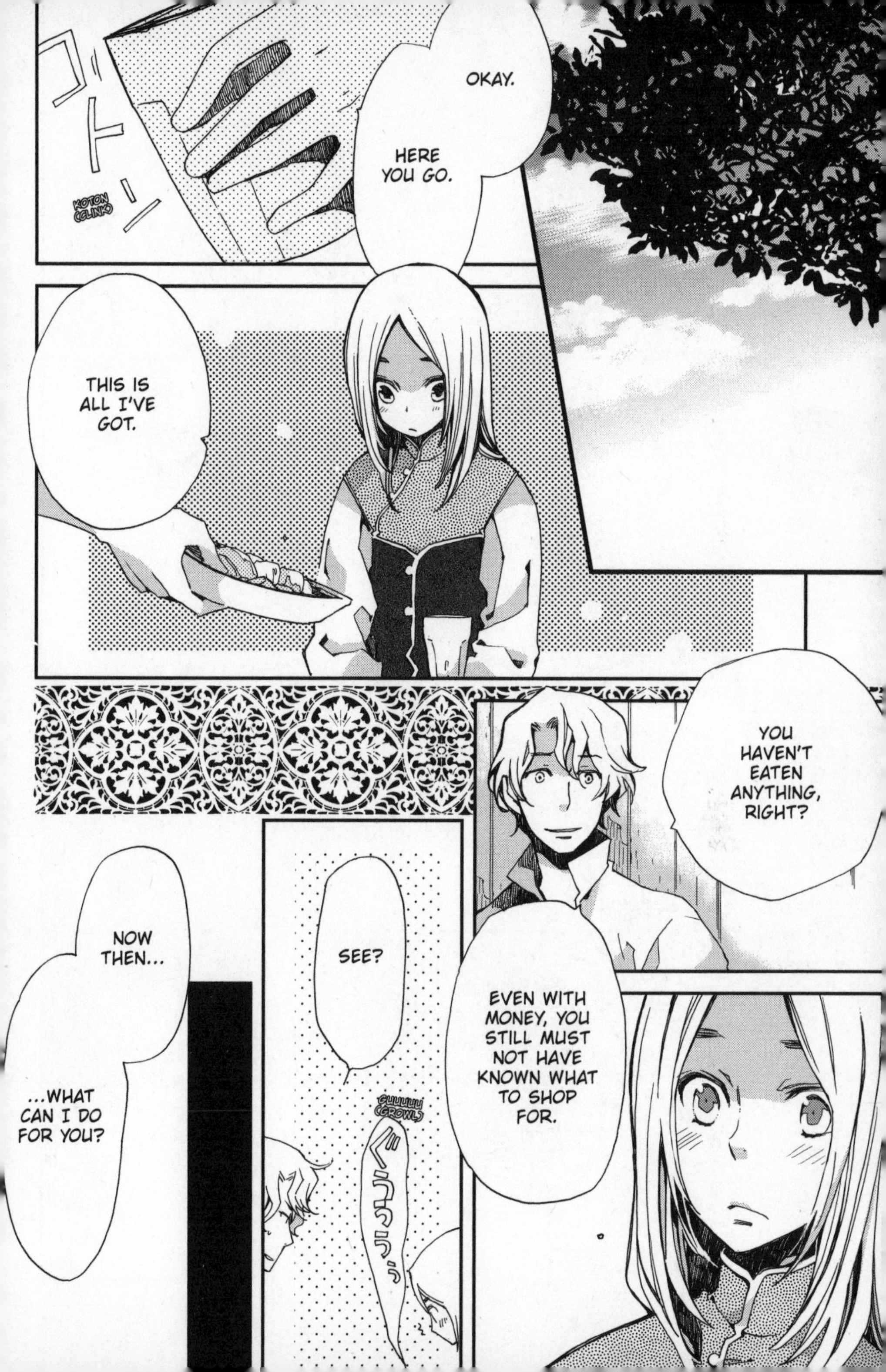
OKAY.
HERE YOU GO.
KOTON (CLINK)
THIS IS ALL I'VE GOT.
YOU HAVEN'T EATEN ANYTHING, RIGHT?
EVEN WITH MONEY, YOU STILL MUST NOT HAVE KNOWN WHAT TO SHOP FOR.
SEE?
GUUUUU (GROWL)
NOW THEN...
...WHAT CAN I DO FOR YOU?

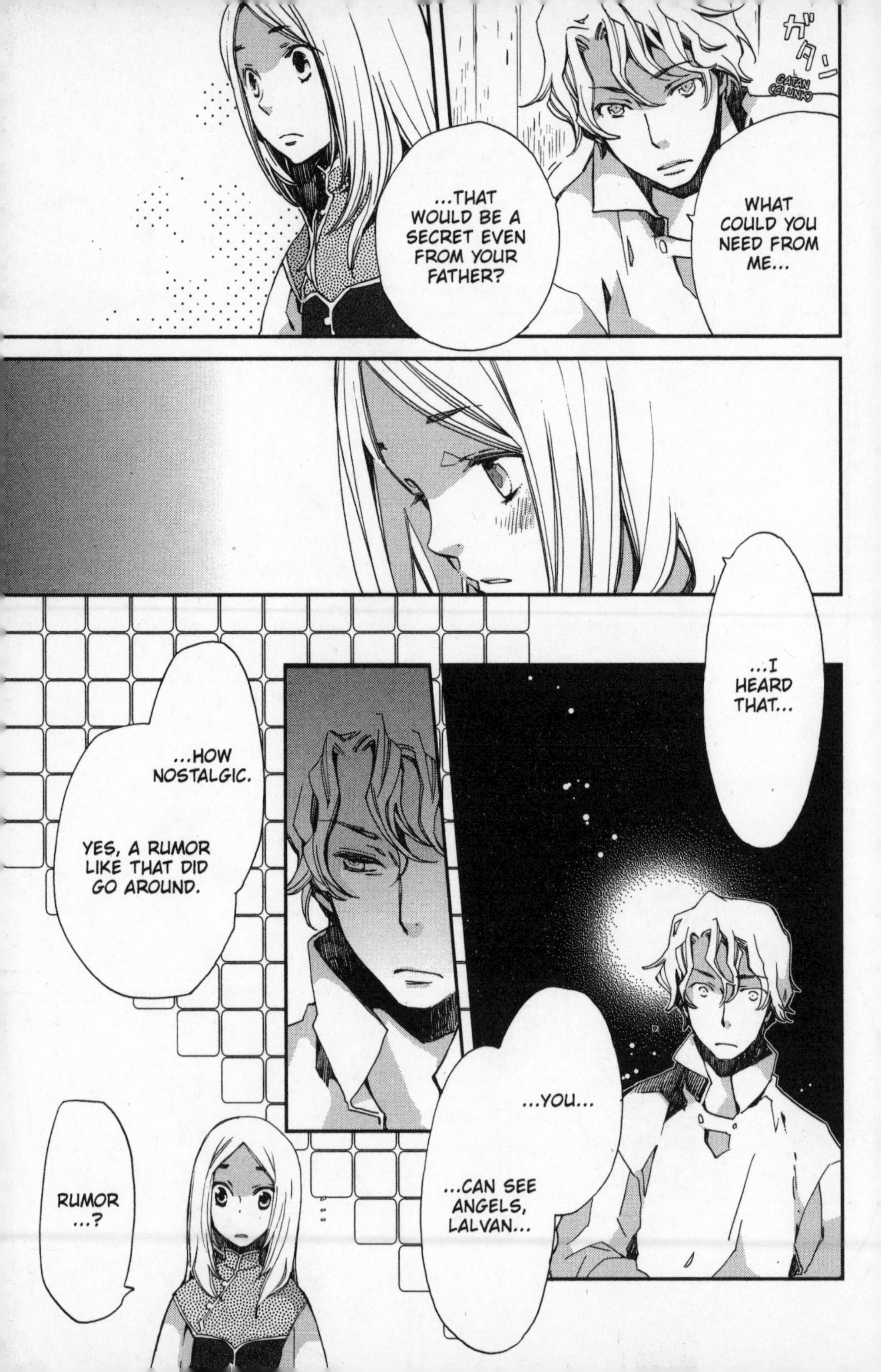
ガタン
GATAN (CLUNK)
WHAT COULD YOU NEED FROM ME...
...THAT WOULD BE A SECRET EVEN FROM YOUR FATHER?
...I HEARD THAT...
...YOU...
...CAN SEE ANGELS, LALVAN...
...HOW NOSTALGIC.
YES, A RUMOR LIKE THAT DID GO AROUND.
RUMOR ...?

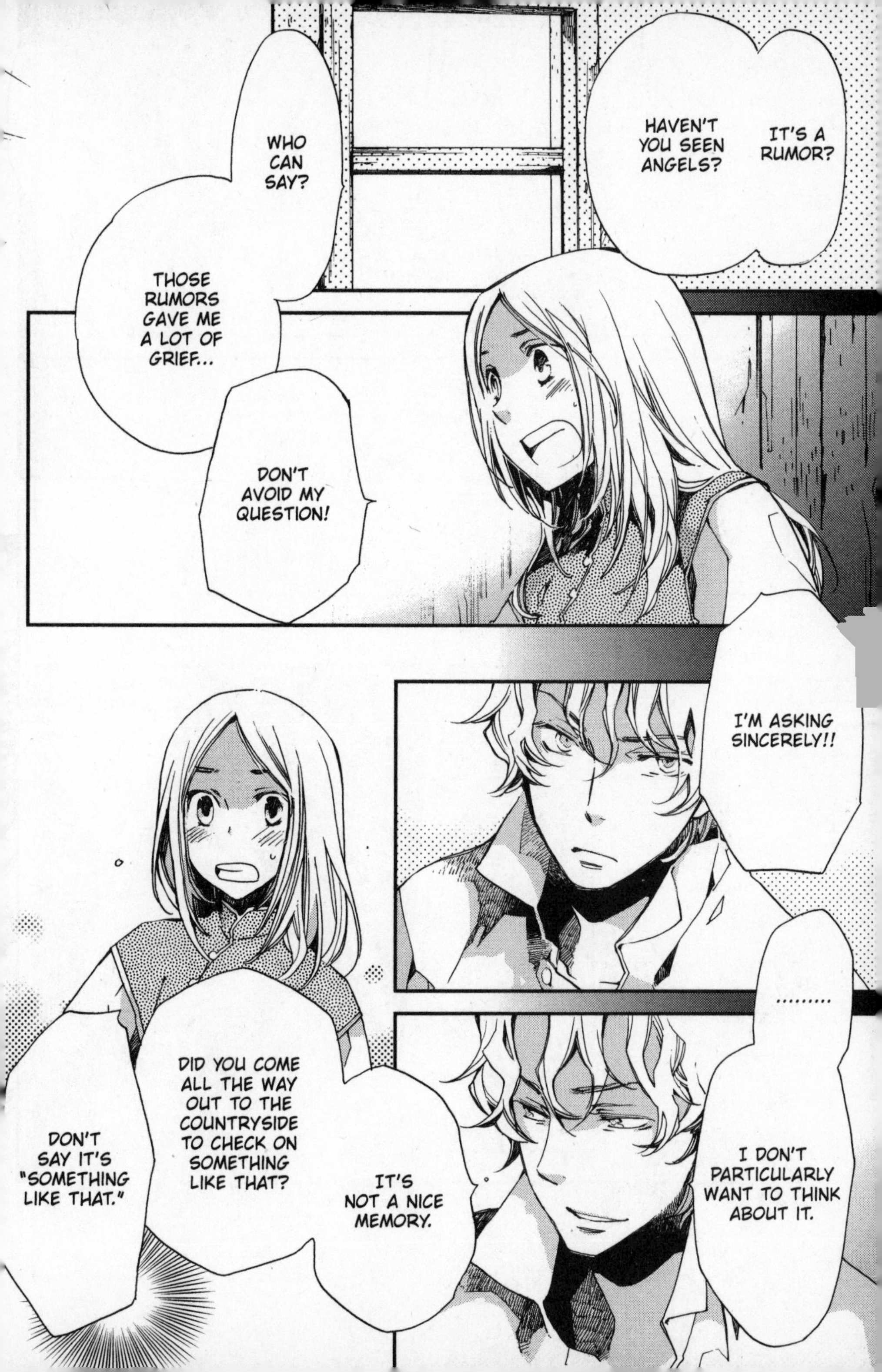
IT'S A RUMOR?
HAVEN'T YOU SEEN ANGELS?
WHO CAN SAY?
THOSE RUMORS GAVE ME A LOT OF GRIEF...
DON'T AVOID MY QUESTION!
I'M ASKING SINCERELY!!
....
I DON'T PARTICULARLY WANT TO THINK ABOUT IT.
IT'S NOT A NICE MEMORY.
DID YOU COME ALL THE WAY OUT TO THE COUNTRYSIDE TO CHECK ON SOMETHING LIKE THAT?
DON'T SAY IT'S "SOMETHING LIKE THAT."

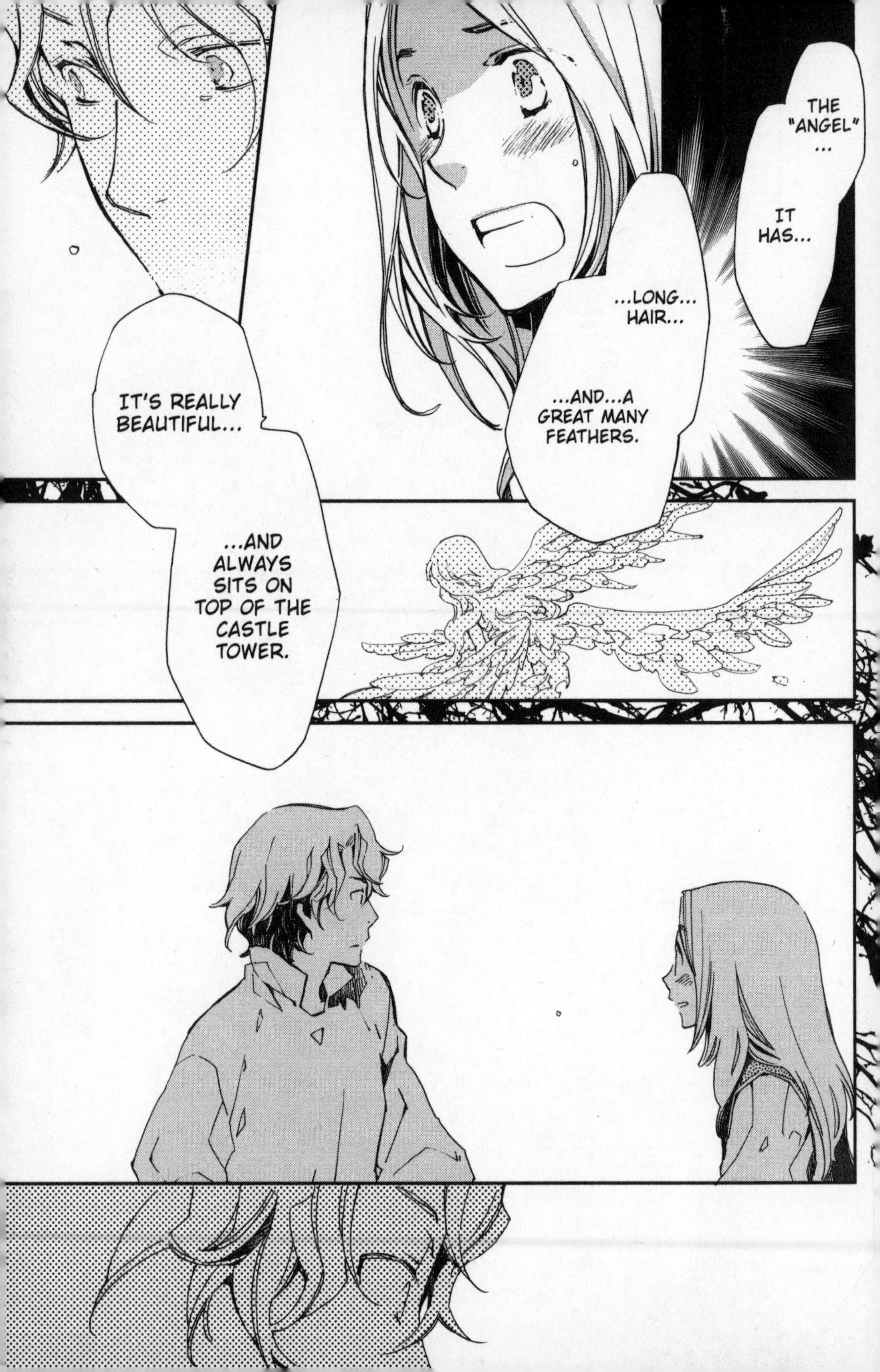
THE "ANGEL"...
IT HAS...
...LONG... HAIR...
...AND...A GREAT MANY FEATHERS.
IT'S REALLY BEAUTIFUL...
...AND ALWAYS SITS ON TOP OF THE CASTLE TOWER.

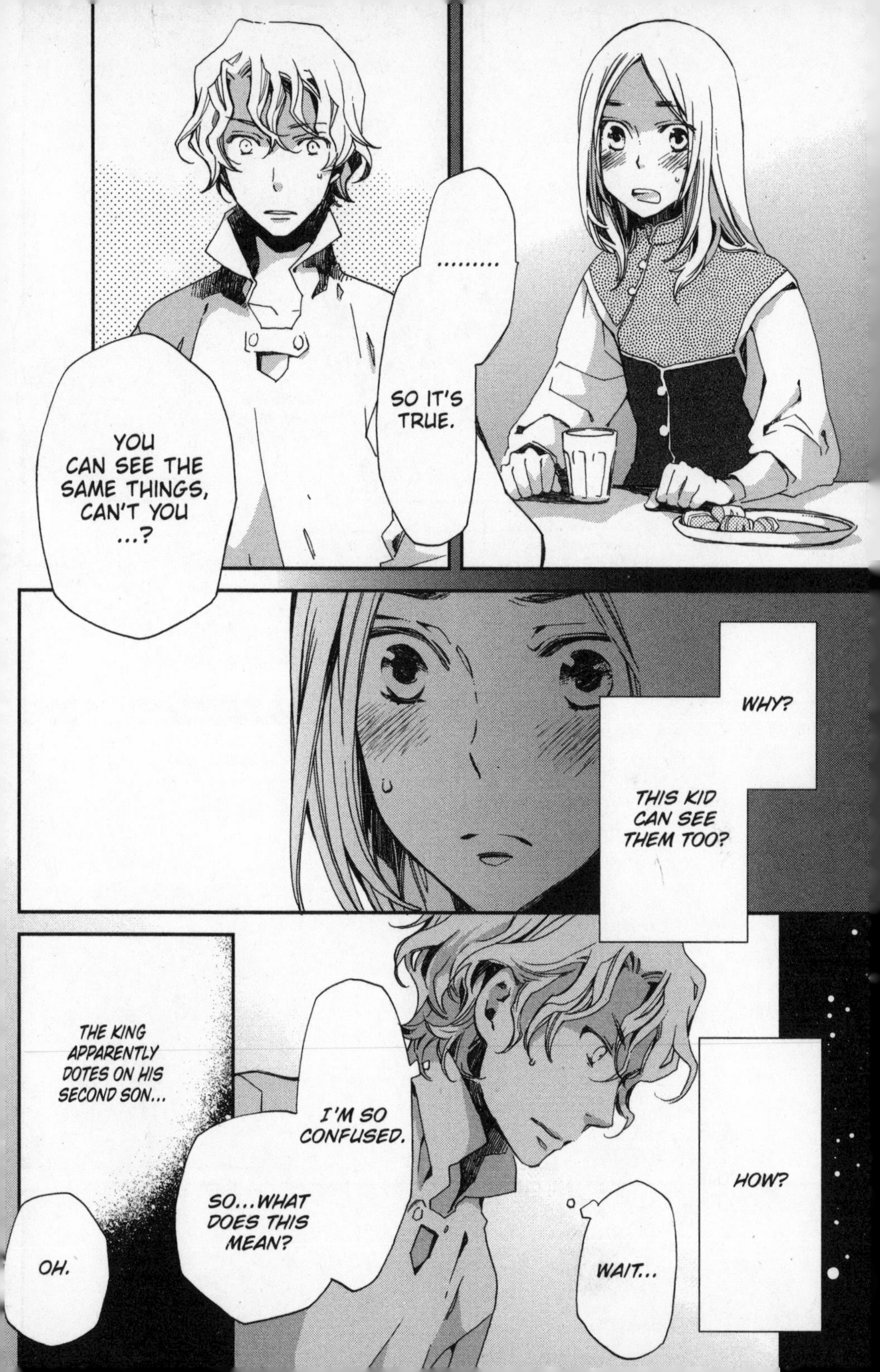

....
SO IT'S TRUE.
YOU CAN SEE THE SAME THINGS, CAN'T YOU ...?
WHY?
THIS KID CAN SEE THEM TOO?
HOW?
WAIT...
I'M SO CONFUSED.
SO...WHAT DOES THIS MEAN?
THE KING APPARENTLY DOTES ON HIS SECOND SON...
OH.

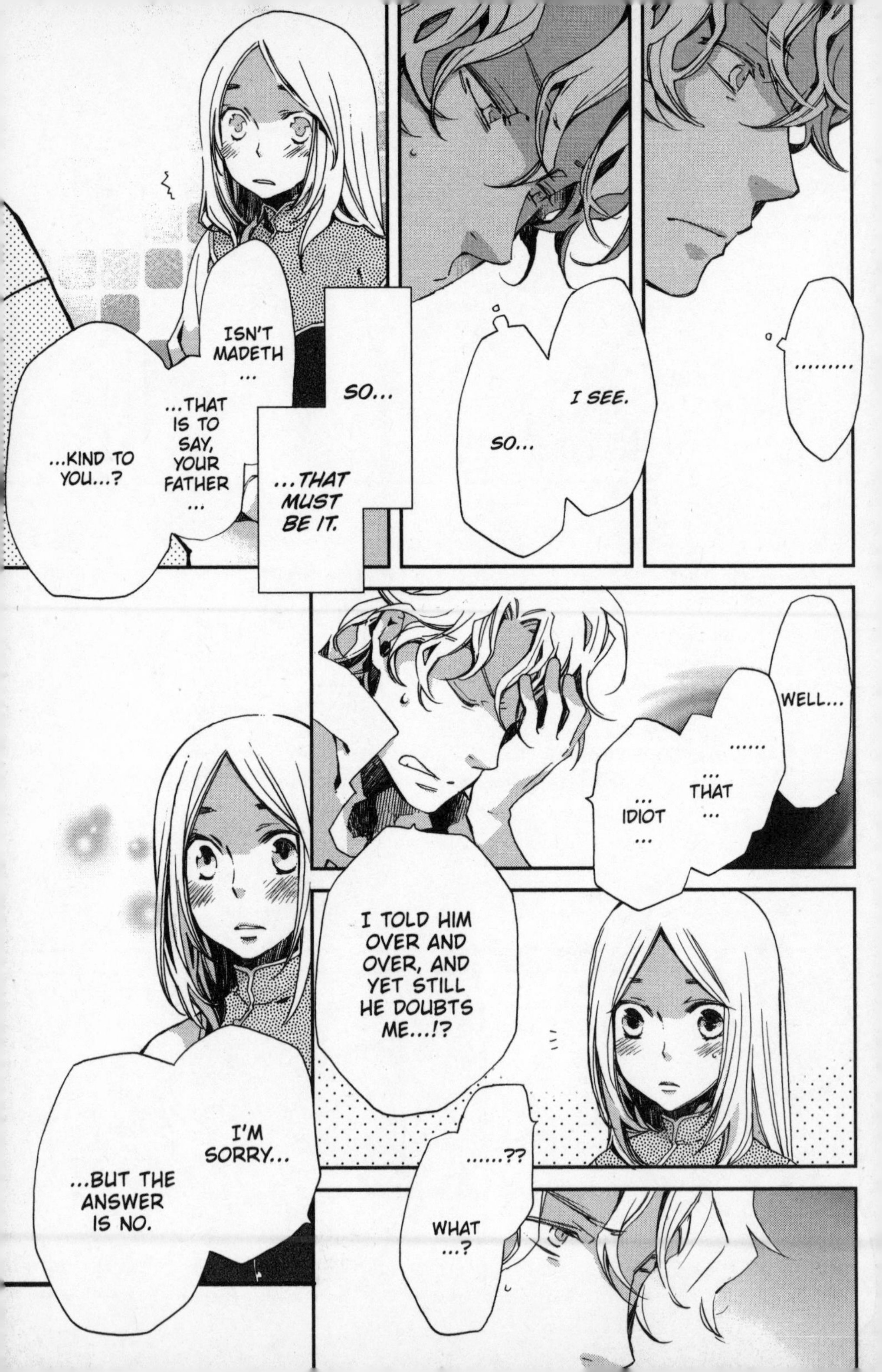
....
I SEE.
SO...
SO...
...THAT MUST BE IT.
ISN'T MADETH ... ...THAT IS TO SAY, YOUR FATHER ...
...KIND TO YOU...?
WELL...
.... THAT ...
... IDIOT ...
I TOLD HIM OVER AND OVER, AND YET STILL HE DOUBTS ME...!?
......??
WHAT ...?
I'M SORRY...
...BUT THE ANSWER IS NO.

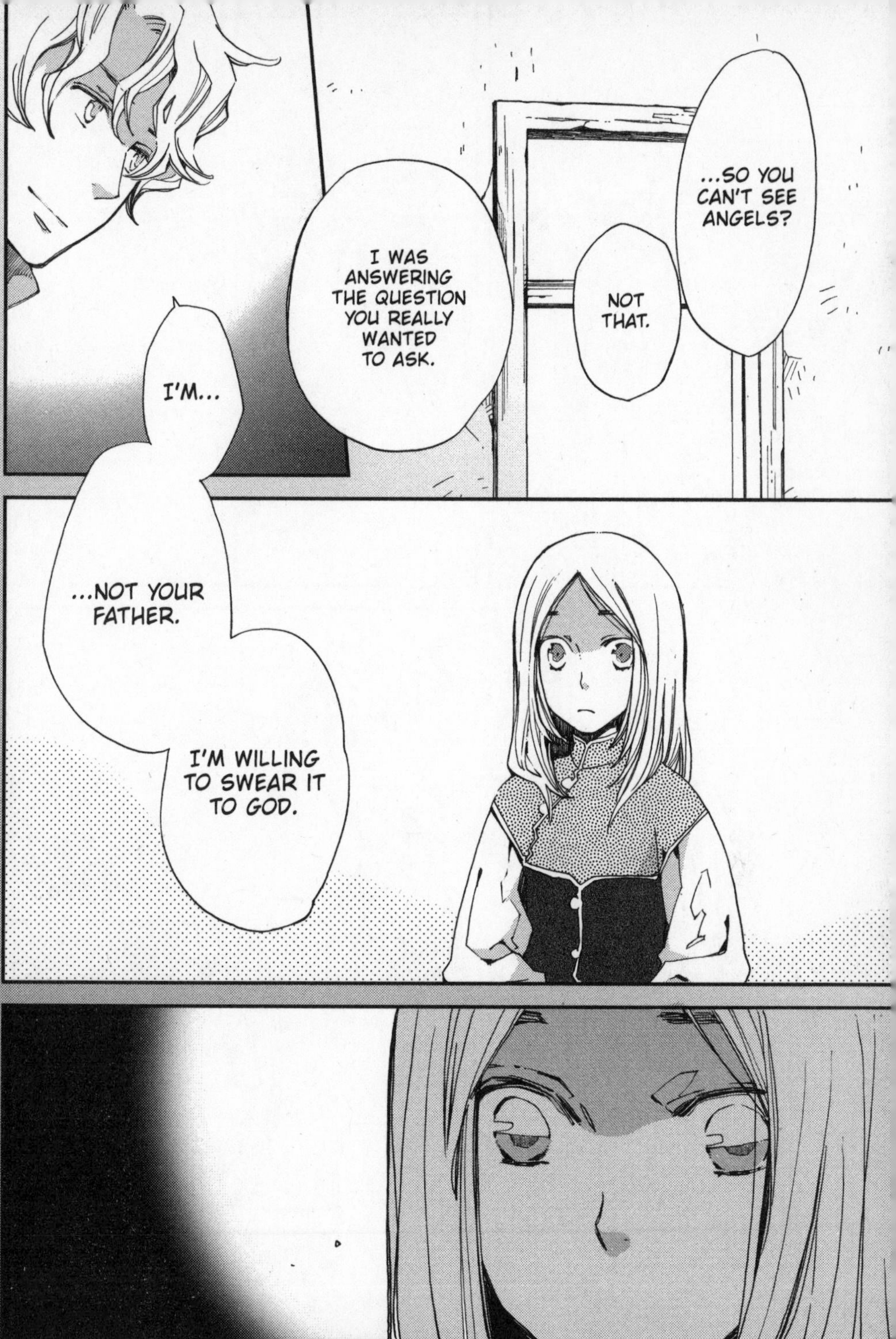
...SO YOU CAN'T SEE ANGELS?
NOT THAT.
I WAS ANSWERING THE QUESTION YOU REALLY WANTED TO ASK.
I'M...
...NOT YOUR FATHER.
I'M WILLING TO SWEAR IT TO GOD.

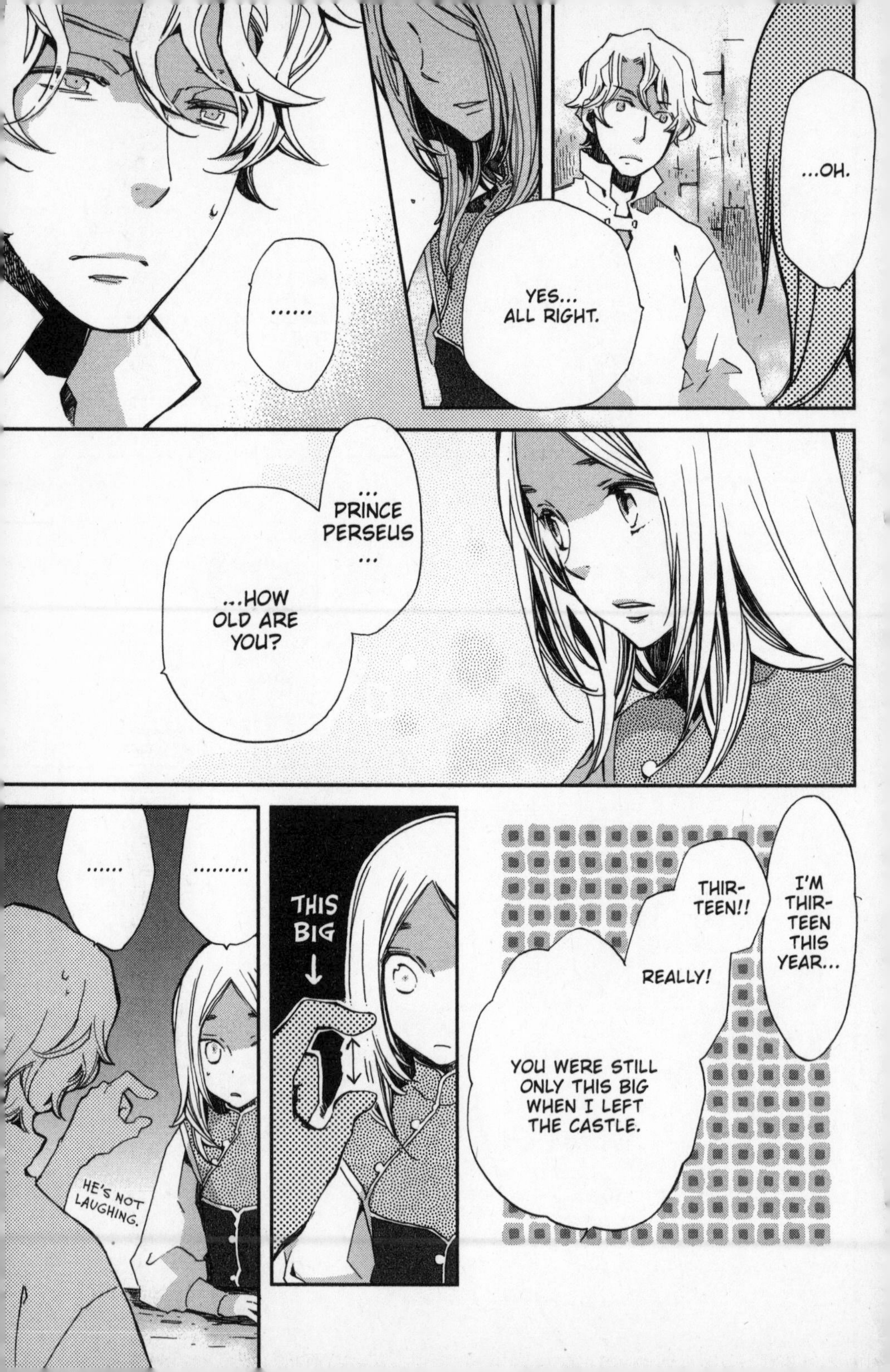
...OH.
YES... ALL RIGHT.
......
... PRINCE PERSEUS ...
...HOW OLD ARE YOU?
I'M THIRTEEN THIS YEAR...
THIR-TEEN!!
REALLY!
YOU WERE STILL ONLY THIS BIG WHEN I LEFT THE CASTLE.
THIS BIG ↓
....
......
HE'S NOT LAUGHING.

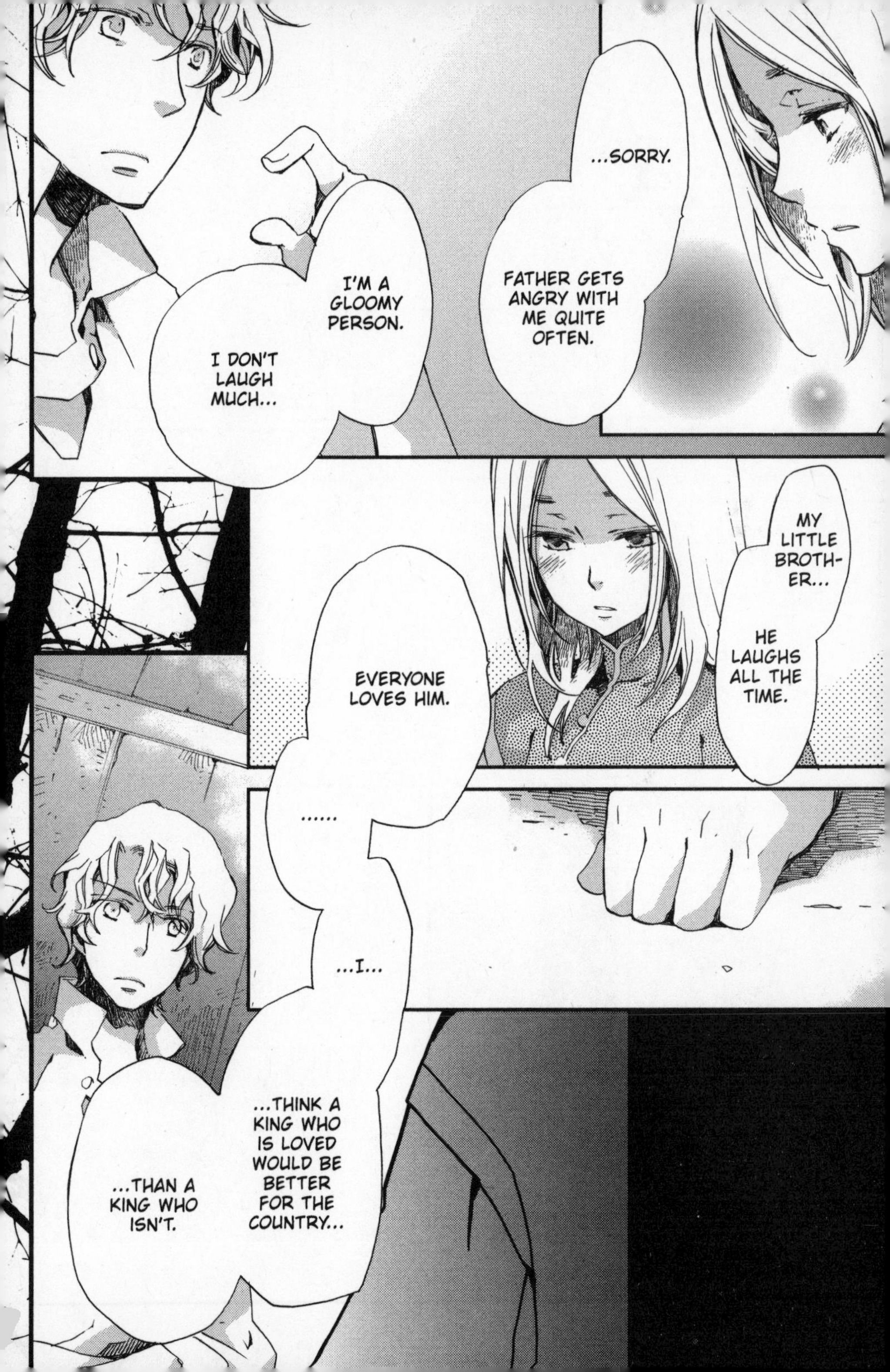
...SORRY.
FATHER GETS ANGRY WITH ME QUITE OFTEN.
I'M A GLOOMY PERSON.
I DON'T LAUGH MUCH...
MY LITTLE BROTH-ER...
HE LAUGHS ALL THE TIME.
EVERYONE LOVES HIM.
......
...I...
...THINK A KING WHO IS LOVED WOULD BE BETTER FOR THE COUNTRY...
...THAN A KING WHO ISN'T.

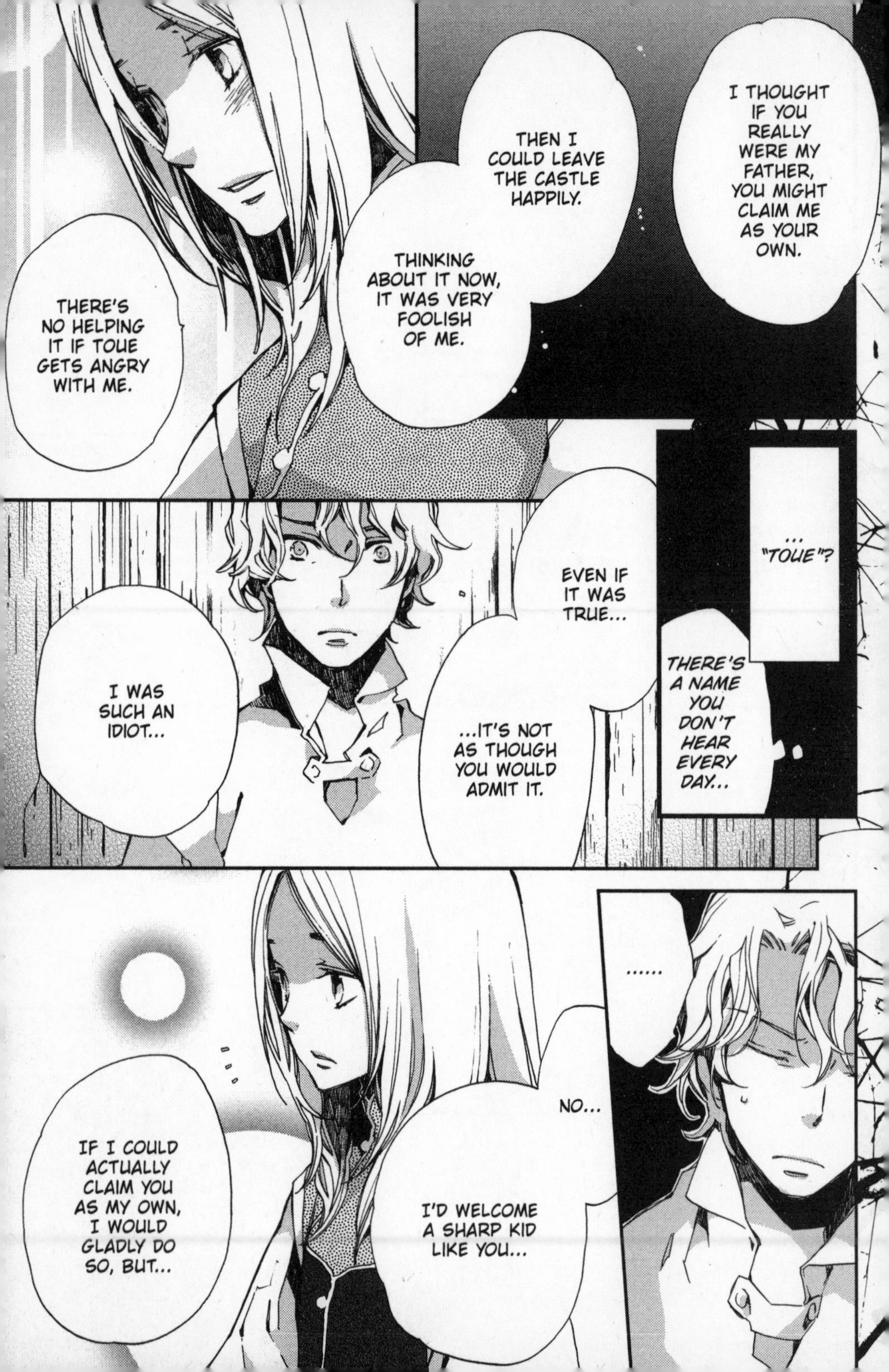
I THOUGHT IF YOU REALLY WERE MY FATHER, YOU MIGHT CLAIM ME AS YOUR OWN.
THEN I COULD LEAVE THE CASTLE HAPPILY.
THINKING ABOUT IT NOW, IT WAS VERY FOOLISH OF ME.
THERE'S NO HELPING IT IF TOUE GETS ANGRY WITH ME.
... "TOUE"?
THERE'S A NAME YOU DON'T HEAR EVERY DAY...
EVEN IF IT WAS TRUE...
...IT'S NOT AS THOUGH YOU WOULD ADMIT IT.
I WAS SUCH AN IDIOT...
......
NO...
I'D WELCOME A SHARP KID LIKE YOU...
IF I COULD ACTUALLY CLAIM YOU AS MY OWN, I WOULD GLADLY DO SO, BUT...

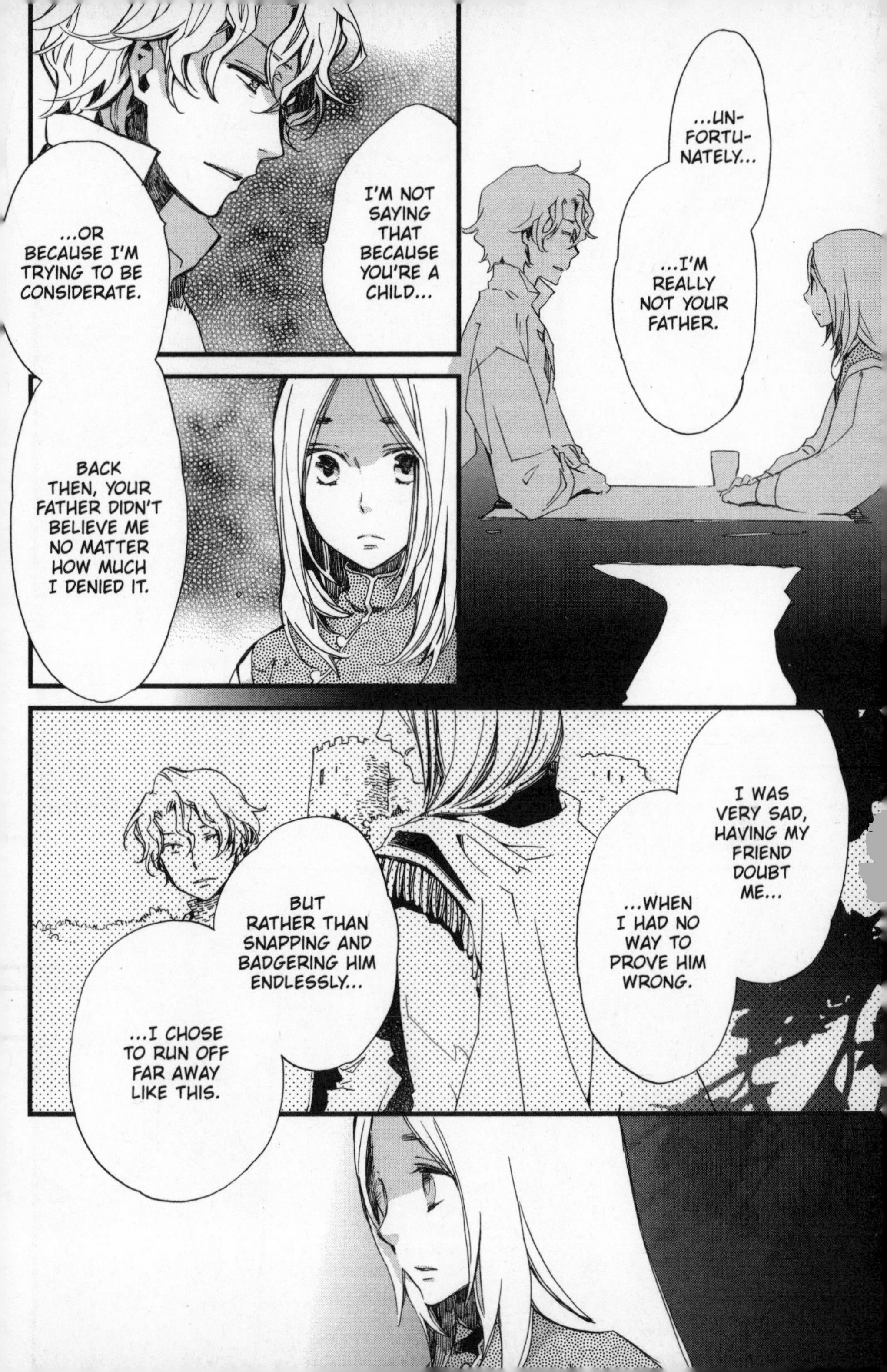
...UN-FORTU-NATELY...
...I'M REALLY NOT YOUR FATHER.
I'M NOT SAYING THAT BECAUSE YOU'RE A CHILD...
...OR BECAUSE I'M TRYING TO BE CONSIDERATE.
BACK THEN, YOUR FATHER DIDN'T BELIEVE ME NO MATTER HOW MUCH I DENIED IT.
I WAS VERY SAD, HAVING MY FRIEND DOUBT ME...
...WHEN I HAD NO WAY TO PROVE HIM WRONG.
BUT RATHER THAN SNAPPING AND BADGERING HIM ENDLESSLY...
...I CHOSE TO RUN OFF FAR AWAY LIKE THIS.

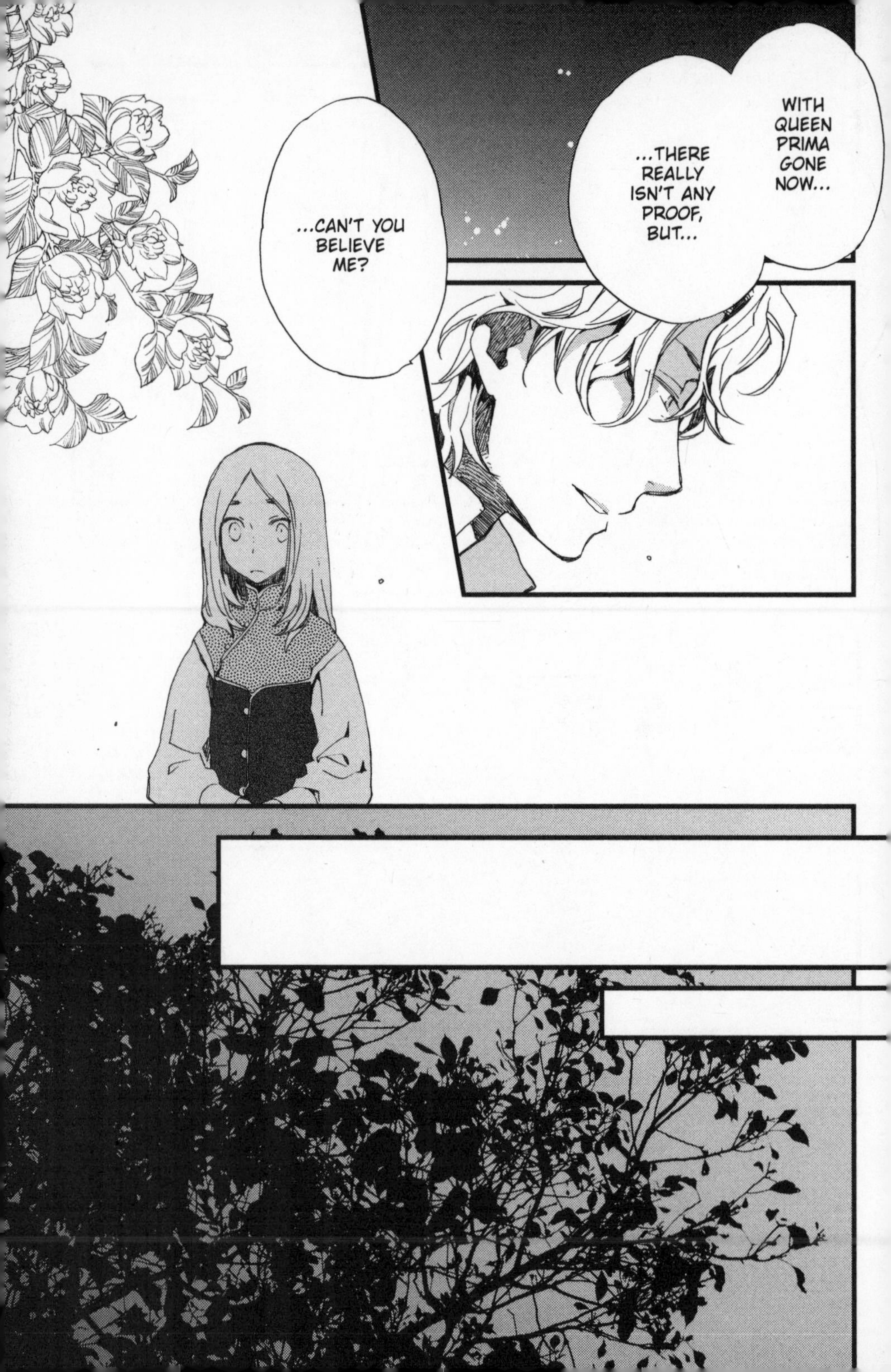
WITH QUEEN PRIMA GONE NOW...
...THERE REALLY ISN'T ANY PROOF, BUT...
...CAN'T YOU BELIEVE ME?

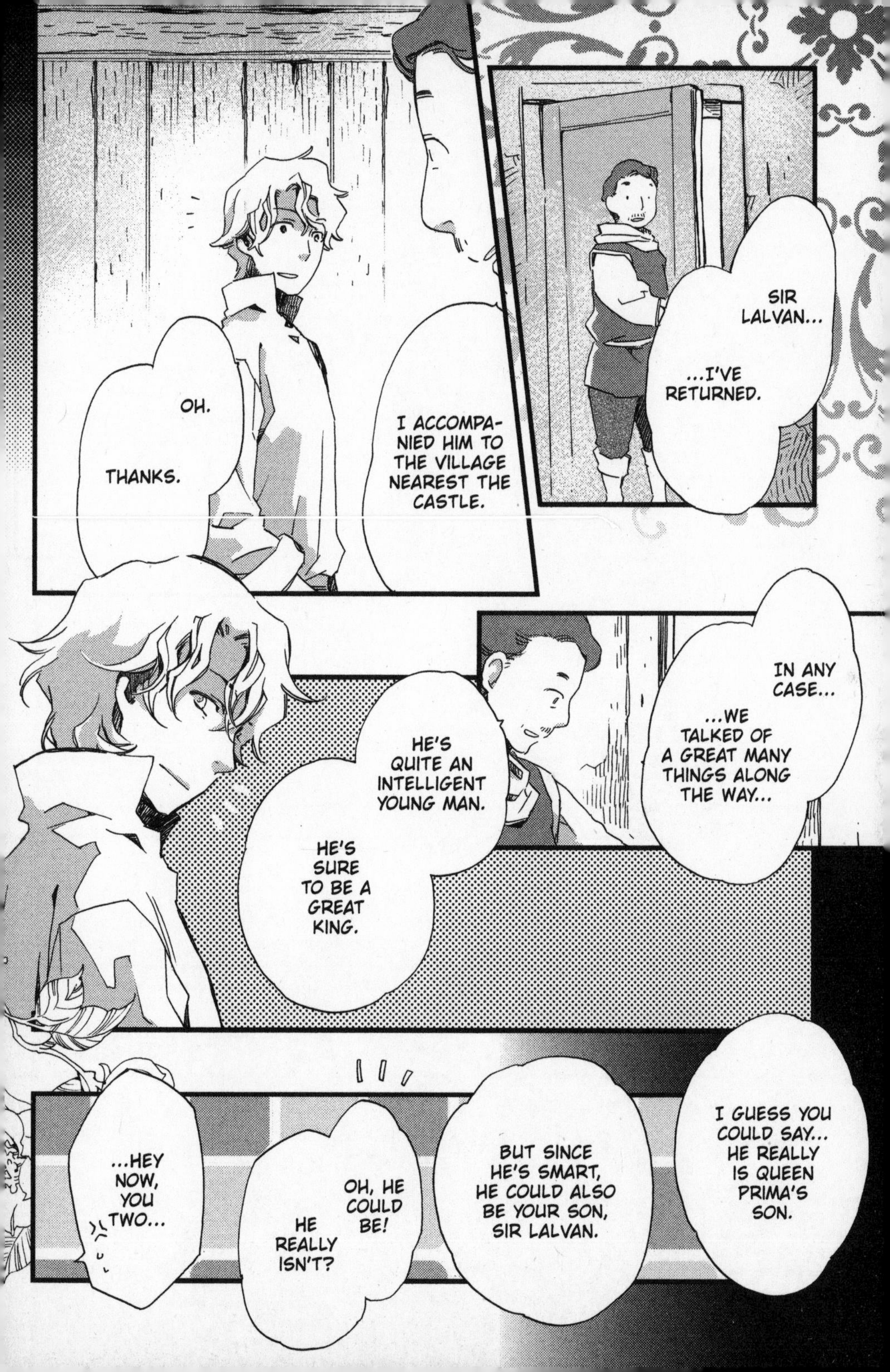
SIR LALVAN...
...I'VE RETURNED.
I ACCOMPANIED HIM TO THE VILLAGE NEAREST THE CASTLE.
OH.
THANKS.
IN ANY CASE...
...WE TALKED OF A GREAT MANY THINGS ALONG THE WAY...
HE'S QUITE AN INTELLIGENT YOUNG MAN.
HE'S SURE TO BE A GREAT KING.
I GUESS YOU COULD SAY... HE REALLY IS QUEEN PRIMA'S SON.
BUT SINCE HE'S SMART, HE COULD ALSO BE YOUR SON, SIR LALVAN.
OH, HE COULD BE!
HE REALLY ISN'T?
...HEY NOW, YOU TWO...

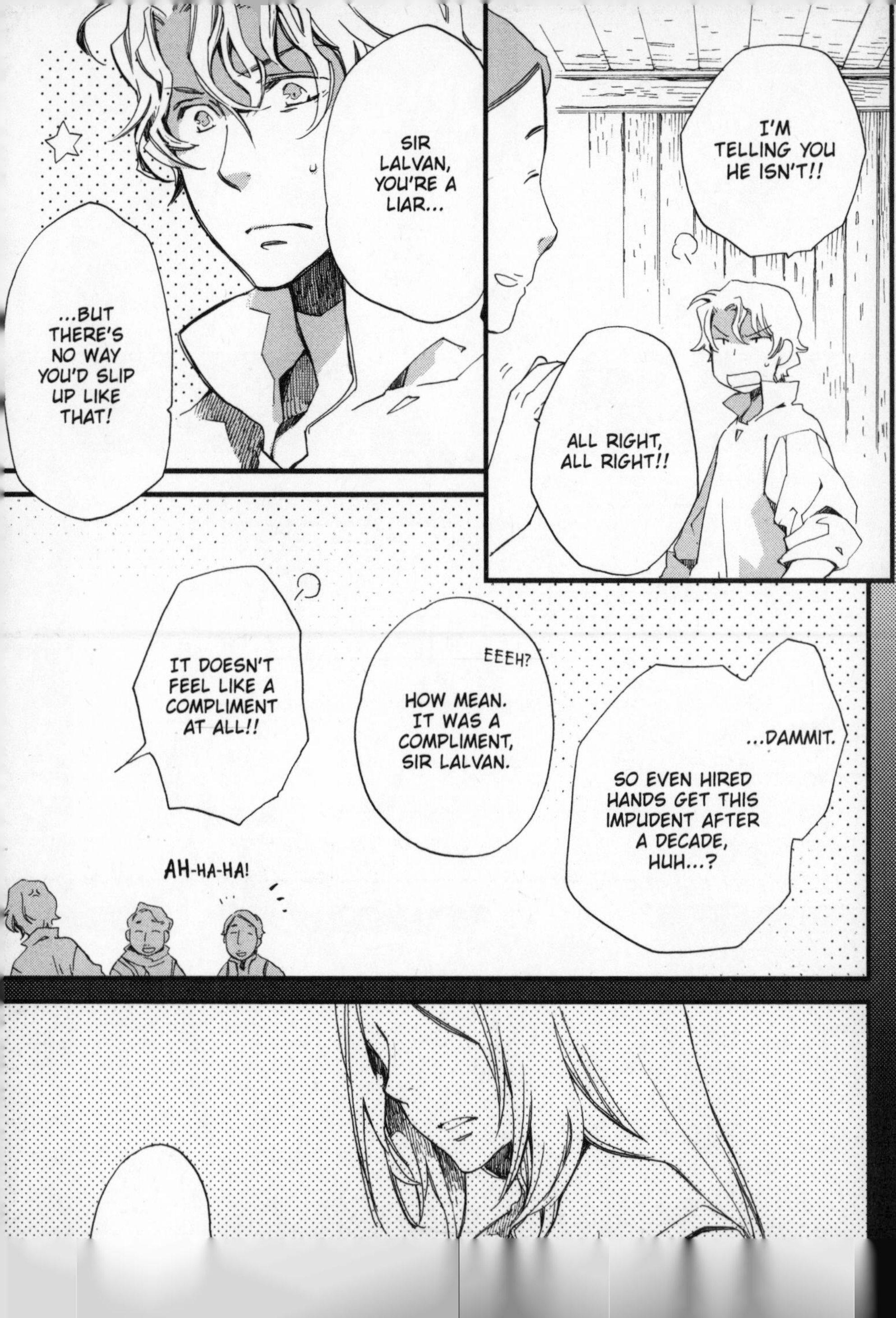
I'M TELLING YOU HE ISN'T!!
ALL RIGHT, ALL RIGHT!!
SIR LALVAN, YOU'RE A LIAR...
...BUT THERE'S NO WAY YOU'D SLIP UP LIKE THAT!
...DAMMIT.
SO EVEN HIRED HANDS GET THIS IMPUDENT AFTER A DECADE, HUH...?
EEEH?
HOW MEAN. IT WAS A COMPLIMENT, SIR LALVAN.
IT DOESN'T FEEL LIKE A COMPLIMENT AT ALL!!
AH-HA-HA!

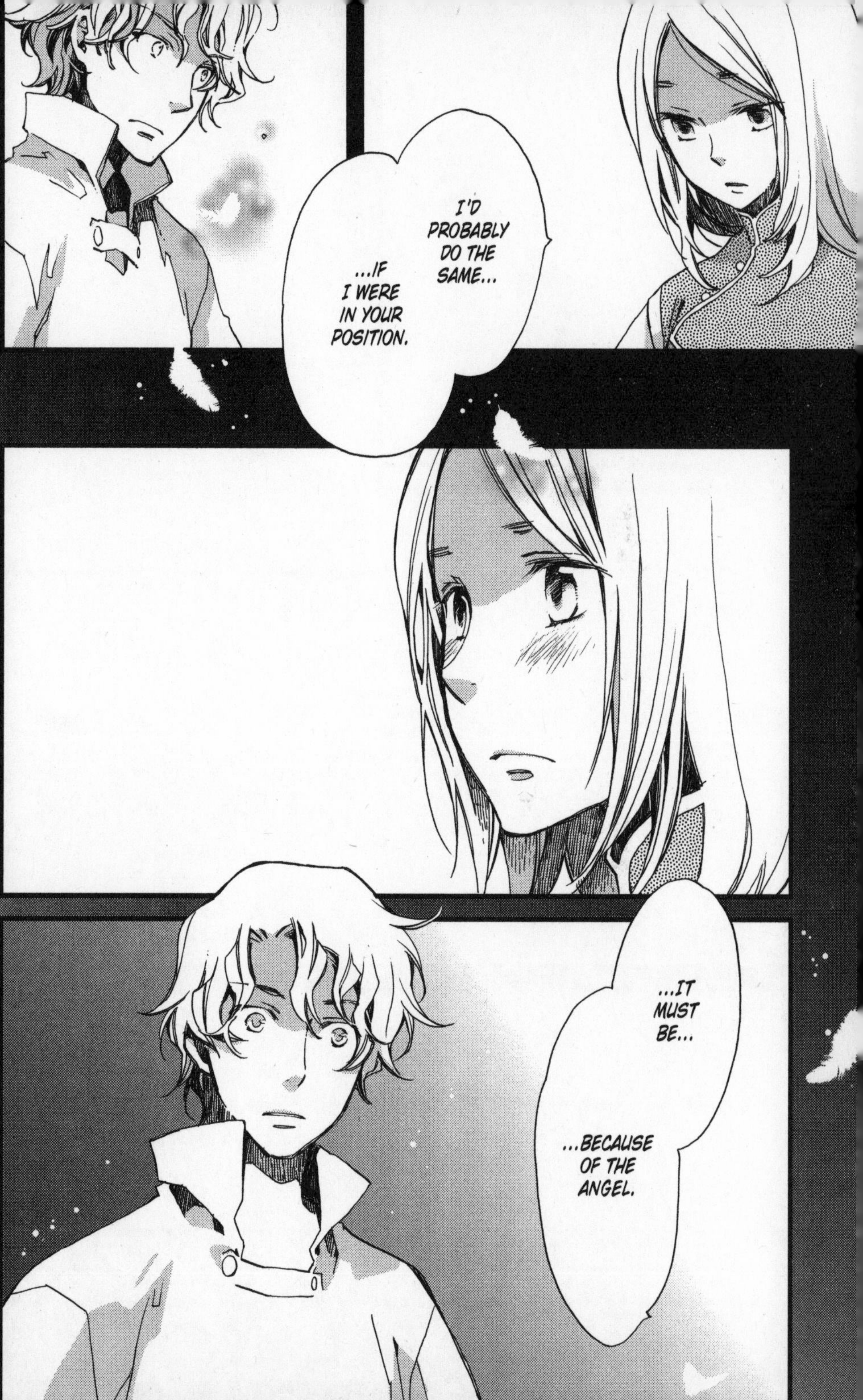
I'D PROBABLY DO THE SAME...
...IF I WERE IN YOUR POSITION.
...IT MUST BE...
...BECAUSE OF THE ANGEL.

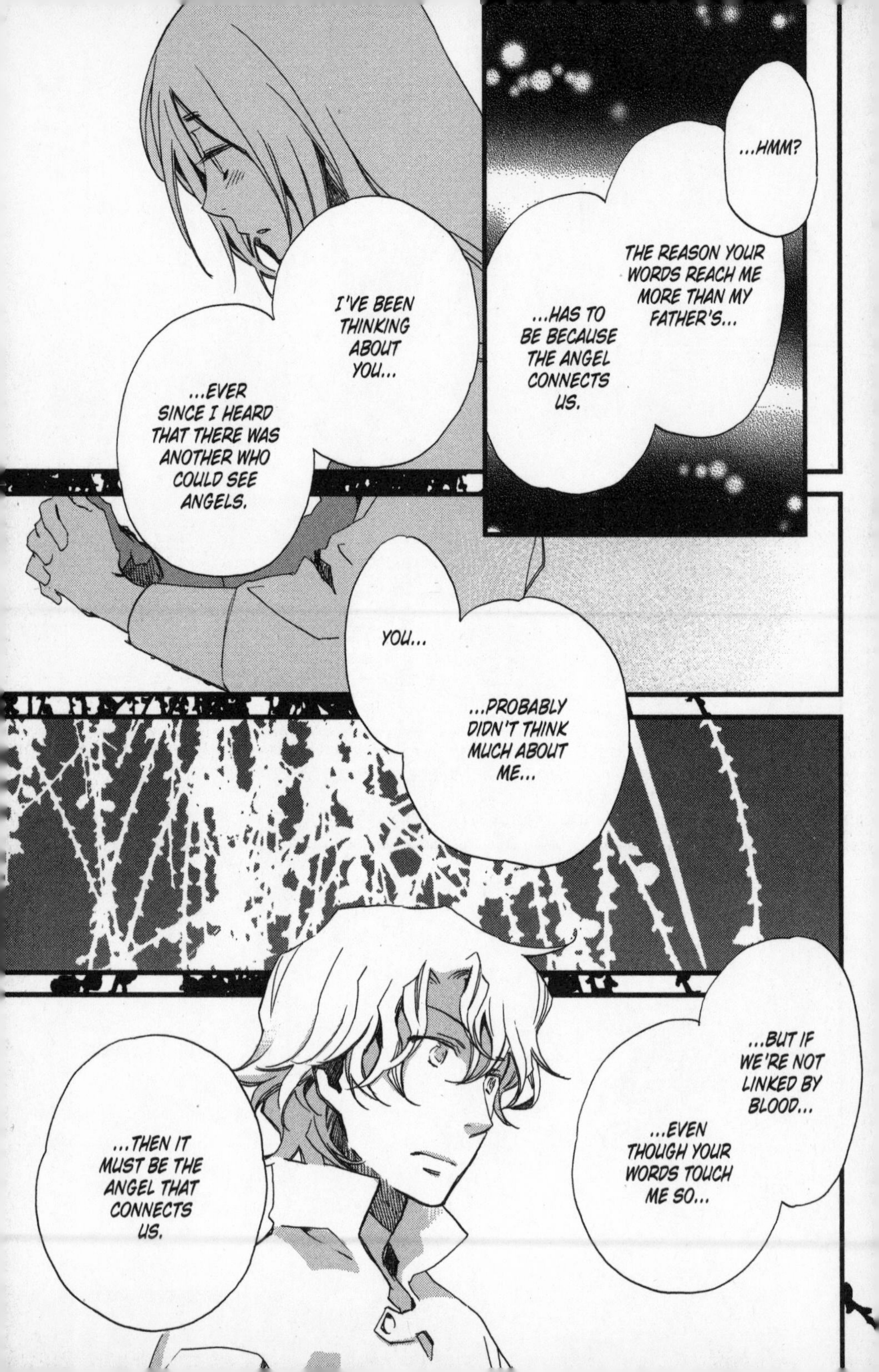
...HMM?
THE REASON YOUR WORDS REACH ME MORE THAN MY FATHER'S...
...HAS TO BE BECAUSE THE ANGEL CONNECTS US.
I'VE BEEN THINKING ABOUT YOU...
...EVER SINCE I HEARD THAT THERE WAS ANOTHER WHO COULD SEE ANGELS.
YOU...
...PROBABLY DIDN'T THINK MUCH ABOUT ME...
...BUT IF WE'RE NOT LINKED BY BLOOD...
...EVEN THOUGH YOUR WORDS TOUCH ME SO...
...THEN IT MUST BE THE ANGEL THAT CONNECTS US.

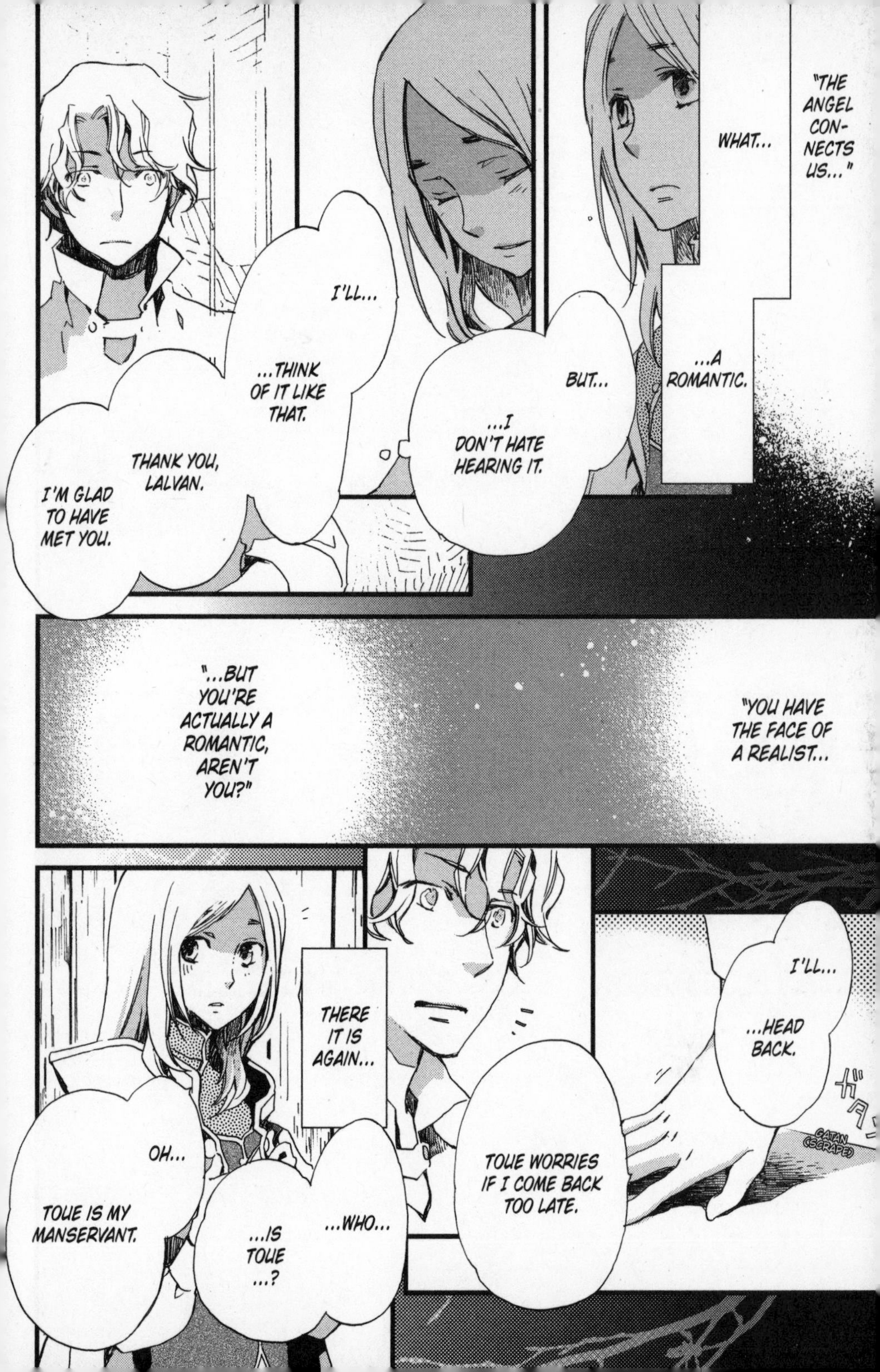
"THE ANGEL CONNECTS US..."
WHAT...
...A ROMANTIC.
BUT...
...I DON'T HATE HEARING IT.
I'LL...
...THINK OF IT LIKE THAT.
THANK YOU, LALVAN.
I'M GLAD TO HAVE MET YOU.
"YOU HAVE THE FACE OF A REALIST...
"...BUT YOU'RE ACTUALLY A ROMANTIC, AREN'T YOU?"
I'LL...
...HEAD BACK.
GATAN (SCRAPE)
TOUE WORRIES IF I COME BACK TOO LATE.
THERE IT IS AGAIN...
...WHO...
...IS TOUE ...?
OH...
TOUE IS MY MANSERVANT.

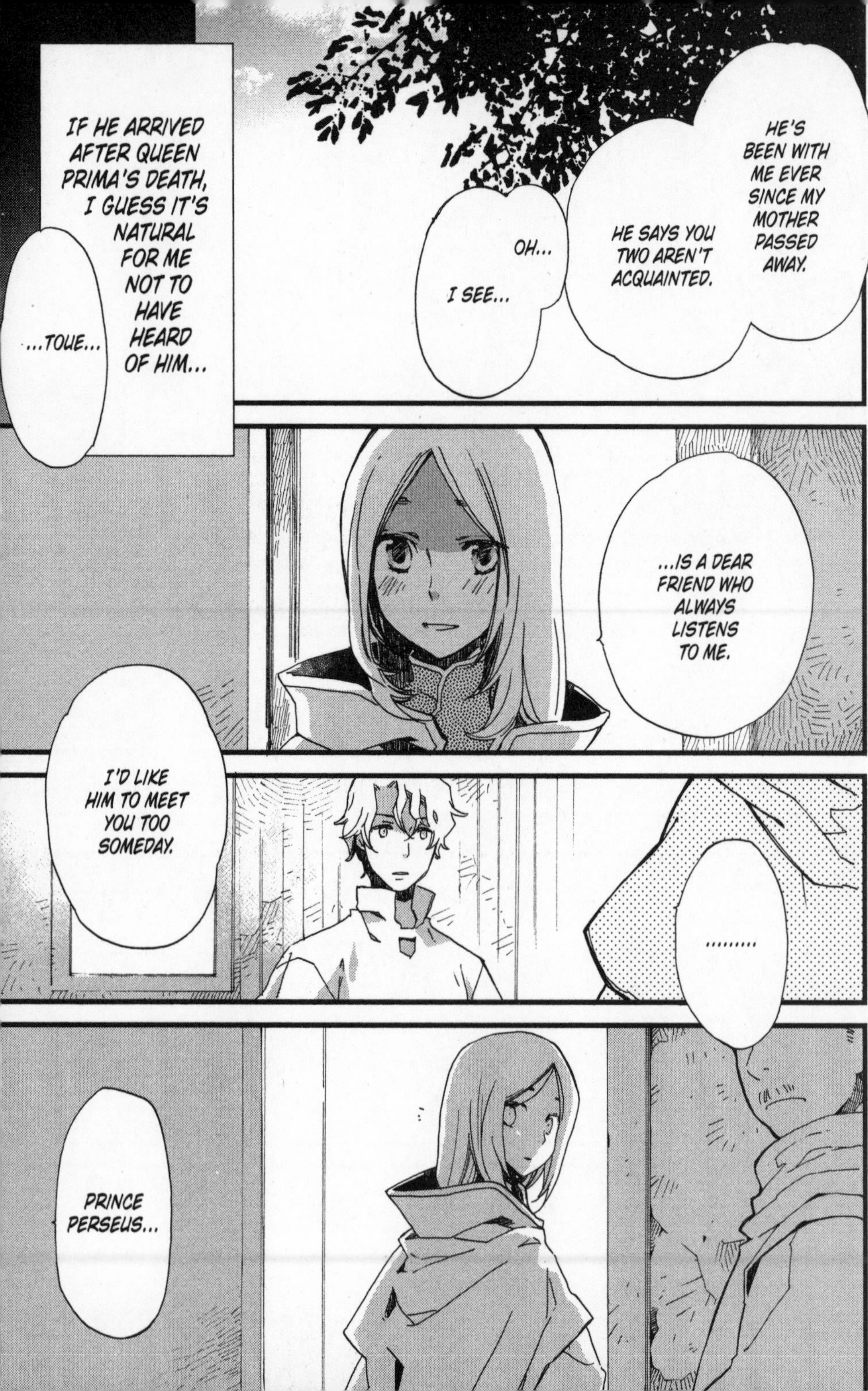
HE'S BEEN WITH ME EVER SINCE MY MOTHER PASSED AWAY.
HE SAYS YOU TWO AREN'T ACQUAINTED.
OH... I SEE...
IF HE ARRIVED AFTER QUEEN PRIMA'S DEATH, I GUESS IT'S NATURAL FOR ME NOT TO HAVE HEARD OF HIM...
...TOUE...
...IS A DEAR FRIEND WHO ALWAYS LISTENS TO ME.
....
I'D LIKE HIM TO MEET YOU TOO SOMEDAY.
PRINCE PERSEUS...

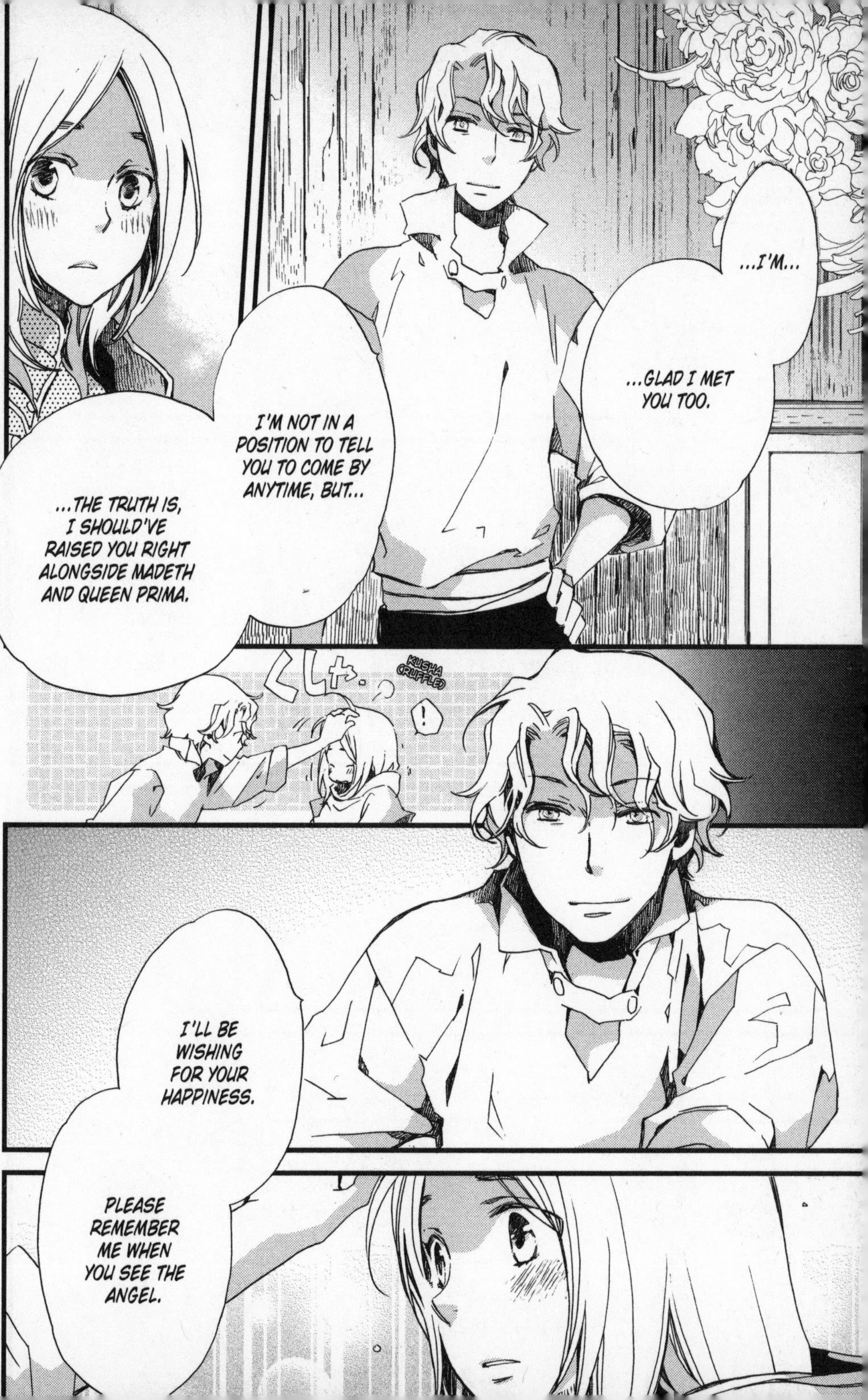
...I'M...
...GLAD I MET YOU TOO.
I'M NOT IN A POSITION TO TELL YOU TO COME BY ANYTIME, BUT...
...THE TRUTH IS, I SHOULD'VE RAISED YOU RIGHT ALONGSIDE MADETH AND QUEEN PRIMA.
くしゃ
KUSHA (RUFFLED)
!
I'LL BE WISHING FOR YOUR HAPPINESS.
PLEASE REMEMBER ME WHEN YOU SEE THE ANGEL.

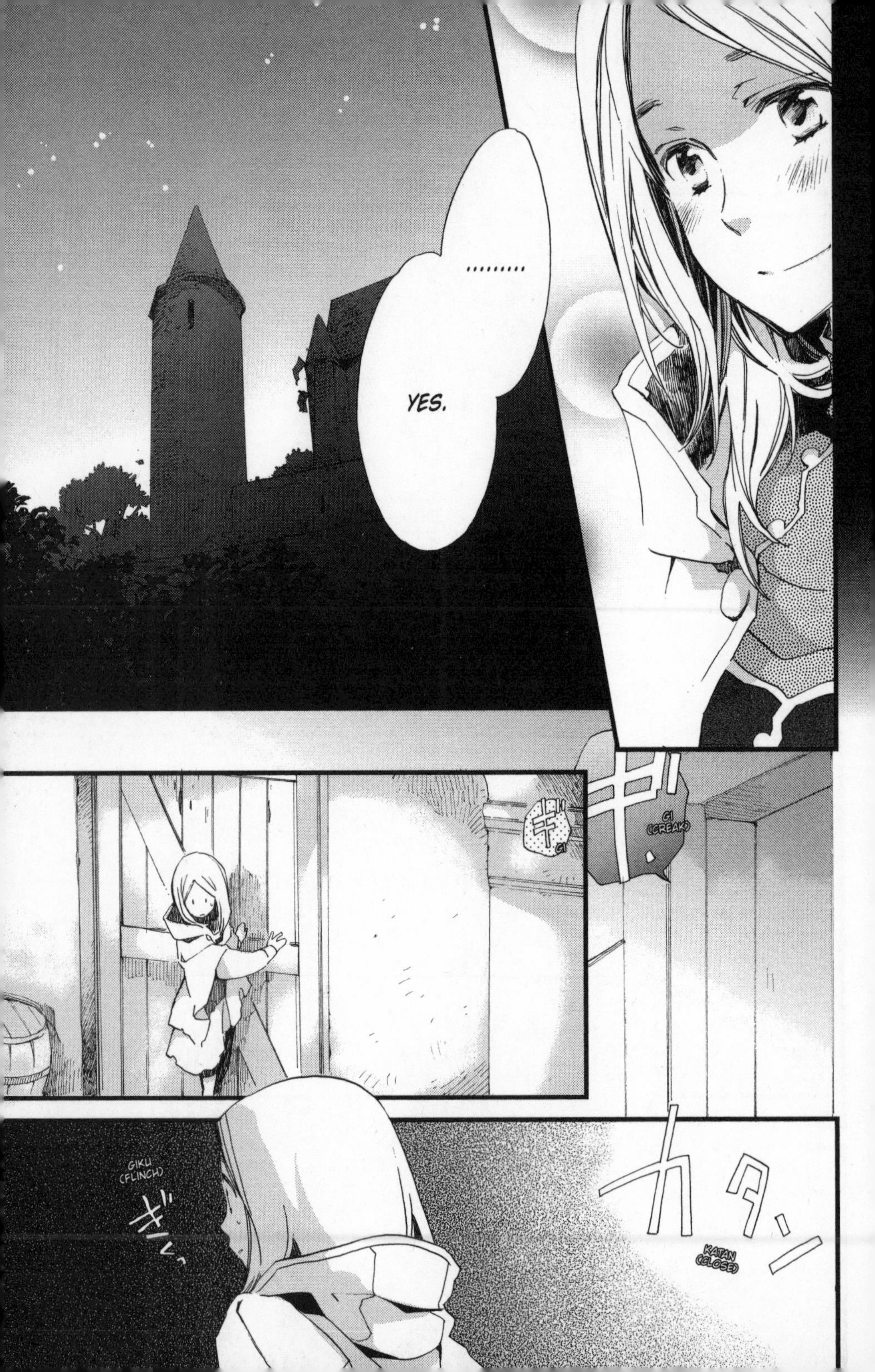

....
YES.
ギ
GI (CREAK)
ギ
GI
カタン
KATAN (CLOSE)
GIKU (FLINCH)

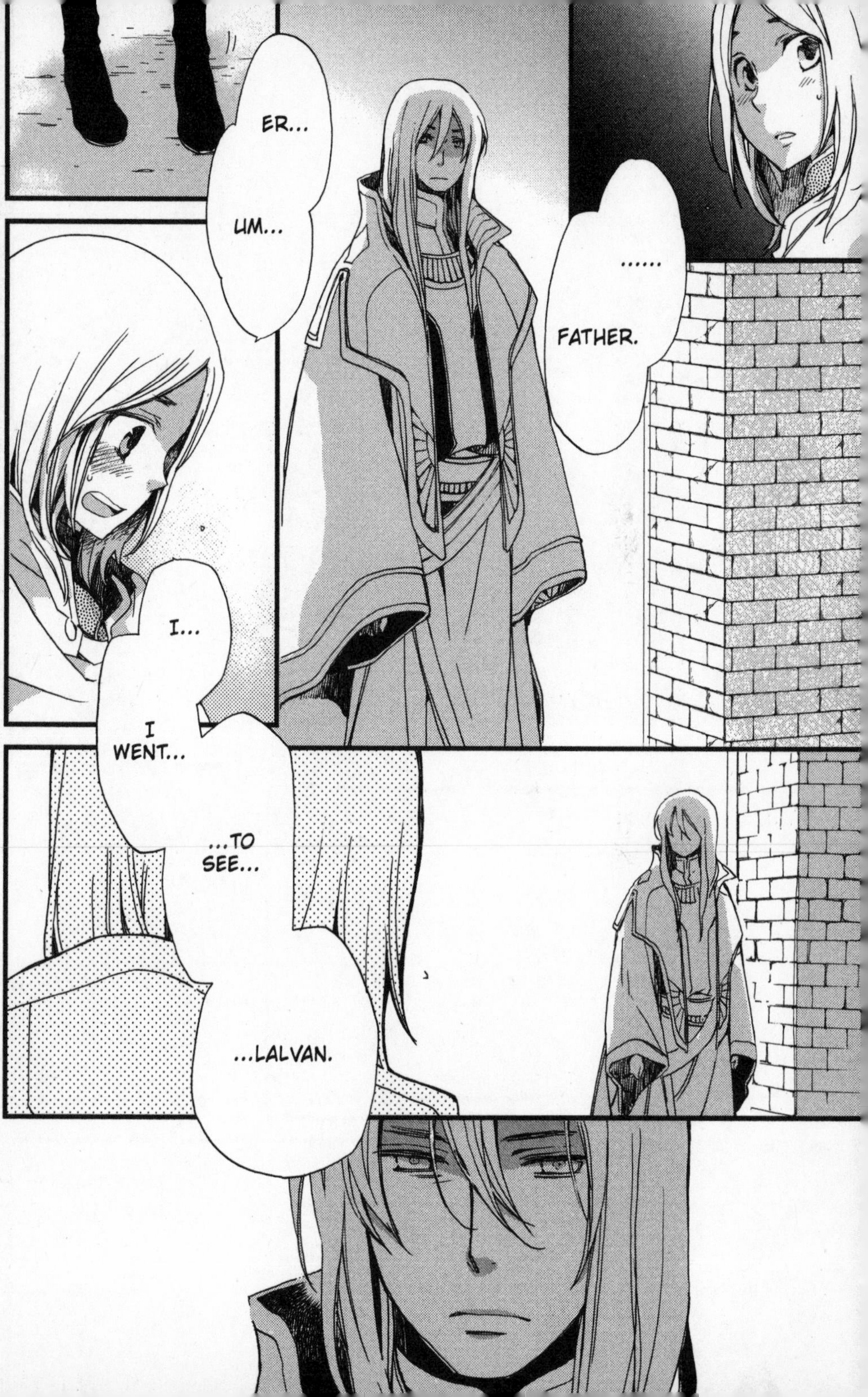

...... FATHER.
ER... UM...
I...
I WENT...
...TO SEE...
...LALVAN.

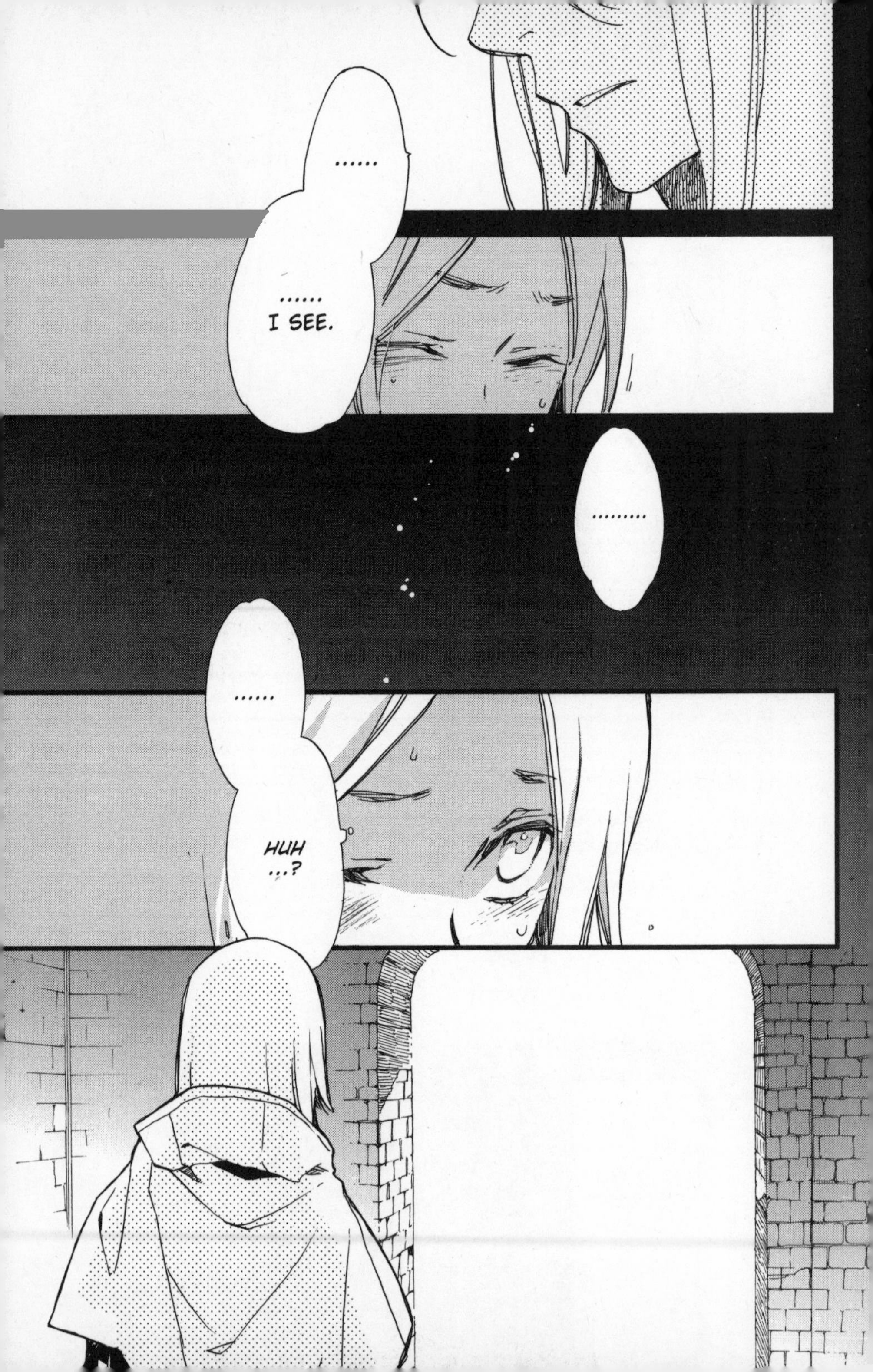
......
......
I SEE.
....
......
HUH
...?

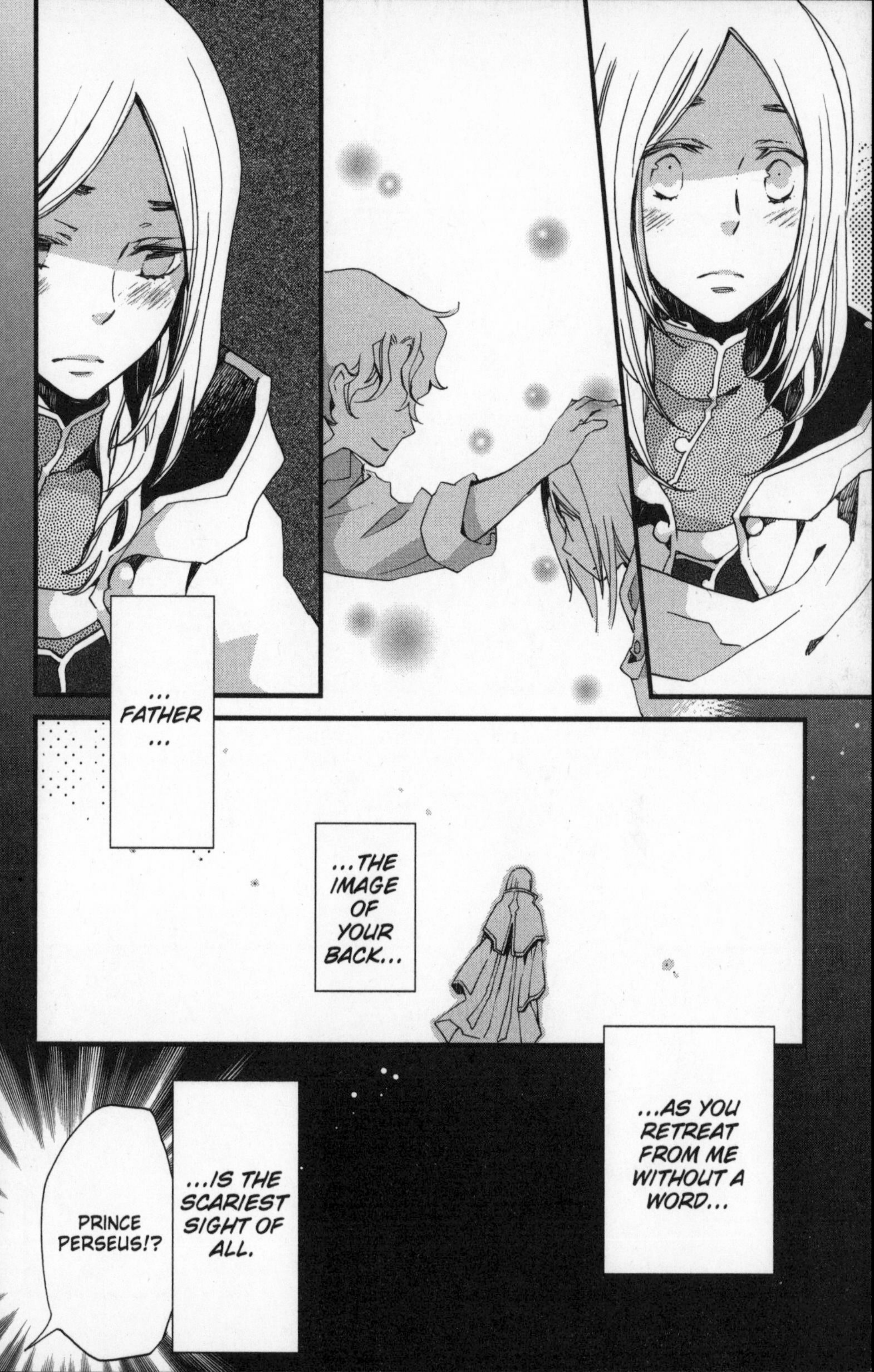
...FATHER...
...THE IMAGE OF YOUR BACK...
...AS YOU RETREAT FROM ME WITHOUT A WORD...
...IS THE SCARIEST SIGHT OF ALL.
PRINCE PERSEUS!?

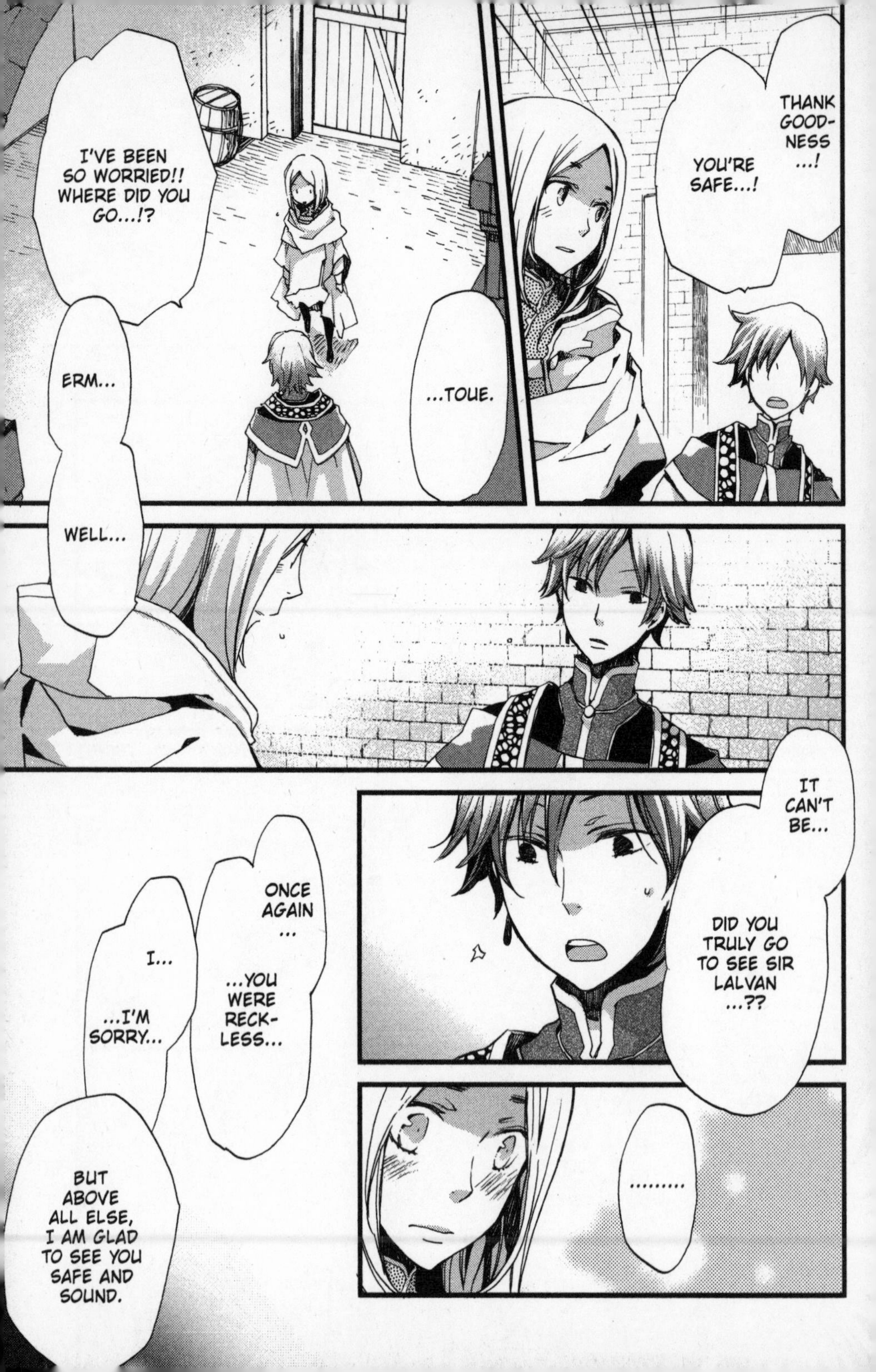
THANK GOODNESS...!
YOU'RE SAFE...!
...TOUE.
I'VE BEEN SO WORRIED!! WHERE DID YOU GO...!?
ERM...
WELL...
IT CAN'T BE...
DID YOU TRULY GO TO SEE SIR LALVAN...??
....
ONCE AGAIN...
...YOU WERE RECKLESS...
I...
...I'M SORRY...
BUT ABOVE ALL ELSE, I AM GLAD TO SEE YOU SAFE AND SOUND.

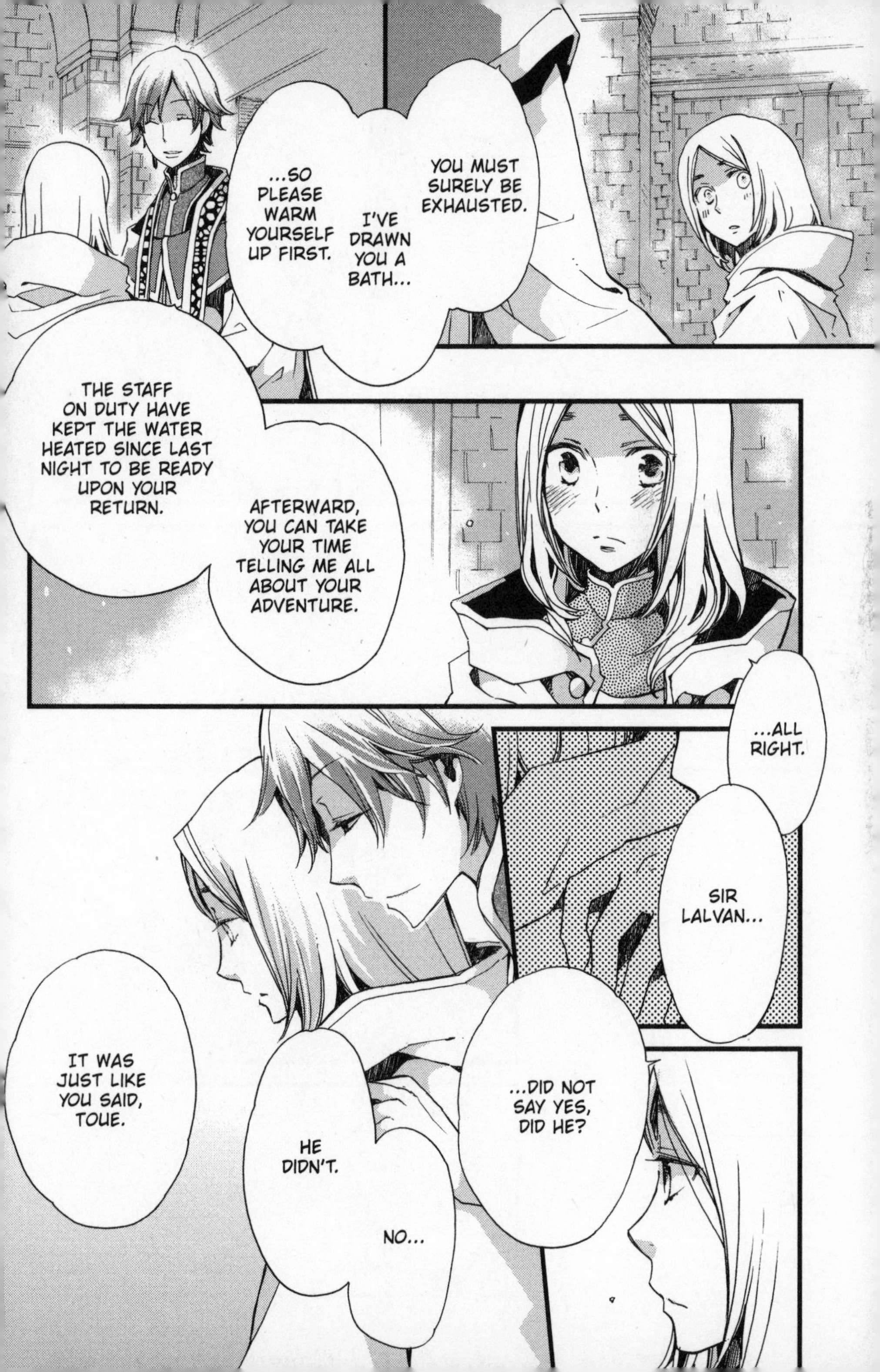
YOU MUST SURELY BE EXHAUSTED.
I'VE DRAWN YOU A BATH...
...SO PLEASE WARM YOURSELF UP FIRST.
THE STAFF ON DUTY HAVE KEPT THE WATER HEATED SINCE LAST NIGHT TO BE READY UPON YOUR RETURN.
AFTERWARD, YOU CAN TAKE YOUR TIME TELLING ME ALL ABOUT YOUR ADVENTURE.
...ALL RIGHT.
SIR LALVAN...
...DID NOT SAY YES, DID HE?
HE DIDN'T.
NO...
IT WAS JUST LIKE YOU SAID, TOUE.

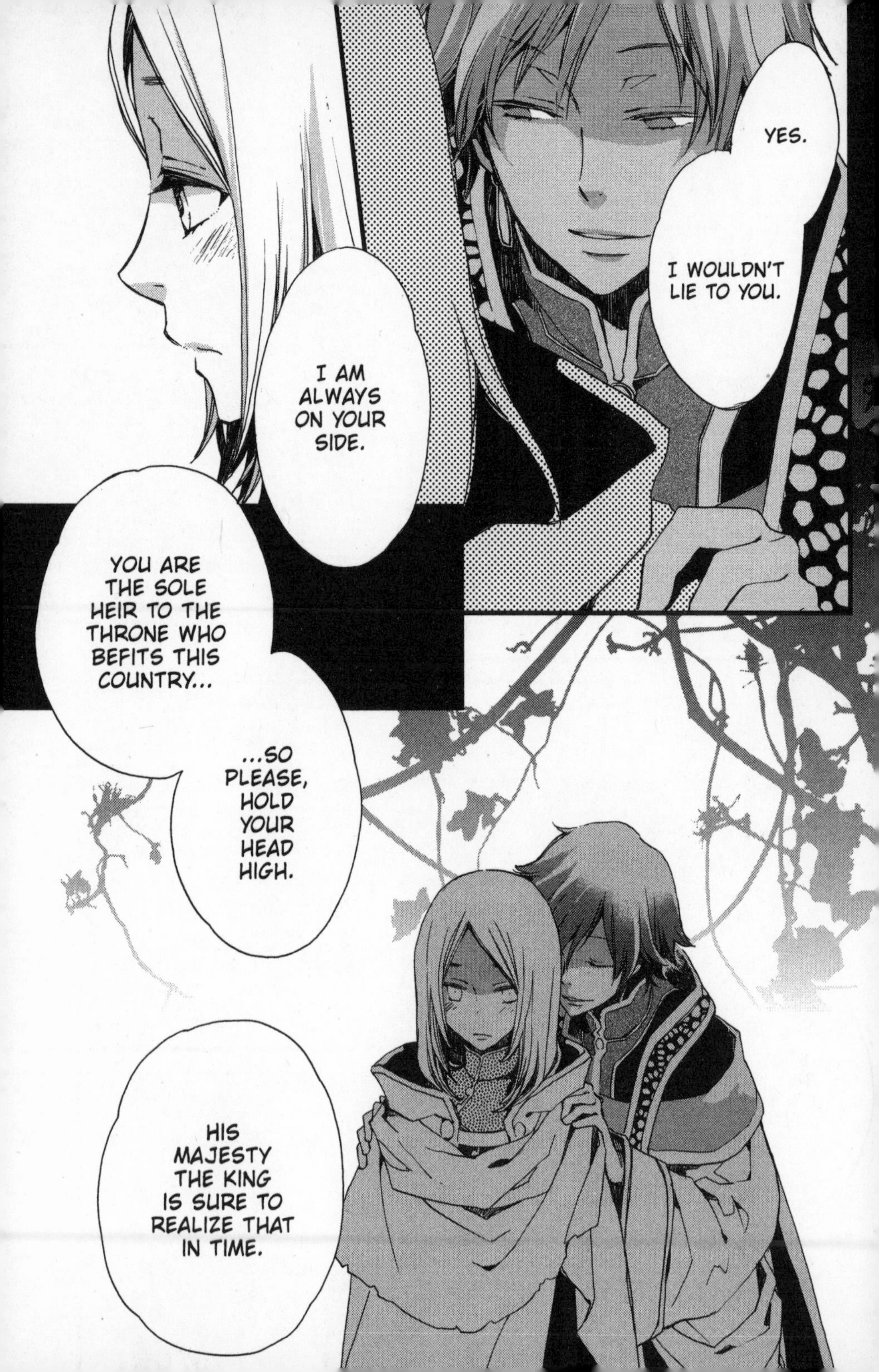
YES.
I WOULDN'T LIE TO YOU.
I AM ALWAYS ON YOUR SIDE.
YOU ARE THE SOLE HEIR TO THE THRONE WHO BEFITS THIS COUNTRY...
...SO PLEASE, HOLD YOUR HEAD HIGH.
HIS MAJESTY THE KING IS SURE TO REALIZE THAT IN TIME.

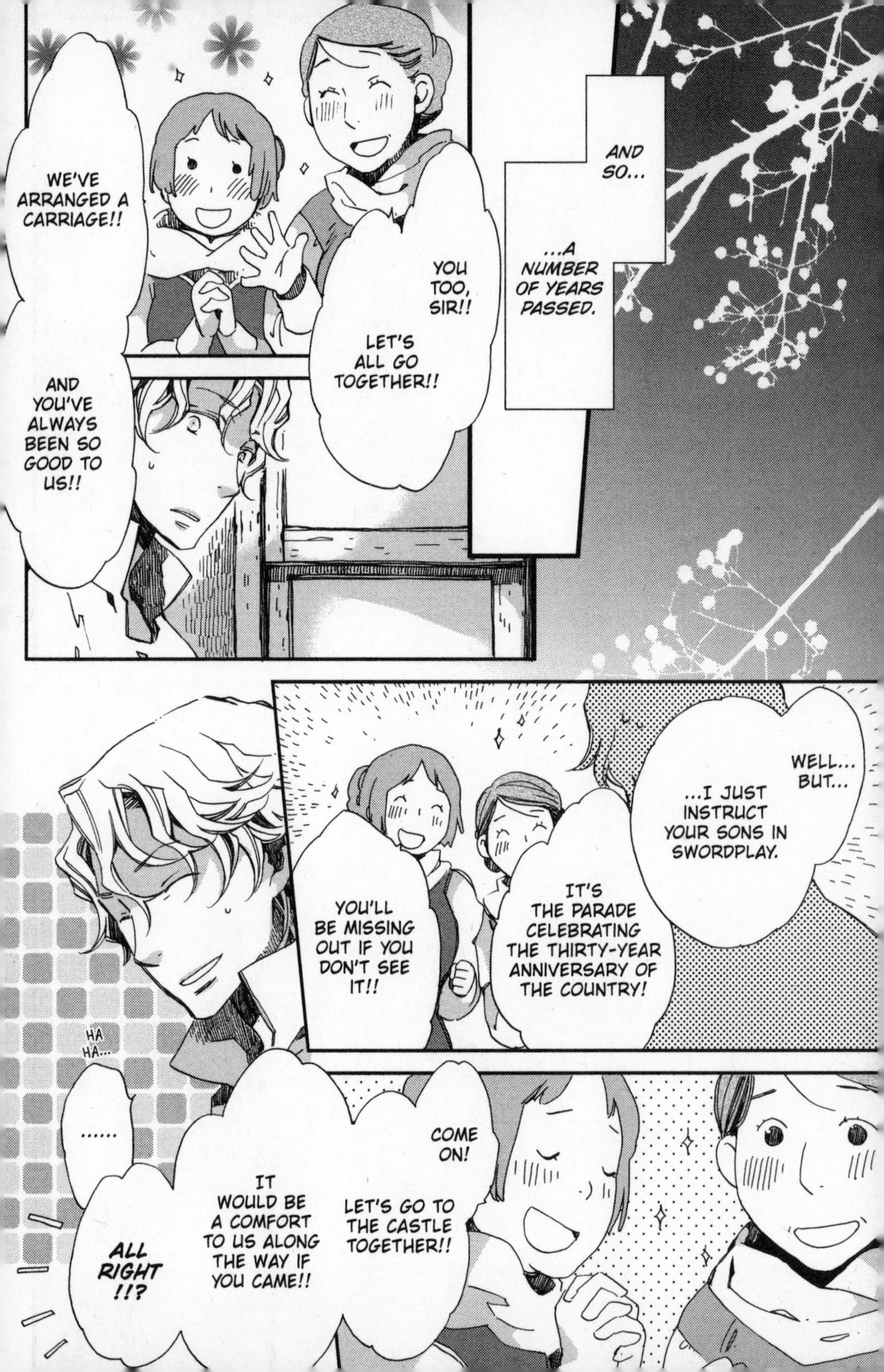
AND SO...
...A NUMBER OF YEARS PASSED.
YOU TOO, SIR!!
LET'S ALL GO TOGETHER!!
WE'VE ARRANGED A CARRIAGE!!
AND YOU'VE ALWAYS BEEN SO GOOD TO US!!
WELL... BUT...
...I JUST INSTRUCT YOUR SONS IN SWORDPLAY.
IT'S THE PARADE CELEBRATING THE THIRTY-YEAR ANNIVERSARY OF THE COUNTRY!
YOU'LL BE MISSING OUT IF YOU DON'T SEE IT!!
HA HA...
COME ON!
LET'S GO TO THE CASTLE TOGETHER!!
IT WOULD BE A COMFORT TO US ALONG THE WAY IF YOU CAME!!
......
ALL RIGHT!!?

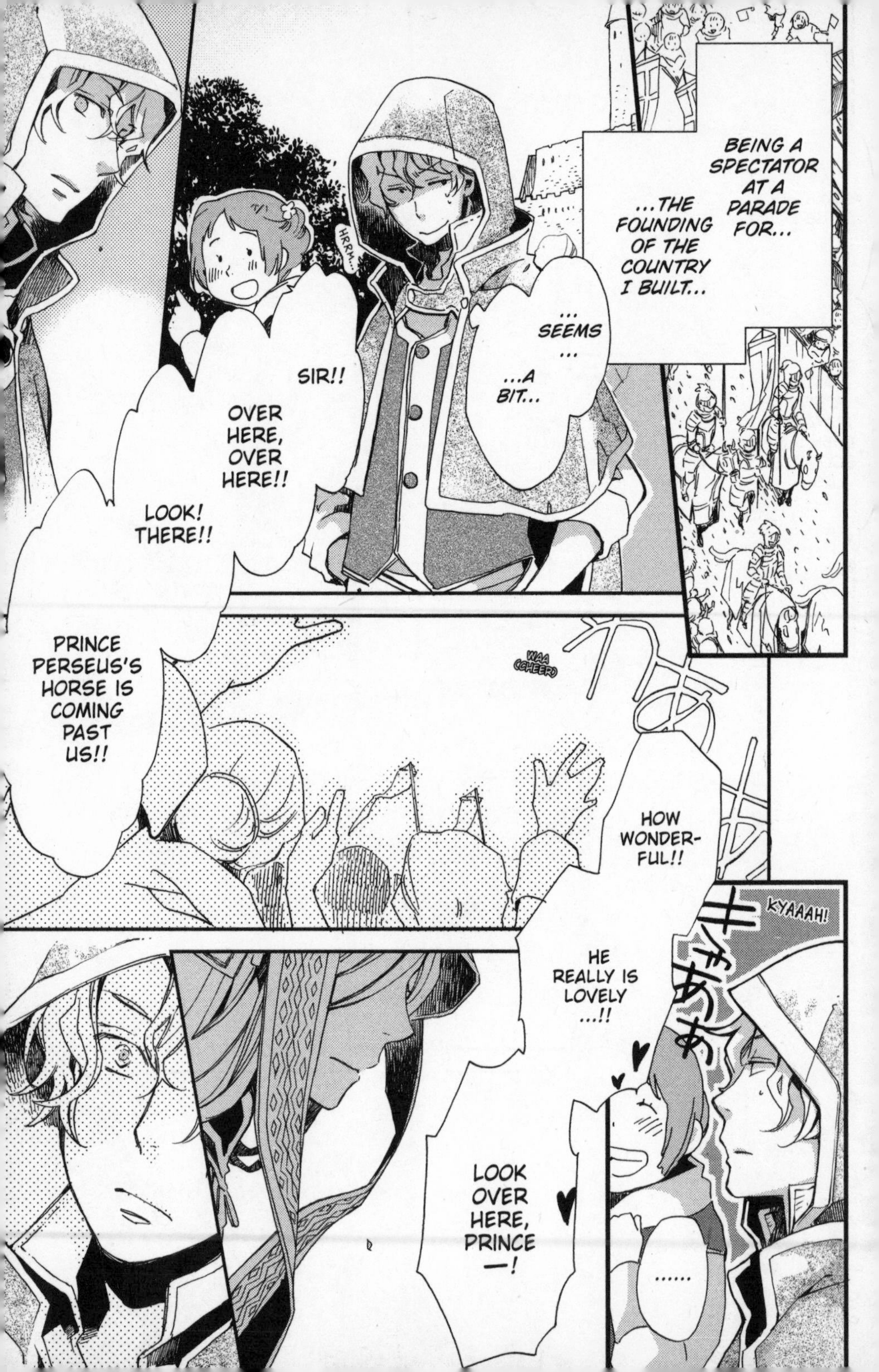
BEING A SPECTATOR AT A PARADE FOR...
...THE FOUNDING OF THE COUNTRY I BUILT...
...SEEMS...
...A BIT...
HRRM...
SIR!!
OVER HERE, OVER HERE!!
LOOK! THERE!!
WAA (CHEER)
HOW WONDER-FUL!!
PRINCE PERSEUS'S HORSE IS COMING PAST US!!
KYAAAH!
HE REALLY IS LOVELY...!!
......
LOOK OVER HERE, PRINCE—!

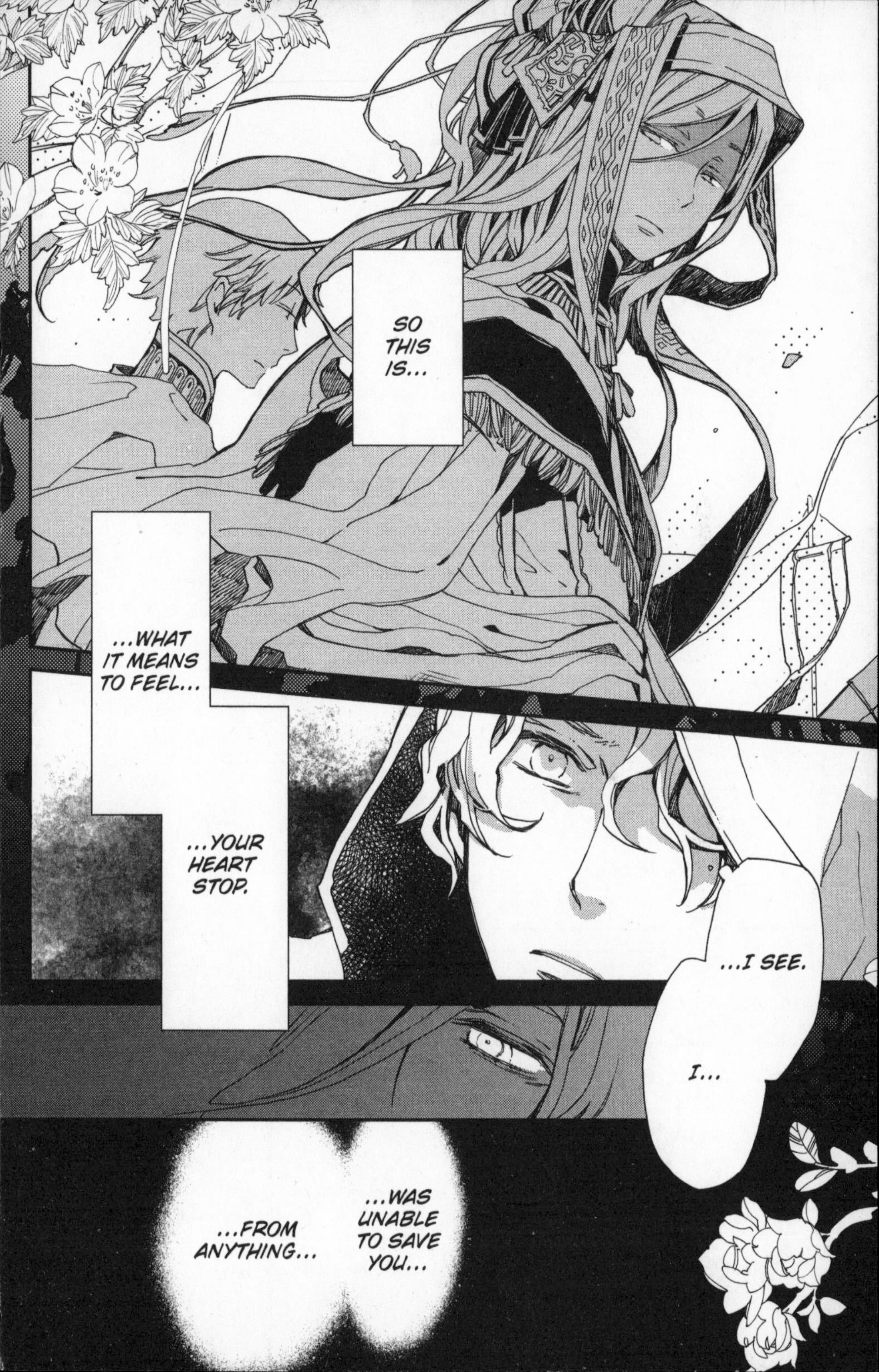
SO THIS IS...
...WHAT IT MEANS TO FEEL...
...YOUR HEART STOP.
...I SEE.
I...
...WAS UNABLE TO SAVE YOU...
...FROM ANYTHING...

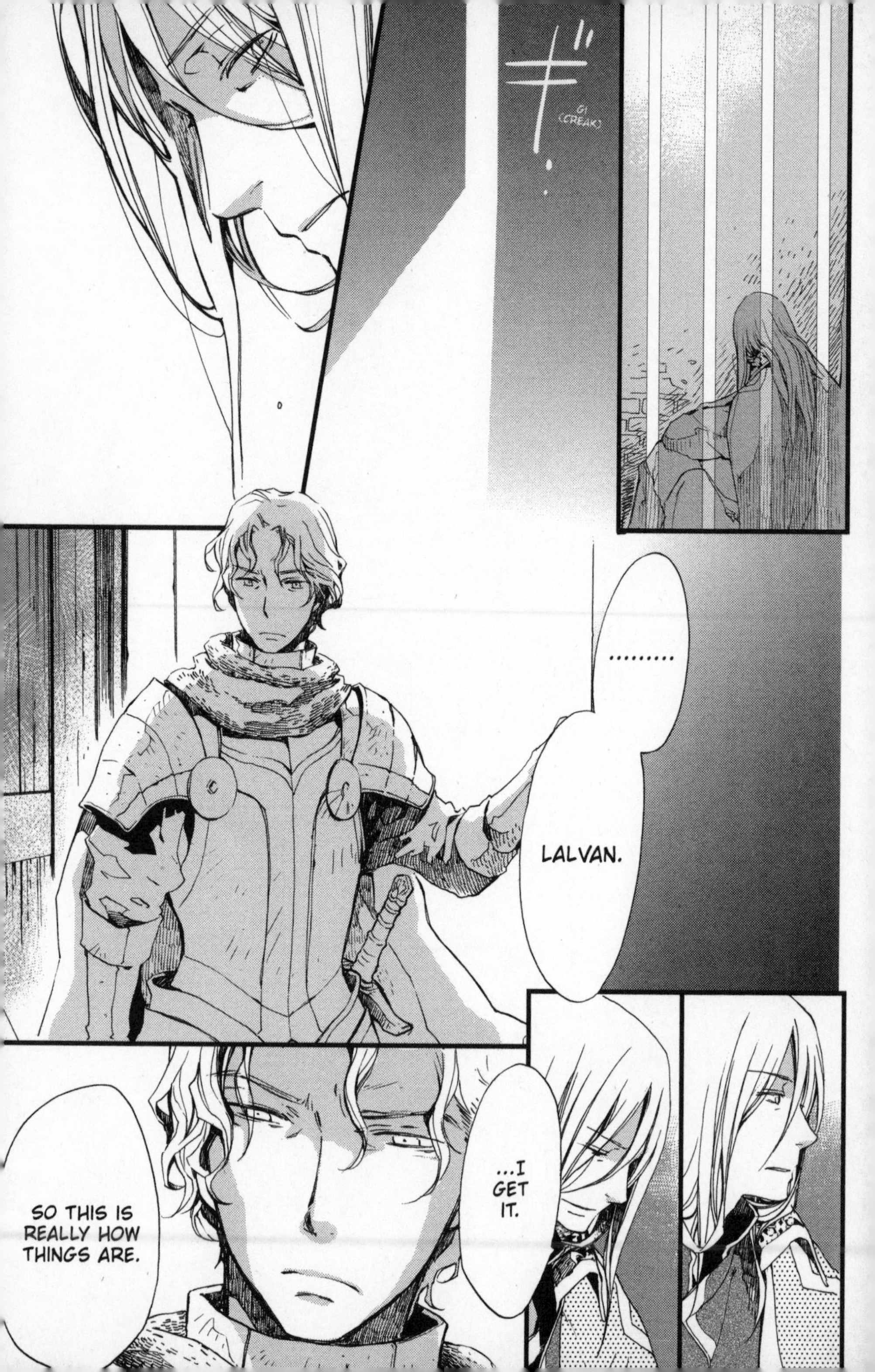
ギ
GI (CREAK)
....
LALVAN.
...I GET IT.
SO THIS IS REALLY HOW THINGS ARE.

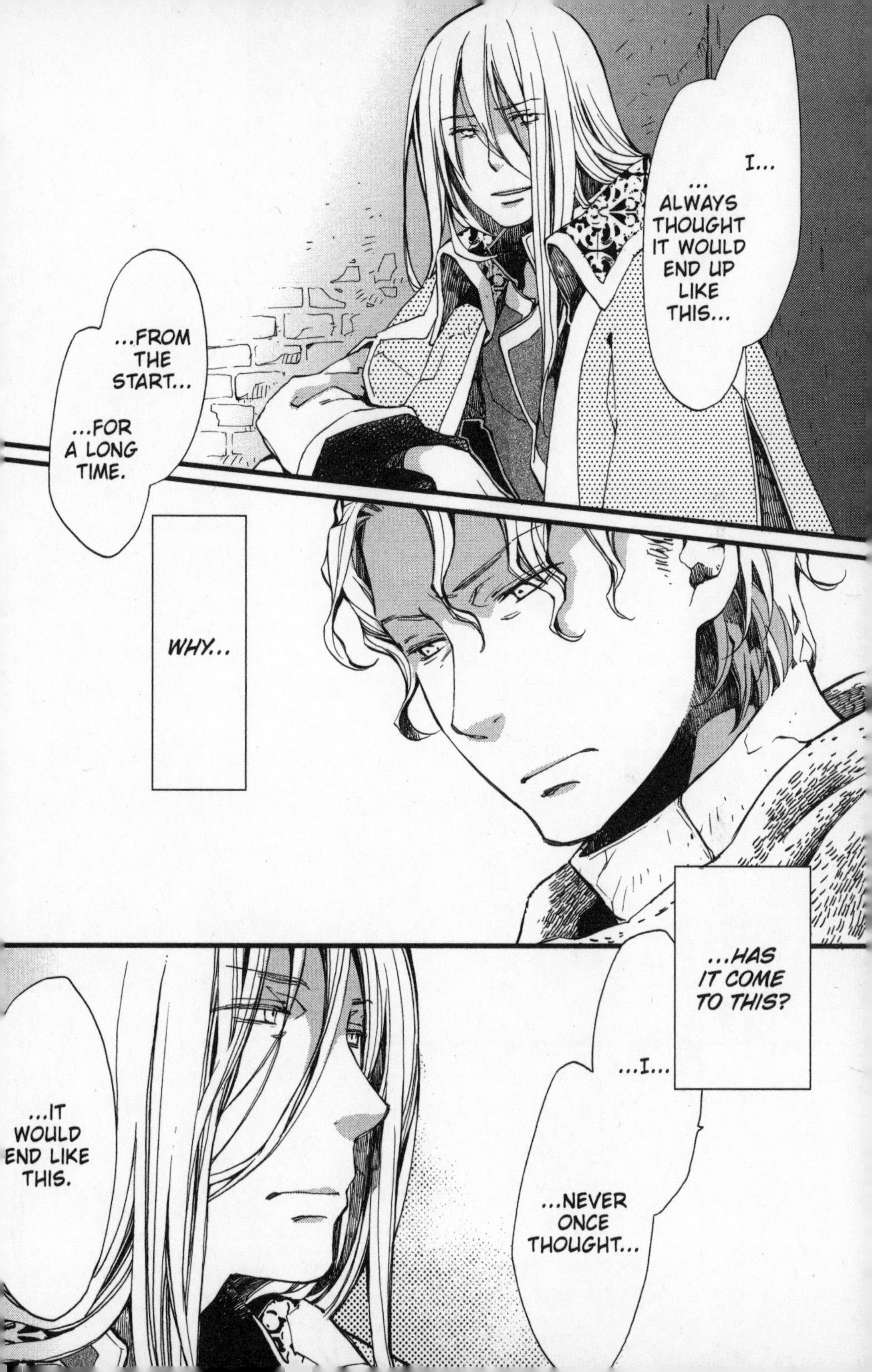
I...
...ALWAYS THOUGHT IT WOULD END UP LIKE THIS...
...FROM THE START...
...FOR A LONG TIME.
WHY...
...HAS IT COME TO THIS?
...I...
...NEVER ONCE THOUGHT...
...IT WOULD END LIKE THIS.

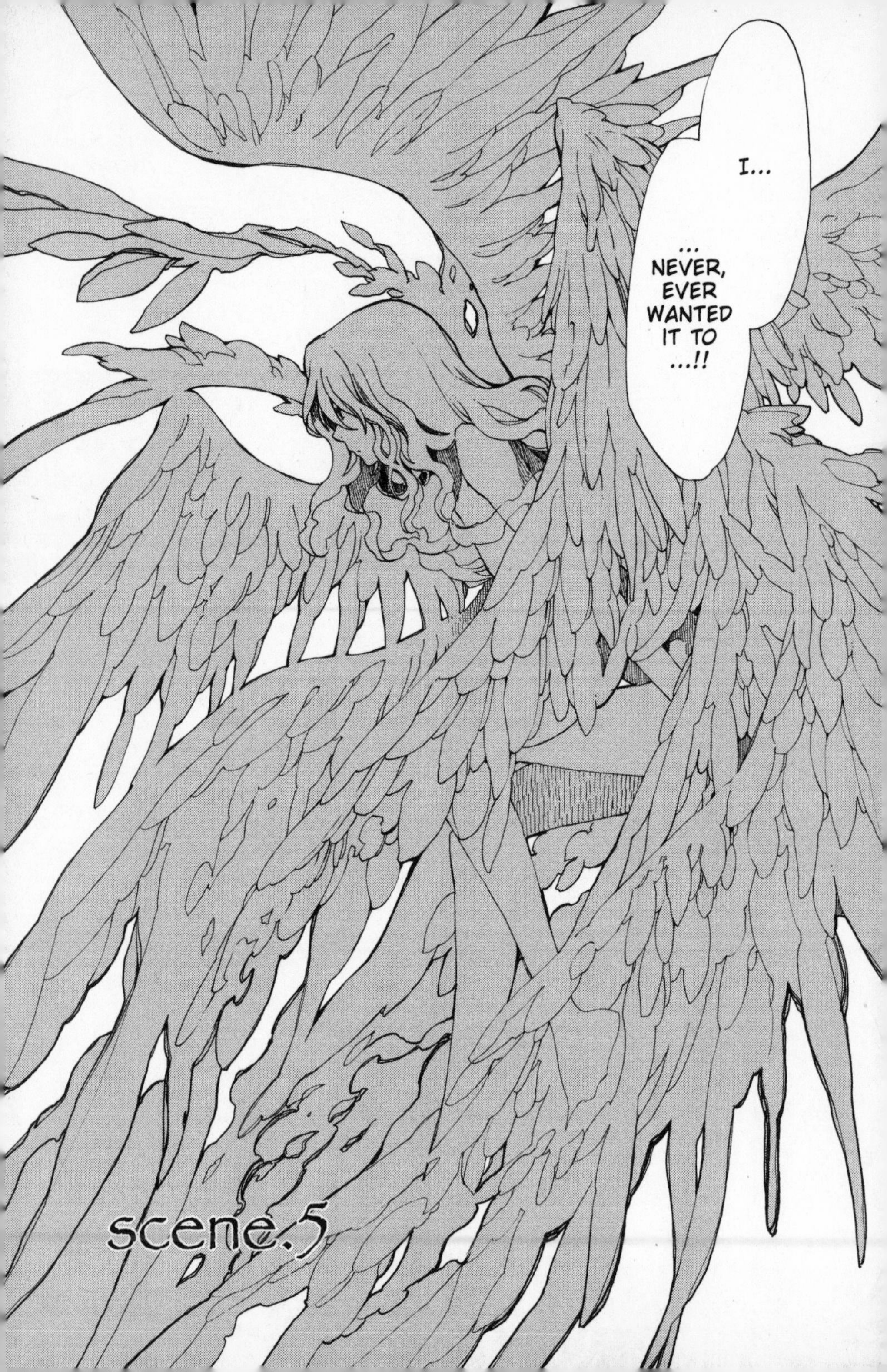
I...
...NEVER, EVER WANTED IT TO ...!!
scene.5

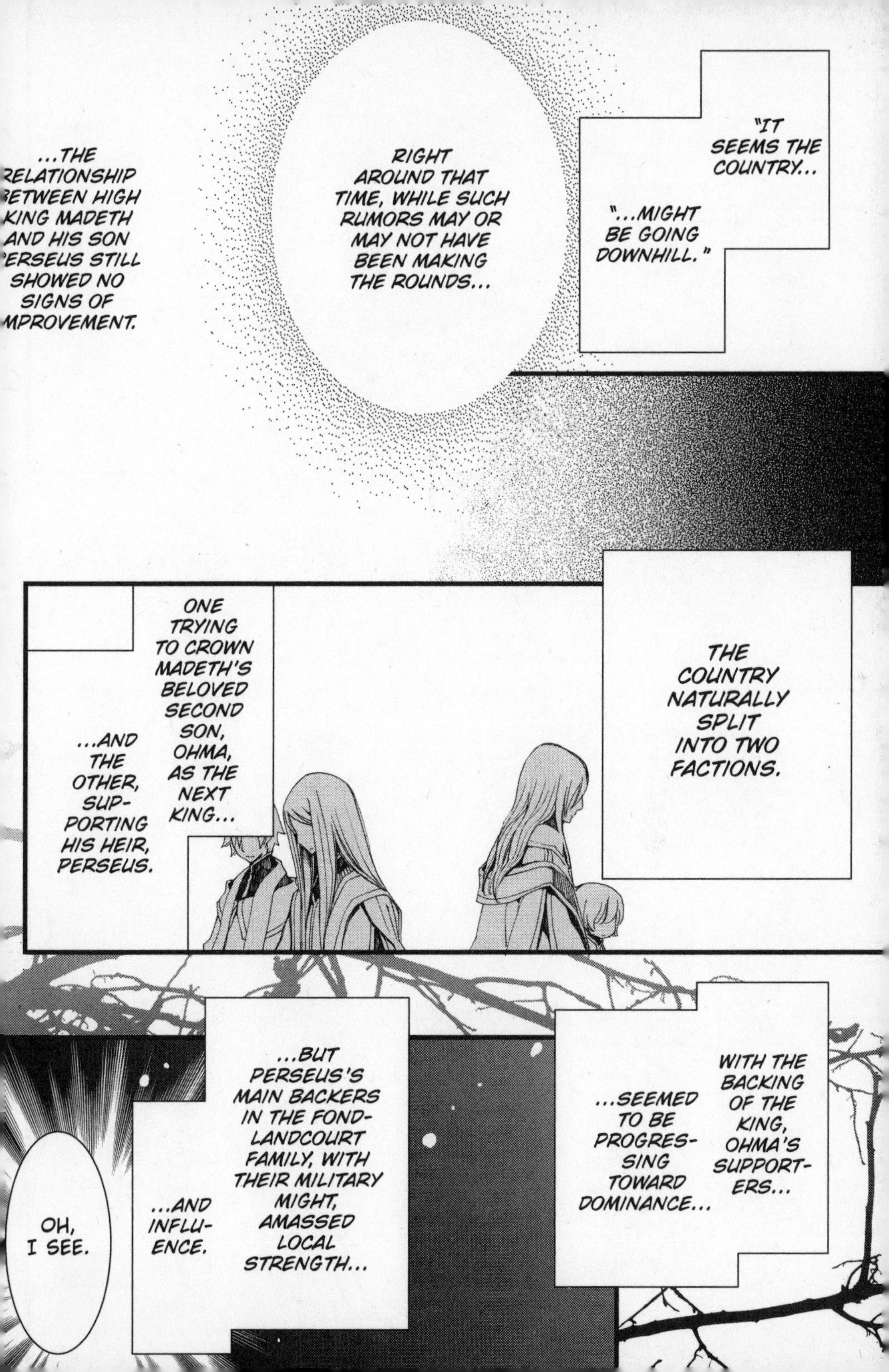
"IT SEEMS THE COUNTRY...
"...MIGHT BE GOING DOWNHILL."
RIGHT AROUND THAT TIME, WHILE SUCH RUMORS MAY OR MAY NOT HAVE BEEN MAKING THE ROUNDS...
...THE RELATIONSHIP BETWEEN HIGH KING MADETH AND HIS SON PERSEUS STILL SHOWED NO SIGNS OF IMPROVEMENT.
THE COUNTRY NATURALLY SPLIT INTO TWO FACTIONS.
ONE TRYING TO CROWN MADETH'S BELOVED SECOND SON, OHMA, AS THE NEXT KING...
...AND THE OTHER, SUPPORTING HIS HEIR, PERSEUS.
WITH THE BACKING OF THE KING, OHMA'S SUPPORTERS...
...SEEMED TO BE PROGRESSING TOWARD DOMINANCE...
...BUT PERSEUS'S MAIN BACKERS IN THE FOND-LANDCOURT FAMILY, WITH THEIR MILITARY MIGHT, AMASSED LOCAL STRENGTH...
...AND INFLUENCE.
OH, I SEE.

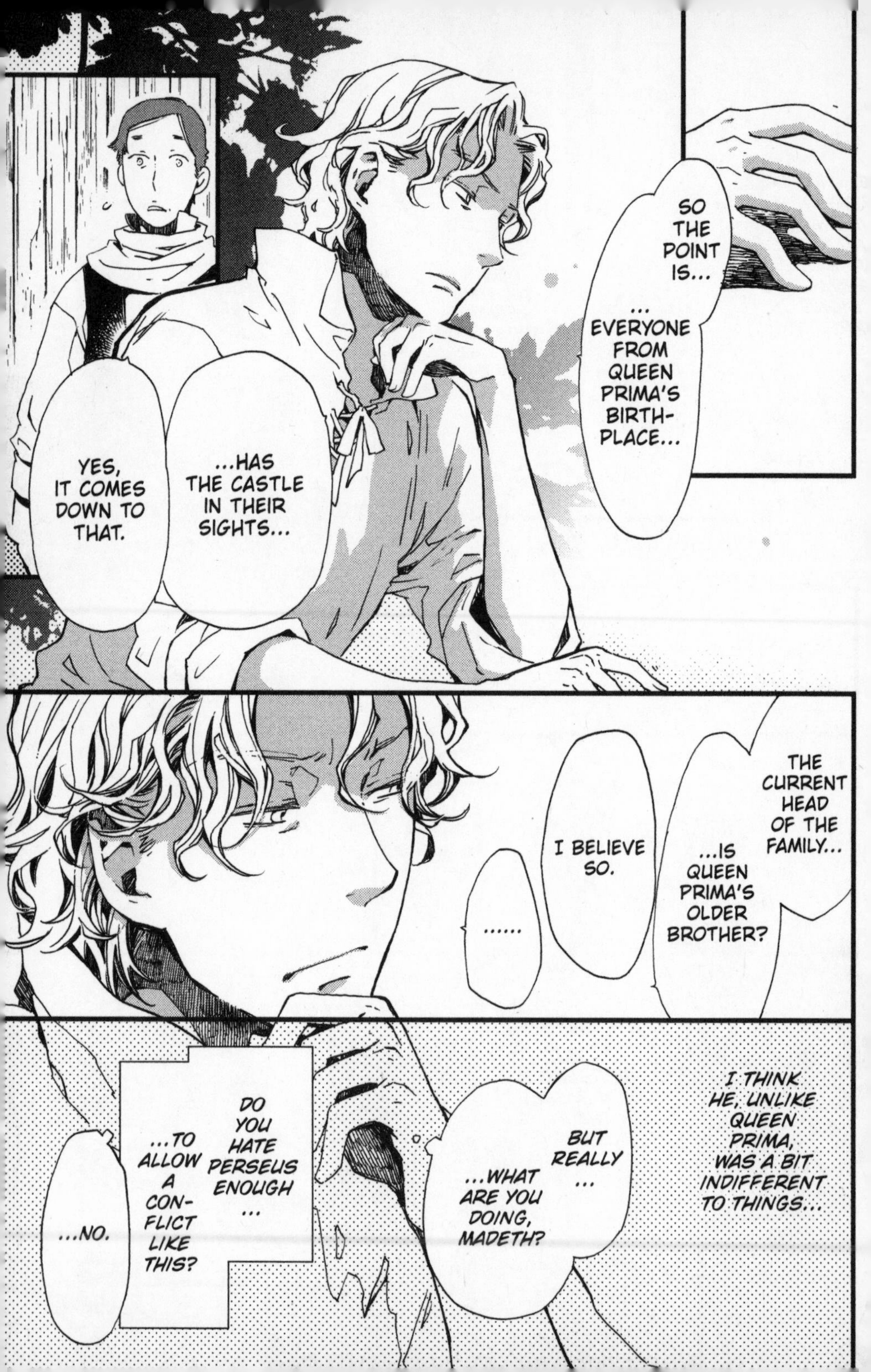
SO THE POINT IS...
...EVERYONE FROM QUEEN PRIMA'S BIRTH-PLACE...
...HAS THE CASTLE IN THEIR SIGHTS...
YES, IT COMES DOWN TO THAT.
THE CURRENT HEAD OF THE FAMILY...
...IS QUEEN PRIMA'S OLDER BROTHER?
I BELIEVE SO.
......
I THINK HE, UNLIKE QUEEN PRIMA, WAS A BIT INDIFFERENT TO THINGS...
BUT REALLY...
...WHAT ARE YOU DOING, MADETH?
DO YOU HATE PERSEUS ENOUGH...
...TO ALLOW A CON-FLICT LIKE THIS?
...NO.

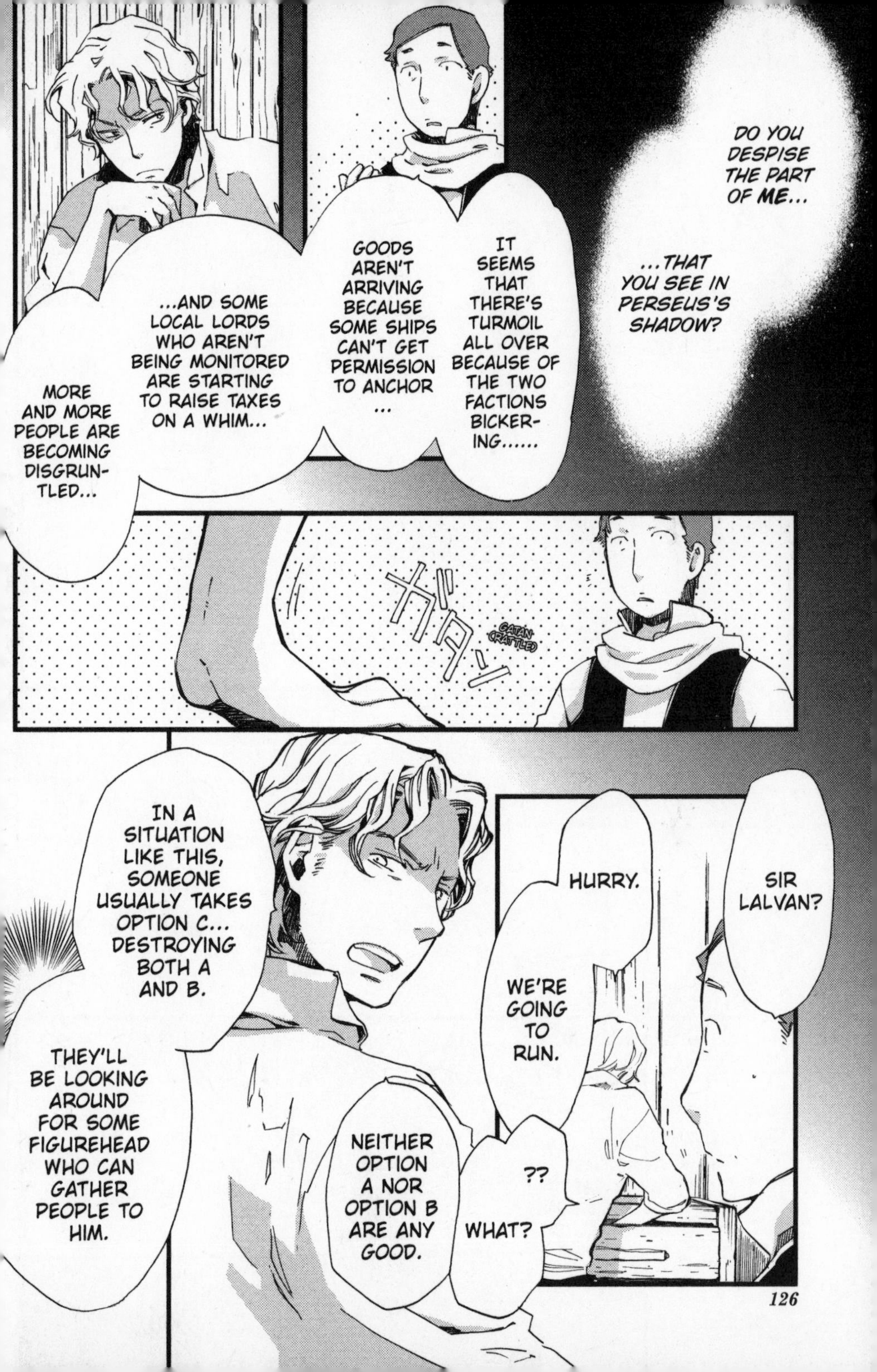
DO YOU DESPISE THE PART OF **ME**...
...THAT YOU SEE IN PERSEUS'S SHADOW?
IT SEEMS THAT THERE'S TURMOIL ALL OVER BECAUSE OF THE TWO FACTIONS BICKERING......
GOODS AREN'T ARRIVING BECAUSE SOME SHIPS CAN'T GET PERMISSION TO ANCHOR ...
...AND SOME LOCAL LORDS WHO AREN'T BEING MONITORED ARE STARTING TO RAISE TAXES ON A WHIM...
MORE AND MORE PEOPLE ARE BECOMING DISGRUNTLED...
GATAN (RATTLED)
SIR LALVAN?
HURRY.
WE'RE GOING TO RUN.
??
WHAT?
NEITHER OPTION A NOR OPTION B ARE ANY GOOD.
IN A SITUATION LIKE THIS, SOMEONE USUALLY TAKES OPTION C... DESTROYING BOTH A AND B.
THEY'LL BE LOOKING AROUND FOR SOME FIGUREHEAD WHO CAN GATHER PEOPLE TO HIM.

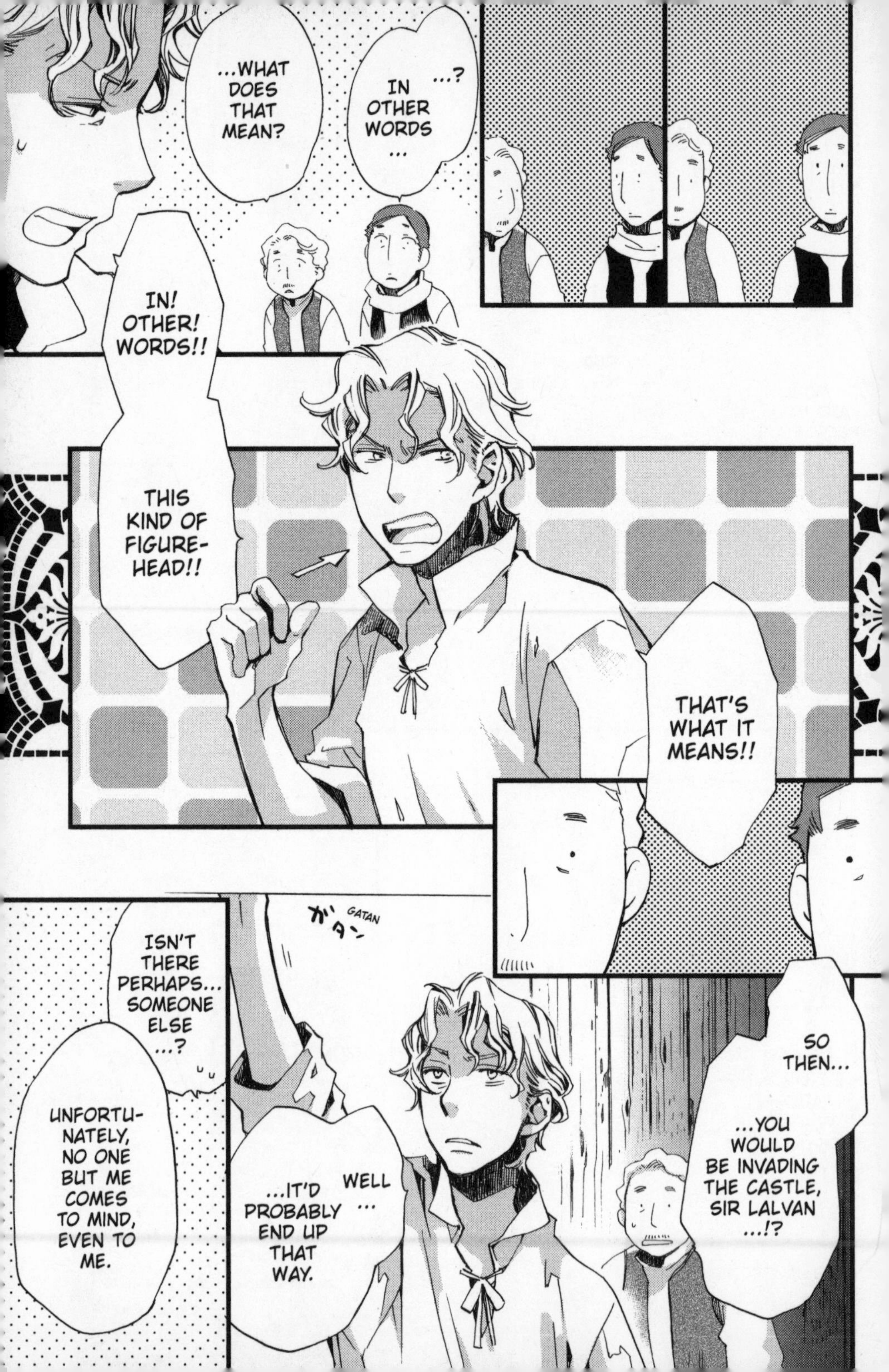
IN OTHER WORDS ...
...?
...WHAT DOES THAT MEAN?
IN! OTHER! WORDS!! THIS KIND OF FIGUREHEAD!!
THAT'S WHAT IT MEANS!!
SO THEN...
...YOU WOULD BE INVADING THE CASTLE, SIR LALVAN ...!?
ガタン GATAN
WELL ...
...IT'D PROBABLY END UP THAT WAY.
ISN'T THERE PERHAPS... SOMEONE ELSE ...?
UNFORTUNATELY, NO ONE BUT ME COMES TO MIND, EVEN TO ME.

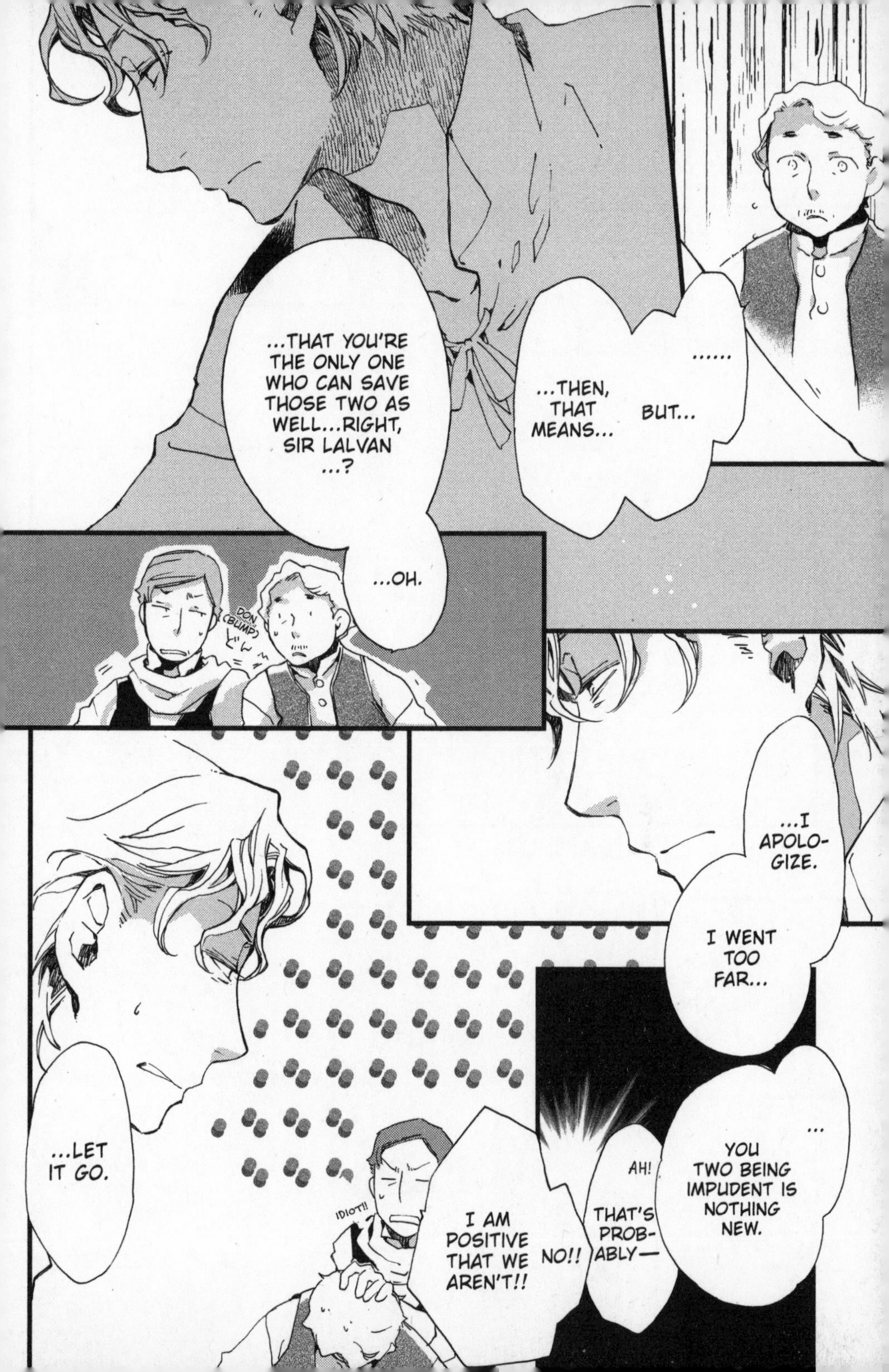
......
BUT...
...THEN, THAT MEANS...
...THAT YOU'RE THE ONLY ONE WHO CAN SAVE THOSE TWO AS WELL...RIGHT, SIR LALVAN ...?
...OH.
DON (BUMP)
...I APOLOGIZE.
I WENT TOO FAR...
...
YOU TWO BEING IMPUDENT IS NOTHING NEW.
AH!
THAT'S PROBABLY—
NO!!
I AM POSITIVE THAT WE AREN'T!!
IDIOT!!
...LET IT GO.

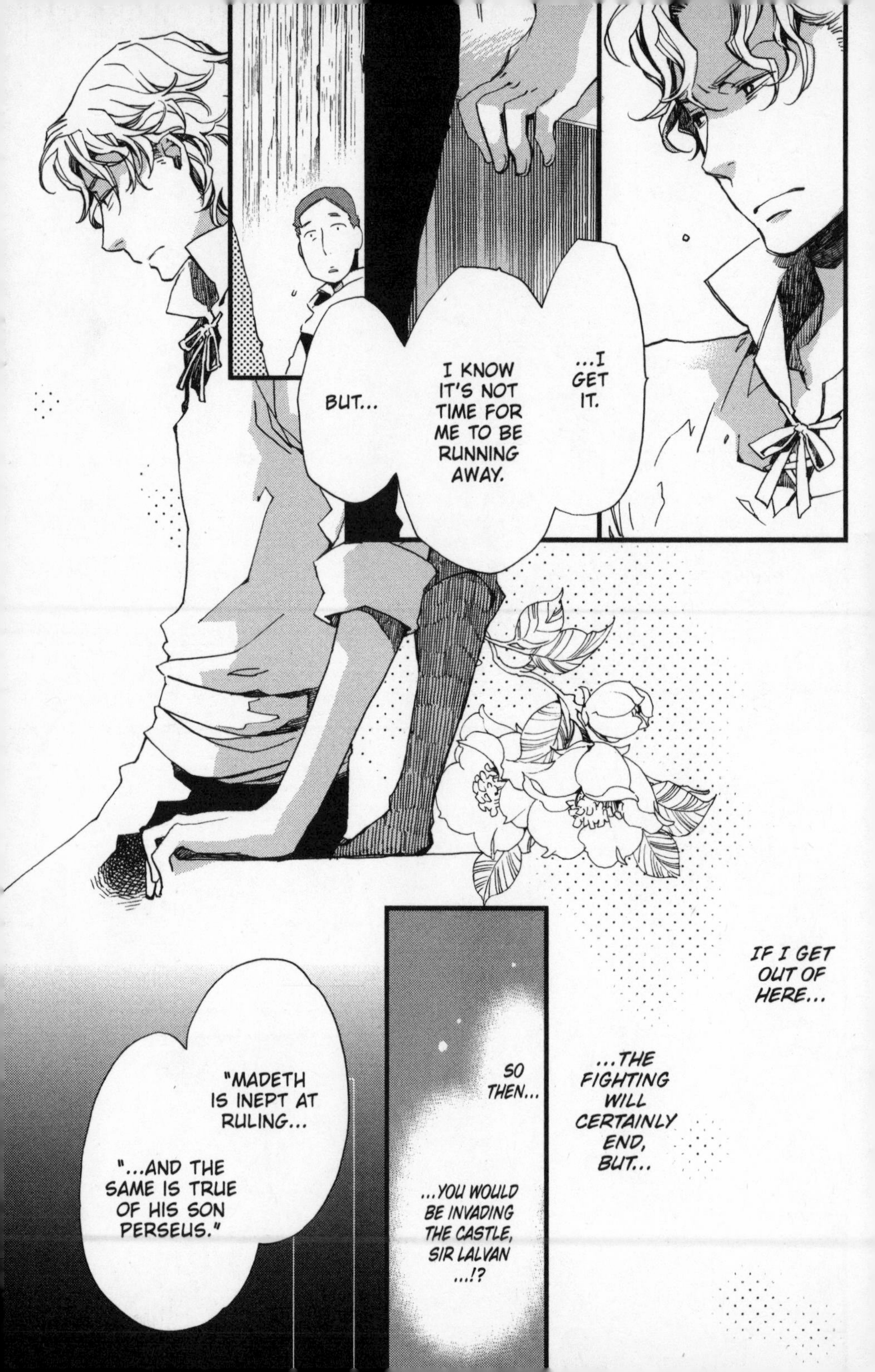
...I GET IT.
I KNOW IT'S NOT TIME FOR ME TO BE RUNNING AWAY.
BUT...
IF I GET OUT OF HERE...
...THE FIGHTING WILL CERTAINLY END, BUT...
SO THEN...
...YOU WOULD BE INVADING THE CASTLE, SIR LALVAN ...!?
"MADETH IS INEPT AT RULING...
"...AND THE SAME IS TRUE OF HIS SON PERSEUS."

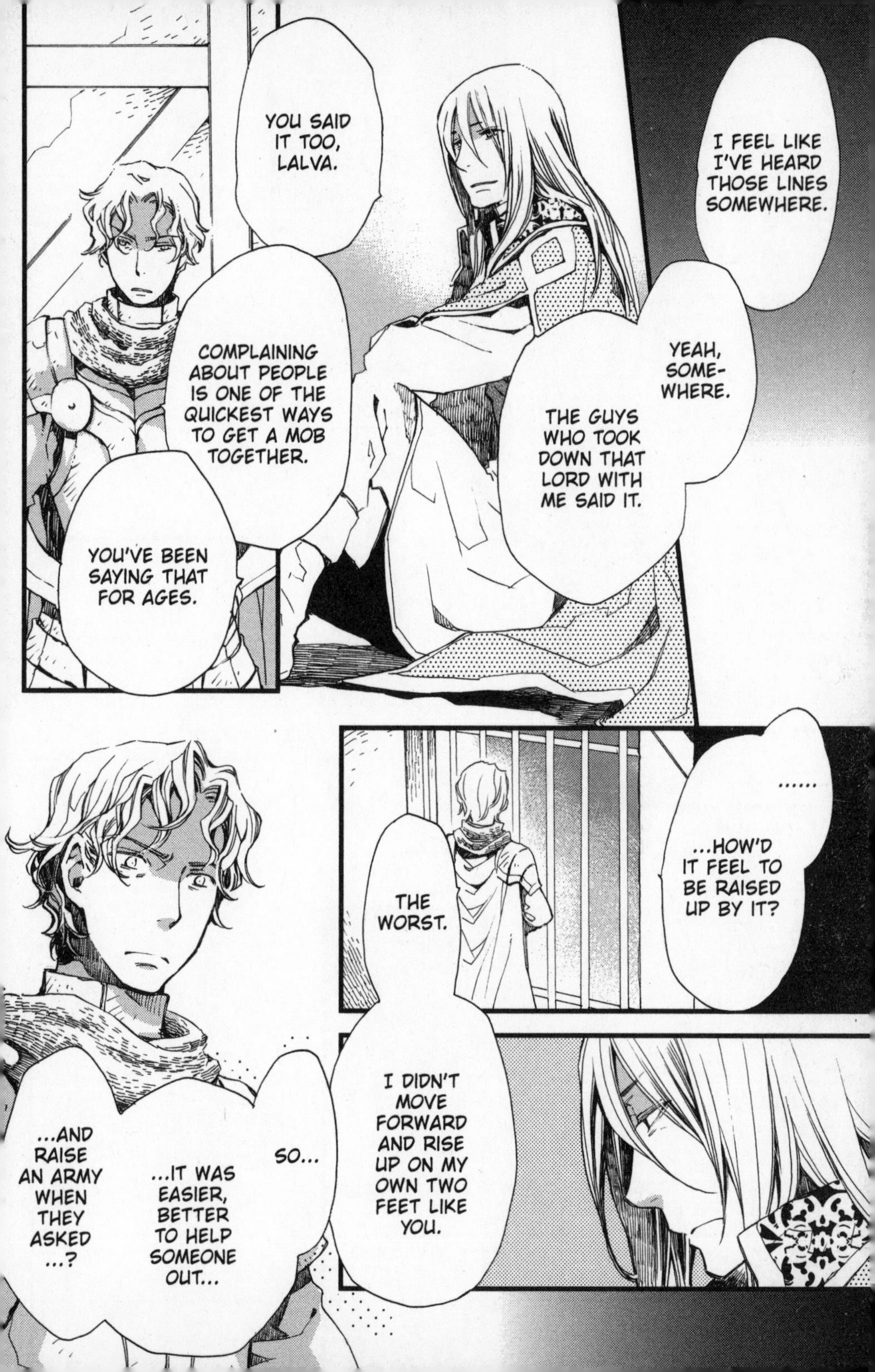
I FEEL LIKE I'VE HEARD THOSE LINES SOMEWHERE.
YOU SAID IT TOO, LALVA.
YEAH, SOME-WHERE.
THE GUYS WHO TOOK DOWN THAT LORD WITH ME SAID IT.
COMPLAINING ABOUT PEOPLE IS ONE OF THE QUICKEST WAYS TO GET A MOB TOGETHER.
YOU'VE BEEN SAYING THAT FOR AGES.
......
...HOW'D IT FEEL TO BE RAISED UP BY IT?
THE WORST.
I DIDN'T MOVE FORWARD AND RISE UP ON MY OWN TWO FEET LIKE YOU.
SO...
...IT WAS EASIER, BETTER TO HELP SOMEONE OUT...
...AND RAISE AN ARMY WHEN THEY ASKED ...?

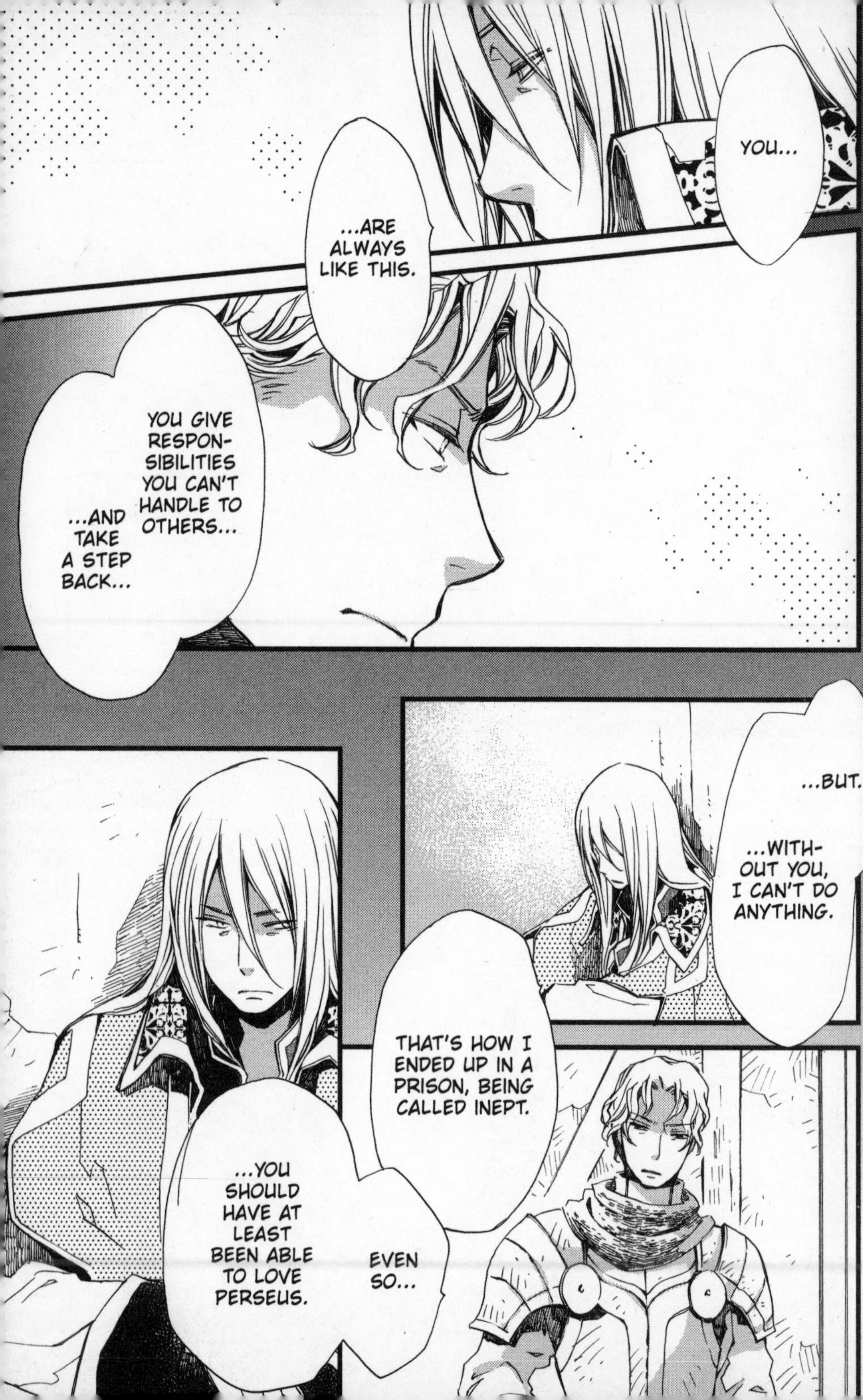
YOU...
...ARE ALWAYS LIKE THIS.
YOU GIVE RESPON-SIBILITIES YOU CAN'T HANDLE TO OTHERS...
...AND TAKE A STEP BACK...
...BUT...
...WITH-OUT YOU, I CAN'T DO ANYTHING.
THAT'S HOW I ENDED UP IN A PRISON, BEING CALLED INEPT.
EVEN SO...
...YOU SHOULD HAVE AT LEAST BEEN ABLE TO LOVE PERSEUS.

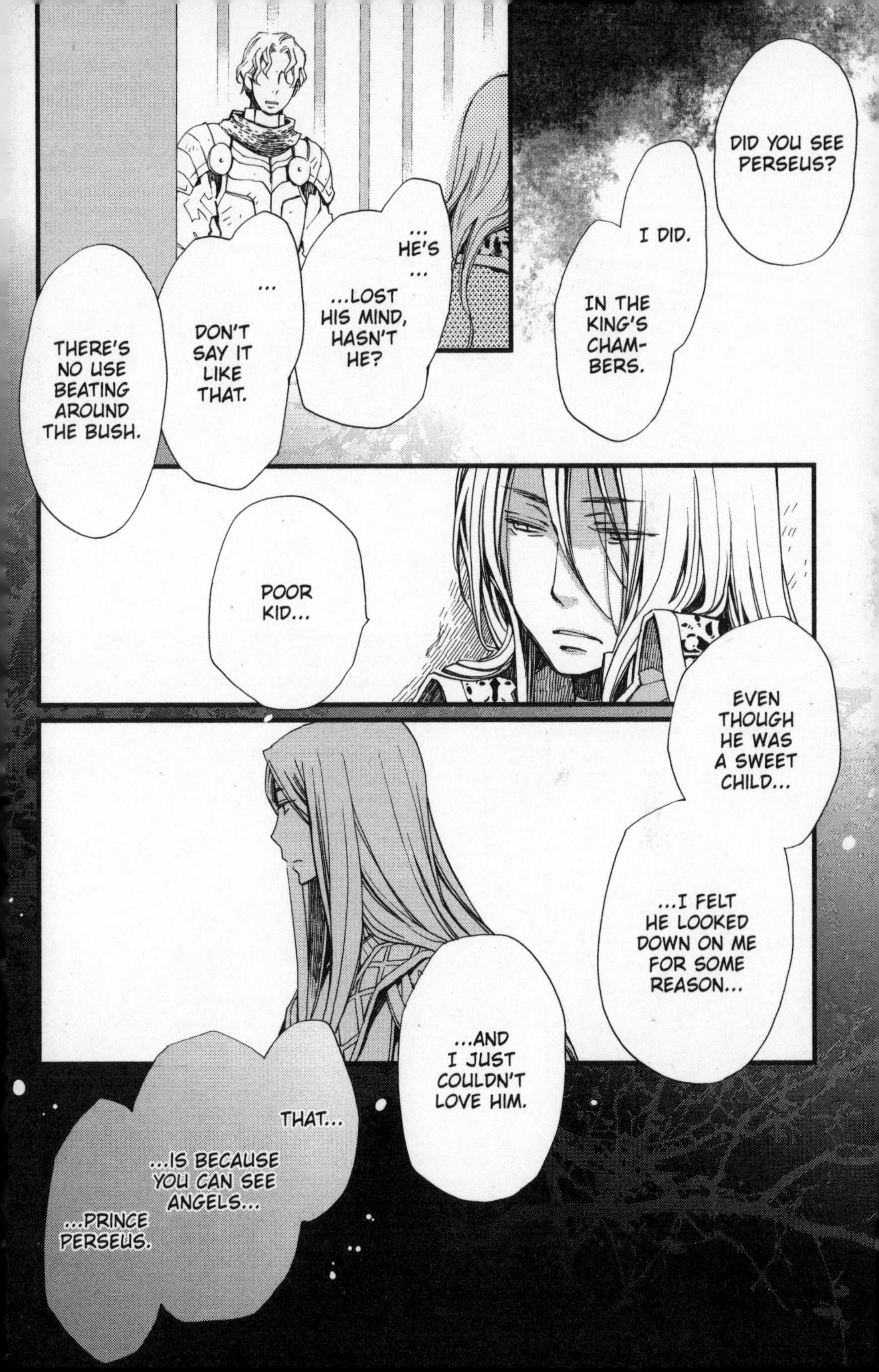
DID YOU SEE PERSEUS?
I DID.
IN THE KING'S CHAMBERS.
... HE'S ...
...LOST HIS MIND, HASN'T HE?
...
DON'T SAY IT LIKE THAT.
THERE'S NO USE BEATING AROUND THE BUSH.
POOR KID...
EVEN THOUGH HE WAS A SWEET CHILD...
...I FELT HE LOOKED DOWN ON ME FOR SOME REASON...
...AND I JUST COULDN'T LOVE HIM.
THAT...
...IS BECAUSE YOU CAN SEE ANGELS...
...PRINCE PERSEUS.

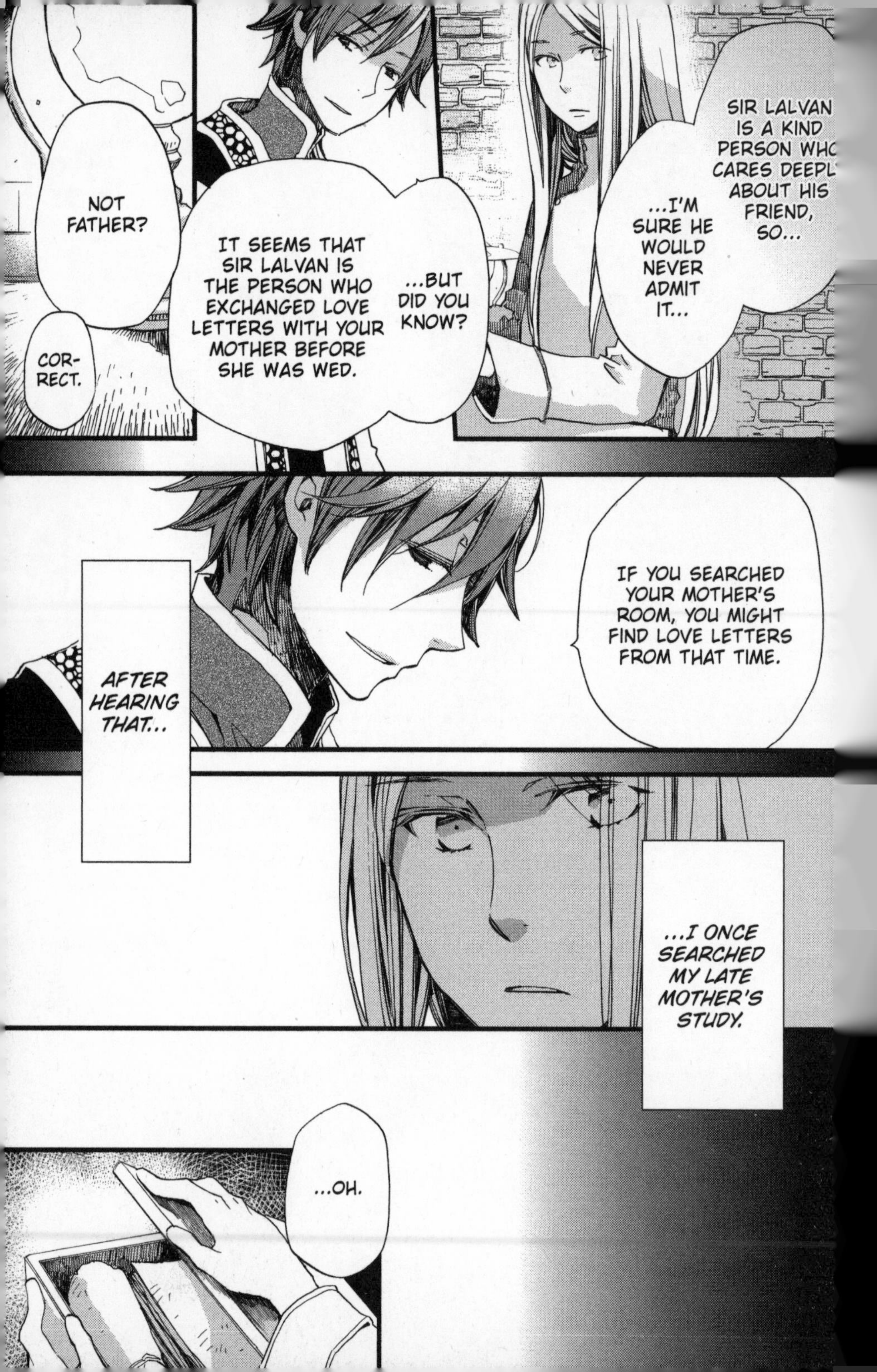
SIR LALVAN IS A KIND PERSON WHO CARES DEEPL ABOUT HIS FRIEND, SO...
...I'M SURE HE WOULD NEVER ADMIT IT...
...BUT DID YOU KNOW?
IT SEEMS THAT SIR LALVAN IS THE PERSON WHO EXCHANGED LOVE LETTERS WITH YOUR MOTHER BEFORE SHE WAS WED.
NOT FATHER?
COR-RECT.
IF YOU SEARCHED YOUR MOTHER'S ROOM, YOU MIGHT FIND LOVE LETTERS FROM THAT TIME.
AFTER HEARING THAT...
...I ONCE SEARCHED MY LATE MOTHER'S STUDY.
...OH.

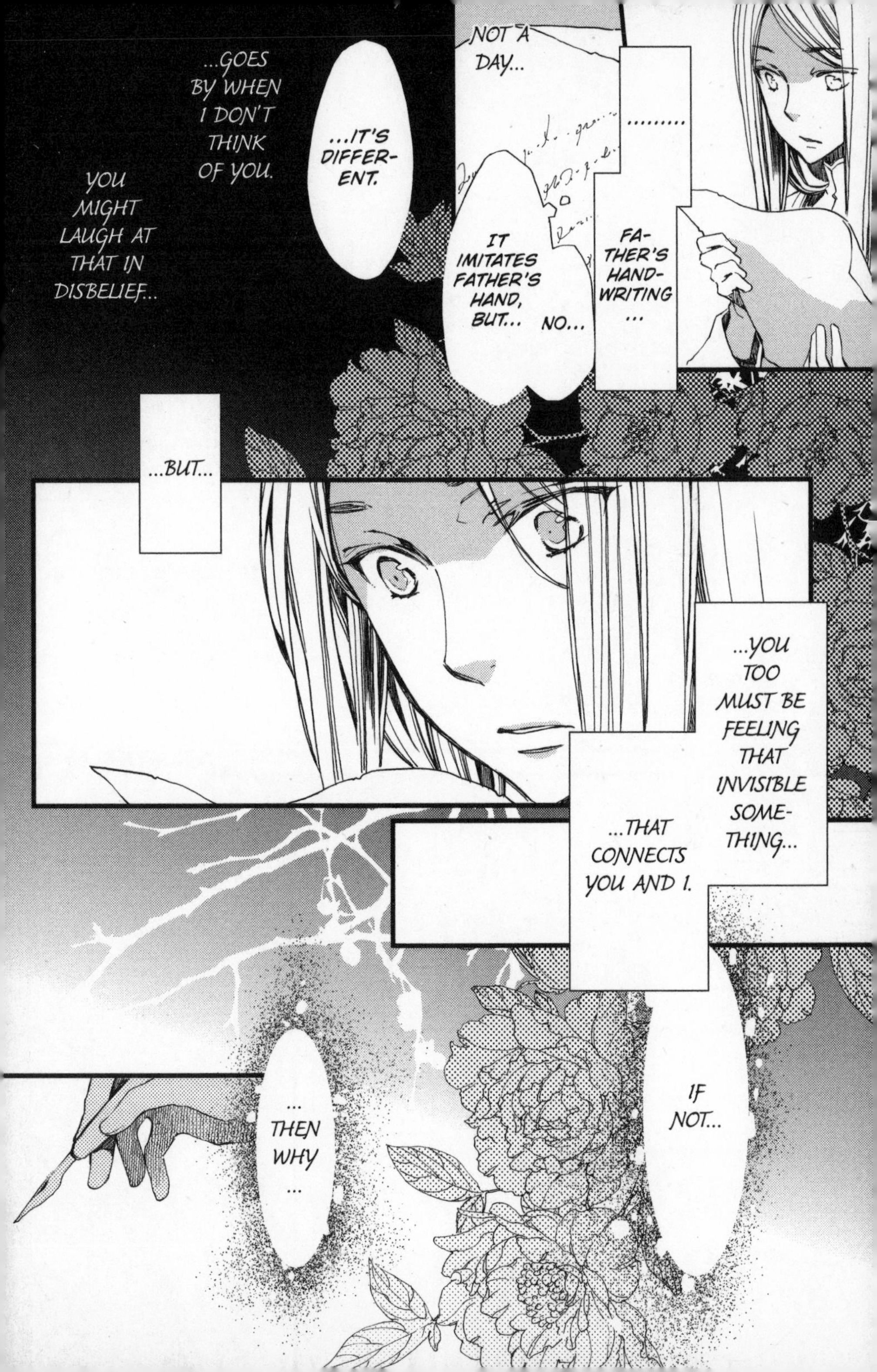
....
FA-THER'S HAND-WRITING...
NOT A DAY...
NO...
IT IMITATES FATHER'S HAND, BUT...
...IT'S DIFFER-ENT.
...GOES BY WHEN I DON'T THINK OF YOU.
YOU MIGHT LAUGH AT THAT IN DISBELIEF...
...BUT...
...YOU TOO MUST BE FEELING THAT INVISIBLE SOME-THING...
...THAT CONNECTS YOU AND I.
IF NOT...
...THEN WHY...

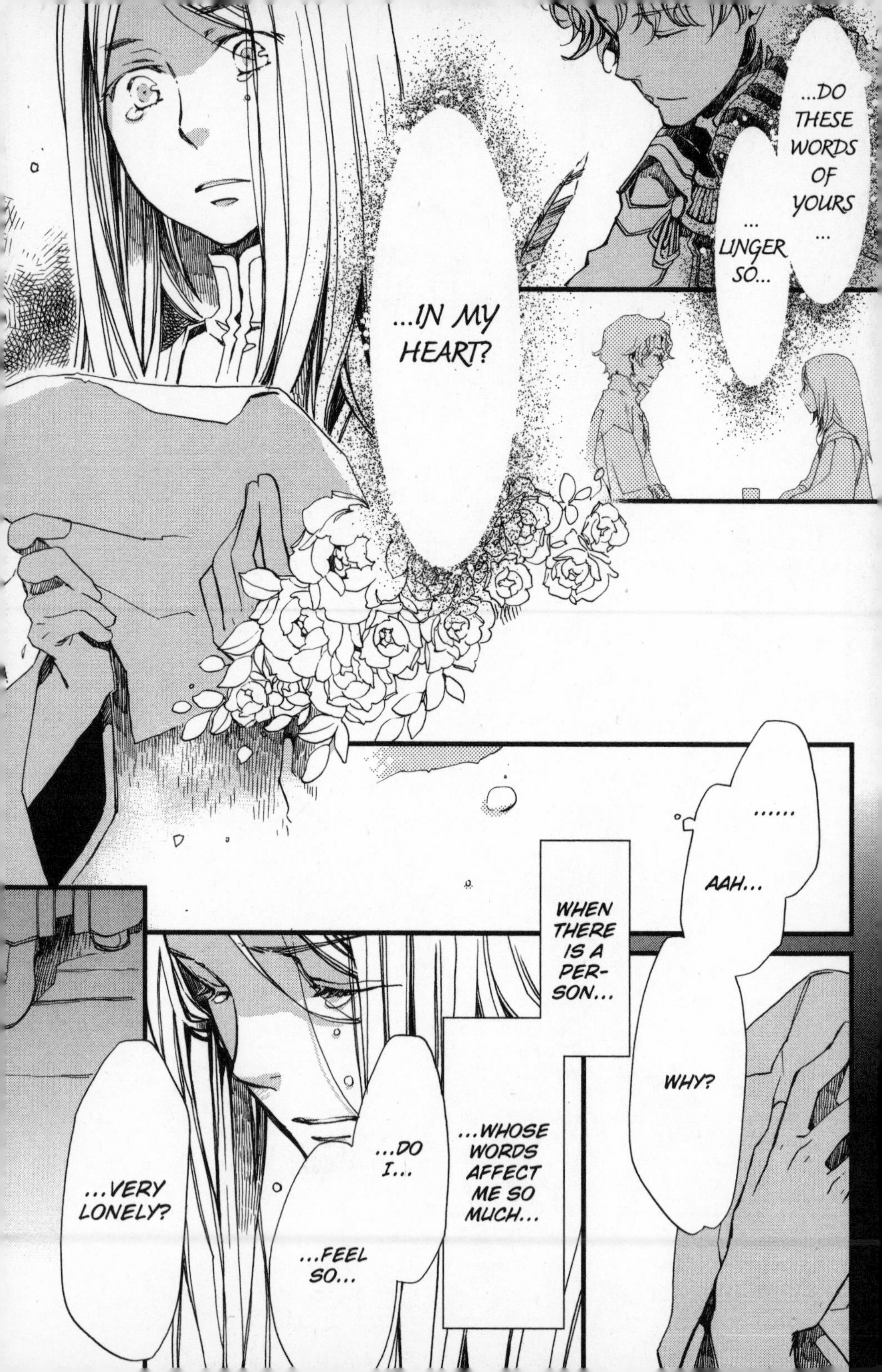
...DO THESE WORDS OF YOURS ...
... LINGER SO...
...IN MY HEART?
......
AAH...
WHY?
WHEN THERE IS A PER-SON...
...WHOSE WORDS AFFECT ME SO MUCH...
...DO I...
...FEEL SO...
...VERY LONELY?

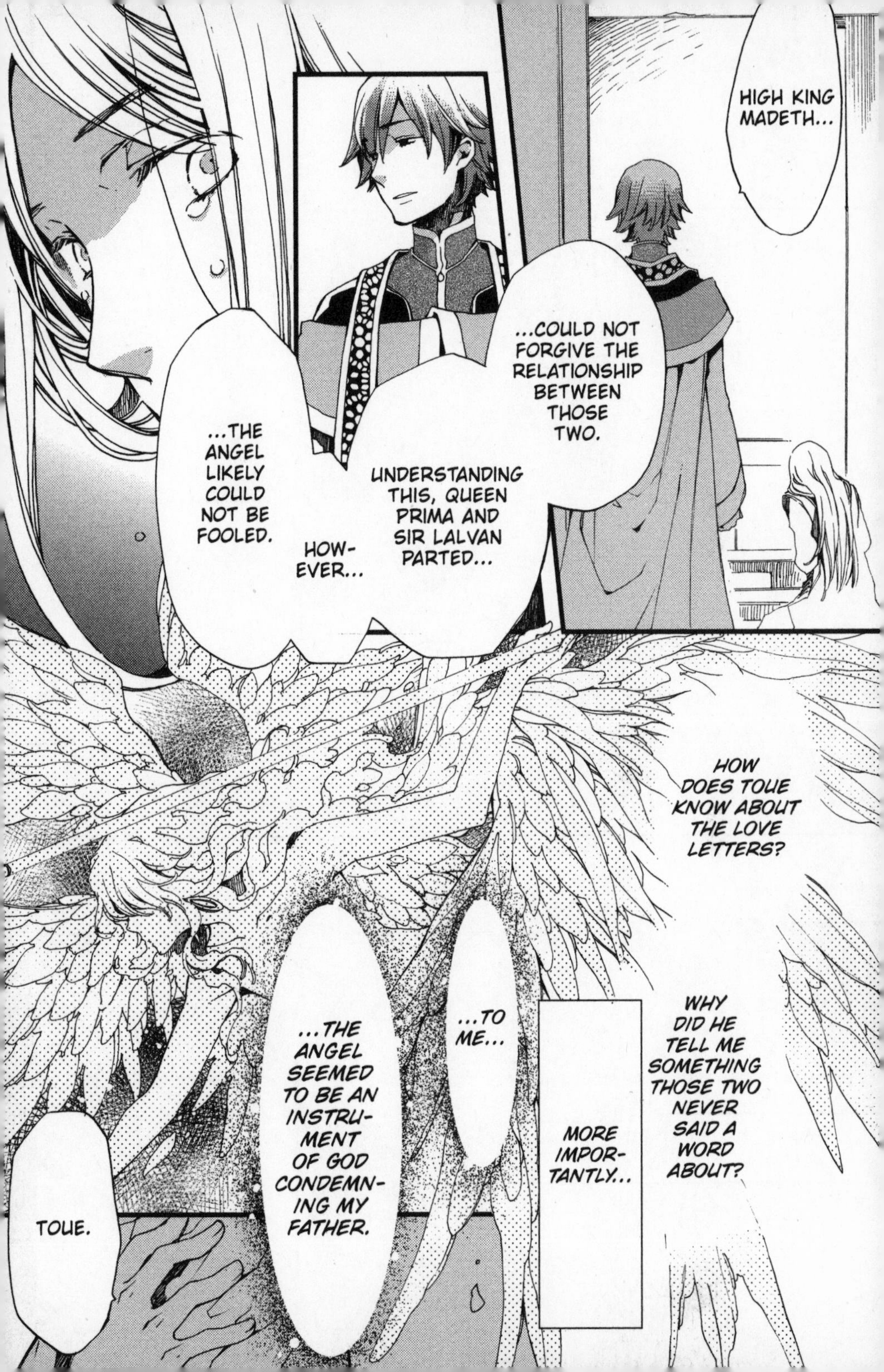
HIGH KING MADETH...
...COULD NOT FORGIVE THE RELATIONSHIP BETWEEN THOSE TWO.
UNDERSTANDING THIS, QUEEN PRIMA AND SIR LALVAN PARTED...
HOW-EVER...
...THE ANGEL LIKELY COULD NOT BE FOOLED.
HOW DOES TOUE KNOW ABOUT THE LOVE LETTERS?
WHY DID HE TELL ME SOMETHING THOSE TWO NEVER SAID A WORD ABOUT?
MORE IMPOR-TANTLY...
...TO ME...
...THE ANGEL SEEMED TO BE AN INSTRU-MENT OF GOD CONDEMN-ING MY FATHER.
TOUE.

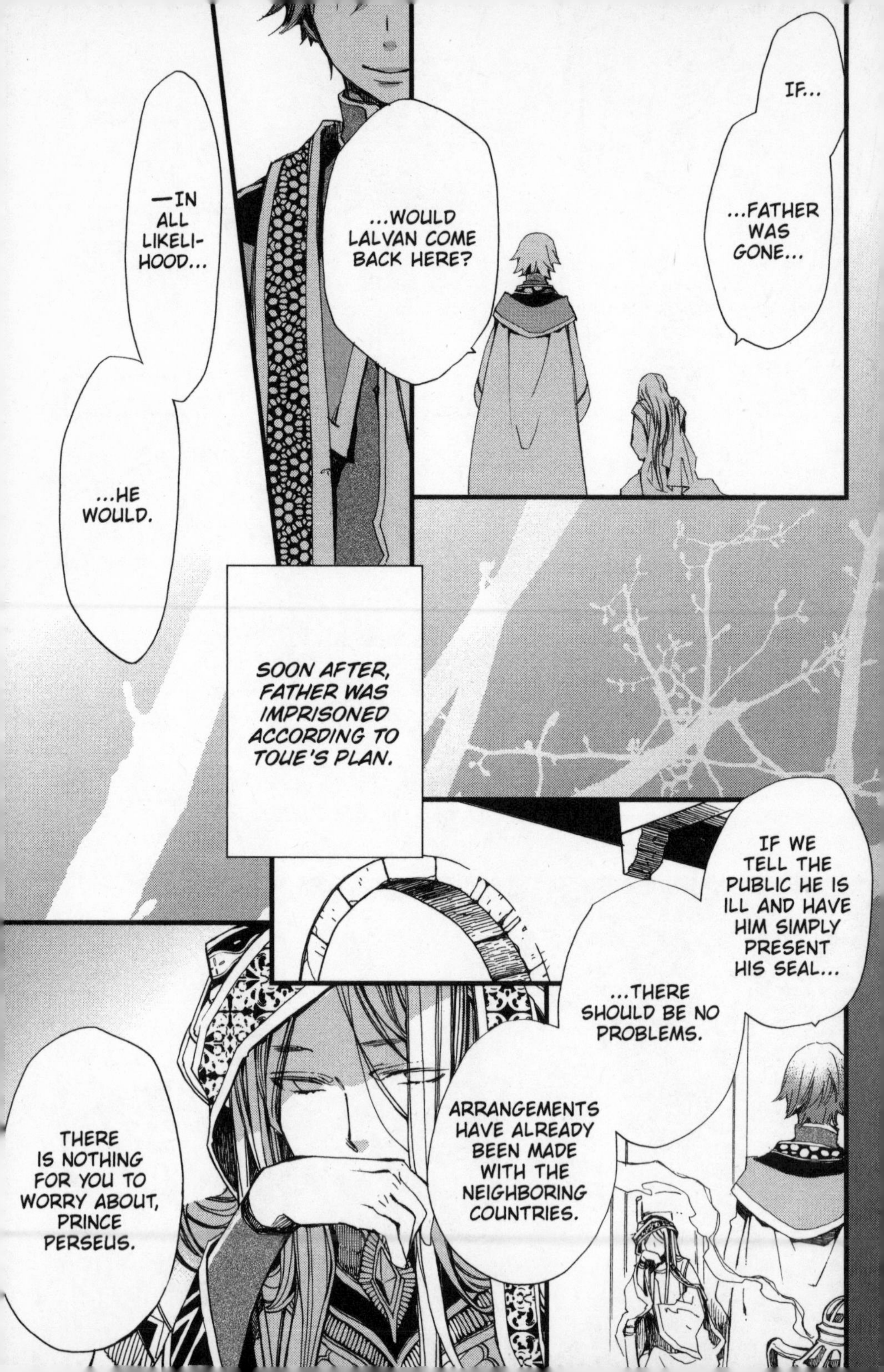
IF...
...FATHER WAS GONE...
...WOULD LALVAN COME BACK HERE?
—IN ALL LIKELI-HOOD...
...HE WOULD.
SOON AFTER, FATHER WAS IMPRISONED ACCORDING TO TOUE'S PLAN.
IF WE TELL THE PUBLIC HE IS ILL AND HAVE HIM SIMPLY PRESENT HIS SEAL...
...THERE SHOULD BE NO PROBLEMS.
ARRANGEMENTS HAVE ALREADY BEEN MADE WITH THE NEIGHBORING COUNTRIES.
THERE IS NOTHING FOR YOU TO WORRY ABOUT, PRINCE PERSEUS.

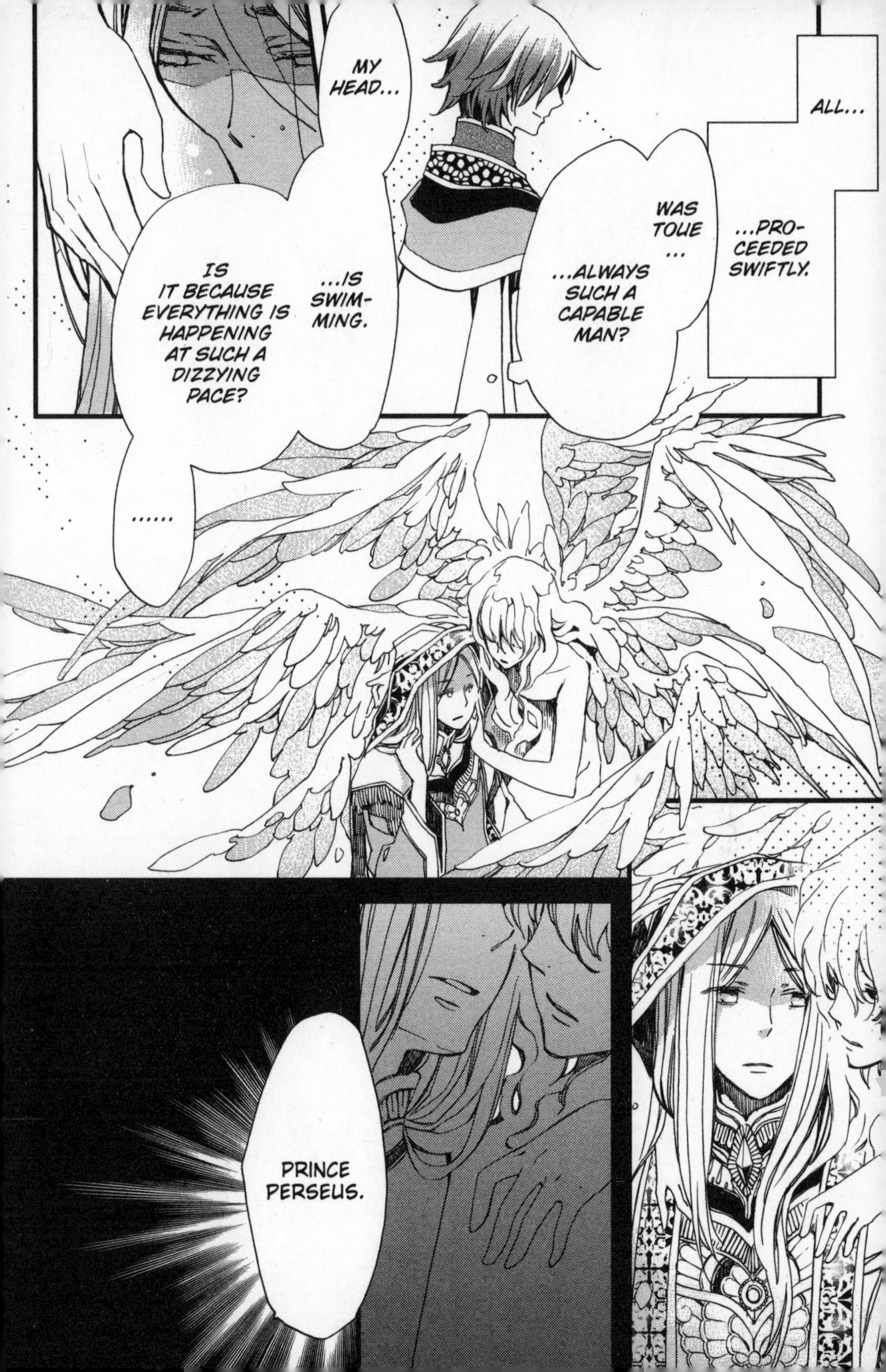
ALL...
...PRO-CEEDED SWIFTLY.
WAS TOUE ...
...ALWAYS SUCH A CAPABLE MAN?
MY HEAD...
...IS SWIM-MING.
IS IT BECAUSE EVERYTHING IS HAPPENING AT SUCH A DIZZYING PACE?
......
PRINCE PERSEUS.

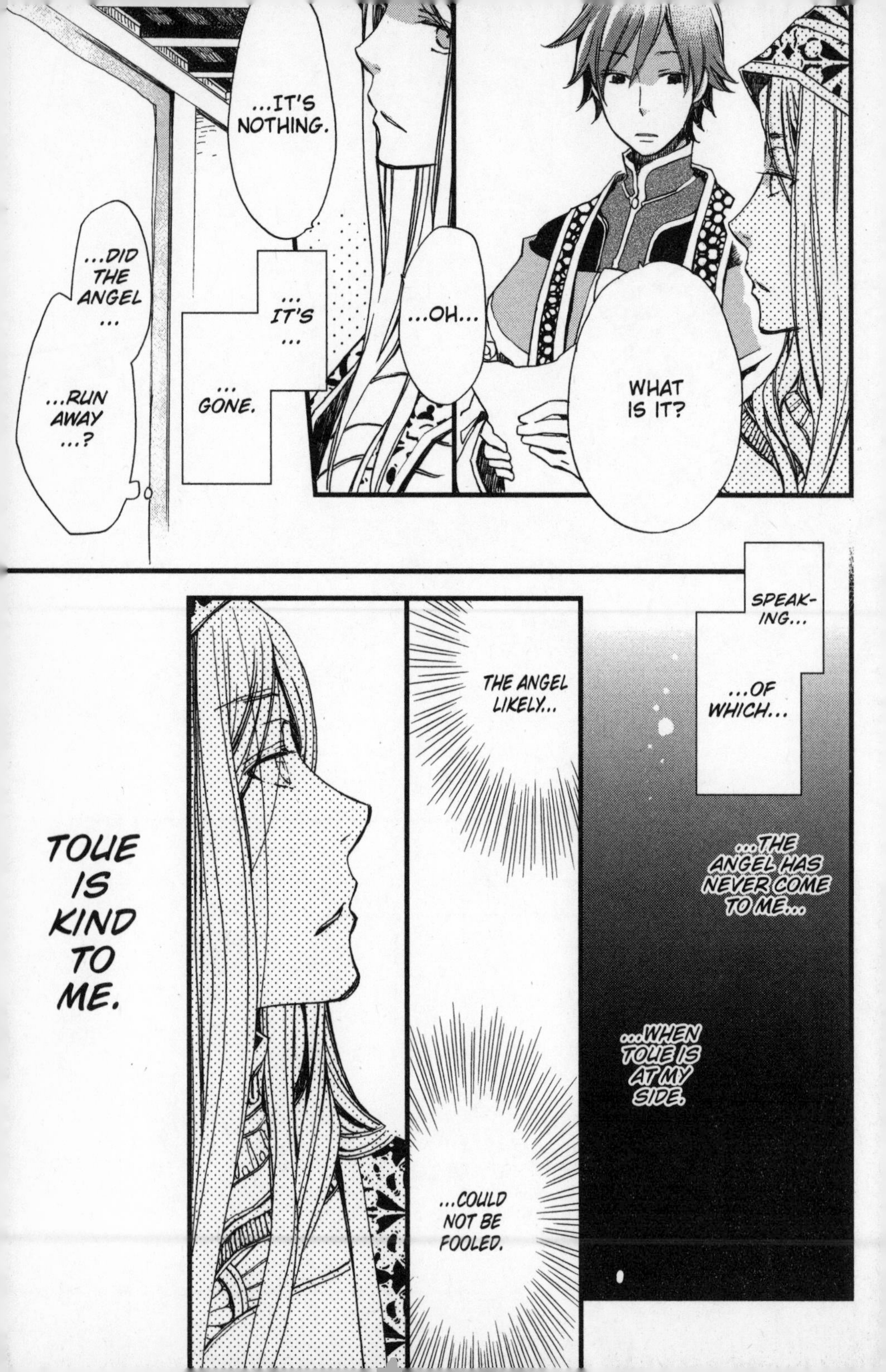
WHAT IS IT?
...OH...
...IT'S NOTHING.
...IT'S... ...GONE.
...DID THE ANGEL... ...RUN AWAY...?
SPEAK-ING... ...OF WHICH...
...THE ANGEL HAS NEVER COME TO ME...
...WHEN TOUE IS AT MY SIDE.
THE ANGEL LIKELY...
...COULD NOT BE FOOLED.
TOUE IS KIND TO ME.

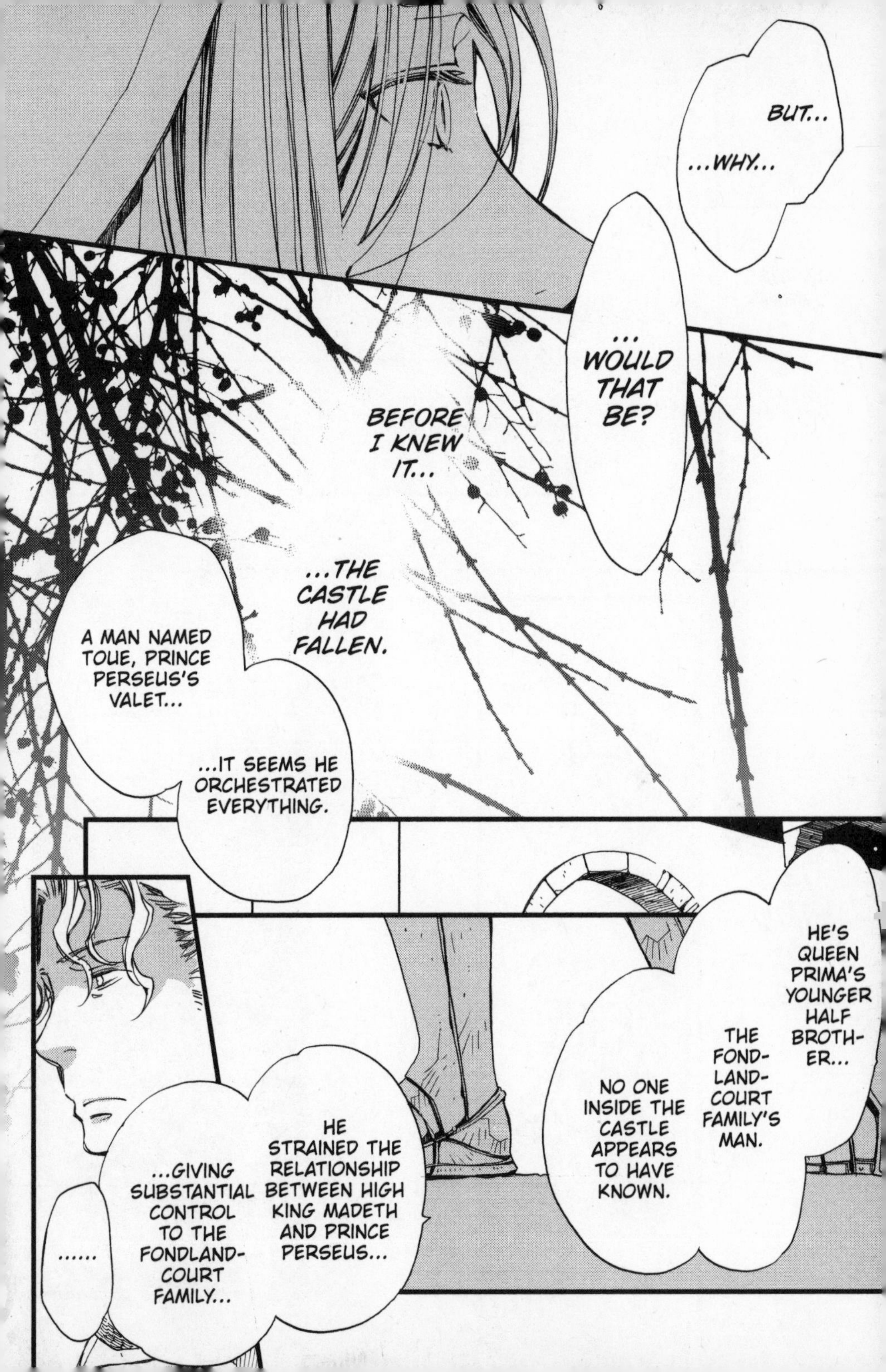
BUT...
...WHY...
...WOULD THAT BE?
BEFORE I KNEW IT...
...THE CASTLE HAD FALLEN.
A MAN NAMED TOUE, PRINCE PERSEUS'S VALET...
...IT SEEMS HE ORCHESTRATED EVERYTHING.
HE'S QUEEN PRIMA'S YOUNGER HALF BROTHER...
THE FONDLAND-COURT FAMILY'S MAN.
NO ONE INSIDE THE CASTLE APPEARS TO HAVE KNOWN.
HE STRAINED THE RELATIONSHIP BETWEEN HIGH KING MADETH AND PRINCE PERSEUS...
...GIVING SUBSTANTIAL CONTROL TO THE FONDLAND-COURT FAMILY...
......

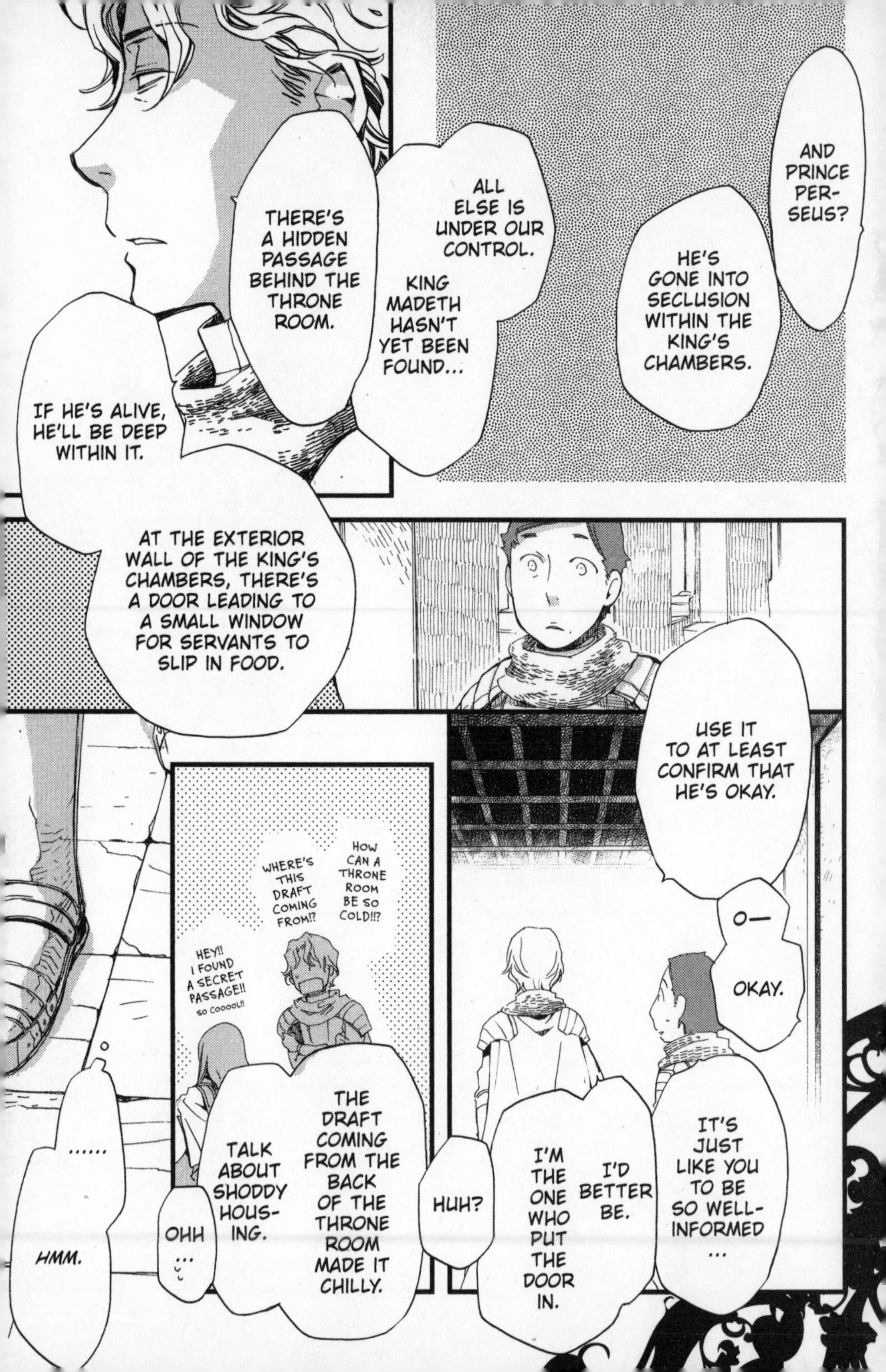
AND PRINCE PERSEUS?
HE'S GONE INTO SECLUSION WITHIN THE KING'S CHAMBERS.
ALL ELSE IS UNDER OUR CONTROL.
KING MADETH HASN'T YET BEEN FOUND...
THERE'S A HIDDEN PASSAGE BEHIND THE THRONE ROOM.
IF HE'S ALIVE, HE'LL BE DEEP WITHIN IT.
AT THE EXTERIOR WALL OF THE KING'S CHAMBERS, THERE'S A DOOR LEADING TO A SMALL WINDOW FOR SERVANTS TO SLIP IN FOOD.
USE IT TO AT LEAST CONFIRM THAT HE'S OKAY.
O— OKAY.
IT'S JUST LIKE YOU TO BE SO WELL-INFORMED...
I'D BETTER BE.
I'M THE ONE WHO PUT THE DOOR IN.
HUH?
HOW CAN A THRONE ROOM BE SO COLD!!?
WHERE'S THIS DRAFT COMING FROM!?
HEY!! I FOUND A SECRET PASSAGE!! SO COOOOL!!
THE DRAFT COMING FROM THE BACK OF THE THRONE ROOM MADE IT CHILLY.
TALK ABOUT SHODDY HOUS-ING.
OHH...
......
HMM.

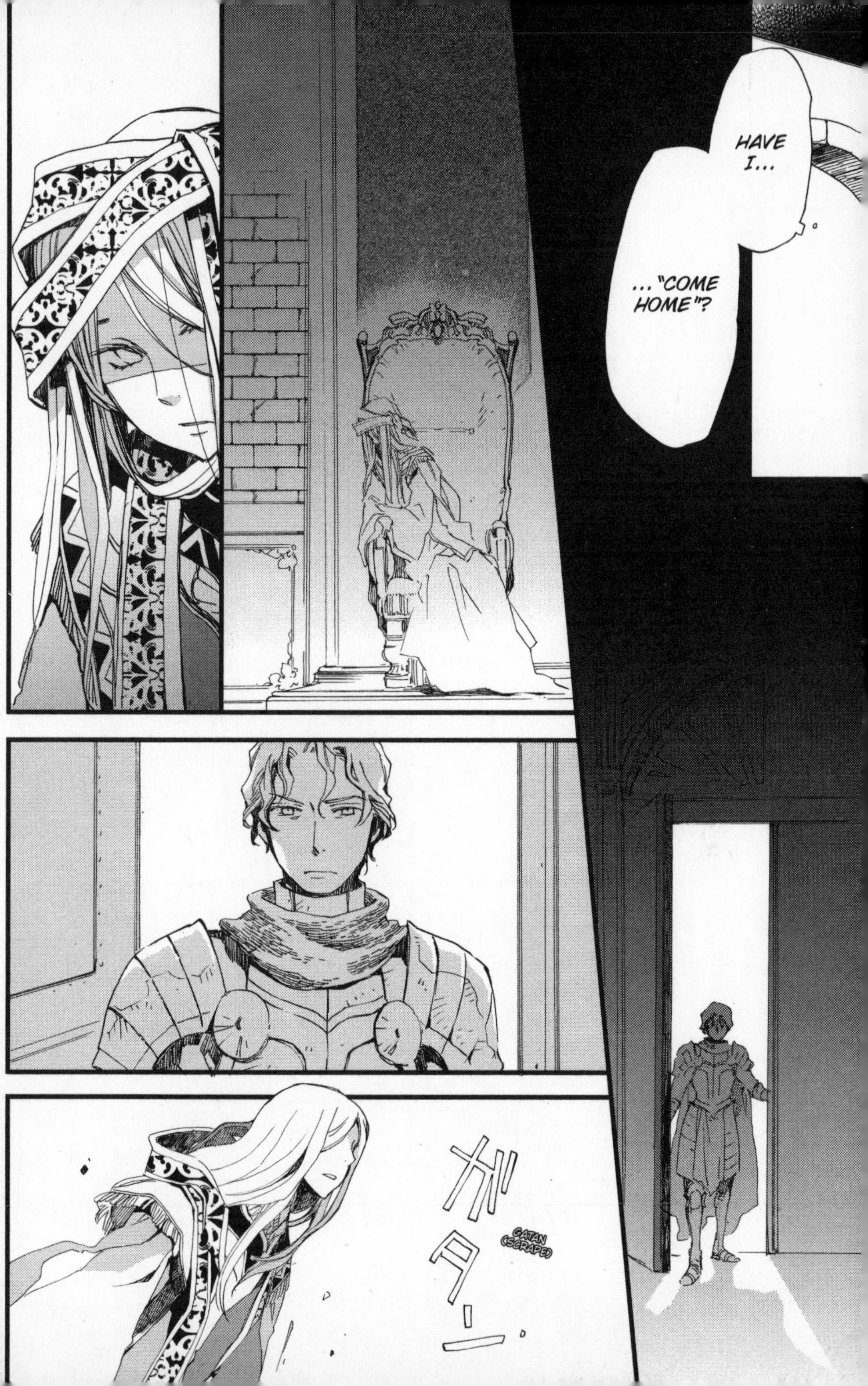
HAVE I...
..."COME HOME"?
ガタン
GATAN (SCRAPED)

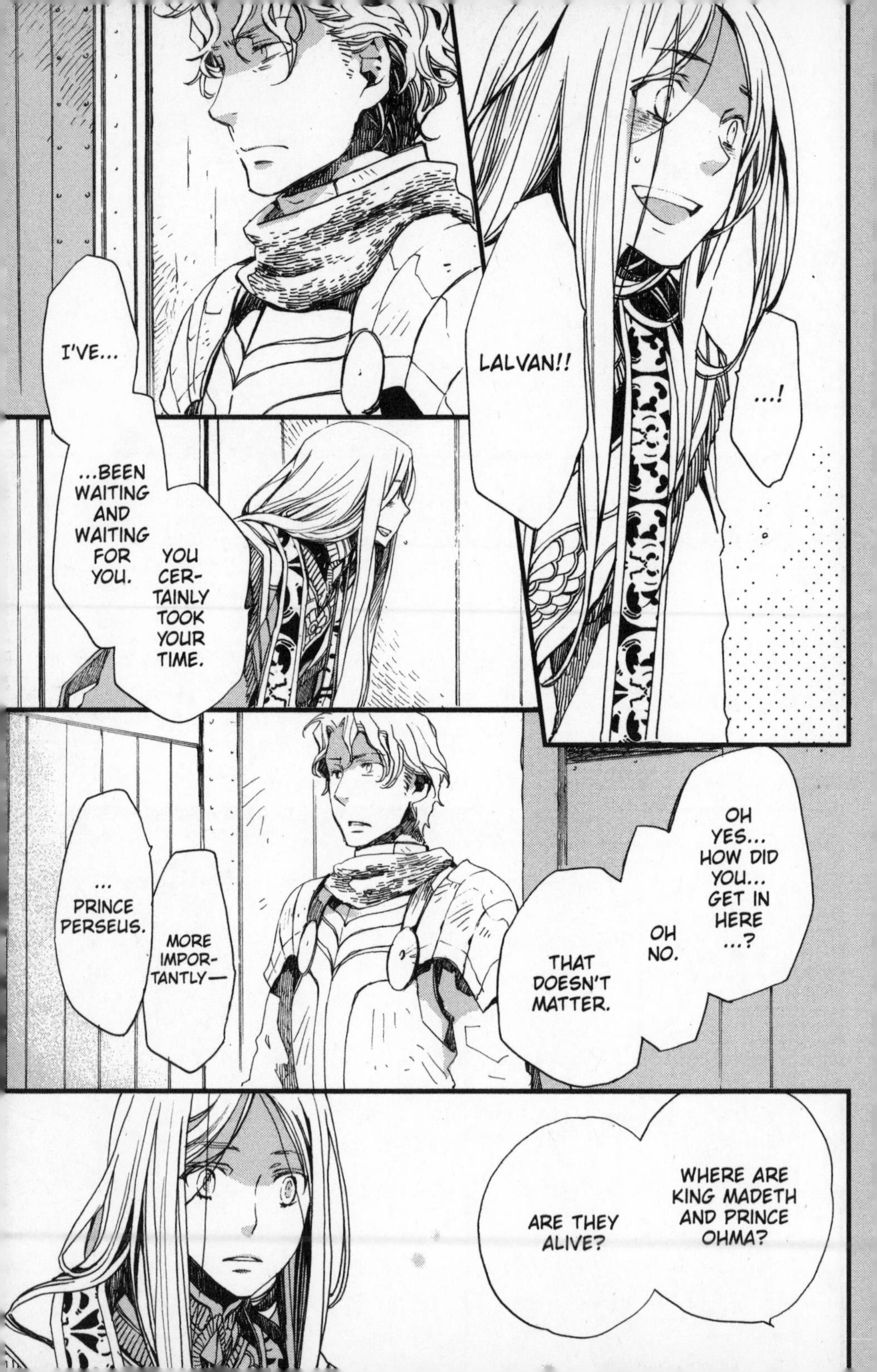
LALVAN!!
...!
I'VE...
...BEEN WAITING AND WAITING FOR YOU.
YOU CERTAINLY TOOK YOUR TIME.
OH YES... HOW DID YOU... GET IN HERE ...?
OH NO.
THAT DOESN'T MATTER.
... PRINCE PERSEUS.
MORE IMPORTANTLY—
WHERE ARE KING MADETH AND PRINCE OHMA?
ARE THEY ALIVE?

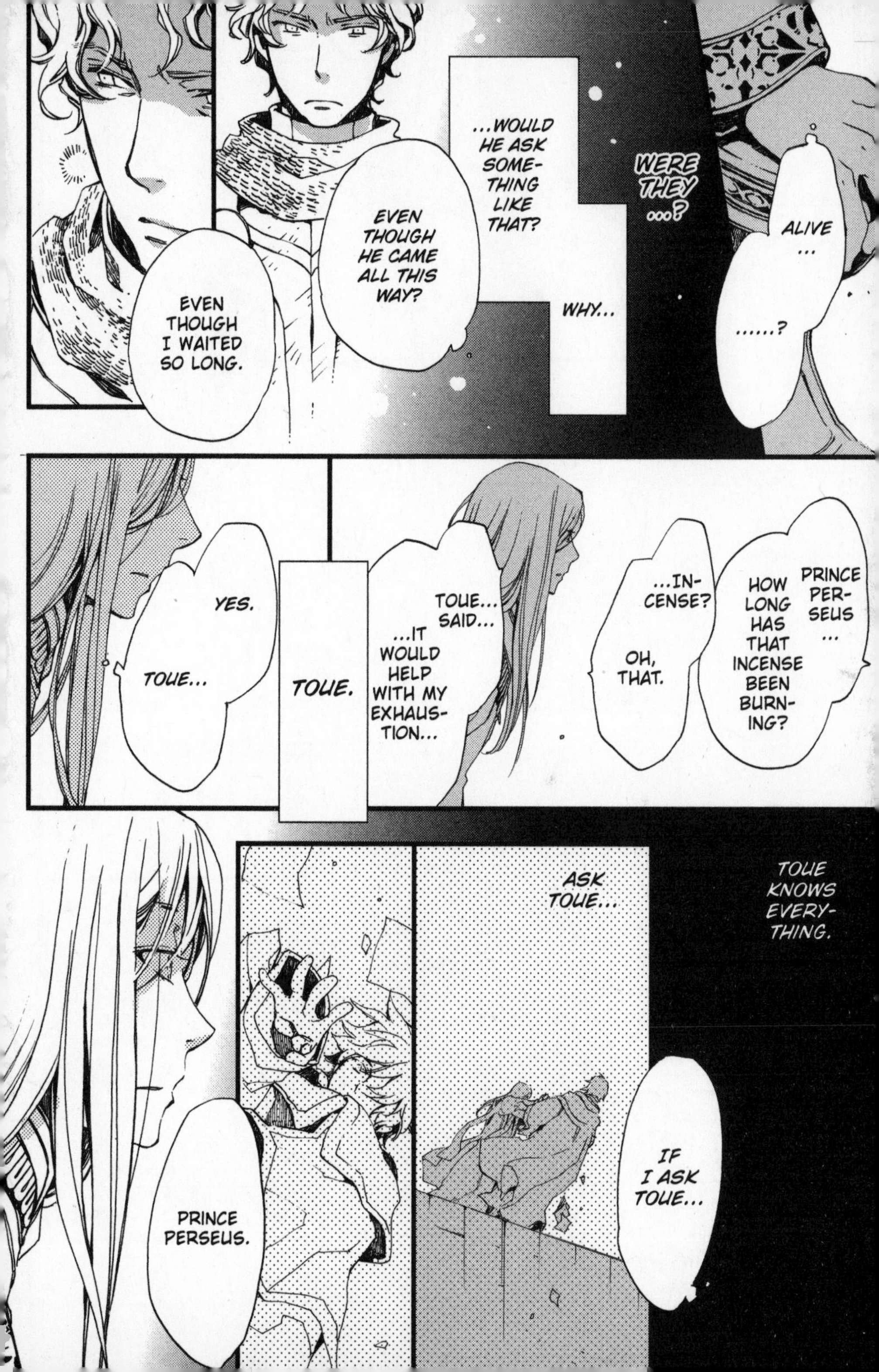
WERE THEY ...?
ALIVE ...
......?
WHY...
...WOULD HE ASK SOMETHING LIKE THAT?
EVEN THOUGH HE CAME ALL THIS WAY?
EVEN THOUGH I WAITED SO LONG.
PRINCE PERSEUS ...
HOW LONG HAS THAT INCENSE BEEN BURNING?
...INCENSE?
OH, THAT.
TOUE... SAID...
...IT WOULD HELP WITH MY EXHAUSTION...
TOUE.
YES.
TOUE...
TOUE KNOWS EVERYTHING.
ASK TOUE...
IF I ASK TOUE...
PRINCE PERSEUS.

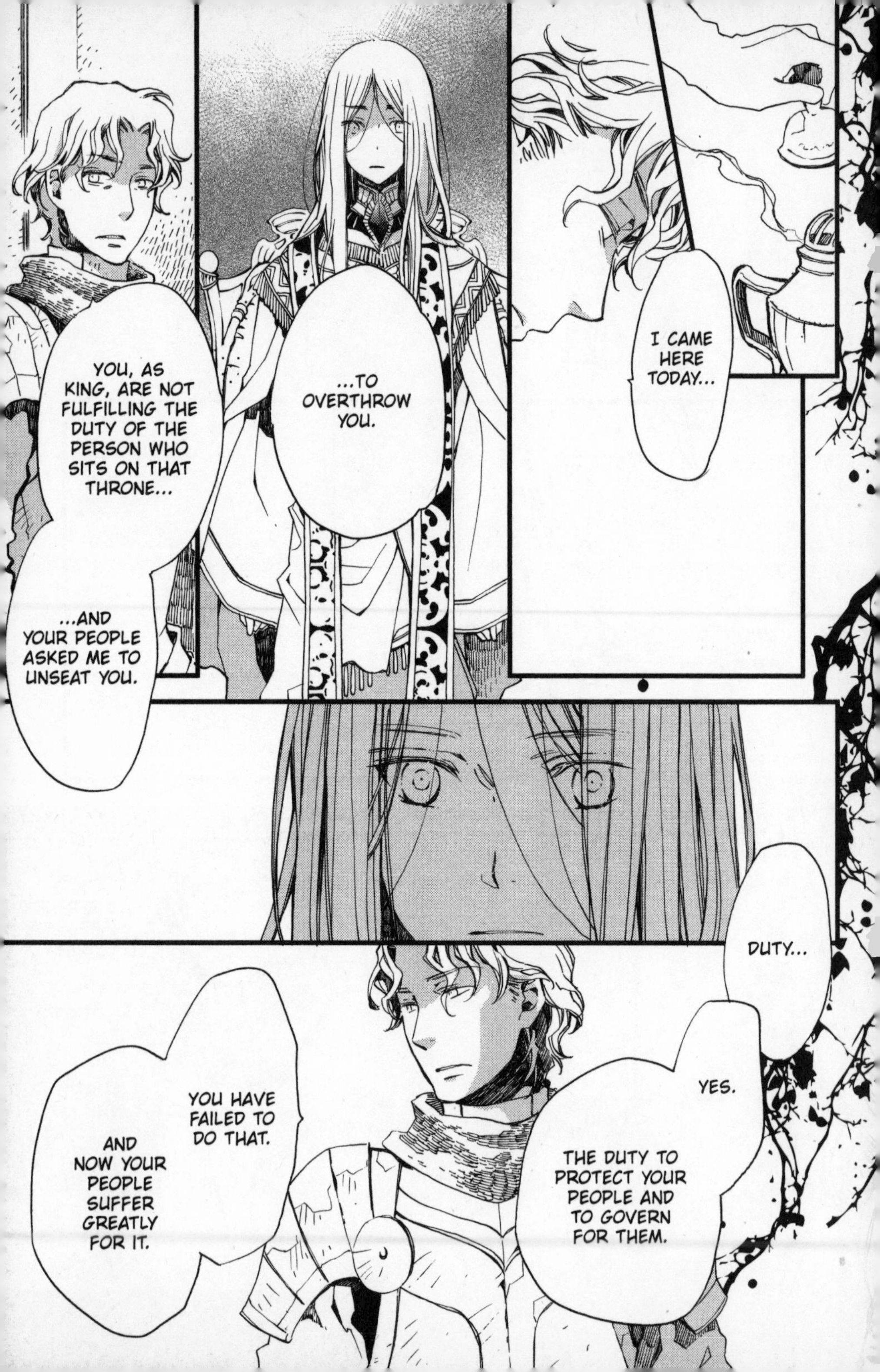
I CAME HERE TODAY...
...TO OVERTHROW YOU.
YOU, AS KING, ARE NOT FULFILLING THE DUTY OF THE PERSON WHO SITS ON THAT THRONE...
...AND YOUR PEOPLE ASKED ME TO UNSEAT YOU.
DUTY...
YES.
THE DUTY TO PROTECT YOUR PEOPLE AND TO GOVERN FOR THEM.
YOU HAVE FAILED TO DO THAT.
AND NOW YOUR PEOPLE SUFFER GREATLY FOR IT.

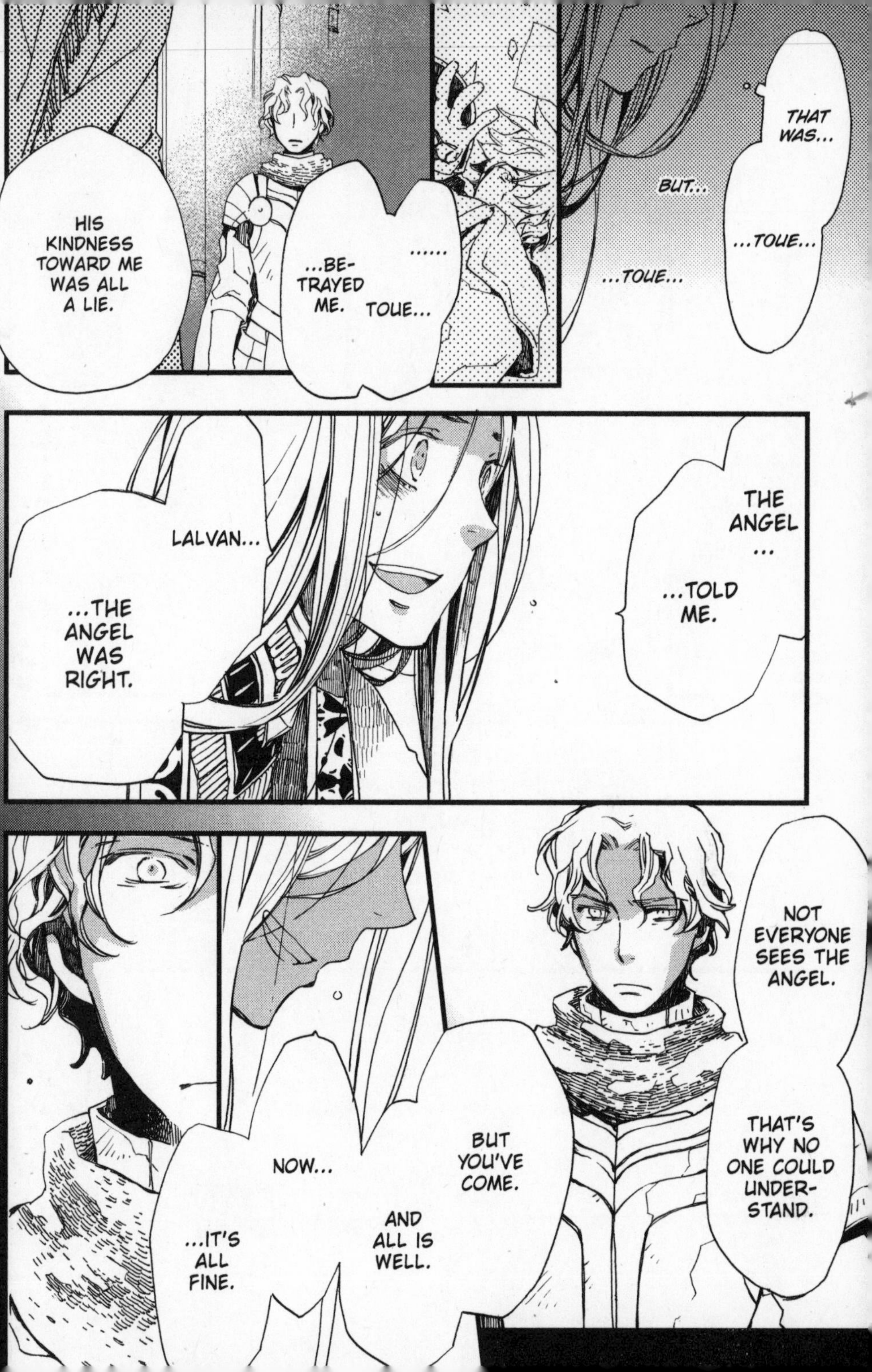
THAT WAS...
...TOUE...
BUT...
...TOUE...
......
...BE-TRAYED ME.
TOUE...
HIS KINDNESS TOWARD ME WAS ALL A LIE.
THE ANGEL ... ...TOLD ME.
LALVAN...
...THE ANGEL WAS RIGHT.
NOT EVERYONE SEES THE ANGEL.
THAT'S WHY NO ONE COULD UNDER-STAND.
BUT YOU'VE COME.
AND ALL IS WELL.
NOW...
...IT'S ALL FINE.

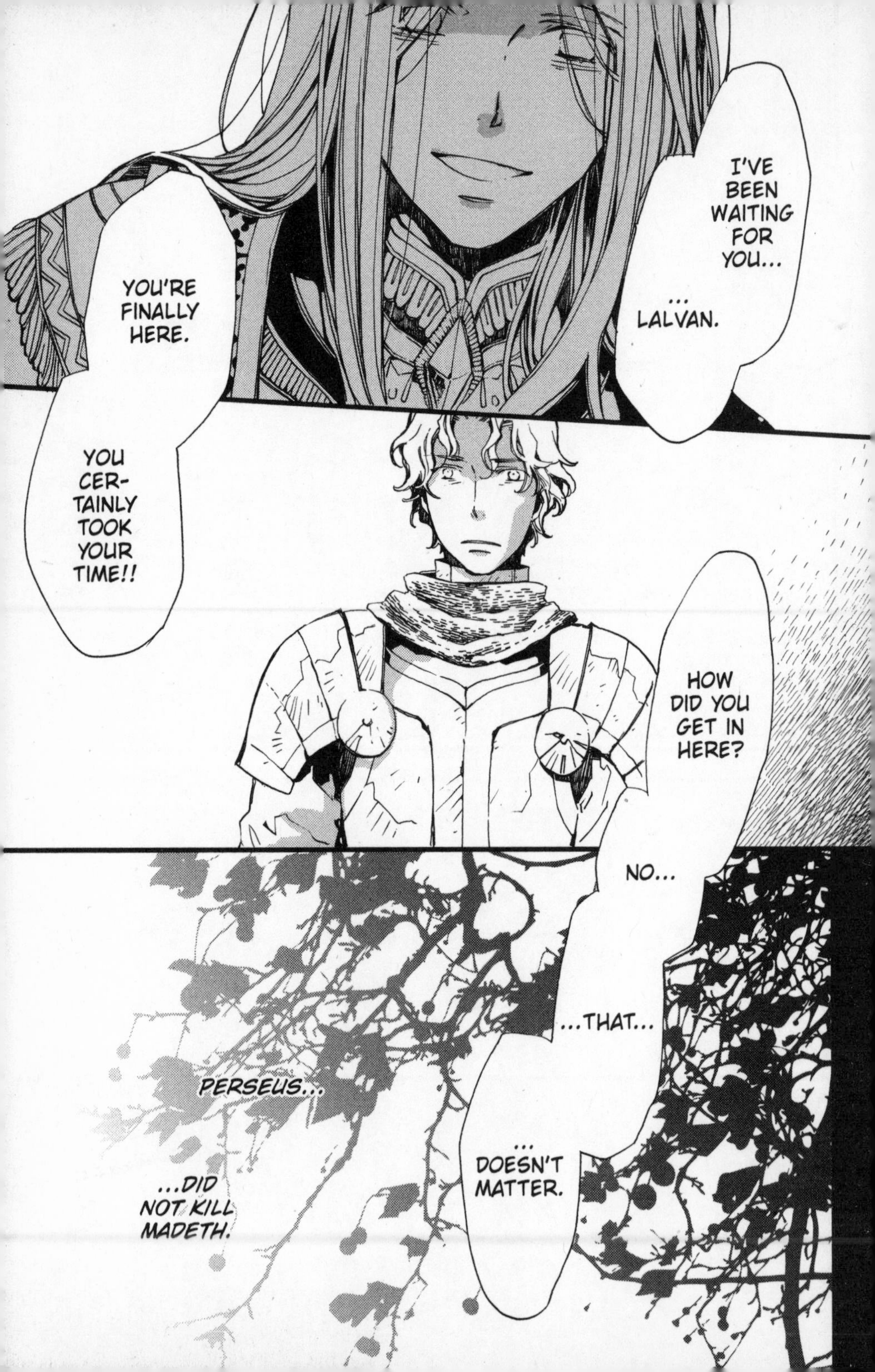
I'VE BEEN WAITING FOR YOU...
...LALVAN.
YOU'RE FINALLY HERE.
YOU CER-TAINLY TOOK YOUR TIME!!
HOW DID YOU GET IN HERE?
NO...
...THAT...
...DOESN'T MATTER.
PERSEUS...
...DID NOT KILL MADETH.

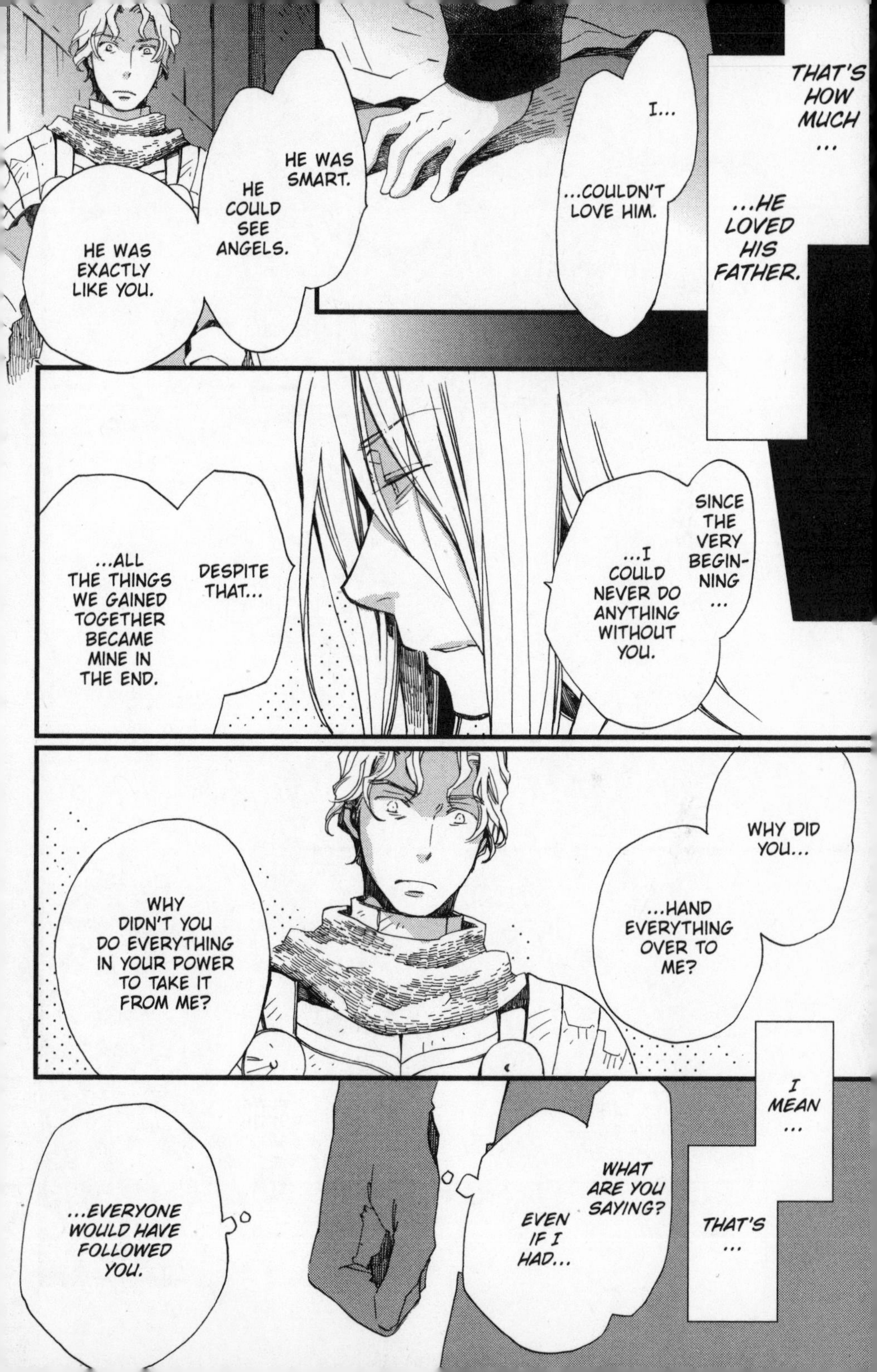
THAT'S HOW MUCH ... ...HE LOVED HIS FATHER.
I...
...COULDN'T LOVE HIM.
HE WAS SMART.
HE COULD SEE ANGELS.
HE WAS EXACTLY LIKE YOU.
SINCE THE VERY BEGIN-NING ...
...I COULD NEVER DO ANYTHING WITHOUT YOU.
DESPITE THAT...
...ALL THE THINGS WE GAINED TOGETHER BECAME MINE IN THE END.
WHY DID YOU...
...HAND EVERYTHING OVER TO ME?
WHY DIDN'T YOU DO EVERYTHING IN YOUR POWER TO TAKE IT FROM ME?
I MEAN ...
THAT'S ...
WHAT ARE YOU SAYING?
EVEN IF I HAD...
...EVERYONE WOULD HAVE FOLLOWED YOU.

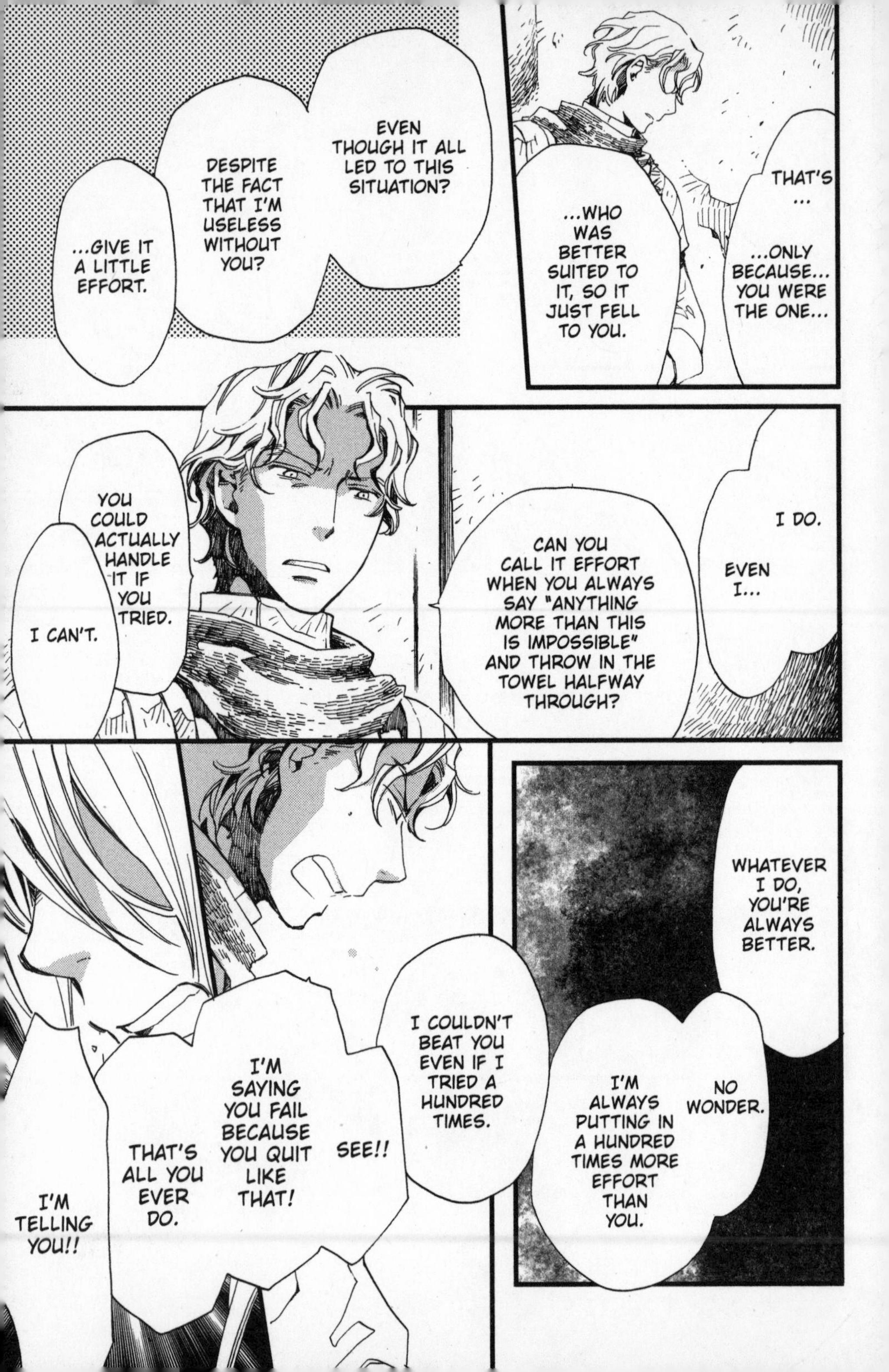
THAT'S...
...ONLY BECAUSE... YOU WERE THE ONE...
...WHO WAS BETTER SUITED TO IT, SO IT JUST FELL TO YOU.
EVEN THOUGH IT ALL LED TO THIS SITUATION?
DESPITE THE FACT THAT I'M USELESS WITHOUT YOU?
...GIVE IT A LITTLE EFFORT.
I DO.
EVEN I...
CAN YOU CALL IT EFFORT WHEN YOU ALWAYS SAY "ANYTHING MORE THAN THIS IS IMPOSSIBLE" AND THROW IN THE TOWEL HALFWAY THROUGH?
YOU COULD ACTUALLY HANDLE IT IF YOU TRIED.
I CAN'T.
WHATEVER I DO, YOU'RE ALWAYS BETTER.
NO WONDER.
I'M ALWAYS PUTTING IN A HUNDRED TIMES MORE EFFORT THAN YOU.
I COULDN'T BEAT YOU EVEN IF I TRIED A HUNDRED TIMES.
SEE!!
I'M SAYING YOU FAIL BECAUSE YOU QUIT LIKE THAT!
THAT'S ALL YOU EVER DO.
I'M TELLING YOU!!

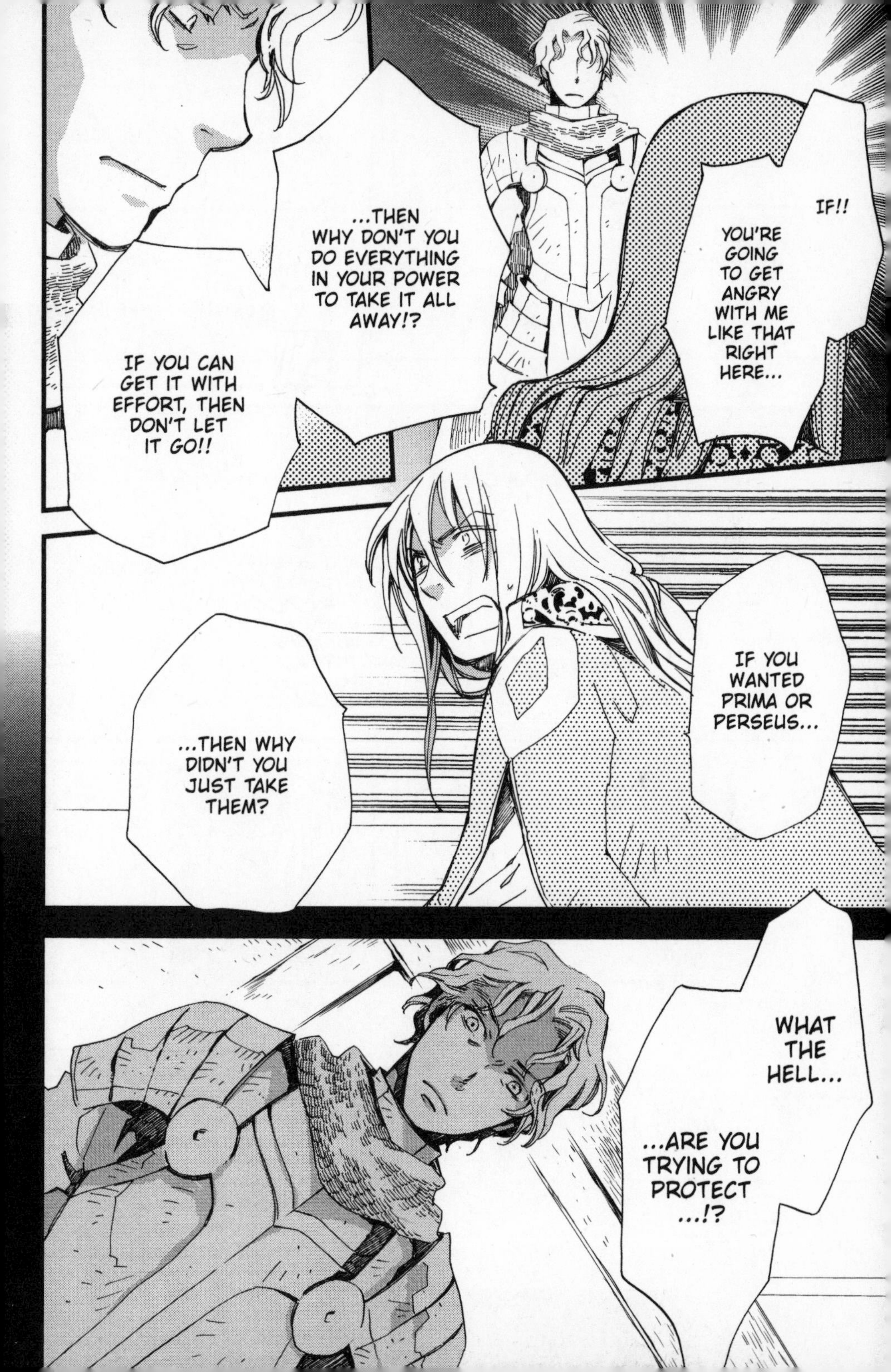
IF!! YOU'RE GOING TO GET ANGRY WITH ME LIKE THAT RIGHT HERE...
...THEN WHY DON'T YOU DO EVERYTHING IN YOUR POWER TO TAKE IT ALL AWAY!?
IF YOU CAN GET IT WITH EFFORT, THEN DON'T LET IT GO!!
IF YOU WANTED PRIMA OR PERSEUS...
...THEN WHY DIDN'T YOU JUST TAKE THEM?
WHAT THE HELL...
...ARE YOU TRYING TO PROTECT ...!?

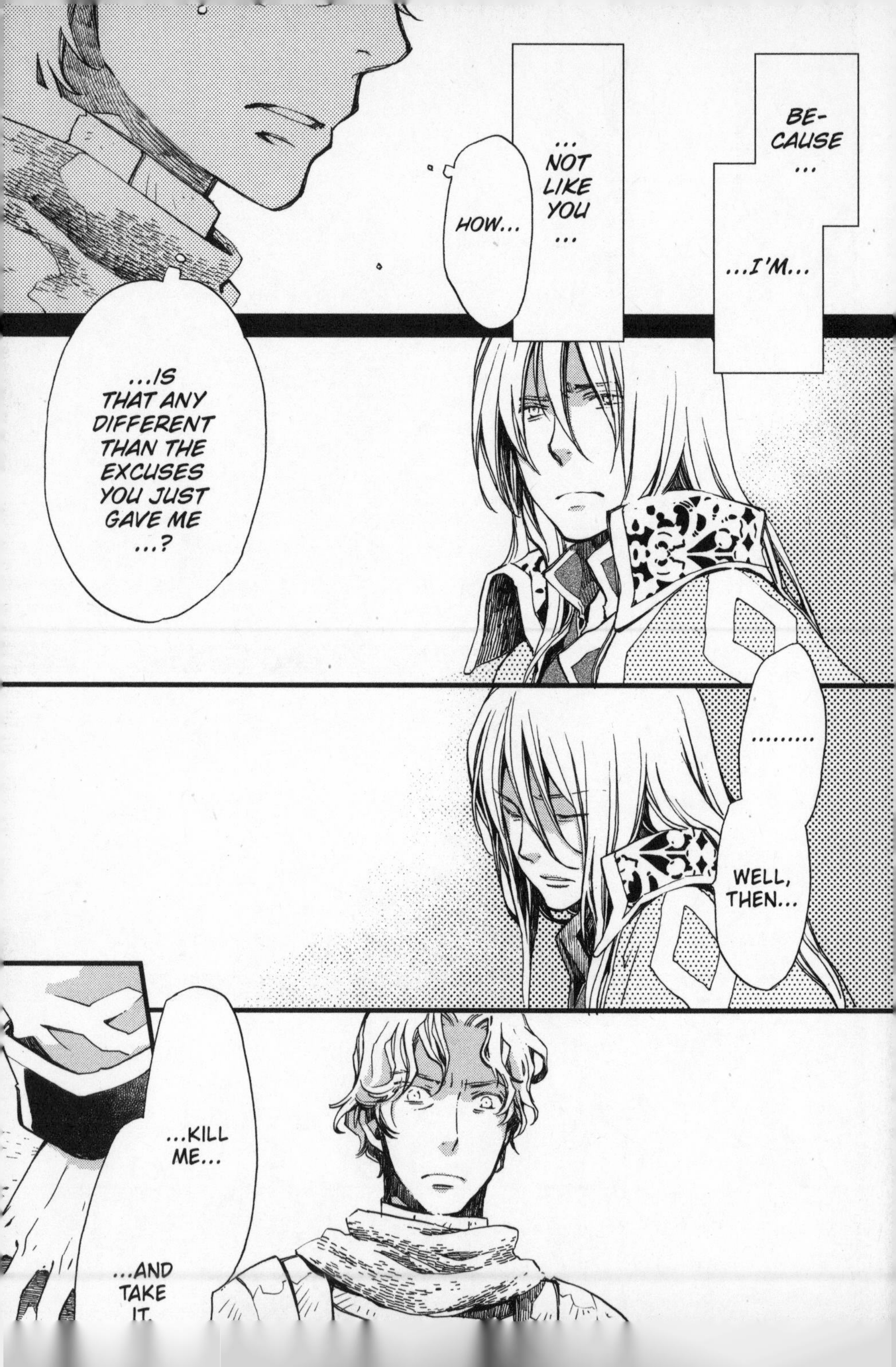
BE-CAUSE...
...I'M...
...NOT LIKE YOU...
HOW...
...IS THAT ANY DIFFERENT THAN THE EXCUSES YOU JUST GAVE ME...?
....
WELL, THEN...
...KILL ME...
...AND TAKE IT.

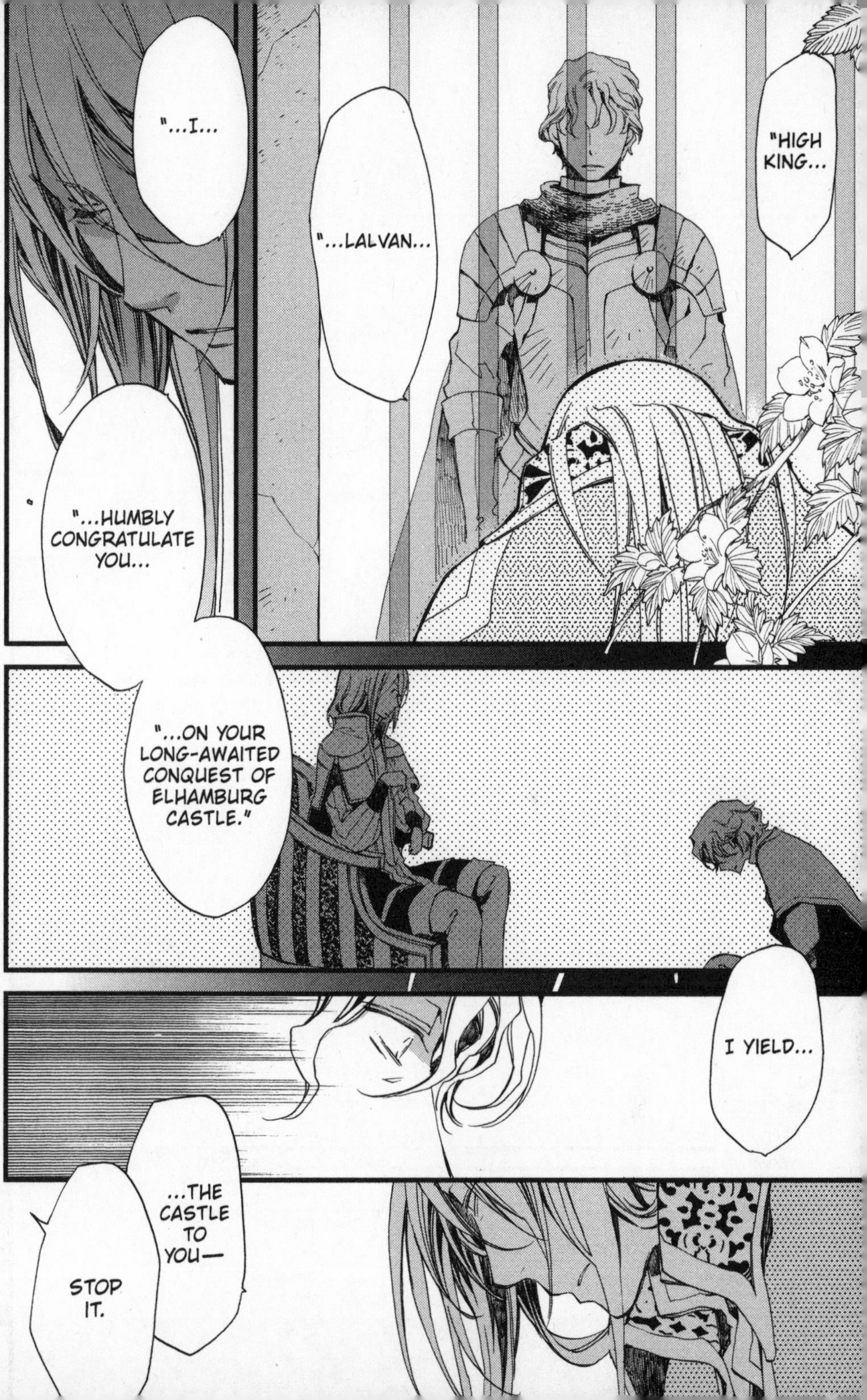
"HIGH KING...
"...LALVAN...
"...I...
"...HUMBLY CONGRATULATE YOU...
"...ON YOUR LONG-AWAITED CONQUEST OF ELHAMBURG CASTLE."
I YIELD...
...THE CASTLE TO YOU—
STOP IT.

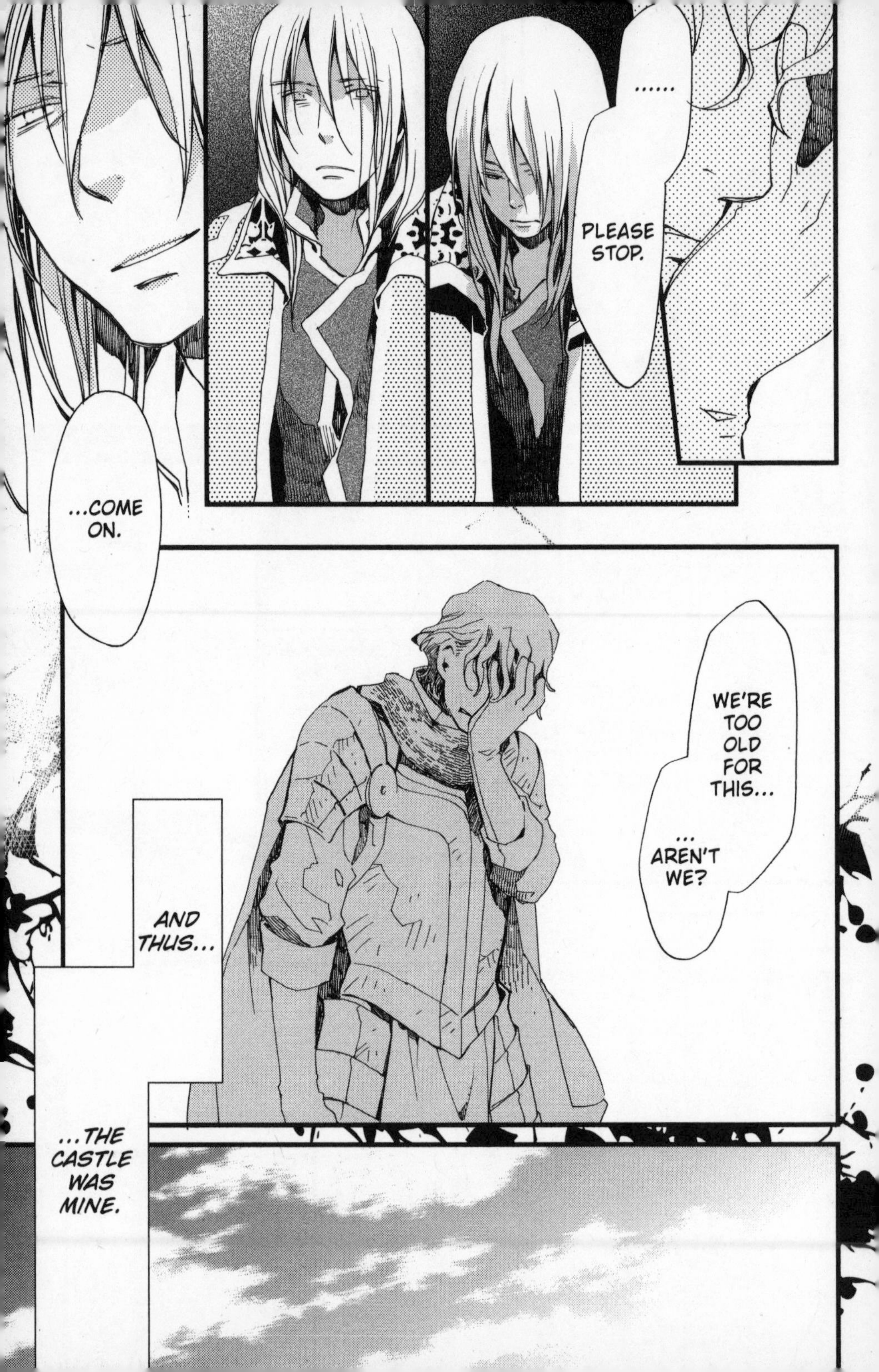
......
PLEASE STOP.
...COME ON.
WE'RE TOO OLD FOR THIS...
...AREN'T WE?
AND THUS...
...THE CASTLE WAS MINE.

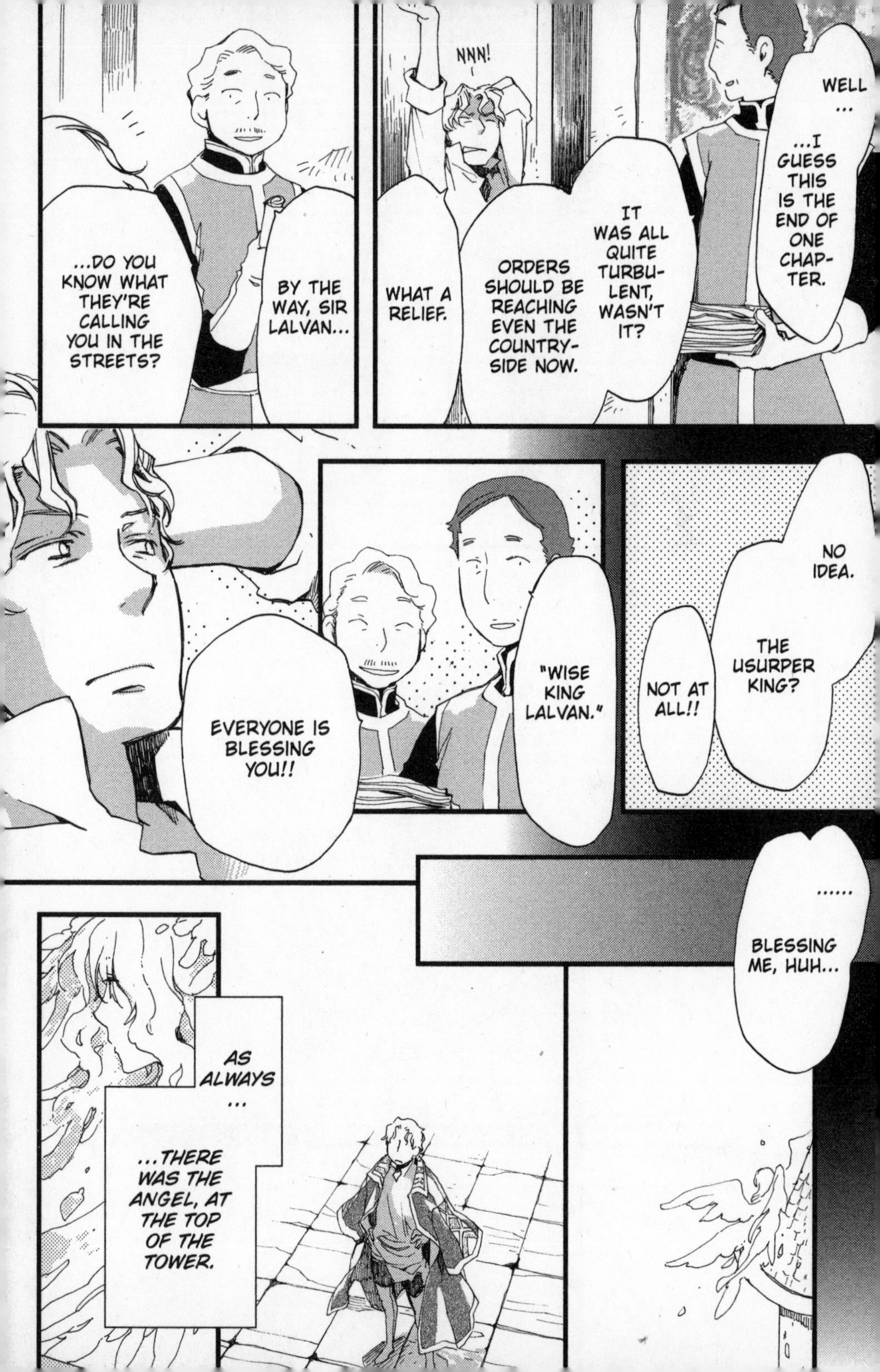
WELL ...
...I GUESS THIS IS THE END OF ONE CHAPTER.
IT WAS ALL QUITE TURBULENT, WASN'T IT?
NNN!
ORDERS SHOULD BE REACHING EVEN THE COUNTRYSIDE NOW.
WHAT A RELIEF.
BY THE WAY, SIR LALVAN...
...DO YOU KNOW WHAT THEY'RE CALLING YOU IN THE STREETS?
NO IDEA.
THE USURPER KING?
NOT AT ALL!!
"WISE KING LALVAN."
EVERYONE IS BLESSING YOU!!
......
BLESSING ME, HUH...
AS ALWAYS ...
...THERE WAS THE ANGEL, AT THE TOP OF THE TOWER.

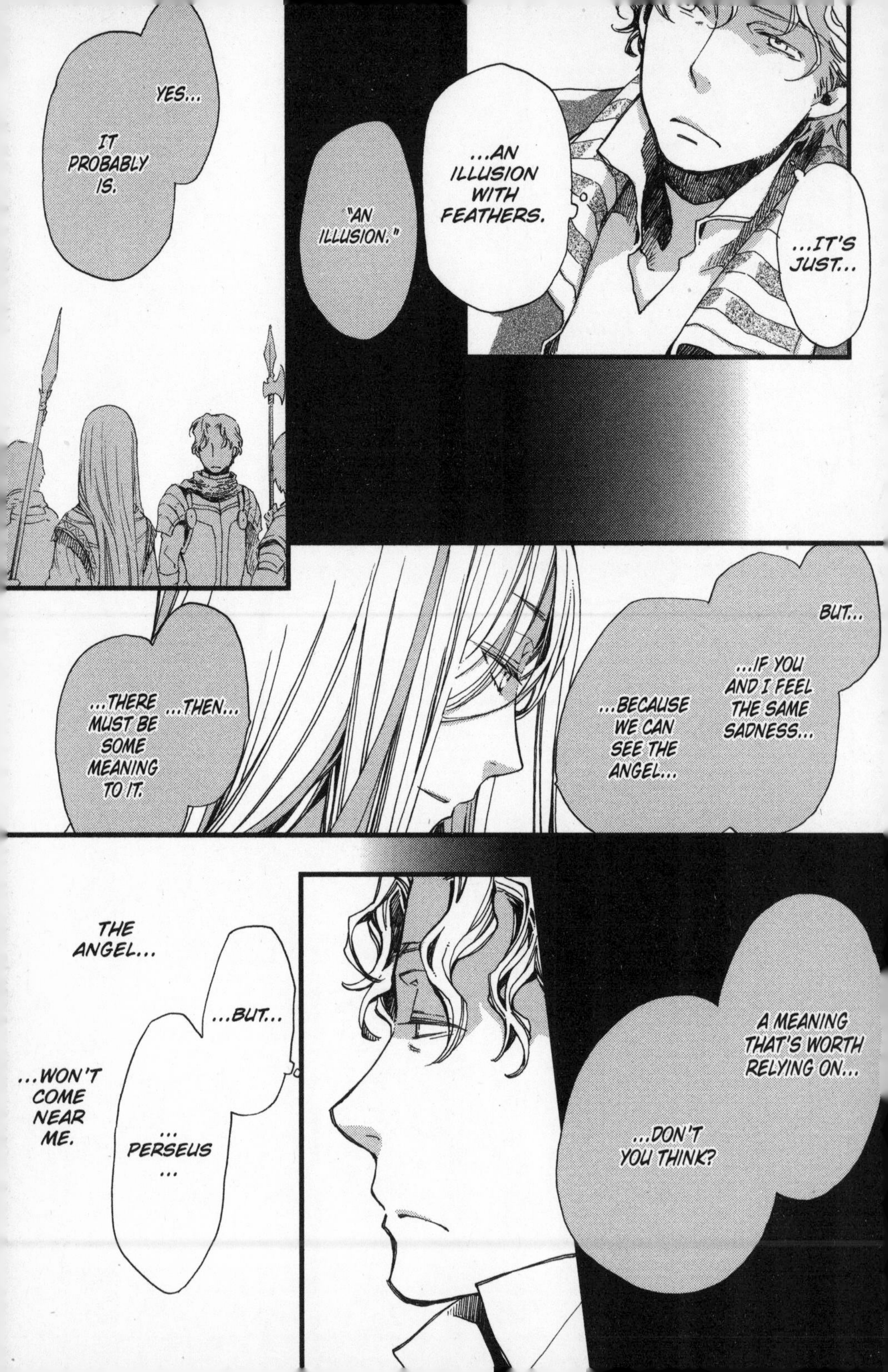
...IT'S JUST...
...AN ILLUSION WITH FEATHERS.
"AN ILLUSION."
YES...
IT PROBABLY IS.
BUT...
...IF YOU AND I FEEL THE SAME SADNESS...
...BECAUSE WE CAN SEE THE ANGEL...
...THEN...
...THERE MUST BE SOME MEANING TO IT.
A MEANING THAT'S WORTH RELYING ON...
...DON'T YOU THINK?
...BUT...
...PERSEUS...
THE ANGEL...
...WON'T COME NEAR ME.

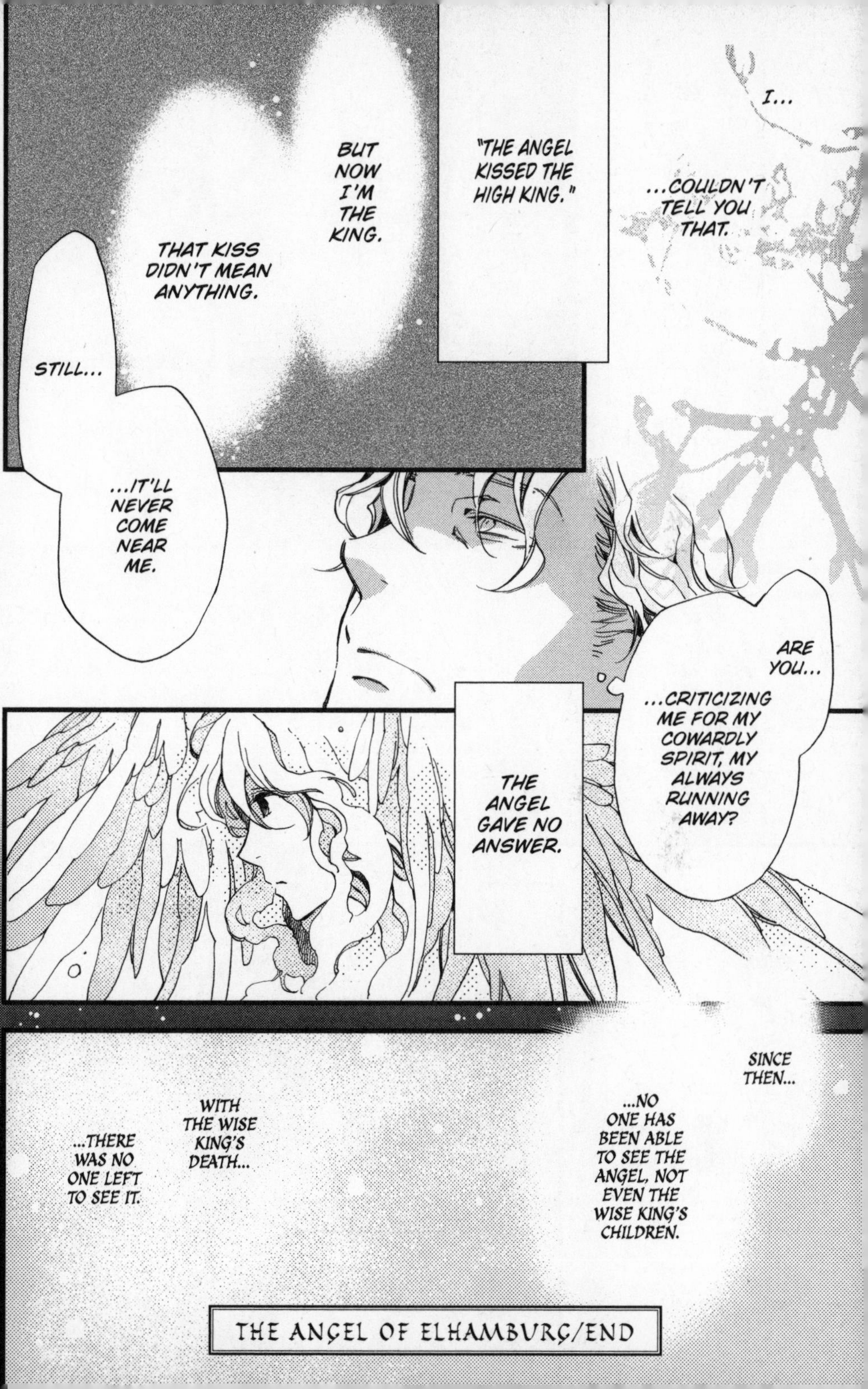
I...
...COULDN'T TELL YOU THAT.
"THE ANGEL KISSED THE HIGH KING."
BUT NOW I'M THE KING.
THAT KISS DIDN'T MEAN ANYTHING.
STILL...
...IT'LL NEVER COME NEAR ME.
ARE YOU...
...CRITICIZING ME FOR MY COWARDLY SPIRIT, MY ALWAYS RUNNING AWAY?
THE ANGEL GAVE NO ANSWER.
SINCE THEN...
...NO ONE HAS BEEN ABLE TO SEE THE ANGEL, NOT EVEN THE WISE KING'S CHILDREN.
WITH THE WISE KING'S DEATH...
...THERE WAS NO ONE LEFT TO SEE IT.
THE ANGEL OF ELHAMBURG/END

At first, I totally intended to make this a one-shot story, but then my editor told me, "I'm really looking forward to seeing what happens next!" (LOL) I had the setting already established, but I never saw myself actually drawing the rest of it, so I came up with the second installment in a rush...

Those are the conditions that this collected volume was published under, but I'd be delighted if you enjoyed reading it all the same.

I actually referenced characters from a play I saw at the time to create the characters of Madeth and Lalvan. Just because the basis for the characters was the same doesn't mean that the story will be as wonderful as the inspiration, though! (LOL) Somehow, Madeth turned into a completely pitiful fellow. But I'm pretty fond of characters that lead people despite being relatively useless. Lalvan is a character that doesn't do very much either, but I'm also pretty fond of hopeless characters that make tons of excuses without doing much of anything, even though they could do a lot if they tried...

It was fun to go on and on drawing the types of characters that I like. Thank you (for a lot of things)! (LOL)

I'd be happy if we could meet again in other books. Really happy, I think. I'd be super-duper happy.

あき Aki 88

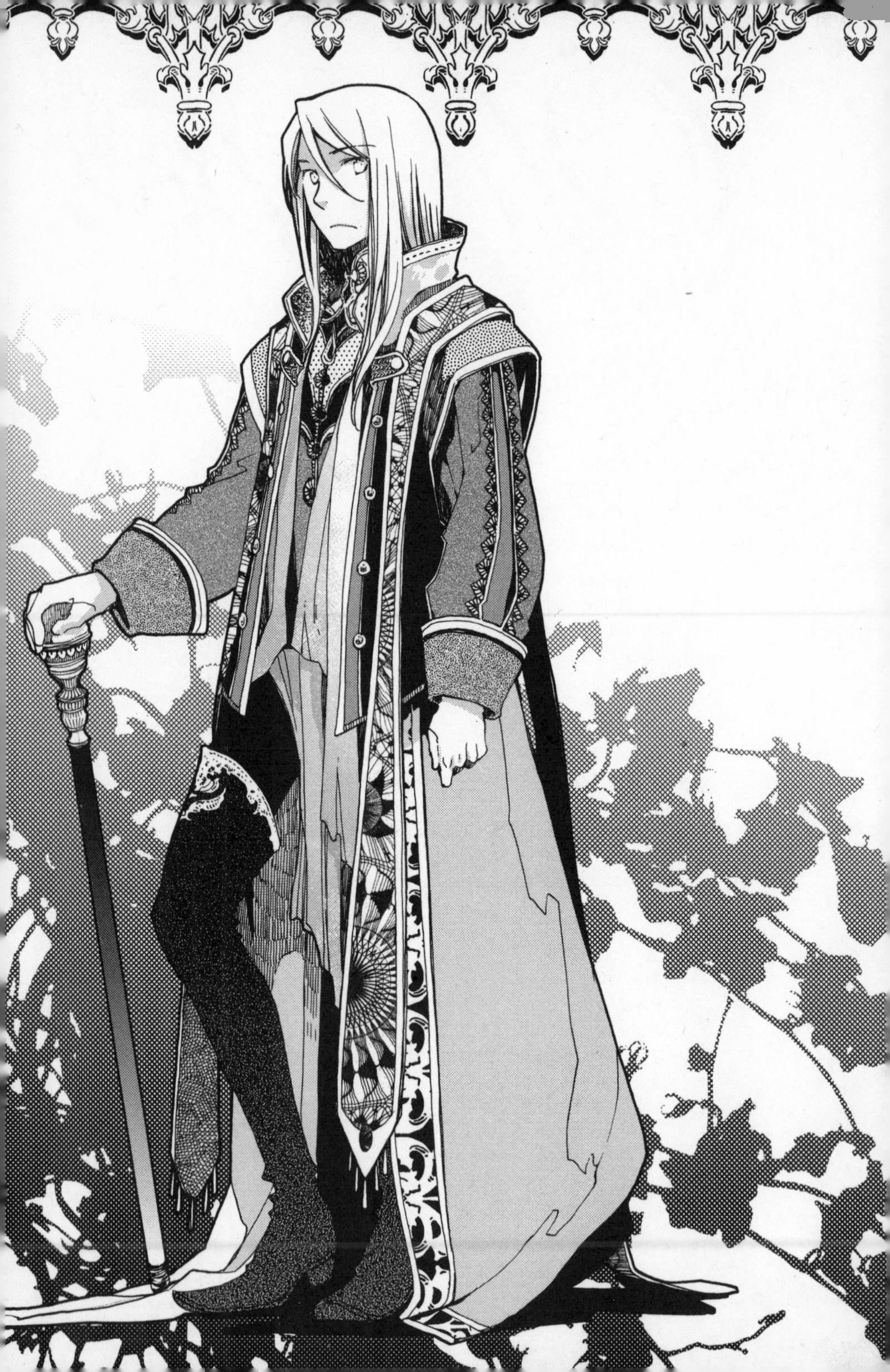